ASIAN MILITARY EVOLUTIONS

Civil–Military Relations in Asia

Edited by
Alan Chong and Nicole Jen

First published in Great Britain in 2024 by

Bristol University Press
University of Bristol
1-9 Old Park Hill
Bristol
BS2 8BB
UK
t: +44 (0)117 374 6645
e: bup-info@bristol.ac.uk

Details of international sales and distribution partners are available at bristoluniversitypress.co.uk

© Bristol University Press 2024

British Library Cataloguing in Publication Data
A catalogue record for this book is available from the British Library

ISBN 978-1-5292-2931-8 hardcover
ISBN 978-1-5292-2932-5 paperback
ISBN 978-1-5292-2933-2 ePub
ISBN 978-1-5292-2934-9 ePdf

The right of Alan Chong and Nicole Jenne to be identified as editors of this work has been asserted by them in accordance with the Copyright, Designs and Patents Act 1988.

All rights reserved: no part of this publication may be reproduced, stored in a retrieval system, or transmitted in any form or by any means, electronic, mechanical, photocopying, recording, or otherwise without the prior permission of Bristol University Press.

Every reasonable effort has been made to obtain permission to reproduce copyrighted material. If, however, anyone knows of an oversight, please contact the publisher.

The statements and opinions contained within this publication are solely those of the editors and contributors and not of the University of Bristol or Bristol University Press. The University of Bristol and Bristol University Press disclaim responsibility for any injury to persons or property resulting from any material published in this publication.

Bristol University Press works to counter discrimination on grounds of gender, race, disability, age and sexuality.

Cover design: Nicky Boroweic
Front cover image: Adobe/Arnav Pratap Singh

Contents

List of Figures and Tables — v
Notes on Contributors — vi
Acknowledgements — x

1   Introduction: Asian Military Evolutions – Entrenching Varieties of Civil–Military Relations and Their Security Initiatives in Asia — 1
Alan Chong and Nicole Jenne

PART I   Southeast Asia

2   Fostering Developmental Guardianship: The Case of Myanmar's *Tatmadaw* — 29
Adhi Priamarizki

3   Business as Usual despite Reform: The Indonesian Military under Jokowi — 46
Dahlia Gratia Setiyawan

4   Militarizing Governance: Informal Civil–Military Relations and Democratic Erosion in the Philippines — 68
Aries A. Arugay

5   Mind the Gap: The Curious Case of Everyday Civil–Military Relations in Singapore — 90
Jun Yan Chang and Shu Huang Ho

6   The Role of the Malaysian Armed Forces in Defence Diplomacy: A Foreign Policy Outworking of Civil–Military Relations in Malaysia — 110
David Han

7   The Architecture and Evolution of Civil–Military Relations in Vietnam — 129
Alexander L. Vuving

8   The Stubborn Illiberalism and Trialectical Dynamics of Thailand's Civil–Military Relations — 149
Gregory V. Raymond

| 9 | Peacekeeping: An Emerging Area of Southeast Asia's Defence and Security Cooperation?
Nicole Jenne | 170 |

PART II Northeast Asia

10	Subjective Conditional Control: Return of the Strongman in China's Party–Army Relations *James Char*	197
11	Military and Politics in Patrimonial North Korea *Jongseok Woo*	229
12	Curing National Insecurity through Developmental Authoritarianism in South Korea's Civil–Military Relations *Il Woo Lee and Alan Chong*	248
13	Image Makeover: The Military Evolution of Japan's Self-Defense Forces *Yee-Kuang Heng*	272

PART III South Asia

| 14 | The Deficient Evolution of Civil–Military Relations in India
Harsh V. Pant and Tuneer Mukherjee | 295 |
| 15 | Defence Diplomacy and Civil–Military Relations: The Case of Bangladesh
Rashed Uz Zaman | 320 |

| 16 | Conclusion: Asian Military Evolutions as a Contribution to Civil–Military Relations Thought
Alan Chong and Nicole Jenne | 340 |

| Index | 349 |

List of Figures and Tables

Figures

4.1	Perceptions of civilian supremacy over the military in the Philippines	74
4.2	Net trust ratings of the Philippine military, 1993–2019	81
4.3	Views on the role of retired generals in Duterte's cabinet	83
4.4	Views on the appropriate mission of the Philippine military	86

Tables

4.1	Legislative oversight of the Philippine military	75
4.2	Independent civilian oversight of the Philippine military	78
7.1	Military representation on the VCP Politburo and Central Committee, 1976–2021	135
9.1	Participation in UN peacekeeping by Southeast Asian countries	176
9.2	Senior appointments in UN peacekeeping by Southeast Asian countries	179
9.3	Southeast Asian peacekeeping centres	183
10.1	PLA senior officers under graft probe since the 18th Party Congress (patron–client ties with Xu Caihou)	207
10.2	PLA senior officers under graft probe since the 18th Party Congress (patron–client ties with Guo Boxiong)	209
10.3	PLA senior officers under graft probe since the 18th Party Congress (patron–client ties with Xu Caihou and Guo Boxiong)	211
10.4	Group Army (GA) affiliations and leadership following the PLA reforms	215

Notes on Contributors

Aries A. Arugay is Professor of Political Science at the University of the Philippines in Diliman. He is also Editor-in-Chief of *Asian Politics & Policy*, published by Wiley-Blackwell and the Policy Studies Organisation. His main research interests are comparative democratization, civil–military relations, ASEAN regionalism, and Philippine foreign and security policy. He has published in academic journals such as the *American Behavioral Scientist, Annals of the American Academy of Political and Social Science, Asian Perspective, Journal of East Asian Studies, Journal of Peacebuilding & Development* and the *Philippine Political Science Journal*, among others.

Jun Yan Chang is Research Fellow at the Institute of Defence and Strategic Studies (IDSS), S. Rajaratnam School of International Studies (RSIS), Nanyang Technological University (NTU). He has published in various academic journals. Prior to joining RSIS, Jun Yan was a combat officer in the Republic of Singapore Navy, participating in various multilateral maritime exercises and operations, such as the Exercise Rim of the Pacific (RIMPAC) and Operation Blue Sapphire (Maritime).

James Char is Research Fellow with the China Programme at RSIS, NTU, Singapore. His research interests centre on the domestic politics and civil–military relations of contemporary China, and the history of warfare in modern China. His articles have appeared in peer-reviewed journals including *Asian Security, Journal of Strategic Studies* and *The China Quarterly*. He is the editor of the special issue 'The People's Liberation Army in Its Tenth Decade', *Journal of Strategic Studies* 44(2) (2021) and the principal editor of the special section 'A New Direction in the People's Liberation Army's Emergent Strategic Thinking, Roles and Missions', *The China Quarterly* 232 (December 2017).

Alan Chong is Senior Fellow at RSIS in Singapore. He has published widely on the notion of soft power and the role of ideas in constructing the international relations of Singapore and Asia. He has edited the books *International Security in the Asia-Pacific: Transcending ASEAN towards Transitional*

Polycentrism (Palgrave, 2018) and, with Pham Quang Minh, *Critical Reflections on China's Belt and Road Initiative* (Cham: Springer Nature under the imprint of Palgrave Macmillan, 2020). He also served as co-editor (with Faizal bin Yahya) of *State, Society and Information Technology in Asia* (Ashgate/Routledge, 2014/2015).

David Han is a PhD candidate in International Relations at the London School of Economics and Political Science. Concurrently, he is a Research Fellow with the Malaysia Programme at RSIS, Singapore. His research interests include foreign policy analysis, international relations theory, international relations of Southeast Asia and the Asia-Pacific and Malaysia's foreign policy. His articles have appeared in peer-reviewed journals such as *Asian Politics and Policy*, *The Chinese Journal of International Politics* and *The Round Table: The Commonwealth Journal of International Affairs*. He has also written commentaries for *The Diplomat* and *East Asia Forum*.

Yee-Kuang Heng is Professor at the Graduate School of Public Policy, The University of Tokyo. Dr Heng graduated from the London School of Economics and Political Science (LSE) with a BSc (First Class Honours) and then PhD in International Relations funded by the UK Overseas Research Students Award Scheme. His current research interests include UK–Japan defence cooperation and wider European military presence in the Indo-Pacific. He has published on Japanese foreign policy in the *Journal of Strategic Studies*, *International Relations of the Asia-Pacific*, *The Pacific Review*, *Defence Studies* and *The Routledge Handbook of Japanese Foreign Policy* (2018).

Shu Huang Ho was Teaching Fellow at the IDSS, RSIS, NTU. He has a BA (Hons) degree in History from the National University of Singapore (NUS), as well as an MSc in Strategic Studies from RSIS. Prior to joining RSIS, Shu Huang worked for the Singapore Armed Forces (SAF) to set up the Army Museum of Singapore. His affiliation with the SAF continued at RSIS where he was involved in the professional military education of its officers.

Nicole Jenne is Associate Professor at the Pontificia Universidad Católica de Chile, Institute of Political Science. She holds a PhD in International Relations from the European University Institute, Florence (2016). Nicole has published on different aspects at the intersection of International Relations and international security, with a geographic focus on Latin America and the Asia Pacific. She was the guest editor, together with Chiara Ruffa and Christoph Harig, of a recent special issue published with the *European Journal of International Security* on civil–military relations

(February 2022). Her book *The Domestic Origins of No-war Communities* will be published with Cambridge University Press.

Il Woo Lee is a former Associate Research Fellow with RSIS, NTU, Singapore. His research interests include military history and foreign policy with a special emphasis on East Asia. Currently, he resides in South Korea where he actively observes the political scene there. He holds a Bachelor's degree in Political Science from the University of Georgia (UGA) and a Master's in International Relations from the London School of Economics and Political Science (LSE).

Tuneer Mukherjee is a researcher of Asian security and his current focus is on naval modernization in South Asia. Previously, he was a Junior Fellow with the Observer Research Foundation's Maritime Policy Initiative in New Delhi, India, where he worked on Indo-Pacific maritime strategy and the impact of artificial intelligence on naval operations. He has also been a researcher with the Asia Maritime Transparency Initiative at the Center for Strategic and International Studies, Washington DC, where he tracked maritime disputes in the South China Sea.

Harsh V. Pant is Professor of International Relations at King's College London. He is Director, Studies and Head of the Strategic Studies Programme at the Observer Research Foundation, New Delhi. He is also Director (Honorary) of Delhi School of Transnational Affairs at Delhi University. His current research is focused on Asian security issues. His most recent books include *New Directions in India's Foreign Policy: Theory and Praxis* (Cambridge University Press), *America and the Indo-Pacific: Trump and Beyond* (Routledge), *India's Nuclear Policy* (Oxford University Press), *Handbook of Indian Defence Policy* (Routledge), and *India's Afghan Muddle* (HarperCollins).

Adhi Priamarizki is Visiting Fellow at the Indonesia Programme, RSIS, NTU. He holds a PhD in International Relations from Ritsumeikan University, Japan, and a MSc in Strategic Studies from RSIS. Adhi wrote a doctoral dissertation on civil–military relations in Indonesia, Myanmar and Thailand. His research interests include Indonesia's military transformation, civil–military relations in Southeast Asia and Indonesian politics.

Gregory V. Raymond is a lecturer in the Strategic and Defence Studies Centre in the Coral Bell School of Asia Pacific Affairs at the Australian National University. His research interests include Southeast Asian security, regional militaries and strategic cultures, memory and national identity, and the relations of mainland Southeast Asia with China. His book on Thailand's strategic culture entitled *Thai Military Power* was published in 2018 by NIAS Press. His new book, *The US–Thai Alliance and Asian International*

Relations: History, Memory and Current Developments (with John Blaxland), was published by Routledge in 2021. Before joining the Australian National University, Greg was a policy advisor in the Australian Government.

Dahlia Gratia Setiyawan is a political historian of Southeast Asia with a focus on Indonesia. She obtained her PhD from UCLA in 2014. Her research interests include the 1965–66 Indonesian mass violence and Cold War-era US–Indonesia relations. In cooperation with the American–Indonesian Cultural and Exchange Foundation she recently completed an archival preservation project related to Americans in Indonesia during the Sukarno and Suharto eras. Dahlia lives and works in Los Angeles. She is a History and Social Sciences faculty member and Associate Director of the Collegiate Division at Windward School.

Rashed Uz Zaman teaches at the Department of International Relations, University of Dhaka, Bangladesh. He was educated at Dhaka, Hull and Reading. Dr Zaman works on foreign policy, strategic and international security issues and has spoken and written extensively on Bangladesh in UN peacekeeping missions. In 2009–11, Dr Zaman was an Alexander von Humboldt post-doctoral research fellow at the University of Erfurt, Germany. He was a Fulbright Visiting Professor in the Department of Political Science at Vanderbilt University in 2012.

Alexander L. Vuving is Professor at the Daniel K. Inouye Asia-Pacific Center for Security Studies. His major areas of research include: the sources of state behaviour, the history of great power competition, the struggle over international order, power and leadership, soft power, Chinese strategy, Vietnamese politics and foreign policy and the South China Sea disputes. He has published in major scholarly journals and presented at leading universities and think tanks around the world. Numerous newspapers and news agencies, including *The New York Times*, *Financial Times*, Associated Press and Bloomberg, have featured and quoted his views.

Jongseok Woo is Associate Professor of Political Science at the University of South Florida. His research interests include security studies, military politics, North Korean politics and political corruption. He has (co)authored three books: *Security Challenges and Military Politics in East Asia* (Bloomsbury, 2011), *Politics in North and South Korea* (Routledge, 2018) and *Political Corruption and Democratic Governance* (Lexington, 2018). His research has appeared in *Contemporary Politics*, *Pacific Focus*, *Communist and Post-Communist Studies*, *Japanese Journal of Political Science*, *Korea Observer*, *Issues & Studies* and *Problems of Post-Communism*. He is currently writing a book on the military and politics in North Korea.

Acknowledgements

It is always the case that edited books come a long way before they are published. This one is no different. Its title is not simply descriptive of a social science phenomenon. It is also a product of our frustrations with adapting mainstream Western concepts to analyse Asian security issues for over a decade both in a think tank and university environment. Interestingly, intellectual umbrage has driven this project to its conclusion, without any official funding involved or other kinds of institutional patronage.

On the sidelines of the International Studies Association's extraordinary Asian conference in Hong Kong in July 2017, we sat down to mull over how a panel on military operations other than war we had put together had triggered such intense reactions from the audience. Over a dinner of sumptuous Hong Kong blended Cantonese roast meats and crunchy vegetables, we thought of cooking up flavours from an Asian grounded perspective to challenge conventional civil–military relations literature.

Starting from our limited preliminary circles, we contacted the present set of authors one by one through personal acquaintances and third-party recommendations. We thank the following by name for each of them are unique contributors: Adhi Priamarizki – for the long conversations outside Ritsumeikan University in Kyoto on Southeast Asian politics; Alexander L. Vuving – for boldness and depth in research about Vietnam's political landscape despite a tremendous workload at the Asia-Pacific Center for Security Studies in Honolulu; Aries A. Arugay – for gamely stepping up to write on Philippine civil–military relations with a masterly wealth of personal research on the subject when few dared to accept such an assignment; Dahlia Gratia Setiyawan – for having accompanied the project with academic foresight and gentle patience since its very beginning; David Han – for enthusiastically joining his doctoral work on Malaysian politics and foreign policy to our late hour invitation to be part of the project; Gregory V. Raymond – for offering impressive insights, advice and support always; Harsh V. Pant and Tuneer Mukherjee – for their most insightful writing on India while wrapping their arguments creatively around recent scholarship on military bureaucratic politics; Il Woo Lee – for being critical towards South Korean politics and reaffirming his co-author's intellectual hunches on the colonial and authoritarian climates of Korea in the 1930s through 1970s; James Char – for having kept supplying fascinating insights into the PLA despite all odds; Jun Yan Chang and Shu Huang Ho – for their friendship, generosity and sharp insights into Southeast Asian politics; Rashed Uz Zaman – for his eagerness and continued communications of the kind that make academic cooperation worthwhile; Yee-Kuang Heng – for having taught us so much about Japanese culture and what it tells us about the Japanese Self-Defense Forces and for being a believer in this project from the start; and Jongseok Woo, for his collegiality and for making us aware of not one, but two stories of North Korean politics and the military.

For their most valuable editorial assistance we thank Ian Seow and Javiera Correa. We also owe a huge debt of gratitude to Stephen Wenham at Bristol University Press for trusting our convictions about the long term value of this pan-regional update on civil-military relations. Sophia Unger has likewise persevered with us through multiple rounds of editing. The following pages are the beautiful result of these efforts.

Nicole Jenne would also like to sincerely thank those current and retired members of the armed forces across Southeast Asia who are willing to share their experiences.

Finally, Alan Chong would like to dedicate this book to the memory of his late mentor, teacher and friend, Associate Professor Ishtiaq Hossain, of the International Islamic University of Malaysia. We are indebted to him for supplying background insights into Bangladesh and India in crafting the initial book proposal.

Alan Chong
Nicole Jenne
December 2022

1

Introduction: Asian Military Evolutions – Entrenching Varieties of Civil–Military Relations and Their Security Initiatives in Asia

Alan Chong and Nicole Jenne

The date 6 January 2021 has gone down in US political history as the day of a Trumpian insurrection against democratic procedures in the wake of a lost presidential bid. Closer scrutiny, however, reveals that this was also a timely reminder that the lived realities of civil–military relations in the United States are not radically different from the issues that Asian civil–military relations deal with. The 'Battle of the Capitol' revealed that citizens who were soldiers and policemen cast aside constitutional niceties to define what they personally felt were patriotic actions to defend the Republic. The policemen defending the premises of the Capitol, members of Congress and senators accused pro-Trump rioters of violating their professional oath of protecting the constitution. This was plausible in one direction because a good number of the rioters were retired military personnel who believed President Trump was the saviour of white supremacist causes in the country *and* legitimately won the presidential elections of 2020. It was no small irony that the rioters with military experience threw the same challenge against those defending the Capitol and the legislators within it: the enforcers of law and order *were themselves breaking the oath* of protecting the constitution (Steinhauer, 2021). Reflecting on the incident of 6 January, a former US Marine and intelligence officer wrote an editorial for *The New York Times* and commented:

> Our all-volunteer force, combined with two decades of pervasive war, has created a vast civil–military divide in America. Increasingly,

civilians don't understand the military, and vice versa. Republics with large standing militaries and endemic political dysfunction have not fared well over the course of history. (Ackerman, 2021)

In Asia, where the vast majority of political systems are republics in name only, and mostly afflicted with 'endemic political dysfunction' under the tumultuous challenges of nation and state-building, civil–military divides are deliberately fudged as a strategy. In many instances, the fudge transformed into a fusion to expedite national construction, political coalition, the consolidation of national identity and even defence diplomacy.

At the beginning of the 21st century, civil–military relations in Asia have evolved in several trajectories that have indubitably stretched the study of the subject in unprecedented ways. In this book, we argue that civil–military relations in Asia ought to be analysed under the concept of *Asian military evolutions*. Civil–military relations have conventionally been derived as a subject worthy of political and scholarly attention because it addresses the question of the viability of a democracy while it has to constitutionally control its so-called 'armed guardian'. The theme of Asian military evolutions addresses both deliberate and accidental political efforts to defuse disputes between civilian politicians and military leaders over the operation of political order, *and* builds on innovative attempts to treat civil–military relations as a productive field for defence diplomacy and military operations other than war (MOOTW). Of course, the 'threat to democracy' *problematique* the study of civil–military relations has conventionally dealt with has not completely lost relevance as events over the past two decades have shown across Myanmar, Thailand, Indonesia and Bangladesh. However, the blurring of the civilian and the military spheres is increasingly becoming recognized as a key component of strategies to deal with Asia's broadening national and transnational security agendas, what has become popularly known also as non-traditional security or human security (Kerr, 2007). In order to probe Asia as broadly as possible for our social scientific purpose, this volume includes contributions from Southeast Asia, Northeast Asia and South Asia. We chose what we believe to be a reasonable sample of chapters to broach the idea of Asian military evolutions. In this regard, we geographically omit Iran in the Western extremity and exclude Central Asia and Russia to the north.

While the military is traditionally trained to anticipate and plan for physical and hostile human invasions across a demarcated sovereign border, it is theoretically less adept at using the 'soft power' needed to solve humanitarian crises, conduct non-invasive search and rescue operations, coordinate multinational sea patrols and build confidence for future MOOTW engagements. This aloofness towards 'soft' missions is rapidly changing. Additionally, civil–military relations in Asia have taken on the patina of a multilateral defence diplomacy that promotes regular formal and informal dialogues between serving members of each country's defence think tanks, schools and selected military units. It might even be said that Asian civil–military relations have expediently evolved an international public relations wing. It will become evident once we start surveying the state of the field that Asian military evolutions assume a *hybridized distinctiveness* that fills a lacuna in the literature. These are 'evolutionary' practices since most Asian militaries, along with the scholars who study them, have tried to incorporate standard Western derived frameworks of civil–military relations into both praxis and theory but have seen the necessity to adapt them to suit local circumstances. Asian practice will reveal creative fusions and some novel departures in rendering civil–military relations an asset in furthering national security objectives.

The purpose of the following survey is to point out the limitations of existing frameworks of civil–military relations. Foremost in orthodox civil–military relations theorizing is the question of democratic control followed by the adjoining, newer paradigm of 'control, effectiveness and efficiency'. We will further review a section of localized civil–military relations literature, which we label as 'Civil–Military Relations for Development?', with a dedicated focus on Asian Global South civil–military relations perspectives. Finally, before we introduce the chapters of the book, we will treat the increasingly conscious overlap between Asian civil–military relations and MOOTW under the label 'Civil–Military Relations as an Asset in Human Security: The Practice of Asian Defence Diplomacy'. Notably, the idea of development is key to understanding that across Asia security equals development and that understanding of security *qua* development encompasses human security in many aspects. Development is therefore to be understood in Asia as the pursuit of the consolidation of statehood and nationhood, actions ensuring political stability that do not exclude violent put downs of civilian 'misrule', and the involvement by militaries in direct contributions to the economy, social rehabilitation and disaster relief.

In almost all the chapters, the idea of development and human security priorities in ordering civil–military relations are either twinned or blend easily from one into the other, eliminating the divide between the civilian and the military that is fundamental to traditional civil–military relations paradigms. In positing Asian military evolutions, we are conscious of distinguishing this book from the two major works edited by Muthiah Alagappa two decades ago, which posited that Asian civil–military relations still revolved around zero-sum curtailment of predatory military behaviour in politics (Alagappa, 2001a; 2001b). The realities of Asian civil–military practices are such that coercion and Huntingtonian-type military professionalism are blended into the grand cause of development. The public discourses on civil–military relations in most of our cases do not prioritize democratic considerations. Instead, they jointly embed development and nationalism as primary missions.

The question of democratic control

Peter Feaver, one of the foremost interpreters of the traditional mould of studying civil–military relations, summed up this approach in the question 'How do civilians control the military?' (Feaver, 2003, p 1). Inspired by the United States of America's deep historical suspicion of tyrannical authority exercised through the force of arms, this approach takes after the paradox of needing an adequately armed military to protect a contractual political community from all external threats, and yet fearing that the very military destined for protection may ironically harm the very society it is supposed to protect. The latter, dire scenario can occur through the military assuming the role of chief executive instead of acting as a mere guardian of society and draining that society of its resources to fund defence. Moreover, a 'rogue military' could conceivably act as a Frankensteinian-like foreign policy agent, dragging the society it deigns to protect into conflicts with other societies that run contrary to the interests of the former (Feaver, 2003, p 5).

Peter Feaver's scholarly inspiration, Samuel Huntington, famously described this paradox as a principal tension between the functional imperative of soldiering and societal pressures outside the control of the military. When Huntington refers to the core of civil–military relations being the relationship of the officer corps to the state, he is implying that the superior ranks of the military confront daily difficult choices in discharging their function of defending the state. This defence of the state usually implies that soldiering is a profession derived from the challenge of mastering winning security strategies, maintaining discipline among their subordinates and relating their mission to the possibilities of technology and intelligence availability (Huntington, 1957, pp 3–14). Societal pressures, on the other hand, emanate from the assumed civilian nature of the state, including the population contained within it. Societal pressures are generated by 'social forces, ideologies, and institutions dominant within the society' (Huntington, 1957, p 2). Huntington warned that the military could not always conform to any of these pressures for to do so may well compromise operationally the functional imperative. For instance, the military ought not to be expected to practise an unadulterated form of democracy in its hierarchy since this would undercut the chain of command and the professional ethic of obedience by subordinate ranks to the superior ones. Likewise, when the military rehearses for lethal combat against an armed opponent that is most likely to be another comparable military organization from a hostile sovereignty, this same logic cannot be applied to the policing of criminal violence in civilian settings.

The exception to the latter may be the imposition of martial law by the sitting government. Even then, it is not expected that martial law would be invoked as a norm in a liberal democracy. Huntington's thesis is in the main a US liberal democratic reading of 18th- and 19th-century British and European continental traditions updated to the World War Two era lessons of German and Japanese militarism at home. He unambiguously condemns the excesses of allowing the functional imperative of the military to override the societal pressures it must manage in order to preserve a working form of liberal democracy. It is therefore no surprise that Huntington's acolyte, Peter Feaver, refines civil–military tensions into a probe of the complexities between the US civilian government acting as political 'principal' issuing mission orders to its security 'agent' or executor of policies, the military. If the agent defies the principal, the latter can employ a range of constitutional and 'extra-legal' punishments to force compliance (Feaver, 2003, pp 87–95). Subsequent research by others on the portents and prospects of 'democratic armies' in Africa, Asia and the Middle East stems from such a line of argument (Barany, 2012). Even so, such research reads an excessive silver lining into how non-Western civil–military relations models align with the Huntington–Feaver approach by relying on a number of extremely 'safe' country studies like India, Bangladesh, post-1998 Indonesia and South Korea to support its claims. Additionally, the treatment of Pakistan and Thailand veers towards unwarranted optimism for democratic development (Barany, 2012, pp 178–211; 245–74).

Read in this light, the Huntington–Feaver 'school' universally places a premium on the fact that civil–military relations ought to only be measured against the yardstick of a functioning liberal democracy. It reflects a thoroughly North American warning of militarization, and by most scholarly extensions worldwide, a Western approach to civil–military relations that ignores the many hybridized perspectives that do not necessarily condemn the militarization of society as an unmitigated evil.

The new civil–military relations? Control, effectiveness and efficiency

Some Western scholars have helpfully adopted in the early 2000s a critical perspective on the question of democratic control while hardly straying from the latter's framework. As Thomas Bruneau and Florina Matei put it, the obsession with democratic transition and consolidation in post-military dictatorship polities was unhealthily reinforced by the popular fervour that greeted the so-called Third Wave of democratization beginning in the mid-1970s and that lasted through the collapse of communism in Eastern and Central Europe (Matei, 2013, p 29). Leading studies in Comparative Politics, such as those by Juan Linz, Alfred Stepan, Philippe Schmitter and Adam

Przeworski anchored their examinations of the erstwhile Third World polities in the institutionalization and political culture-building of new democracies by treating the military as 'actors' and another 'variable' in the consolidation of the new participatory regimes. While noble, even idealistic and practical by turns, this focus on the military under democratization had the effect of over-privileging democratic security over national security (Matei, 2013, p 30). Most studies prioritized analysis of a depoliticized military 'tradecraft' or the failures of military and paramilitary intelligence institutions measured against benchmarks of professionalism in technical terms. In this regard, we must acknowledge the contribution of Morris Janowitz, who continued where Huntington left off by arguing that military professionalism ought to be put under the sociological microscope by virtue of the fact that 'modern technology has produced such a high level of specialization that men are likely to think of themselves as members of a specific skill group, rather than as members of a social class' (Janowitz, 1960, p 7). Following on the heels of scholarship focussing on 'military professionalism', the circumstances of the post-9/11 US military administration of 'postwar' Afghanistan and Iraq served to usher into a new phase of civil–military relations scholarship (Matei, 2013, p 30). The emphasis lay in transitioning from combat operations to stabilization operations, that in its more genteel phrasing, are better dubbed 'nation-building'. The latter phrase is peculiar to the US-centric discourse, for when we survey non-Western literature on civil–military relations in the next section, 'nation-building' is but one dimension of the broader effort mustered by the military in pursuing development.

The *Routledge Handbook of Civil–Military Relations* edited by Florina Matei and Thomas Bruneau attempts to shift the paradigm of civil–military relations scholarship towards a more equilibrated, tripartite conceptualization of control, effectiveness and efficiency. As Matei put it, the struggle between civilians and the military for control of the destiny of the state may conveniently cut to the heart of debates about democratic consolidation but does not address how effectively the relative control each side exerts against the other expedites or hinders missions that aim to advance national and international security (Matei, 2013, p 29). Matei adduces examples of counterterrorist policing and preventive operations from Bali to Moscow that exemplify a new form of civil–military 'synergy'. Moreover, US and NATO involvement in so-called Peace Support Operations redirect the focus on civil–military relations to deliver new combinations of policing and nation-building powers to rehabilitate war-torn societies. The aim is therefore to study civil–military relations in terms of 'what armed forces, police forces and intelligence agencies actually do in the twenty-first century, how well they do it, and at what cost in personnel and treasure' (Matei, 2013, pp 29–30).

Control now assumes a supervisory position in terms of monitoring compliance with mission mandates, the scrutiny of institutional mechanisms that facilitate the application of relevant national and international laws in civil–military relations, and the harmonization of civilian-led organizational units with military units in an operation. Effectiveness, the second of the new civil–military relations paradigm's three elements, is assessed upon how the military, and where applicable their civilian partners, perform in missions. Matei admits that effectiveness is very difficult to measure since the indicators of successful achievement depend on a variety of subjective goals and on unambiguously declared political objectives, the specification of margins of error in executing missions and so forth (Matei, 2013, p 32). Matei and Bruneau's third grand concept is that of efficiency, evidently borrowed from rational choice theory. As Matei confidently declares, 'efficiency in the use of resources refers to the ability to fulfil assigned roles and missions at the optimum cost' (Matei, 2013, p 32). Thereafter, she quickly warns that efficiency is fundamentally slippery, not least because waging wars 'successfully', curbing terrorism and stabilizing peace in post-conflict situations may potentially be existential endeavours. Efficiency in civil–military relations is therefore a 'red herring' in the field of security unless one is completely wedded to the operating assumptions behind defence economics where everything from equipping the military to assessing its performance on the battlefield or peace enforcement contexts can be coded and consequently measured through statistics (Matei, 2013, p 33). Consequently, Thomas Bruneau, Aurel Croissant, Florina Matei and Carolyn Halladay have argued that the question of control stands out as a contested construct between western democracies and non-western semi-democracies and autocracies. Effectiveness however allows for better comparative analyses across all country cases, since the concept assesses civil-military relations in terms of how militaries transform political guidance into efficacious action in everything from conventional military operations to MOOTW (Bruneau and Croissant, 2019; Matei et al, 2022). This turn towards comparing effectiveness of national militaries comes closest to what our book explores via the notion of Asian military evolutions. Asian military effectiveness is attained by conflating ideology, control and development in all cases.

Closely associated with the work of Matei and Bruneau is the approach of security sector reform (SSR) sketched by Timothy Edmunds. As the term implies, SSR 'aims to reform security institutions to make them better at creating a secure environment for individuals and communities, in a way that is consistent with democratic norms and principles of good governance' (Edmunds, 2013, p 48). Edmunds adapted this definition from the Organization for Economic Cooperation and Development (OECD) but evidently embeds the Huntington–Feaver line along with the control, effectiveness and efficiency dynamics of Matei and Bruneau. SSR is clearly aimed at rehabilitating civil–military relations in developing nation contexts (that is, Global South), or post-conflict contexts, where the local military and police forces were an active factor in either retarding development or contributing to unrest, thus even reversing it. This can even be stretched to include discussion of civil–military relations under the involvement of private military and security companies, which unsurprisingly distracts from indigenous interpretations of civil–military relations (Heinecken, 2014). In this regard, the SSR approach condescendingly frames Global South civil–military relations exclusively into questions of democratic professionalism. Such an approach clearly neglects the voices of determination from the Global South pertaining to their own derivations of civil–military relations.

Civil–military relations for development? Studying the Asian Global South

When one discusses the ambiguity of MOOTW today as an area where civilian and military spheres are deliberately and by definition tousled, it is helpful to consider that this has antecedents in the role of the military in development in what we call the Global South today, or the 'Third World' of newly decolonized states in the 1950s through 1970s. As Shils wrote in 1962 against the backdrop of military regimes ruling in Pakistan, Iraq, Sudan, the United Arab Republic and South Korea, 'the ascendancy of the military in the domestic life of these states has been a response to the difficulties which the new states have encountered in their efforts to establish themselves as modern sovereignties' (Shils, 1962, p 8). Shils echoed the view articulated by Samuel Huntington, Neil Smelser, Cyril Black and Walt Rostow – all of whom were scholars of developmental sociology or political economy – that modernization implied that the new state had to be democratic, build institutions to practise and safeguard that democracy, while also making the economy and democracy relevant to the people's needs. At the same time, the entire new society should be 'dynamic' in adjusting to new scientifically oriented education designed to produce a technologically oriented labour force for a modern industrial and agricultural economy. This also meant ownership of land had to be redistributed or repurposed for a modern economy. Additionally, the advent of new occupations meant displacing traditional power elites. The latter was dismissed by Shils as 'the *ancien regime* of landlords, sheikhs, chiefs, rajahs and grand viziers' who were assumed in most developmental contexts to stand in the way of modern democracy and economy since they stood to lose influence and authority (Shils, 1962, p 9). Therefore, the elite that dares to push through transformative policies runs the risk of triggering reactionary resistance from these quarters. This resistance can be operated within a democratic constitution, or temptingly, outside it for a quicker result. This is where the political space opens up for the military to skew modern civil–military relations in favour of military government for modernization.

Lucian Pye's contribution to the same volume that Shils contributed to, that is *The Role of the Military in Underdeveloped Countries*, edited by John J. Johnston, makes a bold prediction of the transformative figure of the military in a developmental context. In this regard, Pye's words are worth quoting in some detail:

> [T]he good soldier is also to some degree a modernized man. Thus it is that the armies in the newly emergent countries come to play key roles in the process by which traditional ways give way to more Westernized [ie as modern] ideas and practices. The very fact that the recruit must break his ties and associations with civilian life and adjust to the more impersonal world of the army tends to emphasize the fundamental nature of this process, which involves the movement out of the particularistic relationships of traditional life and into the more impersonal and universalistic relationships of an industrialized society.
>
> Army training is thus consistent with the direction taken by the basic process of acculturation in traditional societies. Within the army, however, the rate of acculturation is greatly accelerated. This fact contributes to the tendency of army officers to underestimate the difficulties of changing the civilian society … In contrast to the villager who is caught up in the process of being urbanized, the young army recruit from the village has the more sheltered, the more gradual introduction into the modern world. It is hardly necessary to point out the disturbing fact that the urbanization process as it has taken place in most Asian, African, and Latin American societies has generally tended to produce a highly restless, insecure population. Those who have been forced off the land or attracted to the cities often find themselves in a psychologically threatening situation. These are the people who tend to turn to extremist politics and to look for some form of social and personal security in political movements that demand their total commitment. (Pye, 1962, pp 80–81)

In this line of reasoning, military government represents salvation amid the turbulence of modernization. This is a familiar story with the initially enlightened missions motivating so many *golpes de estado* in Latin America from Argentina to Brazil to Chile and Nicaragua (Loveman and Davies, 1997; Mullins, 2006). In Asia, the Indonesian military invoked a 'New Order' following the overthrow of the ostentatious, economically inept and ideologically capricious Soekarno in October 1965. Likewise, the military overthrow of Rhee Syng-man's regime in South Korea in 1961 and Ngo Dinh Diem in South Vietnam in 1963, were explained as efforts to overcome corruption in government impeding national prosperity and security. In Myanmar in 1962, and again in 1988, the military explained its takeover of government citing civilian politicians' inability to maintain law and order and mismanagement of the economy. In Thailand too, this book will demonstrate how coups between 1932 and the latest one in 2014 were consistently legitimized based on the normative claims of modernization, national renovation and economic development. Without too much of a stretch, even Japan's disastrous venture into a war of conquest against its Asian neighbours between 1931 and 1945 was explained away as a revitalized form of modernized nationalism. It is rarely possible for the development-oriented military that seizes power in a coup d'état to succeed in keeping its high-minded promises. But the patterns of political recurrence suggest that the salvation roles of Asian militaries remain both permanent and existential for the foreseeable future.

The literature on the developmental aspects of civil–military relations in the Global South is vast. Since it often emerges as country and region-specific case studies, we will adhere to surveying the main civil–military relations literature produced on or within Asia itself. In one of the earliest dedicated edited volumes on the subject published in 1985, Zakaria Haji Ahmad and Harold Crouch preferred the term 'military–civilian relations' instead of civil–military relations. As Ahmad explains it, in Southeast Asian cases, the term civil–military relations implies that the military has intervened vis-à-vis the normality of civilian rule with an assumption that such an intervention will in all likelihood produce a negative result. 'Military–civilian relations' on the other hand suggests that 'militaries that do not intervene in the political process may very well have a political role as well' (Ahmad, 1985, p 4). This is significant given the fact that Ahmad and Crouch's volume still associates with the developmental cum modernization paradigm, while also emphasizing that the military in Southeast Asia should be viewed as a component of each country's political system and society. Ahmad's sole authored introduction points out that the nature of the colonial experience distinguished the evolution of the roles of the military in two ways. The 'gradual' quality of nationalist struggles in Malaysia, Singapore and the Philippines ensured that the respective militaries subordinated themselves to civilian authority by and large. In the second mode, where colonial powers were extremely resistant to granting independence to their colonies – as in Burma/Myanmar, Indonesia, Laos and Vietnam – the respective militaries sought to institutionalize a dominant role in the political landscape by both force and law (Ahmad, 1985, p 5). Ahmad pointed out that the relative degrees of politicization of the officer corps also mattered in terms of how far their militaries would be tempted to increase their visibility in domestic politics. Finally, he argued that 'exogenous factors' were equally crucial in determining the nature of military–civilian relations. Colonial practices in instituting local forms of 'gendarmerie', vigilante corps, home guard equivalents or other armed auxiliaries to aid imperial war efforts outside Southeast Asia could all have left indelible institutional imprints. Likewise, the military experiences of regular and irregular combat in World War Two and the concomitant and *post facto* influences of the US and China in the transition to the post-1945 order would also leave their institutional traces. Of course, the onset of the Cold War would have habituated Southeast Asian militaries to assume political roles, training and operational doctrines in particular ways as well (Ahmad, 1985, pp 5–6).

For nearly a decade, the Ahmad and Crouch-edited volume would remain a standard reference for civil–military relations in Southeast Asia. An edited volume by Viberto Selochan treating civil–military relations across a representative sample of Asian states followed up in 1991 (Selochan, 1991). In the introduction, Robin Luckham distinguished the legacies of militaries formed under colonial tutelage and those formed from protracted armed anti-colonial struggles. The latter was overtly political from their inception. Although Luckham had no reservations about the phrase civil–military relations, he did acknowledge that the experiences and trajectories of evolution of the military in a nascent state were vital ingredients in assessing their subsequent roles in the political system and externally. For instance, he noted that the Indonesian military built up their competence during campaigns to pacify 'a rebellious periphery' with significant material aid and training from both Cold War superpowers (Luckham, 1991, p 5). Moreover, the Sukarno presidency was favourable to the economic fortunes of the Indonesian military by enabling them to gain financial and political autonomy by running the nationalized Dutch colonial enterprises in the post-independence era. This ensured that the military would have a permanent stake in the domestic political economy. Hence when Sukarno's experiment in 'Guided Democracy' gradually handed power over to the communists, by 1965 the armed forces felt sufficiently threatened to stage a coup d'état against Sukarno's regime (Luckham, 1991, p 6).

In myriad ways, the development-oriented civil–military relations literature on the Asia-Pacific added vital variation to the control, effectiveness and efficiency approach to civil–military relations although it has never jettisoned the Huntington-Feaver paradigm. The follow-up volume by R.J. May and Viberto Selochan in 1998 titled *The Military and Democracy in Asia and the Pacific* continued to highlight these variations in Asian civil–military relations (May and Selochan, 1998). In an even bolder volume in 2001, Alagappa called upon contributors to 16 country studies ranging from Bangladesh, China, India, Indonesia, Japan, Malaysia, Burma/Myanmar, Pakistan to even politically placid Singapore and Vietnam to buttress an argument pronouncing the ultimate decline of the political role of the military in Asia (Alagappa, 2001b). One will easily quibble with Alagappa's choice of case studies – India, Singapore, Malaysia, Japan – not normally associated with turbulence in civil–military relations, but fitting the rest into an optimistic overall assessment of decline of the military in politics. The chapters on Thailand, Pakistan in the wake of the coup led by Pervez Musharraf in

1999, and Burma are particularly awkward given the fact that the respective militaries continue to defy the central thesis of the volume and have quite obviously retrenched their roles within constitutional limits and wider political precedents.

More realistic and helpful to our observation about Asian military evolutions are three recent volumes by Aurel Croissant, David Kuehn, Philip Lorenz, Paul Chambers and Terence Lee. Croissant et al revisited the question of 'who guards the guardians' by focussing on the 'agency-structure' problem from the perspective of civilian governments. Drawing upon strands of earlier research on civil–military relations, Croissant et al emphasize the 'political entrepreneurship and strategic actions of civilians' in each of their seven country studies (Croissant et al, 2013, p 15). Civilians can tame the political dispositions and characteristics of the military by 'breaking' existing patterns of less than democratically friendly civil–military relations through putting in place institutions that retard intervention or incentivize the military to adhere to alternative forms of professionalization and role differentiation. Croissant et al go on to deconstruct analytical categories for the relationship between democracy and civil–military relations in terms of 'effective power to govern' as opposed to defining democracies constraining military roles in politics through formal measures of civil liberties, horizontal accountability and political rights (Croissant et al, 2013, p 25). Pushing this argument further, Croissant et al suggest that the analysis of Asian civil–military relations ought to focus on elite recruitment, public policy, internal security, national defence and military organization (Croissant et al, 2013, pp 26–36). This is significant in appreciating the thickness of local contexts and the political mastery of managing political power in micro-processes within and without formal institutions. This belated acknowledgement of Asian particularity also explains why most indigenous scholarship on civil–military relations has in the past tended to avoid theorizing altogether, as it is evident in the earlier mentioned Ahmad and Crouch and Selochan et al edited volumes, where virtually every country study analysed civil–military relations in mostly discrete local articulations.

Terence Lee's 2015 work frames civil–military relations in terms of what he denominates 'military responses to popular protests in authoritarian Asia' (Lee, 2015). It is noteworthy that he accepts that much of Asia is governed in an authoritarian context. Therefore, civil–military relations ought to be approached through analysis of the internal dynamics of regime consolidation, deterioration or downfall. Lee posited that regime longevity is mostly buttressed by power-sharing political institutions supported by a 'minimum winning coalition', even where authoritarian rule is personified in one person (Lee, 2015, pp 30–1). He then goes on to extrapolate how military authoritarian regimes nurture their rule by similar means while potentially, and simultaneously, personalizing the regime in the image of one person. This is handled through a ruling council of senior officers, established usually through elite consent rules and norms for rotating political office, succession and intra-elite dispute resolution. At the same time, the organizational hierarchy within the military is retained. Authoritarian rule is therefore sustained so long as no member of the military elite feels disenfranchised enough to succumb to the temptation to defect to 'the other side' under the provocation of a mass protest by non-elites (Lee, 2015, pp 36–46). Lee illustrates these explanations via case studies of Indonesia, the Philippines, Burma/Myanmar and China.

Lee's study in many ways serves as a culminating point in the study of Asian civil–military relations by emphasizing the possibility that democratization is not the only political game domestically. Making a social contract with the governed population under the terms of an authoritarian well-ordered state may well account for the creative fusions Asian militaries practise in retaining varying degrees of political salience. A related question also beckons with respect to the governance of Asian developmental polities: do Asian states necessarily require liberal democracy to deliver the public goods of order and mass prosperity?

In a remarkable edited volume that was published in 2017, Paul Chambers and Napisa Waitoolkiat add economic welfare to the list of developmental goods desired by the population, and the polity in general, from the Asian military. Leading into the subject is a discussion about how the military supplies violence as a public and private commodity in a 'political security market' (Chambers and Waitoolkiat, 2017, p 4). Violence in this economic, market-oriented developmental sense does not necessarily always entail the actual demonstration of kinetic violence. Instead Asian militaries, as exemplified by those in Southeast Asia, enact roles for 'khaki capital' connoting that entities in military fatigues play a role in the political economy of their respective nation-states. The authors elaborate their concept of 'khaki capital' in terms of:

> a form of income generation whereby the military, as the state-legitimized and dominant custodian of violence, establishes a mode of production that enables it (a) to influence state budgets to extract open or covert financial allocations; (b) to extract, transfer and distribute financial resources; and (c) to create financial or career opportunities that allow for the direct or indirect enhancement of its dividends at both the institutional and the individual level. Such enhancements include military business enterprises, foundations operated by and creating income for elements of (or all of) the military or defence ministry, and individual entitlements (e.g. sinecures). (Chambers and Waitoolkiat, 2017, pp 7–8)

This sort of market-oriented role for Southeast Asian militaries developed roots during the colonial era when the outposts of European empires in the

Dutch East Indies, French-controlled Cambodia, Laos and Vietnam, and the Spanish Philippines all found ways of sustaining themselves through collusions with local comprador and colonial enterprises as a means of supplementing the tenuous financing from their respective European metropoles. Indeed, colonial militaries established a pattern whereby they were closely integrated into the colonial government structures that supervised simultaneously the extractive industries such as the plantations, coal, tin and iron ore.

Not surprisingly, most of the new national armies that both fuelled, and in some cases, led the struggles for decolonization during and after World War Two, likewise developed fairly well-honed experiences with owning large tracts of land, running corporations and operating budgets that supported their own 'national development' activities. This was quite evident in all of Indochina and Indonesia (Chambers and Waitoolkiat, 2017, pp 16–18). Only Brunei, Malaysia, the Philippines and Singapore bucked this trend while their civilian governments found other ways in which the respective militaries could be scripted into narratives of economic defence of nationalist agendas.

Marco Bünte's study of Myanmar suggested that the expansion of a national security state following the military's self-declared failure of the short-lived democratic experiment of 1987–8 facilitated the large-scale expansion of military-run enterprises as a way to not only fund the military's autonomy in running the country, but it also provided funds for modernizing the military's hardware capabilities. In areas where the *Tatmadaw* superficially pacified ethnic insurgencies, the former offered both their erstwhile adversaries and themselves a peace dividend by selling licences for extracting the hitherto conflict-ridden areas' natural resources (Bünte, 2017, pp 102–4). In neighbouring Thailand, the circumstances of the 1932 'Military Coup' that relegated the monarchy to a constitutional one started an era that has lasted into the present whereby the military established for itself a disproportionate say in politics. Military-owned enterprises have been largely treated as political protectorates that provided handsomely for former military officials in their retirement as well as anchoring the loyalty of politicians associated with them. Waitoolkiat and Chambers dubbed this a system of 'military sinecures' since the late 1940s (Waitoolkiat and Chambers, 2017, p 43). As in Myanmar, the significant control of Thai military enterprises boded well for the military's guardianship role in every instance of national crisis such as in 2006, and again in 2014, where civilian democratic politicians and civil society were blamed for fomenting social divisions to the detriment of political stability, hence necessitating acts of military guardianship of the monarchy and national security.

In Carlyle Thayer's study of Vietnam's military economy, he makes the familiar argument that following the reunification of the country at the end of the Vietnam War, the Vietnam People's Army (VPA) was tasked to support development. The instruction from the highest echelons of the Communist Party to volunteer military manpower for civilian reconstruction paved the way for the VPA to establish its own corporate entities for building roads, railways, ports, industrial plants and other civil installations. Today, VPA-controlled businesses pay taxes like other corporate entities and are 'permitted by law to engage in commercial ventures because it earns funds to support genuine military activities that the state budget does not meet' (Thayer, 2017, p 145). In the Philippines, the military was likewise given significant economic reins under martial law during the Marcos administration to buttress the government's base of patronage. Government-controlled companies were assigned to generals and other high-ranking and retired officers to assist their political buy-in into the Marcos system of kleptocratic politics (Hall, 2017, pp 274–5). Even after the post-Marcos democratic transition, the steady involvement of the armed forces in combating local insurgencies enticed members of the deployed units at the murky frontlines to avail themselves of the wealth that could be gained through participation in the underground economies in the conflict zones (Hall, 2017, pp 290–5). Such is the ironic nature of the developmental political economy of Southeast Asian militaries, potentially mirrored elsewhere across developmental Asia. Therein also lies a permanent window of opportunity for the military to anchor itself into a domestic role equal or greater to the one aspired to by civilians.

Civil–military relations as an asset in human security: the practice of Asian defence diplomacy

If militaries in Asia were being acculturated to support a developmental, nation-building oriented mission that ran the gamut from direct participation in the economy to the construction of roads, houses and the delivery of humanitarian relief, it was only logical for them to extend into the realm of defence diplomacy. In the practice of the latter, the aim was generally to build confidence and familiarity with one another's capabilities with the ultimate goal of anchoring bilateral and multilateral friendships between mostly latent armed adversaries. The rapid rise of unprecedented 'webs' of bilateral and multilateral defence diplomacy was accompanied by studies that mapped the extensive use of military exchanges and which debated whether or not the many cooperative activities actually made a difference to Asian security (Capie and Taylor, 2010; Singh and Tan, 2011). Bilateral tensions and residual misgivings, divergent strategic imperatives and the lack of institutional coherence were cited as standing in the way of effective defence regionalism. Regardless of whether the various security dialogues were merely smokescreen (Baldino and Carr, 2016) or actually amounted to more than mere 'talk shops', they nonetheless made an impact domestically in terms of doctrinal rethinking and functional tweaking of missions.

Defence diplomacy, which is mostly understood in line with Cottey and Forster as 'the peacetime cooperative use of armed forces and related infrastructure (primarily defence ministries) as a tool of foreign and security policy' (2004, p 6), poses a definitional problem for Western-inspired civil–military relations scholarship. Defence diplomacy blurs the categories of 'military' and 'civilian', which are intimately linked to the distinction between war and peace that ultimately underpin the particular domestic order of the modern state (Angstrom, 2013). Only by defining civilian versus military roles in war and in peacetime is it possible to establish what are considered legitimate forms of violence and distinguish these from murder and other practices of criminal violence banned in modern societies. Nonetheless, the Asian experience shows that the fudging of the categories of military/civilian and war/peace remains pervasive. China's 'maritime militia' is a case in point. The hundreds of quickly massing fishing boats that exert the PRC's territorial claims in the South China Sea and beyond are not even officially acknowledged by Beijing. Likewise, the global shift towards 'softer' military missions of humanitarian security has not signified the end of politics but implies different forms of contest within and between states, as this volume will show. These softer missions include peace operations, as Nicole Jenne's chapter emphasizes (Chapter 9).

To some extent, the military was eager to participate in defence diplomacy and assume new roles in supplying human security as it stood to lose ground in a post-Cold War era where traditional roles of national defence appeared to be of declining relevance. But while the new roles served to defend economic interests and other prerogatives, defence diplomacy was not wholeheartedly embraced everywhere. The question of who stands to gain, the military or the civilian components of foreign and security policy making, is not easily answered but it is surely true that the overarching goal of the new international engagement has been to camouflage the hard power component represented by the armed forces. Yee-Kuang Heng's study of the Japanese Self-Defense Forces in Tokyo's soft power approach illustrates how well the military's role gets diluted in a soft power package where 'Japan's actions must preferably be seen as non-coercive' and the role of the Self-Defense Forces is described 'as "an international civilian assistance activity", despite the use of naval vessels' (Heng, 2015, p 299). Against the backdrop of organizational rivalry, Heng reports that the Ministry of Foreign Affairs' 'preferred means to support its favoured concept of "human security" tends to rely more on financial and development assistance' rather than the security forces (Heng, 2015, p 304). Clearly, the military is not sidelined in Asian defence diplomacy but neither does it supply the legitimizing discourses and actions central to the new security. As human security missions strain resources that may otherwise be used to perform traditional missions, defence diplomacy both pushed the armed forces away from their previous tasks without allowing them to take full ownership of the new ones. The evolution of Asia's military missions can also be taken to mean that a serious re-definition of practising national defence manoeuvres has taken place.

In a region that has seen its last large-scale armed conflict in 1979, what is officially described as non-traditional missions takes on special relevance for the armed forces. Thus, observers have argued that one important motivation driving the steep increase in joint exercises of China's PLA over the past two decades was the desire to make up for the lack of real combat experience (Blasko, 2010, p 377). Whether these exercises are designed as anti-drug smuggling, border security, anti-terrorist operations or humanitarian assistance and disaster relief (HADR), they are hardly decoupled from national defence considerations. By increasing what the Chinese government called its 'MOOTW capabilities', Asian countries have simultaneously augmented their capacity to project force abroad for purposes including combat (Engstrom, 2013). HADR operations have been used to demonstrate military capabilities as a signal to other regional states and even as a direct substitute for armed competition (Chong and Chang, 2016; Chang and Jenne, 2020). The COVID-19 pandemic has only served to underscore the military's role even in domestic HADR. MOOTW therefore needs to be understood not only as a demonstration project for positive relations, but as a new form of security competition 'by proxy' with potentially worrisome consequences for both regional stability and human security.

Consequently, Asia's defence diplomacy also needs to be read in conjunction with the coercive diplomacy short of armed conflict that has characterized the bilateral relations between India and China, China and Japan, Indonesia and Malaysia and Malaysia and Singapore, to name but four of the region's most troubled country pairs. Clearly, even in Southeast Asia where the web of security cooperation has been densest, defence diplomacy has failed to eradicate the militarization of interstate quarrels. On the contrary, there is sporadic evidence that suggests that the often-cited one thousand meetings Association of Southeast Asian Nations (ASEAN) officials attend every year lead to a situation of moral hazard, allowing for greater willingness to engage in coercive diplomacy due to a strongly felt confidence that low-intensity encounters will be resolved by someone talking to the other side before the situation escalates into serious conflict. That there is no automatic response to militarized crises became evident when a border dispute between Cambodia and Thailand developed into deadly clashes between the two countries in 2011. This rather surprising and isolated confrontation was illustrative of a more general Southeast Asian pattern where sustained and disruptive conflict is generally absent from regional relations, but where societies do not question the need for armed forces, as has been the case in parts of Europe and Latin America. Taken together, the influence of defence diplomacy is part of the deliberately ambiguous pathways of Asian military evolutions examined in this volume.

Orienting inquiry into Asian military evolutions

Drawing upon the preceding literature and trend analyses, we have tasked the contributors to respond directly to at least two of the research questions below:

1. How do colonial legacies influence the evolution of civil–military relations and the military's self-definition of vital roles?
2. Is the Asian military socially, politically and economically embedded to the point that civil–military relations cannot be viewed as a gap between civilian and military elements?
3. Are Asian militaries inclined to view effectiveness in civil–military relations mostly in relation to achieving developmental and modernization goals?
4. If modernization has been attained, especially in the economic realm, do Asian militaries retrench themselves towards a guardianship role vis-à-vis the maintenance of a *status quo* of authoritarian prosperity or do they support democratic prosperity?
5. Is Asian civil–military relations a strength in handling defence diplomacy *qua* HADR and confidence building measures, and in what way?
6. Is Asian defence diplomacy a means of ensuring that international security in the Indo-Pacific operates on two 'synergistic' tracks: mostly civilian roles in fronting formal security discussions while military representatives in and out of uniform float trial balloons in Track II fora?

Consequently, we have seen fit to organize the chapters according to three Asian sub-regions: Southeast Asia, Northeast Asia and South Asia.

Southeast Asia: colonial legacies, developmental modes and authoritarian predilections

In the first chapter, Adhi Priamarizki commences his study from Myanmar's so-called 'democratization' with the 2010 general elections. Nonetheless, the armed forces have maintained their domestic security role until they took power again in early 2021. Myanmar's military, the *Tatmadaw*, has indeed embarked on a modernization plan, but at the same time still emphasized its internal security duty in building its posture. By explaining the perseverance of the military's domestic security role and the 2021 coup despite a period of democratization in the country, Priamarizki's chapter deepens the understanding of the civil–military relations dynamics at work, including its heritage from British colonialism.

In Dahlia Gratia Setiyawan's study of nearby Indonesia, the contemporaneous claim staking by the Indonesian armed forces concerning internal security suggests an augmentation of military authority under the aegis of civilian

President Joko Widodo. Tentara Nasional Indonesia, the Indonesian National Armed Forces' (TNI) counterterrorism strong-arming and the manufacture of fears about proxy warfare, separatism and the revival of Indonesian communism have grown in volume and voracity. What explains the antiquated ideas of the last few years – more than two decades following the *Reformasi* period – and how do they illuminate the TNI's self-perception? To a greater degree than proximate causes, Setiyawan argues that an answer can be found by way of an historical analysis of the Territorial Command structure and the military's civic action programmes. By offering a departure from political histories that focus on elite civil–military relations, this analysis of structural conditions and their (post-)colonial origins suggests at least two things. First, that the issues the TNI is championing now are the result of a path dependent organizational culture. Second, that the TNI's present civil–military manoeuvring is contingent upon the continued influence of the Territorial Commands that went untouched after the political reforms that followed President Suharto's fall from power in 1998.

In Aries A. Arugay's study of Philippine civil–military relations, the socio-political context of the postcolonial polity has conditioned an awkwardly hybrid democratization of civil–military relations. Building on pre-existing civil–military relations literature on the Philippines, Arugay's chapter examines efforts by elected governments to impose civilian control but also to modernize one of Asia's weakest armed forces from 2010 onwards. On the one hand, the country boasts a robust legal framework and clear delineation of responsibilities among the institutions mandated to manage the military and hold it accountable. Arugay, however, argues that effective democratic civilian control is often contradicted by the militarization of civilian structures and the traditional reliance by civilians upon the military on security matters. Their accommodating, substitutive and latent nature profoundly provides political autonomy to the military despite the presence of formal civilian control. Their negative consequences in democratic civil–military relations have been compounded by the erosion of Philippine democracy under the leadership of populist and authoritarian president Rodrigo Duterte. In its conclusion, this chapter suggests that reforms related to building strong representative institutions such as parties, legislatures and other horizontal accountability institutions as well rebooting comprehensive SSR can restore the civil–military balance in the Philippines.

Even in hypermodern Singapore, Jun Yan Chang and Shu Huang Ho posit that civil–military distinctions have been elided as a deliberate act of nation-building by the island republic's nationalist leaders. Despite the numerical strength of the Singapore Armed Forces (SAF), the threat of coups in Singapore is non-existent. Prior scholarship suggests this is because the 'civilian' and 'military' worlds are integrated, with civil–military relations there described as one of "fusion". This chapter goes further in contending that the foundational cultural values of Singapore society and government, and its armed forces, are the same, precluding separate 'civilian' and 'military' worlds in the first place. While there may be a differentiation between 'civilian' and 'military' functions, in Singapore, there is no ontological difference between the solider and the citizen because the civil–military gap, fundamental to the civil–military *problematique* of maintaining control over the military, has never existed. Transcending the classic *problematique*, the authors consequently suggest that Singapore's civil–military relations ought to be understood in terms of their 'everyday' nature, the management of a relationship of roles rather than of two worlds with different identities and values.

In a major update on the seemingly untroubled civil–military relations situation in Malaysia, David Han's chapter describes the process through which the civilian leadership has been able to convince the military to support policies that eschew overly militarized solutions to address changing security challenges domestically and internationally. Thus, the Malaysian Armed Forces (MAF) were steered into supporting foreign and security policies in the form of HADR and peace operations in the late 1980s to facilitate national development. Han argues that this strategy has been particularly successful because military subordination ensured the neat execution of a comprehensive civilian strategy as well as the continuation of a stable civil–military relations balance. It is characteristic of the Asian model of military evolutions, however, that the MAF's apparent apolitical stance has persisted together with the ethnocentric communalism inherent in all facets of the Malaysian state that guarantees Malay supremacy and leadership.

Alexander L. Vuving's chapter on Vietnam offers a slightly contrasting civil–military relations landscape to the preceding five countries: a dominant socialist ruling party twins itself with the military as a base for its legitimacy. Vuving argues that the realities of civil–military relations in Vietnam defy the Western models that dominate the literature. The control architecture underlying this relationship is based on the mutual embeddedness of the military and the Communist Party. While the Party exerts political control over the military, the military's participation and influence in elite politics and policy making are not only legitimate but also an integral part of the architecture, where it plays a dual role as both military officers and Party members. Vuving's chapter demonstrates that, paradoxically, military conflict is not the only and not even the main reason for a surge in the military's influence in Vietnamese politics and foreign policy after the Cold War. The military gained more influence because it was assigned a major political role. While the Party's influence has been on the wane recently, its political control continues to prevail over the trends of commercialization and professionalization.

In neighbouring Thailand, the contours of civil–military relations are likewise defiant of the Western-derived mainstream models. Gregory

V. Raymond posits that Western models of civil–military relations do not apply in Thailand for three key reasons. First, Thailand's status as the sole uncolonized country of Southeast Asia has allowed greater continuity with its pre-colonial era political philosophies than in many other states. The end of the absolute monarchy in 1932, in particular, did not extinguish precolonial ideas of kingship and social order. Today, the division between the military and civilians is less important than a hierarchy that places *kharatchakan* (servants of the king) above business people or other professions, and the military higher than other public servants. Second, visible aspirations for liberal and egalitarian forms of government have been exhibited by disenfranchised groups whose demands for participation in governance have increased over time. Third, the shift in power in international politics, away from the West towards other centres of power, including illiberal and authoritarian states, is reducing the pressure on Thailand to undertake liberal democratic reforms. For these three reasons, Raymond proposes a 'trialectical' framework for Thai civil–military relations. While Thailand remains a hybrid state, in which democratic forces continue to wrestle with traditional elites, at this point in time they are not yet strong enough to force change towards liberal democratic political structures.

With a view to the Southeast Asian region as a whole, Nicole Jenne contributes a pioneering study of the emergence of peacekeeping as a frontier subject for Southeast Asian civil–military relations. Since the 1990s, Southeast Asian states have deployed their militaries in UN (United Nations) peace operations. Often couched in terms of 'Global South' or Asian solidarity, peace operations have become part of Southeast Asia's regionally promoted defence diplomacy that necessarily fuses civil and military functions. It is widely assumed that participation in peace operations will further the consolidation of the ASEAN Political-Security Community by creating convergence in national defence policies and personal contacts among security officials. Jenne's chapter asks whether Southeast Asia's peacekeeping activity effectively constitutes such a form of successful security cooperation. Three factors are examined in this regard: the potential for regional interaction capacity based on national peacekeeping trajectories, the level of regional activity around peace operations as compared to similar cooperation schemes with extra-regional states, and third, cooperation within the framework of individual peace operations. The chapter concludes on a cautious note. Given its liberal origins, peacekeeping challenges but is unlikely to change the quintessential norms of ASEAN cooperation such as face saving and non-interference. But on the positive side, peacekeeping facilitates a non-confrontational discursive diplomatic channel between Southeast Asian militaries and reinforces the civilian nature of the region's sublime, peace-preserving regional international society in the form of ASEAN.

Northeast Asia: democratization coexists with unrelenting elite rule and creative defence diplomacy

Moving on to Northeast Asia, a chapter on China by James Char examines civil–military relations of post-reform China since the 18th Party Congress. To Char, the clearest trend to have emerged has been the strengthening of civilian oversight over the country's armed forces. While that interaction was previously understood through the lens of Party-army relations, developments following the leadership transition in 2012 have since resulted in a new paradigm. By purging past and present PLA elites who had compromised CCP authority as well as promoting their more politically reliable counterparts, Xi Jinping – as the Party's top leader and China's commander-in-chief – has consolidated the trifecta of Party-state-military power, and in the process, centralized overwhelming authority unto himself. Notwithstanding the fact that the CCP's coercive forces have backed their civilian commander-in-chief to dominate the Chinese political landscape in the foreseeable future, whether the latter would be able – and willing – to translate his considerable politico-military clout into a fundamental transformation of an increasingly professional military remains to be seen.

Among the Northeast Asian states, the two Koreas are a natural choice for inclusion given their not too different histories of praetorian politics. Jongseok Woo's chapter on North Korea starts with a basic inquiry given the country's political opacity: what is the political place of the Korean People's Army (KPA) in Pyongyang? How have the three-generation hereditary power successions – from Kim Il-sung, to Kim Jong-il and to Kim Jong-un – been successful without any serious political repercussions, such as partisan infighting or a military coup attempt? What explains the wide gap between frequent mobilization of the KPA for regime security and its political weakness? Contrary to the predominant body of literature on North Korean military and politics, this chapter argues that Pyongyang's political system is an archetype of patrimonial system in which the three Kims have exercised undisputed political and ideological authority. In this setting, major political organs, both the party and the military, become mere servants of the dictator, and the political rise and fall of a particular institution reflects the dictator's ruling method of choice. In the abovementioned formative political changes, the KPA served as the backbone of the Kim family rule.

In Il Woo Lee and Alan Chong's contribution, South Korea merits analysis as a partial mirror image of the North Korean 'national security state'. The authors contend that pre-existing research mistreats South Korean civil–military relations within the framework of liberal democracy in the Western mould. The lingering consequences of Japanese colonialism have predetermined elite military attitudes towards independent South Korea. Beneath the veneer of Korean democracy lies a developmental authoritarianism, an ensemble of measures coordinated to neutralize the South Korean public's susceptibility towards left wing ideologies by delivering middle class prosperity through an industrialized economy and pursuing export-oriented development. In consequence, the failure to fully civilianize remains endemic to the South Korean political system and as Lee and Chong argue, the threat from North Korea serves as a political prop for authoritarian elites.

Finally, the Japanese path of civil–military relations offers yet another avenue of ingenuous Asian improvisation. In Yee-Kuang Heng's observation, in theory Japan may have no 'civil–military' relations to speak of, if one is to take a strict literal interpretation. Its post-World War Two pacifist constitution states that 'land, sea and air forces, as well as other war potential, will never be maintained'. Yet Tokyo maintains one of the most capable military forces in the Indo-Pacific, and it is evolving in quite significant ways for domestic public consumption and regional audiences. Heng's chapter examines the Japan Self-Defense Forces' (JSDF) relationship with its own public and its incrementally significant profile in regional Southeast Asian defence diplomacy. In stark contrast to other regional countries which suffered colonization, the JSDF has to deal with a colonial legacy in that Japan was an imperial colonizer in Southeast Asia. Wartime history and past militarism have also doubtlessly shaped civil–military relations in Japan. As Japanese governments have worked to gain legitimacy and public acceptance for the JSDF both domestically and internationally by utilizing memes from Japanese popular culture, the effectiveness of civil–military relations here may be further viewed in terms of domestic/regional acceptance of the JSDF's existence and roles, on top of the conventional emphasis on achieving developmental and modernization goals.

South Asia: building military leadership through colonial legacies, proxy for activist foreign policy and peacekeeping under civil–military fusion

India's experience with civil–military relations is represented in the chapter by Harsh V. Pant and Tuneer Mukherjee. The latter capture the challenge of India's civil–military relations as a deficit between doctrinal statements about the country's ambitions to serve as 'net security provider' in the Indian Ocean while working tardily towards bolstering military bureaucratic effectiveness. As Pant and Mukherjee argue, India remains rooted in Huntingtonian paradigms that advocate separate domains for the political leadership and the military. Unfortunately, this separation of roles has over time been institutionalized and legitimized to a degree where procedures have taken precedence over the tangible enhancement of military capability. Although there have been successful instances of collaboration between the civilian leadership and the military brass, their overall relationship has been strained by a bureaucracy that continuously seeks to protect its own role in India's civil–military arrangement.

The other significant capture of South Asian civil–military relations comes from the chapter on Bangladesh authored by Rashed Uz Zaman. Zaman focuses on how a military enjoying popular legitimacy embarks on a successful spectrum of MOOTW. Since its creation, the Bangladesh military has expanded its recruitment base and became a geographically, economically, ethnically and religiously representative force. As the military – a key provider of social advancement and other benefits in the country – became more accessible it came to represent greater national cohesion. The Bangladesh Armed Forces' training and education facilities foster international cooperation and regularly host members of foreign militaries. They have also demonstrated increasing capabilities in disaster relief and humanitarian assistance at home and abroad. Bangladesh's involvement in UN peace operations has been instrumental in strengthening the defence diplomacy sector and, according to the author, has become an inseparable part of the military's identity.

References

Ackerman, E. (2021) 'Keep politics far from the US military', *New York Times International Edition*, [online] nd, Available from: https://www.nytimes.com/

Ahmad, Z.H. (1985) 'Configurative and comparative aspects of military–civilian relations', in Z.H. Ahmad and H. Crouch (eds) *Military-Civilian Relations in South-East Asia*, Kuala Lumpur, Selangor: Oxford University Press, pp 3–10.

Alagappa, M. (ed) (2001a) *Military Professionalism in Asia: Conceptual and Empirical Perspectives*, Honolulu (Hawaii): East-West Center.

Alagappa, M. (ed) (2001b) *Coercion and Governance: The Declining Political Role of the Military in Asia*, Stanford (California): Stanford University Press.

Angstrom, J. (2013) 'The changing norms of civil and military and civil–military relations theory', *Small Wars & Insurgencies*, 24(2): 224–36.

Baldino, D. and Carr, A. (2016) 'Defence diplomacy and the Australian defence force: smokescreen or strategy?', *Australian Journal of International Affairs,* 70(2): 139–58.

Barany, Z.D. (2012) *The Soldier and the Changing State: Building Democratic Armies in Africa, Asia and Europe*, Princeton, NJ: Princeton University Press.

Blasko, D. (2010) 'People's Liberation Army and People's Armed Police ground exercises with foreign forces, 2002–2009', in R. Kamphausen, D. Lai and A. Scobell (eds) *The PLA at Home and Abroad*, Carlisle Barracks, PA: US Army War College, pp 377–428.

Bruneau, T.C. and Croissant, A. (2019) 'Civil-Military Relations: Why Control is not Enough' in T.C. Bruneau and A. Croissant (eds) *Civil-Military Relations: Control and Effectiveness Across Regimes*, Boulder, Colorado: Lynne Rienner Publishers, pp 1–18.

Bünte, M. (2017) 'The NLD–military coalition in Myanmar: military guardianship and its economic foundations', in P. Chambers and N.

Waitoolkiat (eds) *Khaki Capital: The Political Economy of the Military in Southeast Asia*, Copenhagen: NIAS Press, pp 93–130.

Capie, D. and Taylor, B. (2010) 'The Shangri-La dialogue and the institutionalization of defence diplomacy in Asia', *The Pacific Review*, 23(3): 359–76.

Chambers, P. and Waitoolkiat, N. (2017) 'Theorizing khaki capital: the political economy of security', in P. Chambers and N. Waitoolkiat (eds) *Khaki Capital: The Political Economy of the Military in Southeast Asia*, Copenhagen: NIAS Press, pp 1–39.

Chang, J.Y. and Jenne, N. (2020) 'Velvet fists: the paradox of defence diplomacy in Southeast Asia', *European Journal of International Security*, 5(3): 332–49.

Chong, A. and Chang, J.Y. (2016) 'Security competition by proxy: Asia Pacific interstate rivalry in the aftermath of the MH370 incident', *Global Change, Peace & Security*, 28(1): 75–98.

Cottey, A. and Forster, A. (2004) *Reshaping Defence Diplomacy: New Roles for Military Cooperation and Assistance*, Oxford: Oxford University Press for the International Institute for Strategic Studies.

Croissant, A., Kuehn, D., Lorenz, P. and Chambers, P.W. (2013) *Democratization and Civilian Control in Asia*, Houndmills, Basingstoke: Palgrave Macmillan.

Edmunds, T. (2013) 'Security sector reform', in T.C. Bruneau and F.C. Matei (eds) *The Routledge Handbook of Civil–Military Relations*, Abingdon: Routledge, pp 48–60.

Engstrom, J. (2013) 'Taking disaster seriously: East Asian military involvement in international disaster relief operations and the implications for force projection', *Asian Security*, 9(1): 38–61.

Feaver, P. (2003) *Armed Servants: Agency, Oversight and Civil Military Relations*, Cambridge, MA: Harvard University Press.

Hall, R.A. (2017) 'Philippine military capital after 1986: norming, holdouts and new frontiers', in P. Chambers and N. Waitoolkiat (eds) *Khaki Capital: The Political Economy of the Military in Southeast Asia*, Copenhagen: NIAS Press, pp 271–304.

Heinecken, L. (2014) 'Outsourcing public security: the unforeseen consequences for the military profession', *Armed Forces and Society*, 40(4): 625–46.

Heng, Y.-K. (2015) 'Smart power and Japan's Self-Defense Forces', *Journal of Strategic Studies*, 38(3), pp 282–308.

Huntington, S. (1957) *The Soldier and the State: The Theory and Politics of Civil–Military Relations*, Cambridge, MA: Harvard University Press.

Janowitz, M. (1960) *The Professional Soldier: A Social and Political* Portrait, Glencoe, IL: The Free Press.

Kerr, P. (2007) 'Human security', in A. Collins (ed) *Contemporary Security Studies*, Oxford: Oxford University Press, pp 91–108.

Lee, T. (2015) *Defect or Defend: Military Responses to Popular Protests in Authoritarian Asia*, Baltimore, MD: Johns Hopkins University Press.

Loveman, B. and Davies, T. (eds) (1997) *The Politics of Antipolitics: The Military in Latin America*, 2nd edn, Lanham, MD: SR Books – an imprint of Rowman and Littlefield.

Luckham, R. (1991) 'Introduction: the military, the developmental state and social forces in Asia and the Pacific: issues for comparative analysis' in V. Selochan (ed) *The Military, the State, and Development in Asia and the Pacific*, Boulder, CO: Westview Press, pp 1–50.

Matei, F.C. (2013) 'A new conceptualization of civil–military relations', in T.C. Bruneau and F.C. Matei (eds) *The Routledge Handbook of Civil–Military Relations*, Abingdon: Routledge, pp 26–38.

Matei, F.C., Halladay, C. and Bruneau, T.C. (2022) 'Introduction: Democratic Civil-Military Relations in the Twenty-First Century', in F.C. Matei, C. Halladay and T.C. Bruneau (eds) *The Routledge Handbook of Civil-Military Relations*, Abingdon, UK: Routledge, pp 1–10.

May, R. and Selochan, V. (eds) (1998) *The Military and Democracy in Asia and the Pacific*, Bathurst, NSW: C. Hurst and Company.

Mullins, M. (2006) *In the Shadow of the Generals: Foreign Policy Making in Argentina, Brazil and Chile*, Aldershot, Hampshire: Ashgate Publishing.

Pye, L.W. (1962) 'Armies in the process of political modernization', in J.J. Johnston (ed) *The Role of the Military in Underdeveloped Countries*, Princeton, NJ: Princeton University Press, pp 69–90.

Selochan, V. (ed) (1991) *The Military, the State, and Development in Asia and the Pacific*, Boulder (Colorado): Westview Press.

Shils, E. (1962) 'The military in the political development of the new states', in J.J. Johnston (ed) *The Role of the Military in Underdeveloped Countries*, Princeton, NJ: Princeton University Press, pp 7–67.

Singh, B. and Tan, S.S. (2011) *From 'Boots' to 'Brogues': The Rise of Defence Diplomacy in Southeast Asia*, Singapore: S. Rajaratnam School of International Studies.

Steinhauer, J. (2021) 'In battle at Capitol, veterans fought on both sides'. *The New York Times International Edition*, [online] 13 February, Available from: https://sure.do/news/at-the-capitol-on-jan-6-veterans-fought-on-both-sides-of-an-american-battle/ [Accessed 12 June 2022].

Thayer, C.A. (2017) 'The political economy of military-run enterprises in Vietnam', in P. Chambers and N. Waitoolkiat (eds) *Khaki Capital: The Political Economy of the Military in Southeast Asia*, Copenhagen: NIAS Press, pp 130–60.

Waitoolkiat, N. and Chambers, P. (2017) 'Arch-royalist rent: the political economy of the military in Thailand' in P. Chambers and N. Waitoolkiat (eds) *Khaki Capital: The Political Economy of the Military in Southeast Asia*, Copenhagen: NIAS Press, pp 40–92.

PART I

Southeast Asia

2

Fostering Developmental Guardianship: The Case of Myanmar's *Tatmadaw*

Adhi Priamarizki

On 1 February 2021, the Myanmar military (*Tatmadaw*) launched a coup against the civilian government that was led by the National League for Democracy (NLD) patron, Aung San Suu Kyi. The coup that occurred during the early period of the COVID-19 global outbreak has certainly tilted the civil–military balance in the country. Furthermore, the military coup confirmed the speculation about the military feeling uneasy towards its civilian counterpart. Prior to the coup, there had been several incidents that displayed the growing enmity of the military. The *Tatmadaw* immediately detained most of the senior NLD members, including Suu Kyi who was put under house arrest by the military. Soon after the coup, the military formed a caretaker government under the so-called State Administrative Council (SAC) in which General Min Aung Hlaing, the coup orchestrator and *Tatmadaw* commander, holds the Chair position (The Myanmar Times, 2021). The installation of the SAC has put the *Tatmadaw* back at the helm of Myanmar's government.

The 2021 coup has mostly destroyed the political transition that was marked by the transfer of authority from a military-led government to a quasi-civilian government in 2011. General Tan Shwe, commander-in-chief of Myanmar's[1] Military (1992–2011), announced the disbandment of the State Peace and Development Council (SPDC) on 30 March 2011.[2] Before it dispersed itself, the SPDC government held general elections in 2010 that were won by the Union Solidarity and Development Party (USDP), which allowed the party to form a majority government and installed former military general Thein Sein as president of the country (2011–16). The 2010 general elections marked a milestone for the so-called democratization, or what others might only see as a temporary transition, from direct to partial military rule in Myanmar. Robert Taylor (2013, p 400) described this reform as a window dressing that failed to bring real change, since the military still maintained significant political control. Such doubt was indeed materialized when the 2021 military takeover occurred.

Existing studies on the *Tatmadaw*'s continued domination after political transition mainly point at the military's control over political liberalization as the enabling factor for the armed forces to maintain its strong political influence (Callahan, 2012; Macdonald, 2013; Croissant and Kamerling, 2013; Egreteau, 2016; Selth, 2018). The military's decision to forgo direct rule is in fact a long process that had been planned many years before (Taylor, 2015). Although the abovementioned studies explain the military's ability to remain in power, they did not explore the reason behind the *Tatmadaw*'s reluctance to fully relinquish its authority and willingness to return to power. The 2021 coup had showcased the *Tatmadaw*'s appetite for political control, though the personal ambitions of General Min Aung Hlaing could be a reason behind such proscribed action (Barany, 2021; Steinberg, 2021). Moreover, the outbreak of COVID-19 generated a complex set of challenges that required a significant amount of resource and bureaucratic mobilization, including the military, to tackle the issue.

This chapter attempts to explain the return of the *Tatmadaw* at the helm of government in Myanmar as well as the military's involvement in COVID-19 management and exploitation to preserve its interests. One element that previous studies have not yet discussed in detail to explain the phenomenon is the influence of doctrinal belief of the *Tatmadaw*, which is heavily inspired by the developmental guardianship idea. The developmental guardianship thinking has driven the *Tatmadaw*'s return to politics as the military aims to maintain its centrality. Moreover, the global outbreak of COVID-19 galvanized the Myanmar military's position as the developmental guardian and justified expansive military involvement in non-defence affairs. The discussion of the role of doctrinal elements, in this case the developmental guardianship paradigm, is this chapter's contribution towards the contemporary literature on military and politics in Myanmar.

In line with the guiding themes presented by Chong and Jenne in the introduction to this volume, the chapter addresses the following general questions: How do colonial legacies shape civil–military evolutions in Myanmar and the *Tatmadaw*'s tutelary belief? How does the *Tatmadaw* perceive civil–military relations? Does the *Tatmadaw* see civil–military relations as primarily related to developmental and modernization goals? In what ways do the 2021 coup and COVID-19 outbreak strengthen the *Tatmadaw*'s guardianship role? To answer the first three questions, this chapter starts with an explanation of the genesis of the *Tatmadaw*'s developmental guardianship. The discussion is then continued with an analysis of the military's doctrinal evolution. To answer the fourth question, the last part of this chapter examines post-political transition dynamics, the 2021 coup and the *Tatmadaw*'s involvement in COVID-19 management.

Genesis of the *Tatmadaw*'s developmental guardianship

Burma was under the British Colonial administration from 1824 until its independence in 1948, except between 1942 and 1945 when Japan occupied the country. The British paved the way for the birth of an early model of military service in Myanmar, in the form of instituting *tat* (volunteer army corps). The Japanese meanwhile accommodated the rise of a local army to support the country's war efforts during World War Two. Previously, the British had excluded ethnic-majority Burmans from the armed forces and only included ethnic-minority groups that antagonized the Burmans. The British, however, permitted many Burman-majority political organizations to establish their own *tat*. These *tats* were not allowed to carry firearms; however, they could perform military drills and war exercises with bamboo staffs. Many former *tat* members later became part of the *Tatmadaw*, which contributed to the attachment of the military to politics.

When Japan invaded Burma, the Burmese government mobilized locals to help in the war. In the wake of this chaotic circumstance, the first form of national army in Burma, the Burma Independence Army (BIA) emerged in December 1941. The BIA consisted of mostly ethnic-majority Burmans unlike the pre-war military that was dominated by Indians and Burmese minorities. By July 1941, 30 young Burmese also known as the so-called 'Thirty Comrades' went to Hainan Island to receive military training from the Japanese, which became the embryo for the Burmese army. The BIA was transformed into Burma's Defence Army in July 1942 and later changed into the Burma National Army (BNA) in 1943 with General Ne Win as commander. The BNA started to develop two characteristics. The first was the importance of anchoring the population's loyalty to the notion of Burmese independence and the necessity of possessing the people's support in achieving this. The other was the urgency to become involved in politics to compete with other political groups and establish what the corps perceived as a correct social and political order (Taylor, 2009, p 236). When Japan's chance to win the war began to fade away, the BNA switched sides to the allies and worked with the British. The BNA later changed into the Patriotic Burma Forces (PBF), in June 1945. Following the Kandy agreement on 7 September 1945,[3] members of the PBF were infused into the regular British Burmese Army under the British colonial authority and later merged into the Burmese Army of Burma.

During its early days, Burma faced numerous armed conflicts, which has forced its military to focus on internal security matters since then. While combating the internal threats, the *Tatmadaw* expanded its influence on the political, economic and social development realms in the name of preserving stability and guarding the state. The prominent threats to the country's sovereignty together with the unstable domestic political situation became two primary reasons for the *Tatmadaw* to stretch its domination to the civilian realm. Many of the ethnic groups in Burma at that time were not entirely supportive towards the creation of the Union, for which the constitution was prepared by the Anti-Fascists People's Freedom League (AFPFL) that was led by General Aung San until his assassination on 19 July 1947. The Communist Party of Burma (CPB) and Karen National Defence Organization (KNDO) became the two major anti-government movements in the civil war that lasted from 1948 to 1952 (Taylor, 1985, p 24). In addition, the rise of Mao Zedong in China in 1949 caused Kuomintang (KMT) soldiers to disperse and flee to northern parts of Myanmar. The remnants of the KMT led by General Li Mi planned to use the northern area as a springboard for attacks against the People's Republic of China (PRC) (Maung Aung Myoe, 2009, p 17). The war against the KMT remnants lasted until the early 1960s when the Chinese People's Liberation Army (PLA) aided the *Tatmadaw* and helped eliminate the rebels.

While the military was combating the insurgents, the civilian politicians in Yangon were too busy quarrelling to gain power in the country. The circumstances triggered a feeling of contempt against the civilian politicians among the *Tatmadaw* officers who perceived themselves as the guardian of the nation. Furthermore, rather than improving the state, many bureaucrats exploited their positions to gain personal benefits. For example, managerial appointments for many state institutions were based on political patronage rather than merit (Richter, 1972, p 225). This type of illegitimate behaviour by civilian politicians triggered further resentment from the military.

The *Tatmadaw*'s doctrinal evolution: galvanizing developmental guardianship

Currently the Burmese military implements a military doctrine with a robust counterinsurgency element; however, the *Tatmadaw* did not always emphasize the internal security realm. Maung Aung Myoe (2009) divides the *Tatmadaw*'s doctrinal development into three phases. During the first phase (1948–65), the *Tatmadaw* developed a doctrine that focused on combating external threats through mechanized warfare. The next phase (1965–88) displayed a dramatic turning point as the military adopted a doctrine emphasizing the concept of the people's war and counterinsurgency. In the third phase (1988–), the *Tatmadaw* improved its doctrine by adding a component of technological development and citing the possibility of foreign invasion through proxy. The current leadership of the *Tatmadaw* also proposed the idea of a 'standard army' that could hint at a new development. In the following we will examine the doctrinal evolution of the *Tatmadaw* from Burma's independence to now.

Burma has been facing insurgency threats since the early days of the Union. However, the early version of the *Tatmadaw* doctrine did not put emphasis on counterinsurgency practice, as the military focused its attention on facing external threats in the form of conventional warfare and using mechanized warfare to counter the danger. The doctrine faced its biggest challenge when the remnants of the KMT force crossed the Burmese border. The endeavour ended in a catastrophic failure for the *Tatmadaw* due to the lack of an appropriate command and control system, a proper logistical support structure and training regime, adequate economic and technological sources as well as efficient civil defence organizations (Maung Aung Myoe, 2009, p 17).

The failure to tackle the threat of KMT remnants forced the Burmese military to review its doctrine and develop a new version that emphasized counterinsurgency. The 1959 *Tatmadaw* conference reviewed the Union's latest internal security situation as well as counterinsurgency operations. During a series of discussions from 1961 to 1964, military officers debated a new doctrine and counterinsurgency strategy for the *Tatmadaw*. The discussions finally produced a fruitful outcome in 1964 with the introduction of the 'People's War' doctrine. The 1964 discussion noted three potential adversaries of the Union: internal insurgents, historical enemies with roughly equal power and enemies with greater power. In addition, the idea of bringing the military and the people together became an important cornerstone of the counterinsurgency operation. The 1964 conference was pivotal for the *Tatmadaw* as it set the foundations for the new military doctrine, which emphasized internal security matters (Maung Aung Myoe, 2009, pp 21–3; Nakanishi, 2013, p 232).

In addition to developing a new doctrine, the *Tatmadaw* began to use militias in the early 1960s, particularly with the intensifying insurgency threats in Shan State as well as communist rebel activities in the northern part of the country. The utilization of militia was further galvanized by the formulation of the Four Cuts counterinsurgency strategy in the 1968 *Tatmadaw* conference. The strategy focused on detaching the insurgents from four resources: food, funding, information and recruits. The strategy was based on the idea of taking the 'fish (guerrilla) out from the water (population)'. The militia came in handy to complement the military in executing this Four Cuts strategy, particularly for mobilizing the population against the insurgents.

The emergence of the new military junta leadership, under the name of State Law and Order Restoration Council (SLORC), in 1988, was also accompanied with change in the internal security environment, which affected the way the *Tatmadaw* was operating. The possibility of Aung San Suu Kyi's NLD cooperating with the ethnic armed groups to undermine the government worried the military junta. Therefore, the SLORC initiated ceasefire negotiations, led by Khin Nyunt, with the ethnic armed organizations (EAOs) (Callahan, 2003, p 215). Between 1989 and 2009, the military government discussed ceasefire agreements with 40 EAOs.[4] The military also believed that with the proliferation of political organizations after the 1988 political upheaval, any mass protest against the military-led socialist government might invite foreign intervention. As a result, the foreign intervention dimension appeared as a new source of threat that required special attention. In addition, the development of new technology, particularly cyberspace, became another consideration for the revision of the *Tatmadaw*'s doctrine.

Despite the additional focus on possible foreign intrusion, the adoption of the People's War notion has still remained at the core of the *Tatmadaw*'s doctrine. According to Maung Aung Myoe (2009, pp 196–197) the *Tatmadaw*'s interpretation of the inclusion of the People's War concept includes the primacy of politics, the primacy of people over weapons, the strategy of using the weak against the strong, the mobilization of the masses to fight a protracted war against invasion and the multiple roles of the *Tatmadaw*. The inclusion of the phrase 'under modern conditions' points at the importance of new battlespace (cyberwar) rather than a change from people-centric into technology-centric warfare. Therefore, the military seems wanting to maintain its status quo relationship with the civilian population by any means, including keeping its political role vigorous.

Meanwhile, the creation of the term 'Three Main National Causes' (non-disintegration of the union, non-disintegration of national unity and perpetuation of national sovereignty)[5] strengthened the guardianship of the military. The term outlined that a clear objective of the state is to maintain the integration and unity of the nation in which the *Tatmadaw* is expected to achieve the goal at all costs. The 'Three Main National Causes' evolved into a kind of mantra that military leaders regularly cited during their speeches. For example, General Min Aung Hlaing, *Tatmadaw* commander-in-chief, argued the need for the armed forces to safeguard the 'Three Main National Causes' in his speech for the 70th Armed Forces Day in 2015. By 2011, the military perceived that external threats had greatly declined; however, the international community might still intervene in Myanmar's internal matters via the 'responsibility to protect' framework (Selth, 2016, p 14).

At the first Union Peace Conference in January 2016, General Min Aung Hlaing introduced the so-called 'standard army' concept to describe the modernization plan within the armed forces. The idea can be seen as an attempt to enhance the current doctrine, which probably required an overhaul given the changing threat environment, especially domestic security.[6] At a meeting with the Union Military Committee in November 2016, Min Aung Hlaing also mentioned the 'standard army' idea, his dream of overhauling the obsolete armaments of the *Tatmadaw* and receiving military drill from the West, as well as gaining wider access to the international arms market (Dunant, 2017). International engagement, together with modernization and defence capability, became the focus of the 'standard army' concept. Moreover, the concept neglected professionalism due to the term's close association with civilian control and the image of being a mercenary army (Thiha, 2017).

Interestingly, Myanmar's 2015 Defence White Paper (DWP) did not mention the 'standard army' concept in its discussion. The white paper nevertheless cited three main security challenges for the country: the 'neighbouring countries' military build-up; the provision of equipment, financial assistance, encouragement by external elements to internal armed groups; and unresolved boundary issues'. Furthermore, the DWP recommended key priorities that the *Tatmadaw* must do as 'guardian of the state'. Ending conflicts with EAOs through peaceful means was among the top priorities as these have been hindering internal security, stability and national development. Furthermore, the white paper advocates wider political involvement of the *Tatmadaw* in brokering peace with EAOs and outlined the necessity for developing MOOTW capabilities to protect Myanmar from non-traditional security threats, such as trade in narcotics, terrorism, human trafficking and transnational crime (Maung Aung Myoe, 2016). The 2015 DWP pretty much galvanized the guardianship of the *Tatmadaw* as it stretched the role of the military into the internal security realm and justified political involvement using the peace process.

The *Tatmadaw*, in February 2018, held its biggest joint military exercise since 1996 in the Ayeyarwady delta region. Interestingly, General Min Aung Hlaing announced that the *Tatmadaw* was still far from being a 'standard army' in a statement following the exercise. He also noted the requirement for the military to forge closer cooperation with the people for defending Myanmar (Shin, 2018). Based on the available, but minimal and vague, information on the 'standard army' idea, we can conclude that the concept primarily aims at modernizing the combat capability of the *Tatmadaw* without creating a gap in civil–military relations. The concept also reflects the military's desire to prolong its political hegemony. Therefore, political domination of the *Tatmadaw* and the non-existence of division in civil–military relations would persist even if there were a new doctrine based on the 'standard army' concept.

The dissolution of the SPDC in 2011 marked the emergence of a new political environment with civilian political players on the rise. The election in 2010 gave way to a new leadership under the USDP, a surrogate party of the military junta. The next election, in 2015, produced the NLD as the winner. These two general elections made the military, at least, share the political arena with emerging civilian leaders. Nonetheless, the landslide victory of the NLD in the 2020 general elections and the party's intention to revise the 2008 Constitution have irritated the military, which resulted in a coup in February 2021. Prior to the coup, the outbreak of COVID-19 has posed a challenge towards civil–military dynamics in Myanmar. Those events have strengthened the status of the *Tatmadaw*'s developmental guardianship, which will be discussed in the following section.

Post-SPDC, COVID-19 and the February 2021 coup

On 1 February 2021, the *Tatmadaw* detained Aung San Suu Kyi, several NLD party leaders and President Win Myint (2018–21), citing election fraud as the reason behind the detentions.[7] The military then blocked roads in the country's capital, Nay Pyi Taw, and the main city, Yangon, disrupted phone and internet connections, forced banks to halt their service and imposed night curfew. The *Tatmadaw* also dissolved the cabinet and appointed Vice President Myint Swe (2016–), who is a former army officer, as acting president (BBC, 2021). The February 2021 coup did not only become the first coup against a civilian government since 1962 but also galvanized the *Tatmadaw*'s continued domination in Myanmar. In fact, the *Tatmadaw* had never fully withdrew from politics and relinquished its political control, not to mention the military's role in orchestrating the political transition in the first place back in 2011.

The process of political change did not only happen in the period of the 2010 general elections and the demise of the SPDC the subsequent year. Instead, it was a concerted and long overdue process that can be traced back to the year 1993 when the first National Convention resumed.[8] The military junta held the 2010 general elections based on the 2008 Constitution. Ironically, the 2008 Constitution provided a safeguard for the *Tatmadaw* to keep its presence in politics, though it did not play the most prominen role. The constitution granted the military a number of privileges and blocked Aung San Suu Kyi's presidential candidacy. The 2008 Constitution gave the military full autonomy in its internal matters. Moreover, the military was given the authority to nominate three ministerial positions (home affairs, defence and border affairs). The constitution intentionally obstructed Daw Suu Kyi's candidacy since it prohibited any person who has family relations with foreign nationals to be president of Myanmar.[9]

In addition, the constitution mandated the formation of the National Defence and Security Council (NDSC) to act as a channel for defence and security consultation with the *Tatmadaw*. In reality, the armed forces made the council another tool to exercise their influence. The NDSC has

11 members of which 6 are appointed by the commander-in-chief. Also, granting amnesty and declaring any state of emergency by the president requires recommendation from the NDSC. In the legislative field, the *Tatmadaw* automatically owns 25 per cent of the Union Assembly or *Pyidaungsu Hluttaw* seats. It provides them a veto power as constitutional amendments can only be done if more than 75 per cent of the total members of the Union Assembly agree. This circumstance made the military representatives prominent players in the parliament as decisions related to constitutional amendment required at least one parliament member from the faction, with the condition that the rest of the parliament has a united voice.

The victory of the NLD in the 2015 general elections did not immediately reduce the domination of the *Tatmadaw*. The party leadership seemed aware of the persistent prominence of the *Tatmadaw* on the political stage. Daw Suu Kyi met General Min Aung Hlaing, who has held the *Tatmadaw* commander-in-chief position since 2011, several times in the aftermath of the 2015 general elections (Maung Aung Myoe, 2017, p 267). The two of them, nevertheless, did not reveal any details of their meetings. One speculation was that the NLD realized the need to form a good enough relationship with the military, which made the meetings possible. On the other hand, General Min Aung Hlaing had signalled the military's hesitation to reduce its grip on the country's political stage by citing the need for the military to stay in politics in order to tame ethnic armed groups (Fisher, 2015). Min Aung Hlaing also believed maintaining political influence and preventing the military from being marginalized or manipulated were paramount for the *Tatmadaw* as he mentioned in his speech on 2 December 2017 to newly graduating officers of the Defence Service Academy in the Pyin Oo Lwin, Mandalay, region (Nyein, 2017).

The NLD leadership, meanwhile, had expressed their concern over the 2008 Constitution and aspired to amend it. The party believed the constitution was the main obstacle for further reform to take place in Myanmar. However, the military has blatantly rejected the idea. In an interview with the BBC in July 2015, General Min Aung Hlaing declared that constitutional amendments will only happen if peace, security and stability have been achieved in Myanmar (Fisher, 2015).

The seemingly good relations between the NLD and the military were at best superficial. Both camps fundamentally opposed each other, particularly over the 2008 Constitution. Despite their disagreement, both the civilians and the *Tatmadaw* avoided criticizing or opposing each other in public. Civilians have also learned that attacking military interests blatantly would be counterproductive.[10] For example, the military did not face any criticism when it launched attacks on ethnic armed groups in northern Shan and Kachin States in late 2016. Daw Suu Kyi instead tried to justify the military operation as a response to Muslim militants' attacks on police posts along Myanmar's border with Bangladesh on 9 October 2016 (Thawnghmung and Robinson, 2017, p 239). The civilian side nonetheless tried to challenge the military's domination in a symbolic way. Until the February 2021 military coup, the NLD government did not arrange a single meeting of the NDSC. On the other hand, Daw Suu Kyi established her own Rule of Law and Tranquillity Committee, headed by Gen (ret) U Tin Oo, a long-term NLD member and Suu Kyi's supporter.[11]

On 29 January 2019, the NLD administration proposed to initiate a constitutional amendment process, which resulted in the formation of the Union of Myanmar Constitution (2008) Amendment Joint Committee (UMCAJC). The party aimed to gradually reduce the military's parliamentary seats, abolish military autonomy and remove Section 59(f) of the constitution, which restricts Aung San Suu Kyi's presidential candidacy (Nyi Kyaw, 2019). The *Tatmadaw* itself meanwhile displayed no intention of tolerating any structural changes that might undermine its national political role in the Constitution, institutional autonomy or the fundamental principles it has set for national unity (Maung Aung Myoe, 2018, p 221).

In the meantime, the internal conflicts that have been haunting Myanmar for decades showed no significant signs of abatement. The peace negotiation between the government and various EAOs under the Nationwide Ceasefire Agreement (NCA) framework seemed to be going nowhere. Continued fighting between the *Tatmadaw* and EAOs, particularly the Karen National Union (KNU) and Restoration Council of the Shan State (RCSS), as well as boycotts from other negotiation participants, such as Ta'ang National Liberation Army (TNLA) and Kachin Independence Army (KIA), had significantly delayed the peace talks (Pauli, 2020). These continuing internal conflicts consequently provided the military a compelling reason for rejecting any attempts to amend the 2008 Constitution by citing national security issues.

The continued electoral ascendancy of the NLD following the 2020 election has alarmed the *Tatmadaw* on the possible overhaul of its autonomy and political role. The military accused the NLD of rigging the 2020 general elections. The political crisis then culminated in a military coup in February 2021, which re-established the military position at the helm of the government through the establishment of the SAC. The international pressure and domestic resistance through the civil disobedience movement (CDM) did little to force the military to revert authority to the civilian side. It was only on 18 October 2021 that the military regime finally accommodated international pressure, notably from ASEAN, by releasing hundreds of political prisoners (Al Jazeera, 2021).

The domestic politics brouhaha happened in the midst of the COVID-19 outbreak and further complicated the already murky situation due to the pandemic. The lack of health infrastructure made the military involvement in COVID-19 management in Myanmar critical as military hospitals became crucial additional sites for quarantine (Lwin, 2020). Despite the urgency, the skirmish between the military and the EAOs did not entirely stop. This continued battle in the rural and conflict areas consequently jeopardized the fight against COVID-19 as many of the civilian facilities, including medical resources, were destroyed (Barklamb, 2020; Hoelzl and Diamond, 2020).

Furthermore, the 2021 coup had further complicated the COVID-19 management following the emergence of the civil disobedience movement (CDM) against the military government. The movement crippled the public sector, including medical services, which consequently paralyzed COVID-19 management (Peter, 2021). The military, however, seemed to be taking advantage of the COVID-19 outbreak to legitimize and strengthen its control. For example, the military cited the breaking of COVID-19 rules to charge Suu Kyi (Myanmar Now, 2021a). Moreover, the detention of CDM movement participants, particularly medical staff and doctors, has further crippled COVID-19 management (Myanmar Now, 2021b). Moreover, the military exploited the pandemic to impose a lockdown and greater political control. The military even put political detainees in prisons unprotected against COVID-19. Many of these political detainees already suffered from underlying conditions or were prone to COVID-19 due to old age, such as the NLD's legal advisor U Nyan Win (Khit, 2021). In addition, the crisis situation turned into an opportunity for some military officers to conduct illicit activities, notably oxygen hoarding (The Irrawaddy, 2021).

From the above discussion we can deduce three propositions regarding the *Tatmadaw*'s developmental guardianship under the contemporary circumstances. First, the political liberalization prior to the 2021 coup did not erode the developmental guardianship mentality of the military. The political liberalization has allowed the rise of civilian political players on Myanmar's political stage. Nonetheless, the debut of civilian leadership did not mean that the military would automatically relinquish its guardianship and hand over the authority to the new player. Instead of doing so, the military has shared the spotlight with civilians, while still possessing the strongest control and influence in the country.

Second, the 2021 coup indicated the persistence of the military in safeguarding its privileges. The takeover has practically ended the civilian's attempt to amend the 2008 Constitution, which guaranteed the political upper hand of the military. The coup also diminished the expanding political influence of the NLD administration. The preservation of the 2008 Constitution is crucial for the military as the continued domination of the military in the country can limit intervention towards the *Tatmadaw*'s internal security campaign.

Third, the COVID-19 outbreak illuminates both the usefulness of the *Tatmadaw*'s developmental guardianship and exploitation of the pandemic to safeguard the military's political interests. The military involvement in COVID-19 management displayed how developmental guardianship thinking drove and justified the *Tatmadaw*'s participation in managing the outbreak. The severe impact of the virus became a call for the military to step forward and take the responsibility even without explicit command from the civilian authority. Following the 2021 coup, the military exploited the pandemic situation to impose a severe political lockdown and even to punish its political opponents.

Conclusion

Prior to the 2021 coup, the *Tatmadaw* had been resisting all attempts to radically alter the political system in Myanmar and seemed to be favouring gradual and administered political transformation. The withdrawal of the military from the government helm certainly did not erode the armed forces' political privilege. Instead, the *Tatmadaw* had carefully designed a safeguard to protect such self-entitlement. The discussion in this chapter showed that the political involvement of the *Tatmadaw* has been part of its developmental guardianship. First, historical legacies set the foundation for the developmental guardianship thinking of the *Tatmadaw*. Political involvement is not a taboo for Myanmar's military. The origin of the *Tamadaw* as part of a political organization induced its political entrenchment. Distrust between the military and ethnic armed groups cultivated during colonialism and the civil war experience contributed significantly in shaping the *Tatmadaw* into a military with a strong focus on domestic security.

Second, the developmental guardianship of the *Tatmadaw* played a crucial role in sustaining its political involvement, as the ideological belief requires the military to be at the forefront of every aspect of public life. The political liberalization did little in altering such a mindset. The military even resisted any attempts to revamp its political domination. Moreover, civil–military relations evolved merely into a tool for supporting the military's guardianship role where the *Tatmadaw* determines the nature of their relationship rather than it being based on a consensus between the two sides. The 2021 coup, which abolished the attempt to amend the constitution and expansion of civilian political power, has proven that the military was willing to go the extra mile to preserve its upper hand position.

Third, keeping the unity of the country at all costs has been the greatest objective of the military. The military perceived the status quo, guaranteed by the 2008 Constitution, as the key in achieving this goal. In addition, threats to the unity of the country in the form of secessionist movements have been regularly cited by the military to justify its rejection of attempts to amend the constitution. Fourth, the military has shown no hesitation to protect and enforce its developmental guardianship role as seen in the 2021 coup and during the COVID-19 outbreak. The outbreak of COVID-19 has galvanized this belief in which the military positioned itself as the spearhead in combating the pandemic. The COVID-19 outbreak provided a great opportunity for the military to enhance its post-coup political domination. There is a blurred distinction between punishing political opponents and managing the pandemic. The implementation of a lockdown policy is an example of such conflated objectives.

Developmental guardianship for the *Tatmadaw* is not only a guiding principle but also the *raison d'être*. Prior to the 2021 coup, the *Tatmadaw* devised its own version of political liberalization in order to fit with the ideal of the military being at the forefront of every aspect of life. The military perceived the alteration as a necessity to safeguard Myanmar and its people. Nonetheless, once an attempt to undermine the centrality of the military occurred, the *Tatmadaw* rolled back the political liberalization process. The military indeed does not perceive rolling back the democratic progress as a problem as long as its authority remains intact. Here we can see that the slow pace of political transformation was implemented in order to preserve the presence and authority of the *Tatmadaw* in politics.

The developmental guardianship indeed played a crucial part in driving the *Tatmadaw*'s decision in maintaining its political influence and privilege. As a result, the emergence of a civilian government did not correlate with the waning political authority of the *Tatmadaw*. The developmental guardianship justified the *Tatmadaw* preserving the 'guardian of the nation' status in which the military perceived contributing to the development of the country as its primary duty. Studies on the military and politics in Myanmar have extensively discussed the *Tatmadaw*'s ability to remain in power. This chapter complements the existing literature by examining the doctrinal element of the military to understand its persistence in maintaining its political supremacy. Furthermore, this chapter showcased that the idea of developmental guardianship has shielded any attempts to undermine the military's political authority.

Notes

1. This chapter uses Burma when discussing events prior to 1989 and Myanmar for the afterwards.
2. SPDC was the name of the military junta government. It was known as State Law and Order Restoration Council (SLORC) from 1988 to 1997. It became SPDC from 1997 until its dissolution in 2011.
3. The agreement regulated the fusion of PBF with other colonial army battalions, such as Karen, Kachin and Chin battalions. The Karen nonetheless withdrew from the agreement by joining the Karen separatist movement in 1949.

4 The central authority since 2009 also proposed the formation of a militia group called Border Guard Force (BGF) to integrate the military wing of the insurgents into the *Tatmadaw*'s structure. The government included the BGF scheme in the negotiation with the rebels. Nonetheless, some of the insurgents rejected the scheme as they see it as part of the military's plan to weaken them. See Buchanan (2016) for a study on the use of militia in Myanmar.

5 The concept appeared when the SLORC planned to hold the 1993 National Convention with ethnic representatives for achieving peace with them. The SLORC on 2 October 1992 pledged six objectives for the convention: (1) Non-disintegration of the Union; (2) Non-disintegration of national unity; (3) Perpetuation of national sovereignty; (4) Promotion of a genuine multiparty democracy; (5) Promotion of the universal principles of justice, liberty and equality; (6) Participation by the defence services in a national political leadership role in the future state. The first three objectives became the 'Three Main National Causes'.

6 The Myanmar government has managed to reach ceasefire agreements with a number of insurgents and includes some of them into the BGF. The *Tatmadaw* also has slowly gained the upper hand in the conflict against the Kachin. The biggest challenges are probably the brouhaha in Rakhine State and the new conflict with the Karen, which started in the early months of 2018.

7 The military accuses NLD of rigging the November 2020 general elections in which the party secured a landslide victory. Although some weakness and errors in voters lists were discovered, the voting in general was conducted in a fair and transparent way (Strangio, 2021).

8 The National Convention started its first session on 9 January 1993 to initiate the reform process. However, the convention was suspended in 1996 as the NLD boycotted it. The NLD members accused the convention as being 'nothing but a ruse by the military to stay in power' (*Asia News*, 2007).

9 Aung San Suu Kyi married a foreigner and her children hold foreign passports.

10 For example, a protest by an NLD MP against the Letpadaung copper mine project, in which a military conglomerate is heavily involved, triggered a boycott from military representatives in the parliament. See Bünte (2017).

11 Author's interview with Dr Andrew Ngun Cun Liang, former member of Myanmar Peace Center, Yangon, 22 November 2017.

References

Al Jazeera (2021) 'Hundreds of political prisoners freed in Myanmar after amnesty', *Al Jazeera*, [online] 19 October, Available from: www.aljazeera.com/news/2021/10/19/hundreds-of-political-prisoners-freed-in-myanmar-after-amnesty [Accessed 8 April 2022].

Asia News (2007) 'National convention ends after 14 years', *Asia News*, [online] 9 April, Available from: www.asianews.it/news-en/National-convention-ends-after-14-years-10215.html [Accessed 6 June 2018].

Barany, Z. (2021) 'Burma: the generals strike back', *Journal of Democracy*, 32(2): 22–36.

Barklamb, J. (2020) 'Under cover of Covid-19, conflict in Myanmar goes unchecked', *The Interpreter*, [online] 8 May, Available from: www.lowyinstitute.org/the-interpreter/under-cover-covid-19-conflict-myanmar-goes-unchecked [Accessed 8 April 2022].

BBC (2021) 'Myanmar coup: Aung San Suu Kyi detained as military seizes control', *BBC*, [online] 1 February, Available from: www.bbc.com/news/world-asia-55882489 [Accessed 8 April 2022].

Buchanan, J. (2016) 'Militias in Myanmar', *Yangon: The Asia Foundation*. https://asiafoundation.org/wp-content/uploads/2016/07/Militias-in-Myanmar.pdf

Bünte, M. (2017) 'The NLD-military coalition in Myanmar', in P. Chambers and N. Waitoolkiat (eds) *Khaki Capital: The Political Economy of the Military in Southeast Asia*, Copenhagen: Nias Press, pp 93–130.

Callahan, M. (2003) *Making Enemies: War and State Building in Burma*, Ithaca and London: Cornell University Press.

Callahan, M. (2012) 'The generals loosen their grip', *Journal of Democracy*, 23(4): 120–31.

Croissant, A. and Kamerling, J. (2013) 'Why do military regime institutionalize? Constitution-making and elections as political survival strategy in Myanmar', *Asian Journal of Political Science*, 21(2), 105–25.

Dunant, B. (2017) 'It's good to be the Tatmadaw', *The Diplomat*, [online] 11 May, Available from: https://thediplomat.com/2017/05/its-good-to-be-the-tatmadaw/ [Accessed 8 April 2022].

Egreteau, R. (2016) *Caretaking Democratization: The Military and Political Change in Myanmar*, London: C. Hurst & Co.

Fisher, J. (2015) 'Myanmar's strongman gives rare BBC interview', *BBC*, [online] 10 July, Available from: www.bbc.com/news/world-asia-33587800 [Accessed 8 April 2022].

Hoelzl, V. and Diamond, C. (2020) 'Myanmar military steps up attacks as coronavirus spreads', *Al Jazeera*, [online] 16 April, Available from: www.aljazeera.com/news/2020/4/16/myanmar-military-steps-up-attacks-as-coronavirus-spreads [Accessed 8 April 2022].

Khit, N. (2021) 'Myanmar's coup leader shows his genocidal intent', *The Irrawaddy*, [online] 21 July, Available from: www.irrawaddy.com/opinion/detained-nld-advisers-covid-death-was-a-political-execution-by-myanmars-junta.html [Accessed 8 April 2022].

Lwin, T. (2020) 'Myanmar military offers more COVID-19 quarantine beds to civilians', *The Irrawaddy*, [online] 17 September, Available from: www.irrawaddy.com/specials/myanmar-covid-19/myanmar-military-offers-covid-19-quarantine-beds-civilians.html [Accessed 8 April 2022].

Macdonald, A.P. (2013) 'From military rule to electoral authoritarianism: the reconfiguration of power in Myanmar and its future', *Asian Affairs: An American Review*, 40: 20–36.

Maung Aung Myoe (2009) *Building the Tatmadaw: Myanmar Armed Forces Since 1948*, Singapore: ISEAS.

Maung Aung Myoe (2016) 'Myanmar military's white paper highlights growing openness', *Nikkei Asia*, [online] 28 March, Available from: https://asia.nikkei.com/Politics/Maung-Aung-Myoe-Myanmar-military-s-white-paper-highlights-growing-openness [Accessed 8 April 2022].

Maung Aung Myoe (2017) 'Emerging pattern of civil–military relations', *Southeast Asian Affairs*, 2017: 259–74.

Maung Aung Myoe (2018) 'Partnership in politics: the Tatmadaw and the NLD in Myanmar since 2016', in J. Chambers, G. McCarthy, N. Farrelly and C. Win (eds) *Myanmar Transformed?: People, Places and Politics*, Singapore: ISEAS, pp 201–30.

Myanmar Now (2021a) 'Suu Kyi hit with second charge of breaching COVID-19 rules', *Myanmar Now*, [online] 12 April, Available from: www.myanmar-now.org/en/news/suu-kyi-hit-with-second-charge-of-breaching-covid-19-rules [Accessed 8 April 2022].

Myanmar Now (2021b) 'Former head of COVID-19 vaccine rollout charged with high treason', *Myanmar Now*, [online] 16 June, Available from: www.myanmar-now.org/en/news/former-head-of-covid-19-vaccine-rollout-charged-with-high-treason [Accessed 8 April 2022].

Nakanishi, Y. (2013) *Strong Soldiers, Failed Revolution: The State and Military in Burma, 1962–88*, Singapore: NUS Press.

Nyein, N. (2017) 'Tatmadaw chief offers cryptic definition of military's political role', *The Irrawaddy*, [online] 2 December, Available from: www.irrawaddy.com/news/burma/tatmadaw-chief-offers-cryptic-definition-militarys-political-role.html [Accessed 8 April 2022].

Nyi Kyaw (2019) 'Democracy first, federalism next? The constitutional reform', *ISEAS Perspective*, no. 93.

Pauli, T.C. (2020) 'Myanmar peace at a crossroads in 2020', *The Asia Foundation*, [online] 30 September, Available from: https://asiafoundation.org/2020/09/30/myanmar-peace-at-a-crossroads-in-2020/ [Accessed 8 April 2022].

Peter, Z. (2021) 'Myanmar's efforts to control COVID-19 crumble since February coup, aid groups say', *VOA News*, [online] 12 April, Available from: www.voanews.com/east-asia-pacific/myanmars-efforts-control-covid-19-crumble-february-coup-aid-groups-say [Accessed 8 April 2022].

Richter, H. (1972) 'The impact of socialism on economic activity in Burma', in T.S. Epstein and D.H. Penny (eds) *Opportunity and Response, Case Studies in Economic Development*, London: C. Hurst.

Selth, A. (2016) 'Strong, fully efficient and modern': Myanmar's new look armed forces'. *Regional Outlook Paper*. www.griffith.edu.au/__data/assets/pdf_file/0017/118313/Regional-Outlook-Paper-49-Selth-web.pdf

Selth, A. (2018) 'All going according to plan? The armed forces and government in Myanmar', *Contemporary Southeast Asia*, 40(1): 1–26.

Shin, A. (2018) 'Tatmadaw seeks closer cooperation with the people in defending country', *The Myanmar Times*, [online] 5 February, Available from: www.mmtimes.com/news/tatmadaw-seeks-closer-cooperation-people-defending-country.html [Accessed 8 April 2022].

Steinberg, D. (2021) *The Military in Burma/Myanmar: On the Longevity of Tatmadaw Rule and Influence*, Singapore: ISEAS.

Strangio, S. (2021) 'Amid coup fears, Myanmar's election commission rejects army election fraud claims', *The Diplomat*, [online] 29 January, Available from: https://thediplomat.com/2021/01/amid-coup-fears-myanmars-election-commission-rejects-army-election-fraud-claims/ [Accessed 8 April 2022].

Taylor, R.H. (1985) 'Burma', in Z.H. Ahmad and H. Crouch (eds) *Military–Civilian Relations in South-East Asia*, Oxford: Oxford University Press. pp 13–49.

Taylor, R.H. (2009) *The State in Myanmar*, London: Hurst & Company.

Taylor, R.H. (2013) 'Myanmar's "pivot" toward the shibboleth of "democracy"', *Asian Affairs*, 44(3): 392–400.

Taylor, R.H. (2015) *The Armed Forces in Myanmar Politics: A Terminating Role?*, Singapore: ISEAS.

Thawnghmung, A.M. and Robinson, G. (2017) 'Myanmar's new era: a break from the past, or too much of the same?', in D. Singh and M. Cook (eds), *Southeast Asian Affairs 2017*, Singapore: ISEAS. pp 237–257.

The Irrawaddy (2021) 'Myanmar military seizes medical oxygen imported by charities', *The Irrawaddy*, [online] 27 July, Available from: www.irrawaddy.com/news/burma/myanmar-military-seizes-medical-oxygen-imported-by-charities.html [Accessed 8 April 2022].

The Myanmar Times (2021) 'Myanmar military announces new state administrative council', *The Myanmar Times*, [online] 2 February, Available from: www.mmtimes.com/news/myanmar-military-announces-new-state-administrative-council.html [Accessed 8 April 2022].

Thiha, A. (2017) 'Understanding the Tatmadaw's "standard army" reforms', *Frontier Myanmar*, [online] 22 June, Available from: https://frontiermyanmar.net/en/understanding-the-tatmadaws-standard-army-reforms [Accessed 8 April 2022].

3

Business as Usual despite Reform: The Indonesian Military under Jokowi

Dahlia Gratia Setiyawan

Across the two administrations of Joko Widodo (popularly known as Jokowi), the Army-dominated TNI (Tentara Nasional Indonesia – Indonesian National Military) has experienced a resurgence. The military's present influence is not what it was during Suharto's New Order (1967–98) when the *dwi fungsi* (dual function) doctrine gave the TNI sweeping political power. Yet, the self-styled civilian reformer has synergized the TNI and its hardline elements. Jokowi has extolled and supported institutional and individual narratives of indispensability to national stability and has opened the door to New Order-era figures' reclamation of political roles.

Since Jokowi assumed the presidency in 2014, regional and national military authority has grown. The TNI has signed Memorandums of Understanding with civilian agencies for the provision of security and has become involved in government initiatives such as rural food self-sufficiency programmes. The TNI's demands for a greater role in counterterrorism operations grew during Jokowi's second term. On top of that, the military has become indispensable to Indonesia's COVID-19 response. On balance, the military is evolving into an institution that seeks an outward facing role while continuing to fulfil its mandate as national guardian.

Under Jokowi the number of ex-TNI hardliners in cabinet positions and courting political office has increased, bringing with them the normalization of intolerance. They have escalated discrimination, threats, intimidation and violence against LGBTQ+ communities and survivors of the state-sponsored anti-communist violence of 1965–6. Talk of proxy wars inform crackdowns against 'subversive elements'. Inflammatory rhetoric about the nation's moral decay, a sustained unapologetic stance about human rights and conservative ideas about state defence prevail.

For progressives, the appearance of hardliners at the helm extinguished hope that Jokowi would honour his promises of meaningful socio-political reform. 'There is now scholarly consensus,' a recent Brookings report states, 'that Indonesia's democracy has not just stagnated but is regressing' (Sambhi, 2021). What explains the antiquated ideas and personalities that have taken centre stage now more than two decades after Indonesia's era of reformation (*reformasi*)? Are the '*dwi fungsi* mindset' (Honna, 2003, p 7) and its adherents experiencing a resurgence? And what does this signify for future Indonesian civil–military relations?

While proximate causes factor in the military's current role retrenchment, the *longue durée* evolution of the structural basis that allows for illiberal actions and rhetoric is equally important to recognize. Narratives that internal and external enemies are besieging Indonesia are nothing new. The resurgence of such spectres does not just indicate the military's gambit for authority and repeated insertion into civilian affairs but is part of the TNI's culture.[1]

The majority of works on the Indonesian military focuses on three eras: how the military entered politics (Crouch, 1978; Sundhaussen, 1982), the TNI under Suharto and military ideology, authoritarianism and human rights abuses at that time (Crouch, 1978; Honna, 2003; Roosa, 2006; Said, 2006; McGregor, 2007; Robinson, 2018), and finally the post-Suharto reformation period (Honna, 2003; Chandra and Kammen, 2011, Haripin, 2020). More recently, Laksamana's (2019) assessment of the Jokowi era finds minimal difference between his management of civil–military relations and that of his predecessors. Echoing the earlier work of Honna (2018), Haripin (2020) suggests that MOOTW have taken on new importance under Jokowi; yet the president has not been revolutionary in that regard, preferring to focus on domestic counterterrorism operations rather than having the TNI participate in multinational initiatives (p 84). Those three scholars, as well as Sambhi (2021) all argue that illiberalism and the strengthened political standing of active and retired TNI figures go hand-in-hand.

The eras that preceded the Jokowi years and the fossilization of the views and values therein, is one factor that has contributed to the TNI's evolution into its present form. This path dependency can be summarized as follows: because civilians are to be mistrusted and only the military knows what is best for the nation, TNI entrenchment in economic, political and social life is both natural and necessary. An additional factor is Jokowi's need for legitimacy, which has compelled him to accommodate figures associated with the New Order. Accordingly, this chapter goes into greater depth than the existing scholarship in analysing the ideology and actions of military hardliners who have surrounded the president. Leaning on and delegating authority to such figures has shifted civil–military relations in favour of the

TNI, particularly when it comes to MOOTW, in numerous ways. This chapter considers several of them: Army counterterrorism manoeuvring, proxy war threat inflation, old guard anti-communism and the TNI's handling of the COVID-19 pandemic. All represent military entrenchment couched in a serious distrust of civilian leadership.

In addressing the guiding questions of this volume, I consider the following three. First, how a colonial legacy – the struggle for independence from Dutch rule – shaped Indonesian civil–military relations in such a way that the Army evolved into a political entity, national guardian and foil to civilian leaders. Second, how civil–military fusion came to be by way of the military's embedding in economics, politics and society. Lastly, how military retrenchment has shored up new/old authoritarian roles for resurgent hardliners and for the TNI.

TNI hardliners take little stock in the Huntingtonian framework referenced in the volume's introductory chapter, instead seeing liberal democracy as more dangerous when present than when absent. Consequently, they seek membership in democratic control structures. And they use both rhetorical devices and platform-seeking strategies to justify a greater socio-political and lateral security role for TNI, one that plays on historical precedent.

Legacies

The Indonesian National Revolution (1945–9) was the military's entry point into politics. The formula was simple. As per Sundhaussen, 'an army charged with large-scale, semi-permanent internal security tasks is, for all practical purposes, involved in internal politics' (1982, p 57). Guerrilla warfare further ensured that 'the roles of political and military leader became almost indistinguishable' (Crouch, 1978, p 25).

The TNI accordingly claimed a special role in securing Indonesia's sovereignty, which bolstered the belief in military circles that militarism surpassed diplomacy. The Army was the nation's saviour. Civilian leadership was to be distrusted. The TNI has clung to that narrative ever since.

In the 1950s, when hostilities with civilian parliamentarians grew (Sundhaussen, 1982, ch 3), General Abdul Harris Nasution, the originator of *dwi fungsi*, began his push for sustained TNI involvement in the nation-building process. In 1958, Nasution increased military authority by establishing the Committee on Army Doctrine. He also inaugurated the first version of Army territorial commands.[2] Henceforth they would be the basis of the military's entrenchment into civilian life and its source of local and national power and influence.

Antagonisms from Sukarno and the Indonesian Communist Party (PKI) – an enemy since the revolution – put the Army on the defensive during Guided Democracy (1957–65). Yet, regional unrest revived the saviour role;

by declaring martial law in March 1957, officers' conviction that only their intervention could save the nation from civilian mismanagement appeared justified (Crouch, 1978, p 24). However, the Doctrine of Territorial Warfare of 1960, which validated the Army's 'growing involvement in virtually all fields on the grounds of strategic needs' (Sundhaussen, 1982, p 141), came at the expense of its popularity and caused its political isolation. That reputational hit together with the rise of the PKI prompted the Army to implement a nationwide civic action programme in 1963.

A failed coup on 30 September 1965 provided anti-communists with a pretext to violently exterminate the PKI. Mere months later, when Sukarno forcibly ceded control to Suharto, between 500,000 and one million people were dead; tens of thousands more were political prisoners (Roosa, 2006; Robinson, 2018, ch 5 and 8). The Army-orchestrated mass killings and extrajudicial detentions of communist cadres, affiliates and others destroyed the TNI's strongest political enemy. The militarized New Order regime stoked fears that communism was an ever-present threat for the next 30 years (Robinson, 2018, pp 256–60).

The adoption of the *dwi fungsi* doctrine in 1966 marked the nadir of the social, political and economic ascendancy of the TNI (then known as Angkatan Bersenjata Republik Indonesia, Indonesian National Armed Forces [ABRI]). *Dwi fungsi* represented operational thinking in development since the Revolution, most strongly informed by Nasution's 'Middle Way' philosophy that imagined the armed forces as a political entity that was neither a dormant nor a hostile power. Yet, the military's further insertion into politics did not indicate a desire to exact total control. The TNI's 'lack of unity, self-confidence and legitimacy' prevented that (Hoadley, 1975, pp 122–3). Nevertheless, the military now claimed socio-political and security roles.

Military modernization saw some attacks on *dwi fungsi* in the final years of the New Order.[3] By the late-1990s, enmity against it surged. Scholars attacked the TNI's authoritarian leadership and human rights abuses (Honna, 2003, ch 2; Said, 2006, ch 2 and 3; McGregor, 2007, ch 5). The slogan *Cabut dwi fungsi!* (Down with the dual function!) embodied public anger at what amounted to 'a euphemism for military surveillance and control of national life' (Honna, 2003, p 3).

In April 2000, the military committed to relinquish its active role in politics. The TNI also agreed to divest management of its businesses by 2009, a harsh blow to the officer corps. *Reformasi* brought to the fore the TNI's image problems. Elite officers' corruption and nepotism translated into a decline not only in quality and professionalism of the armed forces but also in popular trust (Kardi, 1999, p 37). The TNI's abominable human rights record was inescapable. Atrocities committed during the occupation of East Timor (1975–99) prompted the United States and the European Union to cut off arms sales, training and aid in 1999.

Following Indonesia's 'turn toward democracy', forecasts of military reform were circumspect. Some otherwise optimistic regional specialists remarked that, while military coercion might appear to have weakened, the TNI's influence on the political process remained strong (Alagappa, 2001, pp 16–18; Honna 2003, p 200). Other observers likewise urged caution, citing the retention of the territorial command structure as a powerful support mechanism for military authoritarianism and as a bar against true TNI reform (Robinson, 2001, pp 206–56; Honna, 2003, pp 153–57; McGregor, 2006, p xviii).

Consequently, an opportune boost emerged. The US 'War on Terror' prompted the George W. Bush administration to re-establish military ties with Indonesia. In 2010 the United States removed the final roadblocks to the resumption of aid, lifting the sanctions on Indonesia's abusive secret forces, Kopassus.[4] When Jokowi assumed the presidency four years later, the TNI was poised to regain the upper hand in civil–military relations.

All the president's men

Jokowi lost voter confidence and credibility in his inaugural year. Promises of economic stimulation went unfulfilled. He struggled to control infighting within the Indonesian Democratic Party of Struggle, PDI-P, which had backed his candidacy, and to manage competing demands from elite interests. He lacked allies in parliament. A conflict between the police and the Anti-Corruption Commission (KPK), which played out messily in early 2015, further exposed his shortage of authority (Institute for Policy Analysis of Conflict, 2015). Consequently, Jokowi learned a lesson from the civilian presidents who preceded him. Without the support of military officers, politicians' hands are all but tied behind their backs.[5]

Jokowi's appointments of New Order-era figures were concessions to their indispensability. By drawing on past friendships and forging new ties, he sealed his mandate from the electorate. The presence of officers prominent during the Suharto regime was meant to legitimize his presidency. Jokowi, a largely domestic-oriented politician, needed leaders to whom he could delegate matters of national and regional defence and foreign policy.

One of Jokowi's earliest moves was to tap his close friend, retired four-star Kopassus general Luhut Binsar Pandjaitan, as presidential chief of staff. That decision, coming in his shaky first months in office, paid off. Luhut, founder of the elite Detachment 81 counterterrorism unit, shut down ministers' ridicule and mockery of Jokowi and prompted Golkar chair Setya Novanto to offer his party as coalition supporter of the president.[6] Later in 2014, Jokowi named ex-TNI hardliners Ryamizard Ryacudu as Minister of Defence and Gatot Nurmantyo as Army chief of staff; the latter ascended to TNI commander the following year. In his second term, Jokowi chose

Suharto's former TNI commander Wiranto to replace Luhut as chief security minister, a position the latter held following his initial appointment.⁷

Even Jokowi's political rivals have benefitted from his patronage, none more so than Suharto's former son-in-law, Lieutenant General (ret) Prabowo Subianto. Like Wiranto, Prabowo has made multiple unsuccessful bids for national office, two of them as Jokowi's opponent. Yet, when Ryamizard's tenure came to an end in 2019, Jokowi chose Prabowo, fresh off his second unsuccessful bid to unseat the president, to helm the Ministry of Defence. 'He knows more than I do' Jokowi was quoted as saying, citing Prabowo's experience in matters of national defence (Gorbiano, 2019).

Notably, Jokowi's first defeat of Prabowo was what initially raised hopes for an era of civilian leadership in which progressivism, including military reform, would prevail. Prabowo represented all the ugliness of the New Order-era TNI: crony capitalism, corruption and a dodgy human rights record. The victory seemed laden with symbolism. A so-called 'child of the slum' (Cochrane, 2014) lacking lineage to the military or to the political elite had despatched a preeminent beneficiary of New Order aristocratic autocracy.

However, the arrival of Gatot, then Ryamizard, Wiranto and ultimately Prabowo proved otherwise. Divisive Gatot, virulently anti-communist and paranoid about enemies everywhere was a 'blowback to another era' (McBeth, 2017). The appearance of arch-conservative Ryamizard, widely characterized as 'disliked' and 'not all that smart', also troubled many (Bachelard, 2014). Like Gatot, Ryamizard is a master conspiracy theorist, a 1965 denier *par excellence* and deeply uncomfortable with the West, particularly the potential for 'a unipolar order with the United States as the sole superpower' (Singh, 2005, p 70). Aside from his involvement in suppressing the Free Aceh Movement (GAM) in 2003, Ryamizard called the abduction and murder of a Papuan community activist at the hands of Kopassus troops heroic (Haripin, 2016).

As Suharto's TNI commander, Wiranto dealt with enmity toward *dwi fungsi* by backing reform-minded officers' initiatives to remake the military's image. It was an act of political theatre. The United Nations indictment of him in 2003 for crimes against humanity suggests his actual leanings. Prabowo's implication in the kidnapping of pro-democracy advocates as Kopassus head in the late 1990s presented further evidence that Jokowi, as per one activist, 'does not understand that human rights and democracy should be considerations in picking ministerial candidates' (Gorbiano, 2019).

These New Order carryovers either are pseudo-reformers or have no reform credentials at all. Their appointments reflect Jokowi's apathy at producing legitimate military reform. Gatot and Ryamizard are particularly implicated in the threat to human rights that TNI entrenchment and the present civil–military relations imbalance pose. Both used threat inflation to justify calls for the military to amplify its role as a security apparatus and its involvement in politics at the expense of the promotion of democratic values.

In his first term, Jokowi hoped that his new TNI commander would engender loyalty from within the Army corps, but things quickly began to go awry as Gatot's many idiosyncrasies, prejudices, tensions with Jokowi and political aspirations sprang forth. In December 2016, Gatot unilaterally ordered the suspension of the military's defence cooperation with Australia (McBeth, 2017). Then there was a speech to an audience of college students wherein he ruminated on the merits of attracting sharks to devour hypothetical seaborne Chinese refugees (Harvey and Holman, 2017). Gatot's alleged links to the Islamic Defenders Front (FPI) resulted in him being named as the 'main factor' in a rumoured coup against Jokowi.[8] In October 2017 Jokowi angrily admonished the military to stay out of politics.[9] The last straw came days later with Gatot's vocal politicization of his refused entry into the United States (Hutt, 2017). In December 2017, months before Gatot's scheduled retirement, Jokowi appointed the externally oriented Air Marshal Hadi Tjahjanto as TNI commander (Reuters, 2017).

Ryamizard's outsider status as a career combat officer who was never trained abroad made him an attractive cabinet pick, even as it opened him to criticisms of being 'myopic, with little knowledge and exposure to changes in the outside world' (Singh, 2005, p 31). He is one of the finest exemplars of the maintenance of the *dwi fungsi* mentality among Jokowi's old guard generals. His belief as defence minister that the territorial command structure is integral to protect Indonesia from foreign infiltrators or domestic threats was unwavering.

'Terror', believed Ryamizard, 'has been used by the Indonesian Communist Party, GAM, Darul Islam, OPM and other groups using violence to achieve their [political] goals' (Singh, 2005, p 54). Consequently, 'every security apparatus, in particular, the Army, will need to build up a strong intelligence capacity to help the country fight terrorism' (Singh, 2005, p 55). That ideology explains his objective, while serving Jokowi, to further entrench the TNI in the management of the state.

During his 2014–19 tenure as defence minister, Ryamizard's hostility and warmongering directed at Papuan independence at one point seemed to threaten armed conflict. In March 2018, he bellicosely challenged that 'being drawn into a war with the Free Papua Movement (OPM) would take no more effort than making plans for lunch' (*ngajak perang kok seperti ngajak makan soto*) (Bomantama, 2018). Such rhetoric was nothing new for Ryamizard. In 2003 during the Megawati presidency, he had opined that: 'the military's security role should be reinstated due to threats of separatism and other disturbances in the country' (quoted in Sebastian, 2006, p 341). One year later, he claimed there were some 60,000 foreign spies in Indonesia, suggesting again that only the military could address such a threat (Bachelard, 2014; Singh, 2005, pp 91–2).

Ryamizard has kept busy in retirement by pursuing his life's passion: the promotion of national defence. He has continued to advocate for Bela Negara (Defend the State), a civilian defence force that he instituted while defence minister. In 2020, Ryamizard was lauded for his 'true patriotic soul' in service of the national youth (Jyestha, 2020).

Following a failed bid to be taken seriously in the 2019 presidential race, Gatot now professes to be shifting into a new phase of life as a chicken farm impresario. He has rarely missed an opportunity, however, to be quoted in the press on TNI matters or his political views.

The generals who remain in Jokowi's service have even greater influence than ever before. For example, in his role as Coordinating Minister of Maritime Affairs, Luhut now holds authority over wide-ranging security issues. Those include the South China Sea disputes and the international defence cooperation initiatives that the Biden administration seeks with ASEAN members in a doubling-down of Donald Trump's national security strategy. Luhut also leads the Java-Bali Community Activities Restriction Enforcement programme and is Deputy-Chair of the COVID-19 Handling and National Economic Recovery Committee (KPC-PEN).

Luhut and an additional figure worth mentioning, Moeldoko, another former TNI commander and Jokowi's current chief of staff, used their appointments and friendships with the president to become more politically involved. Prabowo, like Gatot before him, has advanced his personal political ambitions at Jokowi's expense. All the aforementioned hardliners fear the TNI's institutional vulnerability and see the military as the nation's saviour. It is in large part due to them that the TNI now claims sweeping new authority in MOOTW.

The TNI and MOOTW

Jokowi envisions Indonesia as a 'global maritime axis' in the Asia-Pacific. Indonesian maritime territory spans greater than two million square miles and includes Pacific and Indian Ocean shipping routes and straits that have functioned as conduits of trade for centuries. With an estimated one half of the world's trading goods and oil passing through its waters (Febrica, 2014, p 13), Indonesia is integral to regional maritime security initiatives and committed to showing its strength. Despite generous Chinese investments in upgrading Indonesian infrastructure, in 2016 Jokowi used the TNI as an indispensable prop of Indonesia's assertion of sovereignty in the South China Sea when he held a cabinet meeting aboard a warship docked in the Natuna Islands. That show of force signalled to China that incursions into Indonesia's exclusive economic zone there would not go unchallenged. Four years later, when Chinese fishing and Coast Guard vessels again entered waters outside of the Natuna Islands, the government scrambled warships and fighter jets to patrol the area (Grossman, 2020).

The South China Sea conflict, piracy and other maritime terrorism in Indonesian waters prompted Jokowi to champion the Navy and the Air Force in his plans to develop an 'integrated three-dimensional defence system' as part of a long-term strategic plan (Shekhar and Liow, 2014). Jokowi announced in 2014 that he would increase the defence budget to 1.5 per cent of gross domestic product (GDP) in five years (Shekhar and Liow, 2014). Current State Defence Policy regulations under Prabowo call for even 'stronger maritime and air surveillance capabilities and integrated TNI units on outlying islands, with particular attention on expanding missile and other area-denial capabilities', which the acquisition of fighter jets and naval assets will support (Ng, 2021).

With the emphasis on maritime affairs and with the Indonesian National Police (POLRI)'s elite Detachment 88 (Densus 88) at the helm of counterterrorism operations, the Army made its move. In 2014 soldiers were embedded in POLRI-led counterterrorism units and TNI territorial commands expanded their intelligence gathering capabilities (Mietzner, 2006, p 41) in service of fighting the Islamic State (ISIS). Then, the TNI saw a chance for even more influence. It drew attention to police failures, particularly as concerned the location and capture of Santoso, Indonesia's 'most wanted' extremist (Institute for Policy Analysis of Conflict, 2015). Subsequently, as part of a joint task force, soldiers joined local police and Densus 88 at the shootout that killed Santoso in July 2016. That participation elevated the TNI's image. Police and judiciary corruption unearthed in the wake of the KPK–POLRI conflict of 2015 presented the military with a further opportunity to 'portray themselves as purer, more loyal and ultimately more reliable than the police' (Institute for Policy Analysis of Conflict, 2015).

In May 2017 – a month after the sensational coup rumours broke – Jokowi called for increased armed forces involvement in counterterrorism efforts. He declared that TNI should join parliament in drafting a much-awaited national security bill, a task from which it had been excluded (Kuwado, 2017). Politicians generally applauded that decision. Human rights activists worried about the military's sweeping new powers, seeing a reversal of the part of the 2004 TNI Law that identified military actions only to be carried out by way of a state decree (The Jakarta Post, 2017). Both Wiranto and Ryamizard backed a direct role for the TNI in counterterrorism operations (Anindya, 2017). So did a significant portion of the public.[10]

The TNI's growing involvement in the counterterrorism realm subsequently produced claims of 'proxy wars', which emboldened it further to take a more substantial role in national defence and civilian affairs. In

2014, Gatot, then Army chief of staff, raised the concept to promote 'back to basics' nationalism (Institute for Policy Analysis of Conflict, 2015, pp 14–15). He crisscrossed the country and took to social media to declare that Indonesia was under attack from unseen forces. Major powers, he alleged, were plotting, if not already attempting, to seize control of the nation's natural resources due to the world's decreasing supply of fossil-based energy resources. According to Gatot, the secession of East Timor in 1999 was proxy warfare at work with the Timor Gap oil field being under threat (Afrida, 2017). After its inclusion in the Ministry of Defence 2015 'White Paper' as part of a discussion about how states seek to 'divide and conquer' nations by way of 'asymmetrical weaponry' such as cyber warfare (Ministry of Defence, 2015) the proxy war gained further legitimacy. In 2016, Gatot called for Indonesians to unite against the proxy warfare menace and protect the nation's food and fuel sources (Kompas, 2016). In September of that year, he asserted that terrorist groups were part of a proxy war owing to their receipt of funding from international sources (Russell, 2016). Gatot then announced a media proxy war defence pact, which 11 organizations signed (ANTARA News, 2016).

Joining Gatot in ringing the alarm was Ryamizard. He developed his own proxy war ideology over a number of years and has been vocal about it since at least the end of the New Order.[11] Ryamizard's emphasis on foreign proxies' infiltration has aimed at blocking political resistance most keen on seeking substantial military reform. His proxy war claims reflected measures to widen the definition of radicalism and terrorism and to criminalize acts of 'insulting the Indonesian state' (Singh, 2016, p 2). Seeing threats 'in areas as diverse as ideology, politics, the economy, social issues, culture, law and security', Ryamizard targeted non-governmental organizations (NGOs) and social interest groups (Russell, 2016). For instance, he suggested that the LGBTQ+ rights movement facilitates human rights observers' destabilization of Indonesia by 'skew[ing] the mindset of our nation away from our base ideology' (Tempo, 2016). In that calculus, the nation is under attack from interests incompatible with 'Indonesian culture', an idea that is grounded in nothing other than Ryamizard's own bigotry.

The TNI's embrace of the proxy warfare concept correlates with the promotion of ultra-nationalism in order to increase public amenability toward the TNI's expanding role in civilian life. Sydney Jones, director of the Jakarta-based Institute for Policy Analysis of Conflict (IPAC) notes that by creating paranoia, the military can 'suggest that Indonesian nationalism needs to be re-ignited' (Fabi and Kapoor, 2016). Those who oppose military expansion thus can be silenced out of fear of being labelled foreign proxies (Russell, 2016). It goes without saying that such an approach is strongly redolent of New Order orthodoxy, as it represents a variation on the internal security theme crafted in the 1960s.

Striking similarities exist between the xenophobia of ex-TNI hardliners and that of former president Trump in the United States, Pauline Hansen in Australia and Nigel Farage in Britain (Russell, 2016). As in those cases, the implication of xenophobic talk goes beyond revealing political elite demagoguery. Presidential candidates, ministers and other government officials who demonize both citizens and non-citizens alike normalize intolerance and violence against vulnerable populations.

It is no coincidence that illiberalism has grown during Jokowi's presidencies (Human Rights Watch, 2017, pp 270–6). Take the large anti-LGBTQ+ protests of the last several years in Jakarta or parliamentary proposals to criminalize same sex relations and extramarital sex. Those expressions threaten social stability and suggest that the government is acquiescent to harassment, violence and intimidation of its citizens. But they have also sparked further concern about the military's increasing influence in civilian affairs. Some even have posed a threat to Jokowi himself, such as the 2017 smear campaign against Jakarta's former governor Basuki Tjahaja Purnama who was imprisoned on charges of religious blasphemy. As TNI hardliners were said to be behind those protests and, moreover, certainly did not come to Jokowi's aid in their midst, an escalation in the unrest could have posed serious problems for the president. Luckily for Jokowi, support came from one of his main allies, POLRI chief Tito Karnavian, who quelled the turmoil.

Of all of the currents of intolerance – against foreigners and minority groups – none is arguably stronger or deeper than that against what has come to be known as the latent threat of communism (*bahaya latent komunisme*). That terminology, traceable to the New Order, presents the PKI as an undying threat and promotes the trope of communist-as-terrorist.

For over 50 years, territorial commands have been the lynchpin of the TNI's counterterrorism strategy to ferret out communist activity. They have done so even as the official state position about the 1965–66 mass killings vacillated between silence and denial (Robinson, 2018, pp 306–13). The territorial commands, therefore, were complicit in transforming a once-legal political party into a terrorist organization that needed to be 'pacified'.[12] They helped to implement and propagate the propaganda campaign launched following the abortive coup in 1965, which popularized the notion that communism equalled terrorism.[13] They also coordinated and facilitated death squads and anti-communist militias.

In Jokowi's first term, local military commands repeatedly persecuted citizens who they alleged were promoting communism (Fabi and Kapoor, 2016; Reuters, 2018; Vann, 2019). Predictably, retired members of the military were complicit in attempts to generate hysteria about a communist resurgence. Their efforts gained traction following a government-sponsored symposium in 2016 that granted survivors of the mass violence and their descendants a forum to openly share their narratives of persecution and suffering. Civilian anti-communist hardliners from the FPI and a group of retired New Order-era generals denounced the symposium and convened their own meeting to address, 'the threat of the PKI and other ideologies' (The Jakarta Post, 2016). Ryamizard claimed that he had received indications that the PKI was going to be revived (The Jakara Post, 2016).

Among the polemics alleged to be part of ideological training at military bases is that the nation is under threat from something called New-Style Communism (*Komunisme Gaya Baru*), or KGB (Honna, 2018, pp 265–6). As that thinking goes, KGB seeks to infiltrate the populace by inuring them to things such as 'free healthcare and education programs'. More nefariously, the KGB 'agent' is bent on 'separating the army from [the] people [and] using human rights and democracy issues while positioning oneself as a victim to gain sympathy' (Nairn, 2017). Jokowi himself has been labelled a communist, or, at the very least, the descendant of a PKI family. That allegation arose during the 2014 presidential election and emerged again in 2019.

Generals (ret) Kivlan Zen and Gatot are among the most active of the ex-TNI rabble-rousers. The former was behind the group who protested the 2016 symposium. He then backed the FPI and other organizations that terrorized the participants of a different seminar (Wieringa, 2017; Lane, 2018, p 4). Amid still other FPI-organized anti-communist rallies Gatot called on military commanders to hold mandatory screenings of the Suharto-era docudrama, *Pengkhiantan G30S/PKI* (*The Treachery of the Indonesian Communist Party*) for their troops (Allard and Da Costa, 2017; Lane, 2018, p 5).

That show of force sought to intimidate Indonesians into accepting that the New Order narrative of the tragedy of 1965–66 is the only acceptable interpretation of events. Jokowi, for one, received the message loud and clear. Unwilling to stand up for the rights of the most vulnerable citizens at the expense of his own neck, in June 2017 he used the occasion of a speech at Muhammadiyah University to emphatically declare his opposition to communism. 'If you can show me [evidence of a PKI resurgence], I will strike them down this very second,' he declared (Wibowo, 2017). Such rhetoric was a direct echo of New Order terminology (Robinson, 2018, p 164).

The persistence of red-baiting rumours thus prompted Jokowi to shed the conciliatory tone of his first term, when it appeared that he would issue a formal apology to survivors, their families and the descendants of the dead. However, that tone was what opened him up in the first place to such fierce criticism, gave his ex-TNI antagonists more fodder against him, and, if there is any grain of truth to the rumours, provided the impetus for the alleged coup plot. The renewed use of the latent threat of communism trope to justify the TNI's political relevance in advance of the last election is further notable. Indeed, it suggests that Indonesia remains unable 'to dilute heavy historical legacies … and establish firm civilian control over the armed forces' (Mietzner, 2011, p 13). Consequently, TNI hardliners' persecution of so-called KGB agents and PKI sympathizers – for there is scant possibility that there actually are communist proselytizers in the country – are poised to continue.

TNI hardliners' distrust of civilian political leaders and the general public, who they see as susceptible to liberal thinking, endures. Fears of susceptibility even extend to the TNI's own rank and file. Their targets remain the socio-political sectors most likely to seek military reform: NGOs and special interest groups. The *dwi fungsi* mindset continues unabashed while the path toward democratic transition remains muddied and uncertain as civil–military asymmetry occurs at the Indonesian people's expense.

The COVID-19 pandemic unquestionably has furthered TNI role retrenchment. From the pandemic's onset in 2020 military figures have been in positions of influence and decision-making at the national and territorial levels (Sambhi, 2021). The volume of personnel able to fight the virus' spread and its large network of military-owned and operated healthcare facilities, have made the TNI's upper hand in civil–military relations feel natural and necessary. The military now is identified, according to numerous public opinion surveys, as Indonesia's 'most trusted state institution' (Purba, 2022).

Seeing COVID-19 crisis management as an approximation of an external security threat requiring military primacy (Vatikiotis, 2020), the TNI acted quickly. Initiatives were carried out jointly with POLRI. Throughout the pandemic tens of thousands of TNI–POLRI troops were deployed and redeployed as contact tracers and vaccinators; TNI–POLRI further was instrumental in mobilizing healthcare professionals to serve in those roles and in holding mass inoculation events once Indonesia obtained the vaccine (Fitri, 2021).

The territorial commands were instrumental to the Army's programme; accordingly, the pandemic created an increased reliance upon, and public appreciation of, them particularly as cases of the virus threatened in 2021 to overwhelm Indonesia. The pandemic thus allowed for TNI authority to grow in the realm of HADR, which already in the pre-pandemic times 'allowed the military to accommodate an old political interest of maintaining the territorial command system and defend it with new justification' (Haripin, 2020, p 61).

Owing to the pandemic's impact on the economy, the health system and social stability (Sambhi, 2021) Jokowi continues to delegate authority and the administration of crisis management to the TNI. The military is happy to encourage the idea that, as in past moments of national turmoil, Indonesia cannot function without its leadership. As one scholar has recently warned, without a stronger civilian bureaucracy, 'this trend will be difficult to reverse' (Sambhi, 2021).

Conclusion

Creating a more nuanced understanding of contemporaneous civil–military relations necessitates viewing its new/old dimensions. To historicize events of the present illuminates how TNI hardliners' *modus vivendi* and *modus operandi* continue to echo modes of understanding forged in the past. Moreover, it contextualizes, clarifies and explains how path dependence has become part of the TNI's present evolution as a guarantor of external security and, simultaneously, of political order.

The applicable value of the historically grounded approach to civil–military relations is not unique to Indonesia. It can be applied elsewhere such as Myanmar, for example. Recognizing the historical enmity of the *Tatmadaw* toward civilian politicians partially explains why it appears to be as unwilling as the TNI to withdraw from politics (Prager-Nyein, 2011, pp 24–44; see also Chapter 2 in this volume).

The TNI's current remaking as a defence diplomacy and MOOTW leader speaks to an institutional 'capacity for self-reflection', which might even be an argument against the Indonesian military being typecast as 'conformist, rigid and intellectually stagnant' (Honna, 2003, p 207). Yet traces of orthodoxy – and obfuscation – linger. Indeed, 'the main selling point of the proxy narrative is the ambiguity and elasticity of the concept [which] makes it easy to pin … on even the flimsiest of issues, often to the point where it can be equated with conspiracy theories' (Agastia, 2016). By increasing paranoia among the public and legislators, the TNI can justify an expanded role for itself, silence its critics and opponents, promote its own concept of nationalism and preserve the territorial commands (Institute for Policy Analysis of Conflict, 2015).

In the 2000s, writes Kingsbury, the military 'developed a new type of power by only becoming close to politicians on its own terms' (2003, p 230). Prominent officers helped to install Suharto's successor and subsequently achieved electoral success when socioeconomic stasis and political instability led to a loss of confidence in civilian political leadership. The retention of the territorial commands allowed the TNI to 'tap into economic resources at the grassroots and defend their role as a significant player in local politics' (Mietzner, 2006, p viii).

TNI proximity to politics in the post-Suharto period has paid dividends. Because of a loophole in the 2004 TNI law that mandated military economic divestment, officers have continued to hold the reins of a number of corporations and enterprises, both legal and illicit. The TNI enjoys protection from oversight and exemption from civil persecution. Hardliners remain unconcerned with improving their own image or that of the Army relating to human rights, preferring to deny, conceal, or threaten, even when condemned for past or current actions.

The TNI and its affiliated hardliners stand to continue to benefit from the desire of the United States and Russia to draw closer to Indonesia. Former Defence Secretary James Mattis broached the topic of resuming military training between US and Indonesian Special Forces and partnering in counterterrorism operations. He also proposed further sales of F-16s (Storey, 2018, pp 6–7). Prabowo's purchase of Sukhoi jets allows Indonesia to avoid being overly reliant on the US and has helped stem Russia's geopolitical isolation following the 2022 invasion of Ukraine (Llewellyn, 2022). Having Russia as an ally is in line with Indonesia's maritime security hopes and fears as it concerns a strong China. It certainly adds clarity to Indonesia's abstention from the April 2022 UN General Assembly vote to remove Russia from the Human Rights Council and Jokowi's continued insistence on President Vladimir Putin's attendance at the 2022 G20 Bali Summit (Beech et al, 2022).

Current TNI Commander General Andika Perkasa, a leader with a passion for military law, has instigated some military reform by abolishing a number of New Order-era military policies. Two, which took effect in 2022, stand out among them. In all branches of the military, female recruits are no longer subjected to the physical exam known as the 'virginity test'; Andika also further decided that being a 'PKI descendant' can no longer bar a person from the recruitment process (Saptohutomo, 2022).

Despite those glimmers of hope, significant military reform and more symmetrical civil–military relations remain unlikely. The military's 'saviour' role and the blurring of the categories of civilian and military are here to stay, especially in light of the TNI's leadership in the COVID-19 crisis. If a recent lawsuit against the 2004 TNI law is any indication, a campaign is underway not only for longer terms and larger roles for officers, but for a greater internal security role for the TNI itself. The G20 meetings and postponed national elections, both scheduled for November 2022, are two reasons why the TNI is pushing hard for that mandate (Purba, 2022).

As for Prabowo, he has not abandoned his hopes to become president in 2024, although, by this point, even he knows that he is unlikely to win. Prabowo remains attractive at the grassroots level; another attempt at the top office will help him to net future electoral successes for his party, Gerindra. With Andika possibly poised to enter the race and TNI popularity having reached new heights, will comfort with the *dwi fungsi* mindset become the tipping point in determining the presidency in 2024?

On balance, I have shown that the Huntingtonian framework is not a philosophy that Indonesian military elite hardliners share. For they do not countenance the view that the absence of liberal democracy means that militarization takes place at society's detriment. As adherents of a formidable institutional history dating back to the Revolution, they believe that liberal democratization and too much civilian control are destabilizing and dangerous to Indonesia. As their own theory goes, the military must exert itself in issues of national governance. This is what the TNI will continue to do, even as it further evolves.

Notes

1. There is no single TNI stance that renders Indonesian civil–military relations dichotomous. Indeed, such an argument would be presumptuous; as Jun Honna has observed, the TNI as an institution is incapable of 'adjusting its policies, roles and position based on consensus and shared political values' (2003, p 202).
2. The territorial commands were rooted in Nasution's battle strategy against the Dutch wherein the Army's division of itself into strategic pockets ensured its survival.
3. In fact, criticism of the doctrine first emerged within the TNI at least a decade earlier during a time when it still was forbidden to speak against it.
4. Among its human rights violations are torture, sexual assault and rape, murder and disappearances.
5. Likewise, as Abdurrahman Wahid experienced, excessive involvement in the military's affairs is also a formula for failure (Honna, 2003, pp 180–96). For more on this dilemma as related to Jokowi, see Laksamana, 2019.
6. This backing was crucial for Jokowi who could not then and cannot still rely on PDI-P support alone; Golkar's present factionalism makes it equally reliant on Jokowi who represents government support (Suryadinata, 2018, p 6).
7. Observers of Indonesian politics suggest that Luhut's removal was meant to placate anti-communist military and religious hardliners who were incensed with a planned investigation into the 1965–66 violence. On Jokowi's order, Luhut was – reluctantly – planning to request data on mass graves from human rights organizations (Hutton, 2016).
8. During the crisis the president turned to hardline General A.M. Hendropriyono, who was implicated in crimes that include the assassination of the human rights activist Munir in 2004 (Nairn, 2017).
9. Without naming Gatot explicitly, in an interview around the same time, Lieutenant General (ret) Agus Widjojo stressed that a military commander should be subordinate to the president. He offered the following analogy: 'although the chauffeur more often holds the steering wheel of the car, we should remember that the car is owned by the employer. So the chauffer who drives the car, only drives the car under the orders of the employer' (quoted in Herlianto, 2017, pp 4–5).
10. According to a 2017 *Kompas* survey, '93% of respondents supported the TNI having some role in counterterrorism, while 38% supported the idea of TNI autonomy in combating terrorism. More than half or 55% of respondents believe the TNI should remain under the command of POLRI, although the number who support autonomy is still significant' (Anindya, 2017).
11. In the New Order's final years, fears of foreign intervention ran high due to World Bank/IMF actions to liberalize the banking sector. Hardliners also found threatening foreign pressure for Indonesia to grant independence to East Timor (Russell, 2016).
12. Some scholars have adhered to the military's perspective in their own analyses and essentially find the PKI responsible for its own destruction. See, for instance, Sundhaussen (1982, pp 218–19). However, the suggestion that PKI aggression was primarily to blame for the atrocities that followed is inordinately problematic.
13. Army officials frequently used terms like 'PKI terrorists' to stoke public anger toward the PKI and their inflammatory rhetoric appeared frequently in print media of the era.

References

Afrida, N. (2015) 'TNI chief strikes alarmist tone on proxy war', *The Jakarta Post*, [online] 15 December, Available from: www.thejakartapost.com/news/2015/12/15/tni-chief-strikes-alarmist-tone-proxy-war.html [Accessed 23 March 2017].

Agastia, I.G.B.D. (2016) 'A case against the military's newfound "proxy war" obsession', *The Jakarta Post*, [online] 22 December, Available from: www.thejakartapost.com/academia/2016/12/22/a-case-against-the-militarys-newfound-proxy-war-obsession.html [Accessed 23 March 2017].

Alagappa, M. (ed) (2001) *Coercion and Governance: The Declining Political Role of the Military in Asia*, Stanford: Stanford University Press.

Allard, T. and Da Costa, A.B. (2017) ' "Red scare" puts pressure on Indonesian president', *Reuters*, [online] 27 September, Available from: www.reuters.com/article/us-indonesia-politics-military/red-scare-puts-pressure-on-indonesian-president-idUSKCN1C21AQ [Accessed 11 April 2018].

Anindya, C. (2017) 'TNI's role in counterterrorism: impact on military reform', *RSIS Commentary*, No 224/2017.

ANTARA News (2016) 'Menguasi media salah satu "proxy war"', *ANTARA News*, [online] 28 September, Available from:www.antaranews.com/berita/587161/menguasai-media-salah-satu-proxy-war [Accessed 23 March 2017].

Bachelard, M. (2014) 'Jokowi's cabinet of compromises', *Sydney Morning Herald*, [online] 27 October, Available from: www.smh.com.au/world/indonesia-jokowis-cabinet-of-compromises-20141027-11ce1d.html [Accessed 30 March 2018].

Beech, H., Dahir, A.L. and Lopez, O. (2022) 'With us or with them: in a new Cold War, how about neither', *New York Times*, [online] 24 April, Available from: www.nytimes.com/2022/04/24/world/asia/cold-war-ukraine.html [Accessed 25 April 2022].

Bomantama, R. (2018) 'Ditantang OPM, menhan: dia jual, kita beli', *Tribun News*, [online] 29 March, Available from: www.tribunnews.com/nasional/2018/03/29/ditantang-opm-menhan-dia-jual-kita-beli [Accessed 31 March 2018].

Chandra, S. and Kammen, D. (2011) *A Tour of Duty: Changing Patterns of Military Politics in Indonesia in the 1990s*, Classic Indonesia, Book 13, Jakarta, Kuala Lumpur: Equinox Publishing.

Cochrane, J. (2014) 'A child of the slum rises as president of Indonesia', *New York Times*, [online] 22 July, Available from: www.nytimes.com/2014/07/23/world/asia/joko-widodo-populist-governor-is-named-winner-in-indonesian-election.html [Accessed 7 June 2017].

Crouch, H. (1978) *The Army and Politics in Indonesia*, Ithaca: Cornell University Press.

Fabi, R. and Kapoor, K. (2016) 'Indonesia's "red scare" stokes unease over military's growing influence', *Reuters*, [online] 18 May, Available from: www.reuters.com/article/us-indonesia-military/indonesias-red-scare-stokes-unease-over-militarys-growing-influence-idUSKCN0Y933F [Accessed 15 December 2017].

Febrica, S. (2014) *Explaining Indonesia's Participation in Maritime Security Cooperation*. PhD thesis, University of Glasgow.

Fitri, A. (2021) 'TNI-POLRI and the national vaccination program', *Info Singkat*, XII(4/II): 25–30.

Gorbiano, M.I. (2019) '"He knows more than I do": Jokowi picks Prabowo as defense minister', *The Jakarta Post*, [online] 23 October, Available from: www.thejakartapost.com/news/2019/10/23/he-knows-more-than-i-do-jokowi-picks-prabowo-as-defense-minister.html [Accessed 27 April 2022].

Grossman, D. (2020) 'Why is China pressing Indonesia again over its maritime claims?', *World Politics Review*, [online] 16 January, Available from: www.worldpoliticsreview.com/articles/28476/why-is-china-pressing-indonesia-again-over-the-natuna-islands [Accessed 2 May 2022].

Haripin, M. (2016) 'Ryamizard's proxy wars', *New Mandala*, [online] 8 March, Available from: www.newmandala.org/ryamizards-proxy-wars/ [Accessed 15 December 2017].

Haripin, M. (2020) *Civil–Military Relations in Indonesia: The Politics of Military Operations Other Than War*, Routledge Security in Asia Series, Abingdon, Oxon; New York, NY: Routledge.

Harvey, A. and Holman, J. (2017) 'Panglima TNI mengancam pengungsi Cina', *Republika*, [online] 6 January, Available from: www.republika.co.id/berita/internasional/abc-australia-network/17/01/06/ojc233-panglima-tni-mengancam-pengungsi-china [Accessed 1 April 2018].

Herlianto, J. (2017) 'The current state of military reform in Indonesia: interview with Lieutenant General (Retired) Agus Widjojo (Part I)', *ISEAS Perspective*, 91/2017.

Hoadley, J.S. (1975) *Soldiers and Politics in Southeast Asia: Civil–Military Relations in Comparative Perspective*, Cambridge, MA: Schenkman.

Honna, J. (2003) *Military Politics and Democratization in Indonesia*, London: Routledge Curzon.

Honna, J. (2018) 'Civil–military relations in an emerging state: a perspective from Indonesia's democratic consolidation' in K. Tsunekawa and Y. Todo (eds) *Emerging States at Crossroads*, New York: Springer, 2018, pp 255–70.

Human Rights Watch (2017) *World Report: 2018*, New York, NY: Seven Stories Press.

Hutt, D. (2017) 'Was the Indonesian military chief's US flight incident a political stunt?', *The Diplomat*, [online] 2 November, Available from: https://thediplomat.com/2017/11/was-the-indonesian-military-chiefs-us-flight-incident-a-political-stunt [Accessed 3 April 2018].

Hutton, J. (2016) 'Indonesia moves to investigate anti-communist atrocities', *New York Times*, [online] 27 April, Available from: www.nytimes.com/2016/04/27/world/asia/indonesia-1965-massacre-graves.html [Accessed 3 February 2018].

Institute for Policy Analysis of Conflict (2015) *The Expanding Role of the Indonesian Military*, Jakarta: Institute for Policy Analysis of Conflict, Report No 19.

Jyestha, V. (2020) 'Mantan menham Ryamizard Ryacudu dinilai layak menyandang predikat "bapak bela negara"', *Tribun News*, [online] 2 October, Available from: www.tribunnews.com/nasional/2020/10/02/mantan-menhan-ryamizard-ryacudu-dinilai-layak-menyandang-predikat-bapak-bela-negara [Accessed 23 October 2021].

Kardi, K. (1999) 'TNI kembali ke jati diri', in A. Wirahadikusumah (ed) *Indonesia Baru dan Tantangan TNI: Pemikiran Masa Depan*, Jakarta: Pustaka Sinar Harapan, pp 33–60.

Kingsbury, D. (2003) *Power Politics and the Indonesian Military*, New York: RoutledgeCurzon.

Kuwado, F.J. (2018) 'Tak ikut menjaring cawapres Jokowi, ini alasan Luhut Pandjaitan', *Kompas*, [online] 13 March, Available from: https://nasional.kompas.com/read/2018/03/13/11431791/tak-ikut-menjaring-cawapres-jokowi-ini-alasan-luhut-pandjaitan [Accessed 29 March 2018].

Kompas (2016) 'Panglima TNI: "Proxy War" mengancam Indonesia', *Kompas*, [online] 19 May, Available from: http://nasional.kompas.com/read/2016/05/19/14103921/panglima.tni.proxy.war.mengancam.indonesia [Accessed 23 March 2017].

Laksamana, E. (2017) 'What can we expect from Indonesia's new defence chief?', *The Strategist*, [online], 13 December, Available from: www.aspistrategist.org.au/what-can-we-expect-from-indonesias-new-defence-chief/ [Accessed 30 March 2018].

Laksmana, E. (2019) 'Civil–military relations under Jokowi: between military corporate interests and presidential handholding, *Asia Policy*, 14(4): 63–71.

Lane, M. (2018) 'The further erosion of an Indonesian political taboo', *ISEAS Perspective*, 6/2018.

Llewellyn, A. (2022) '"Not G-19": Why Indonesia won't bar Russia from the G20', *Al Jazeera*, [online] 22 April, Available from: www.aljazeera.com/news/2022/4/22/not-g19-why-indonesia-wont-bar-russia-from-the-g20 [Accessed 25 April 2022].

McBeth, J. (2017) 'Widodo, his paranoid general and a "rotting" situation in Indonesia', *South China Morning Post*, [online] 15 January, Available from: www.scmp.com/week-asia/politics/article/2062023/widodo-his-paranoid-general-and-rotting-situation-indonesia [Accessed 1 April 2018].

McGregor, K. (2007) *History in Uniform: Military Ideology and the Construction of Indonesia's Past*, Honolulu: University of Hawaii Press.

Mietzner, M. (2006) *The Politics of Military Reform in Post-Suharto Indonesia: Elite Conflict, Nationalism, and Institutional Resistance*, Policy Studies Series 23, Washington, DC: East-West Center Publications.

Mietzner, M. (2011) 'Conflict and leadership: the resurgent political role of the military in Southeast Asia' in M. Mietzner (ed) *The Political Resurgence of the Military in Southeast Asia: Conflict and Leadership*, New York: Routledge, pp 1–23.

Ministry of Defence (2015) *Buku Putih Pertahanan Indonesia*, Jakarta: Indonesian Ministry of Defence.

Nairn, A. (2017) 'Trump's Indonesian allies in bed with ISIS-backed militia seeking to oust elected president', *The Intercept*, [online] 18 April, Available from: https://theintercept.com/2017/04/18/trumps-indonesian-allies-in-bed-with-isis-backed-militia-seeking-to-oust-elected-president/ [Accessed 23 April 2017].

Ng, J. (2021) 'How Indonesia's defence ministry has changed under Prabowo Subianto', *The Diplomat*, [online] 22 October, Available from: https://thediplomat.com/2021/10/how-indonesias-defense-ministry-has-changed-under-prabowo-subianto [Accessed 23 October 2021].

Nugroho J. (2018) 'Indonesia's days of pseudo-military leaders are not over yet', *Today*, [online] 31 March, Available from: www.todayonline.com/commentary/indonesias-days-pseudo-military-leaders-are-not-over-yet [Accessed 18 April 2018].

Prager-Nyein, S. (2011) 'The armed forces of Burma: the constant sentinel' in M. Mietzner (ed) *The Political Resurgence of the Military in Southeast Asia: Conflict and Leadership*, New York: Routledge, pp 24–44.

Purba, K. (2022) 'Gen. Andika wants longer term and bigger TNI roles', *The Jakarta Post*, [online] 11 February, Available from: www.thejakartapost.com/opinion/2022/02/11/how-gen-andika-moves-to-expand-militarys-power.html [Accessed 25 April 2022].

Reuters (2017) 'Indonesia president nominates air chief to replace controversial military head' *Reuters*, [online] 4 December, Available from: www.reuters.com/article/us-indonesia-politics-military/indonesia-president-nominates-air-chief-to-replace-controversial-military-head-idUSKBN1DY0T8 [Accessed 15 December 2017].

Reuters (2018) 'Indonesia jails activist under controversial anti-communist law', *Reuters*, [online] 24 January, Available from: www.reuters.com/article/us-indonesia-communism/indonesia-jails-activist-under-controversial-anti-communist-law-idUSKBN1FD189 [Accessed 10 April 2018].

Robinson, G. (2001) 'Indonesia: on a new course?' in M. Alagappa (ed) *Coercion and Governance: The Declining Political Role of the Military in Asia*, Stanford: Stanford University Press, pp 206–56.

Robinson, G. (2018) *The Killing Season: A History of the Indonesian Massacres, 1965–66*, Princeton: Princeton University Press.

Roosa, J. (2006) *Pretext for Mass Murder: The September 30th Movement & Suharto's Coup d'État in Indonesia*, Madison: University of Wisconsin Press.

Russell, T. (2016) '"Proxyphobia" in Indonesia', *New Mandala*, [online] 17 November, Available from: www.newmandala.org/proxyphobia-indonesian-militarys-fear-campaign-trumps-trumps/ [Accessed 15 December 2017].

Said, S. (2006) *Legitimizing Military Rule: Indonesian Armed Forces Ideology, 1958–2000*, Jakarta: Pustaka Sinar Harapan.

Sambhi, N. (2021) 'Generals gaining ground: civil–military relations and democracy in Indonesia, *Brookings*, [online] 22 January, Available from: https://www.brookings.edu/articles/generals-gaining-ground-civil-military-relations-and-democracy-in-indonesia/ [Accessed 5 April 2022].

Saptohutomo, A.P. (2022) 'Terobosan panglima Jendral Andika Perkasa, hapus tes keperawanan sampai keturunan PKI bisa ikut seleksi prajurit', *Kompas*, [online] 31 March, Available from: https://nasional.kompas.com/read/2022/03/31/14443361/terobosan-panglima-jenderal-andika-perkasa-hapus-tes-keperawanan-sampai?page=all [Accessed 25 April 2022].

Sebastian, L.C. (2006) *Realpolitik Ideology: Indonesia's Use of Military Force*, Singapore: Institute of Southeast Asian Studies.

Shekhar, V. and Liow, J.C. (2014) 'Indonesia as a maritime power: Jokowi's vision, strategies and obstacles ahead', *Brookings*, [online] 22 January, Available from: www.brookings.edu/articles/indonesia-as-a-maritime-power-jokowis-vision-strategies-and-obstacles-ahead/ [Accessed 23 March 2017].

Singh, B. (2005) *Ryamizard: In the Footsteps of Gadjah Mada*, Sydney: Bookhouse.

Singh, B. (2016) 'Revising Indonesia's anti-terrorism laws', *RSIS Commentary*, 57/2016.

Singh, B. (2018) 'The emergence of an Asia-Pacific diplomacy of counterterrorism in tackling the Islamic State threat' in A. Chong (ed) *International Security in the Asia-Pacific: Transcending ASEAN Towards Traditional Polycentrism*, New York and Basingstoke: Palgrave MacMillan, pp 287–304.

Storey, I. (2018) 'The Trump administration's 2017 national security strategy and 2018 national defense strategy: implications for Southeast Asia', *ISEAS Perspective*, 9/2018.

Sundhaussen, U. (1982) *The Road to Power: Indonesian Military Politics, 1945–1967*, Kuala Lumpur and New York: Oxford University Press.

Suryadinata, L. (2018) 'Golkar's leadership and the Indonesian president', *ISEAS Perspective*, 5/2018.

Tempo (2016) 'Minister: LGBT movement more dangerous than nuclear warfare', *Tempo* [online] 23 February, Available from: https://en.tempo.co/read/747534/minister-lgbt-movement-more-dangerous-than-nuclear-warfare [Accessed 25 October 2021].

The Jakarta Post (2016) 'Hard-line groups to protest 1965 apology at state palace', *The Jakarta Post*, [online] 2 June, Available from: www.thejakartapost.com/news/2016/06/02/hard-line-groups-to-protest-1965-apology-at-state-palace.html [Accessed 12 June, 2017].

The Jakarta Post (2017) 'Military involvement in counterterrorism last resort: commission', *The Jakarta Post*, [online] 31 March, Available from: www.thejakartapost.com/news/2017/05/31/military-involvement-in-counterterrorism-last-resort-commission.html [Accessed 7 June 2017].

Vann, M. (2019) 'Book raids, red-baiting and culture wars in the Indonesian presidential election', *The Asia Dialogue*, [online] 21 February, Available from: https://theasiadialogue.com/2019/02/21/book-raids-red-baiting-and-culture-wars-in-the-indonesian-presidential-election/ [Accessed: 21 October 2018].

Vatikiotis, M. (2020) 'Coronavirus is paving the way for a return to military rule in Asia', *South China Morning Post*, [online] 4 April, www.scmp.com/week-asia/opinion/article/3078346/coronavirus-paving-way-return-military-rule-asia?module=perpetual_scroll_0&pgtype=article&campaign=3078346Available from: [Accessed 28 April, 2022].

Wibowo, K.S. (2017) 'Jokowi: tunjukkan di mana ada PKI, detik ini juga saya gebuk!', *Tempo*, [online] 3 June, Available from: https://nasional.tempo.co/read/881225/jokowi-tunjukkan-di-mana-ada-pki-detik-ini-juga-saya-gebuk [Accessed: 10 June 2017].

Wieringa, S.E. (2017) 'When a history seminar becomes toxic', *Inside Indonesia*, [online] 2 November, Available from: www.insideindonesia.org/when-a-history-seminar-becomes-toxic [Accessed 30 November 2017].

4

Militarizing Governance: Informal Civil–Military Relations and Democratic Erosion in the Philippines

Aries A. Arugay

Much time has passed since formal democratic rule was restored in the Philippines, but the military remains a powerful institution enjoying spheres of autonomy and various political prerogatives. Since the end of martial law in 1986, the country undertook re-democratization that sought to re-impose civilian supremacy and control over the armed forces through legal and institutional reforms. Though necessary, this has not been sufficient in keeping the military in the barracks during serious political crises and preventing its exercise of undue influence in different policy areas as well as matters related to defence and security (Arugay, 2011). Furthermore, by focusing on the military during the democratic transition, other institutions within the security sector such as the police and the intelligence services failed to undergo significant reform efforts.

Like other third wave democracies, the Philippines attempted to embark on reforming the military given the critical role it played as an institutional partner of the Marcos dictatorship. The push for democratizing civil–military relations was reinforced by the experience of numerous mutinies and political interventions carried out by military officials during periods of legitimacy crises faced by civilian governments. Thus, the Aquino administration (1986–92) was subjected to seven coup attempts from politicized and disgruntled junior officers, some of whom were the leaders of the putsch that led to the 1986 People Power Revolt (Final Report, 1990). Military intervention led by the top brass resulted in the ousting of democratically elected president Joseph Estrada in 2001. The military withdrew its allegiance from the president and transferred it to the constitutional successor Vice-President Gloria Macapagal Arroyo. This paved the way for a more politicized role of the military under the settings of a polarized elite conflict from 2001 to 2010 (Arugay, 2011). Since then, the military made significant commitments to transform itself as an institution through the framework of SSR, particularly the adoption of democratic principles such as transparency, accountability, respect for human rights and political neutrality (Hernandez, 2014). The government also embarked on a modernization programme that aims to equip the military with a 'credible defence posture' to defend the territorial integrity of the republic (de Castro, 2014) and divert the military mission from internal security to external defence.

The civil–military relations literature on the Philippines has extensively documented the political dynamics emanating from the relationship between soldiers and politicians since 2010 (see Lee, 2020). The apparent consensus revolves around the observations that civilian control over the Philippine military remains tenuous despite democratization and political reform and that an imbalance favouring the armed forces remains a possibility. Scholars who have studied the military have pointed to the role of colonial legacies, particularly the formative role of US colonialism in the organization and the domestic-oriented missions of the military (Hedman, 2001; McCoy, 2009). As this is well established in the existing literature, this chapter concentrates on addressing the following guiding question of this edited volume, namely: *Is the Philippine military socially, politically and economically embedded to the point that civil–military relations cannot be viewed as a gap between civilian and military elements?*

In the context of the Philippines' fledgling democracy, the military's politicization has often been a process initiated by civilian politicians inviting them to unduly intervene in politics (Arugay and Slater, 2019). This is also the case of populist authoritarian leader Rodrigo Duterte. From its bloody 'war on drugs' to its varied policies toward the lingering communist insurgency and Mindanao conflict, the Duterte administration has relied on the security sector, particularly the military and the police in accomplishing its security goals (Esguerra, 2019). Clearly favouring military officials for their apparent efficiency and obedience, by 2017 President Duterte had appointed more than the usual number of retired generals in the executive branch of government. Though defence and security institutions such as the Department of National Defence are usually led by former military officials, the Duterte administration has set itself apart from its predecessors since it has also appointed them to cabinet departments such as environment and social welfare and even the office in charge of several internal peace processes.

This chapter focuses on the developments in Philippine civil–military relations from 2010 onwards. It argues that the change of the military's original reformist stance favouring democratic civilian control towards one of a more politicized disposition can be explained by two interrelated structural factors. The first is the presence of *informal institutions* such as the militarization of civilian structures and the traditional reliance on the military regarding security matters. Their competing, substitutive and latent nature profoundly provides political autonomy to the military despite the presence of formal civilian control guaranteed by laws and institutions. The second factor is the *erosion of the country's democratic regime* instigated by a populist leader. The chapter discusses how the interaction of these two structural factors influenced the current civil–military imbalance based on different sources, including an original survey of members of the Philippine 'strategic community' comprising uniformed personnel from the country's security sector as well as government officials, researchers and academics representing the civilian sector.[1] This non-random elite survey reveals the polarized perceptions and evaluations of the respondents on the state of civil–military relations under Duterte, lending support to the explanatory power of the two factors proposed.

An analysis of more recent civil–military relations in the Philippines reinforces already existing knowledge on Asian military evolutions, especially the contradictions that co-exist with the adoption of more democratic, civilian frameworks of controlling the military institution. Like other Asian cases, the Philippines reveal the co-mingling of institutional logics toward democratizing civil–military relations together with more informal, indigenous practices and norms that may confound formal democratic arrangements. This implies that there is no mutual exclusivity between the formal and informal institutions that undergird the relationship of the military with civilian power. Informal aspects of civil–military relations in the Philippines will likely have an impact on future attempts at modernization, professionalization and democratization of the armed forces.

The next section provides the background on the evolution of civil–military relations in the Philippines emphasizing its ebb and flow toward establishing democratic civilian control. After this, the chapter assesses the state of civilian oversight and control over the Armed Forces of the Philippines (AFP) and offers a discussion of the role of informal institutions and democratic erosion in shaping civil–military relations under Duterte. The role of informality makes the Philippines an interesting case of a democratizing country that has largely adopted Western norms of civil–military relations on the surface but nevertheless remains committed to practices and norms that undermine democratic civilian control. By way of conclusion, this chapter presents key lessons drawn from the Philippines' experience in democratizing civil–military relations and some of the future challenges.

Civil–military relations before Duterte

At the outset, the *de jure* mission of the AFP was to defend the country from foreign aggression. In practice, however, the military has concentrated on internal security. The presence of US bases, acting as the country's defence shield, prevented the AFP from achieving competence in their original mission. As training and equipment acquisition conducive to external security took a back seat, the AFP evolved into an entity made up of a disproportionately large army (engaged in guerrilla warfare) and an underdeveloped navy and air force, even though this is inconsistent with the country's geopolitical and strategic needs as an archipelago with a vast coastline. Further, US socialization helped the AFP acquire a heavy anti-communist bias and led them to treat future insurgents as enemies of the state that needed to be crushed (Greitens, 2016).

The gradual acquisition of roles associated with counterinsurgency since the 1950s saw its institutionalization during the Marcos period. Relentless internal conflicts on two fronts – a communist insurgency and Moro secessionism – made civilian governments dependent on the military for domestic security. The dictatorship ushered changes that included the continuous enlargement of military functions to include non-traditional military roles, the institution of structural changes that 'merged' the police with the military through the single leadership of the Philippine Constabulary and the Integrated National Police within the AFP, and the suppression of civil liberties, including elections, freedom of expression and association. As a 'partner in national development,' the military institution became the principal wielders of power over a highly personalized authoritarian regime' (Hernandez, 1997, p 44). The political empowerment of the military by the late dictator is the 'original sin' in Philippine civil–military relations.

While other presidents before Marcos gave the military non-traditional missions, Marcos was different since under his rule, along with the politicization of the military came the destruction of democratic institutions of civilian oversight. As the personalist dictator concentrated power, he also undermined other sources of civilian oversight such as the legislature, judiciary, the bureaucracy and even non-state actors such as the media and civil society (Hernandez, 1979; 1997). The immediate effects of this 'explosive cocktail' would be seen in the (failed) coups in the 1980s under the Corazon Aquino administration.

Even if the Philippine military did not exercise the moderating power as the 'nation's guardian' often seen in liberation armies, it found itself playing a major role during the authoritarian period (Loveman, 2004). The way officials from the military were selectively used by Marcos for his own purposes, as well as the fact that it was a few disgruntled officers who instigated the failed coup that ultimately led to the 1986 'People Power

Revolt', revealed the splits in the military. Thus, rather than being a unified political actor speaking with one voice and protecting a set of core interests, the military is a mélange of different factions mostly aligned with segments of the Philippine political and economic elite. This was displayed again in the multiple political crises from 2001 to 2010, dubbed as the Philippines' lost decade of democracy (Arugay, 2019). This time was characterized by the ouster of an elected president, military mutinies and street protests. Rather than let elite factions compete for political legitimacy, the military was less a neutral body and more a willing participant in the pernicious polarization that pervaded the body politic during this time (Arugay and Slater, 2019). The election of President Benigno Simeon Aquino, the son of transition president Corazon Aquino, restored the civil–military balance in 2010.

Civilian control over the military: problems and challenges

A pioneering Philippine study concluded that there is an adequate constitutional legal and institutional framework for democratic civil–military relations in the country (ISDS, 2010). The 1987 Constitution explicitly provides for democratic civilian control over the military. This fundamental document is supported by statutes, executive decrees, and policy pronouncements by government agencies. The pertaining institutions are either created by the Constitution itself, its bylaws or by the rules formulated by the military (ISDS, 2010).

The legal framework is also explicit in defining the responsibilities of the different security forces. Though practice is still far from what is legally intended, the legal provisions make it clear that there needs to be both an institutional and functional separation between the military and the police. Also, specific government agencies in the executive, legislative and judicial branches are mandated the task of civilian oversight over the military. The legal framework further defines the process of exacting accountability. For example, Republic Act 3019 (Anti-Graft and Corrupt Practices Act) and Republic Act 6713 (Code of Conduct and Ethical Standards for all Government Officials and Employees) provide for how government officials, including those in the military, can be made answerable and sanctioned if proven guilty of any violation. Internally, the military has a Code of Ethics far stricter than that for public officials.

Accountability within the security sector is further exercised by independent bodies such as the Office of the Ombudsman, which has a special deputy ombudsman in charge of the military and other law enforcement agencies. This institution is mandated by the Constitution to act on complaints against officers or employees of the government and enforce their administrative, civil and criminal liability in order to promote efficient government service.² The law specifically states that the Ombudsman shall give priority to complaints filed against high-ranking government officials and complaints involving grave offenses and large sums of money and/or properties.³ However, Congress has yet to pass a law to empower citizens to demand access to government information. This is particularly significant for information regarding the security forces since these are conventionally perceived to be a very secretive part of government. Another independent institution created by the 1987 Constitution is the National Commission on Human Rights (CHR). One of the Commission's functions is strengthening the 'capacities of actors in the security sector, the justice system, front line service providers, and decision and policymakers'.⁴

Given the principle of separation of powers within the Philippine presidential system, there is limited connectivity and interface between civilian institutions of accountability and the internal mechanisms of accountability within the armed forces. Internal accountability is often exercised by the Office of Military Affairs under the Office of the President and the Undersecretary for Internal Control of the Department of National Defence. These are the government agencies tasked to receive complaints and other related matters involving the military and police personnel, respectively. However, they often function separately from the Ombudsman, the CHR and the legislature. This incongruence often results in limited effectiveness, inefficiency and unclear lines of responsibility over the security sector (ISDS, 2010).

Despite this, there is evidence that civilian supremacy is a well-accepted principle governing civil–military relations in the Philippines. According to the abovementioned survey, 7 out of 10 respondents believe that the security sector respects legitimate civilian authority (see Figure 4.1). As expected, those in strongest agreement with this statement are members of the security sector and most of the disagreement came from civilian respondents.

As the executive branch of the Philippine government has inescapable ties with the military, the more independent and stricter civilian control institutions are the legislature and independent bodies such as the Ombudsman. The bicameral Philippine Congress is empowered to conduct parliamentary or legislative oversight of the military.⁵ In 2021, it was composed of the 304-member House of Representatives, which has district representatives (80 per cent) and party-list representatives (20 per cent), and the Senate (with 24 members nationally elected). Congress is mandated to carry out oversight functions mainly through its investigatory powers in aid of legislation, as well as its role in confirming appointments and promotions of officials from the military.⁶

Oversight of the military is a critical generic function of the Philippine Congress.⁷ By enacting an annual General Appropriations Act, it can mandate the military through the Department of National Defence, to report on their

Figure 4.1: Perceptions of civilian supremacy over the military in the Philippines

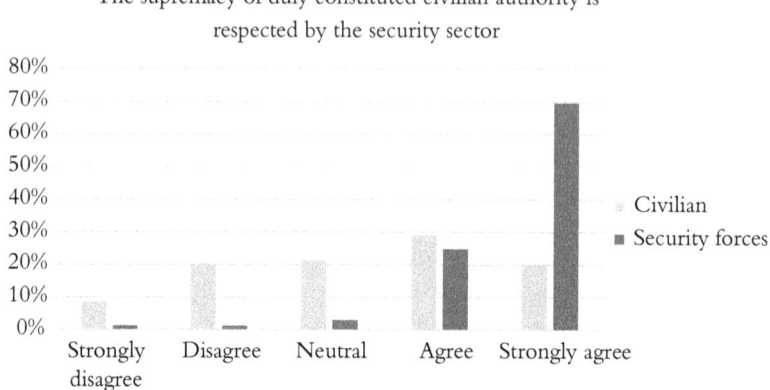

Source: Author's compilation based on data from Julio S. Amador III, Aries A. Arugay, Charmaine Misalucha-Willoughby and Justin Keith Baquisal (2020) 'National Security Agenda of the Philippines: Perceptions from the Filipino Strategic Community', Quezon City: Amador Research Services; www.amadorresearchservices.com/publications/national-security-priorities-and-agenda-in-the-philippines

own performance, justify funding requests and answer relevant questions from members of the congressional committees tasked to approve the budget. The Philippine Congress is generally empowered by laws and its own rules to perform oversight.[8] Both chambers may conduct formal inquiries or investigations in aid of legislation in accordance with their respective rules.[9] Legislative oversight is conducted through several committees, which can be permanent, ad hoc or joint between the two chambers. One of the most important congressional committees relevant to civilian oversight is the Commission on Appointments (CA) led by the senate president. They have the power to confirm executive appointments of military officials from the rank of colonel (army and air force) or captain (navy) and the heads of the major commands.

Existing assessments of the quality of legislative oversight in the Philippines support the observation that a robust legal framework and a clear institutional set-up are in place. However, the main problem lies in the quality of oversight given the lack of effective ability and political willingness (attitude) to exercise oversight following the principles of democratic civilian control. Transparency International, an international NGO that advocates for democratic governance, considered the Philippine Congress as having moderate independence and effectiveness in exercising security sector oversight.[10]

From Table 4.1, one can see the relatively low scores on indicators related to civilian oversight of the military since 2010. This is despite the clear presence

Table 4.1: Legislative oversight of the Philippine military

Question	2013 (Independent assessor)	2015 (Independent assessor)	2015 (Government)
Is there formal provision for effective and independent legislative scrutiny of defence policy?	3	2	Disagree (3)
Does the country have an identifiable and effective parliamentary defence and security committee (or similar such organization) to exercise oversight?	3	2	Disagree (3)
Is there a legislative committee (or other appropriate body) responsible for defence budget scrutiny and analysis in an effective way, and is this body provided with detailed, extensive and timely information on the defence budget?	2	2	Disagree (3)
Is there an effective internal audit process for defence ministry expenditure (that is, for example, transparent, conducted by appropriately skilled individuals and subject to parliamentary oversight)?	1	2	Agree
Is the legislature (or the appropriate legislative committee or members of the legislature) given full information for the budget year on the spending of all secret items relating to national security and military intelligence?	1	1	Disagree (2)
Are audit reports of the annual accounts of the security sector (the military, police and intelligence services) and other secret programmes provided to the legislature (or relevant committee) and are they subsequently subject to parliamentary debate?	0	1	Disagree (3)
Does the country have legislation covering defence and security procurement and are there any items exempt from these laws?	2	2	Disagree (4)

Note: Scores range from 0 (worst) to 4 (best). A score of 4 means best practice. The score of the assessor (independent expert) is reviewed by a government official from the defence sector as well as three reviewers, two academics and one from Transparency International. 'D' stands for Disagree while 'A' stands for Agree with reference to the assessor's score while the number in parentheses refers to the preferred score of the government reviewer.

Source: Author's compilation based on data from the 2015 report of the Transparency International's Government Defence Anti-Corruption Index: https://government.defenceindex.org/countries/philippines/

of formal laws and institutions mandated to carry out this important function. It is also noteworthy that the government representative disagrees with the assessment of the independent expert in almost all questions pertaining to the quality of civilian control over the military in the Philippines.

This assessment is focused solely on anti-corruption and accountability, which is only one of the principles of democratic civilian control. It, however, exposed the risks associated with poor legislative oversight of the military. The Philippines has gradually improved in minimizing its political risk from 45 (2013) to 49 (2015) per cent and its procurement risk from 30 (2013) to 39 (2015) per cent. However, these scores are still within the country category of Band D (A being the highest and E the lowest), which the Philippines shares with countries like Indonesia, Malaysia, Turkey, India, Russia and Kenya.

What can explain the poor quality of legislative oversight in the Philippines? First, these risks stem from the weakness of the political party system, prevalence of patronage and horse-trading, and divided government. Second, there is no formal network of oversight institutions in the two chambers of Congress, making the performance of their functions inefficient, repetitive and redundant. The two chambers also do not coordinate in conducting investigatory hearings, which is important since legislation requires the concurrence of both.

Third, there are gaps in civilian oversight, such as the exemption of PNP officials from being confirmed by the CA. Moreover, Congress lacks a formal oversight function regarding the AFP's peacekeeping missions. Some observers have noted that the legislators' investigative power is often exercised for personal and political motivations and, therefore, prone to abuse. Fourth, there is a big gap between expectations and capability among civilian oversight institutions. For example, the Committee on National Defence and Security of the House of Representatives has 93 members with eight sub-committees but only seven staff members. Beyond the shortage of staff members, a more pressing concern is the development of skills for members of Congress, their personal staff, and the committee staff for civilian oversight through education and training.

Turning to independent civilian oversight institutions apart from Congress, such as independent constitutional bodies (CHR) and the Ombudsman, this chapter finds a similar assessment of poor performance. The risks lie in the lack of ability and appropriate attitude of internal and external institutions to exercise oversight of the security sector. The weak political institutions in the country make it difficult for these institutions to implement their formal mandates. Presidential prerogatives and patronage politics prevent the exercise of independent and effective oversight even if a formal legal framework is provided and institutions are in existence. Available assessments validate the presence of the risks that undermine security sector oversight.

There has been some improvement from 2013 to 2015 in improving oversight of the defence sector in the Philippines. But more importantly, there is a stark disagreement between the independent assessor (academic) and the government reviewer in terms of the performance of civilian oversight from independent institutions as shown in Table 4.2. This exposed the wide gap between how civilian control over the military is perceived by specialists and by government officials. The lack of consensus is troubling since either the government overestimates its own performance in exercising oversight or academic experts are not knowledgeable or underestimate performance.

In a nutshell, civilian oversight of the military in the Philippines exposes a chasm between the formal and the actual. To have a substantive sense of whether the military behaves in accordance with democratic norms and principles, what the empirical evidence suggests is to go beyond the trappings of formal laws and institutions. The next section discusses the informal institutions and practices that undergird civil–military relations in the Philippines and how they have undermined reform efforts.

Informal institutions and civil–military relations

Informal institutions are 'socially shared rules, usually unwritten, that are created, communicated, and enforced outside officially sanctioned channels' (Helmke and Levitsky, 2006, p 4). The critical element of an informal institution is its enforcement by political actors mainly outside formal and established avenues. What is also important to note is the fact that informal institutions can often exist side-by-side with formal institutions. This means that there is a bifurcated sense of reality: one that exists in the formal and therefore superficial sense, and one that mirrors reality more closely but often in a clandestine and difficult to verify way. Informal institutions are also easy to dismiss by political actors who could invoke technical rules to deny their existence and/or power.

There are several types of informal institutions, depending on the effectiveness of formal institutions and whether their outcomes diverge from those of informal institutions. Those that tend to generate more democratic outcomes can either be *complementary* informal institutions that strengthen the commitment of political actors toward formal institutions or *accommodating* informal institutions that alter the effects of formal ones but do not necessarily undermine them. This chapter focuses on types of informal institutions that undermine formal ones and therefore have negative repercussions for democracy. *Substitutive* informal institutions emerge because of the inability of their formal counterparts to achieve their purported objectives. *Competing* informal institutions distort, undermine and overwhelm formal ones. Being the most common type, they assume that formal and informal institutions are mutually exclusive as the latter is intended to subvert the

Table 4.2: Independent civilian oversight of the Philippine military

Question	2013 (Independent assessor)	2015 (Independent assessor)	2015 (Government)
Are there independent, well-resourced, and effective institutions within defence and security tasked with building integrity and countering corruption?	1	2	Disagree (3)
Are there regular assessments by the defence ministry or another government agency of the areas of greatest corruption risk for ministry and armed forces personnel, and do they put in place measures for mitigating such risks?	0	1	Disagree (3)
Does the country have a process for acquisition planning that involves clear oversight, and is it publicly available?	2	2	Disagree (3)
Is there effective and transparent external auditing of military defence expenditure?	1	2	Disagree (3)
Are the policies, administration and budgets of the intelligence services subject to effective, properly resourced and independent oversight?	1	2	Agree
Is independent and transparent scrutiny of asset disposals conducted by defence establishments, and are the reports of such scrutiny publicly available?	0	2	Disagree (3)
Are audit reports of the annual accounts of the security sector (the military, police and intelligence services) and other secret programmes provided to the legislature (or relevant committee), and are they subsequently subject to parliamentary debate?	0	1	Disagree (3)

Table 4.2: Independent civilian oversight of the Philippine military (continued)

Question	2013 (Independent assessor)	2015 (Independent assessor)	2015 (Government)
Are personnel promoted through an objective, meritocratic process? Such a process would include promotion boards outside of the command chain, strong formal appraisal processes and independent oversight.	1	2	Disagree (4)
Are defence procurement oversight mechanisms in place, and are these oversight mechanisms active and transparent?	1	2	Disagree (3)

Source: Author's compilation based on data from the 2015 report of the Transparency International's Government Defence Anti-Corruption Index: https://government.defenceindex.org/countries/philippines/

principles and goals of formally established institutions. Competing and substitutive informal institutions, for example, have the tendency to 'crowd out' formal institutions inhibiting their full implementation and development. They could also hinder further democratization since they prevent formal institutional change and democratic progress. As political actors become comfortable with informality, which originally was a 'band-aid' solution, they might encourage the preservation of these institutions (Helmke and Levitsky, 2006).

Pion-Berlin (2010) analysed the occurrence of informality in civil–military relations in Venezuela. Informal institutions generate behaviours:

> that do not follow the official script, that are not always situated in official venues, and that depart from statutory rules of conduct. They are real enough, often guided by unscripted yet mutual understandings, unofficial codes of conduct and norms. These understandings are usually self-generated and sometimes self-enforced by those who reside within the informal set of relations. (Pion-Berlin, 2010, p 529)

Among the informal institutions he studied were: (1) meetings initiated by the military that bypass the defence minister, (2) presidential 'tampering' of promotion systems and (3) influential retired officers' clubs. Pion-Berlin concluded that not all informal institutions have negative effects upon democratic civil–military relations as some may provide 'band-aid' solutions to a tense and difficult situation between soldiers and politicians. However, it is important to examine the consistency of the impact of informal institutions in undermining democratic (and objective) civilian control to the point that they become the dominant focal points of civil–military interactions that are supposed to be based on formal rules and institutional processes.

The remainder of this chapter discusses two informal institutions in civil–military relations under Duterte. The first is the militarization of civilian structures through the appointment of retired generals in the civilian bureaucracy, which is an example of a competing informal institution. The second is the dominance of the military's voice in security policy making and implementation, illustrating a type of substitutive informal institution that replaces civilian supremacy over security policy matters.

A competing informal institution: the militarization of civilian structures

At present, the AFP is enjoying a much-improved reputation since re-democratization in 1986. While some may attribute this to Duterte's exaltation and constant praise of the institution, a major factor has been its reformist and modernizing stance in the past decade. Since 2010, the Philippine government has embarked on SSR to improve the military's effectiveness and accountability. SSR is a major principle stated in the country's National Security Policy from the Benigno Aquino III Administration (2010–16). The push for professionalism and democratic accountability by the country's civilian leadership, coupled with the military's voluntary cooperation, has increased public trust and confidence in the military. A December 2019 poll revealed that the AFP enjoyed its highest trust ratings since public opinion polling began. An astounding 79 per cent of Filipinos trusts the military (Mangosing, 2020).

The steady improvement of the military's image was a by-product of its openness to embrace reform and substantive professionalism. Among others, this included setting up internal human rights offices, the adoption of a transformation roadmap with the guidance of reputable members of the civilian bureaucracy, academe, media and civil society, and cooperating with politicians to deal with peace and development challenges at the local level.

Due to the challenges of territorial defence and the country's stake in the South China Sea disputes, the last decade saw the military repositioning itself to be more oriented toward addressing external security threats. As an addition to the military's doctrine, this perspective aims to fully modernize the AFP and make it a professional armed force focused on the republic's external defence and security (Figure 4.2).

The popular Duterte administration saw a popular and more powerful military as a potential political ally. From its bloody war on drugs to its fight against terrorism and the lingering communist insurgency, the Duterte

MILITARIZING GOVERNANCE

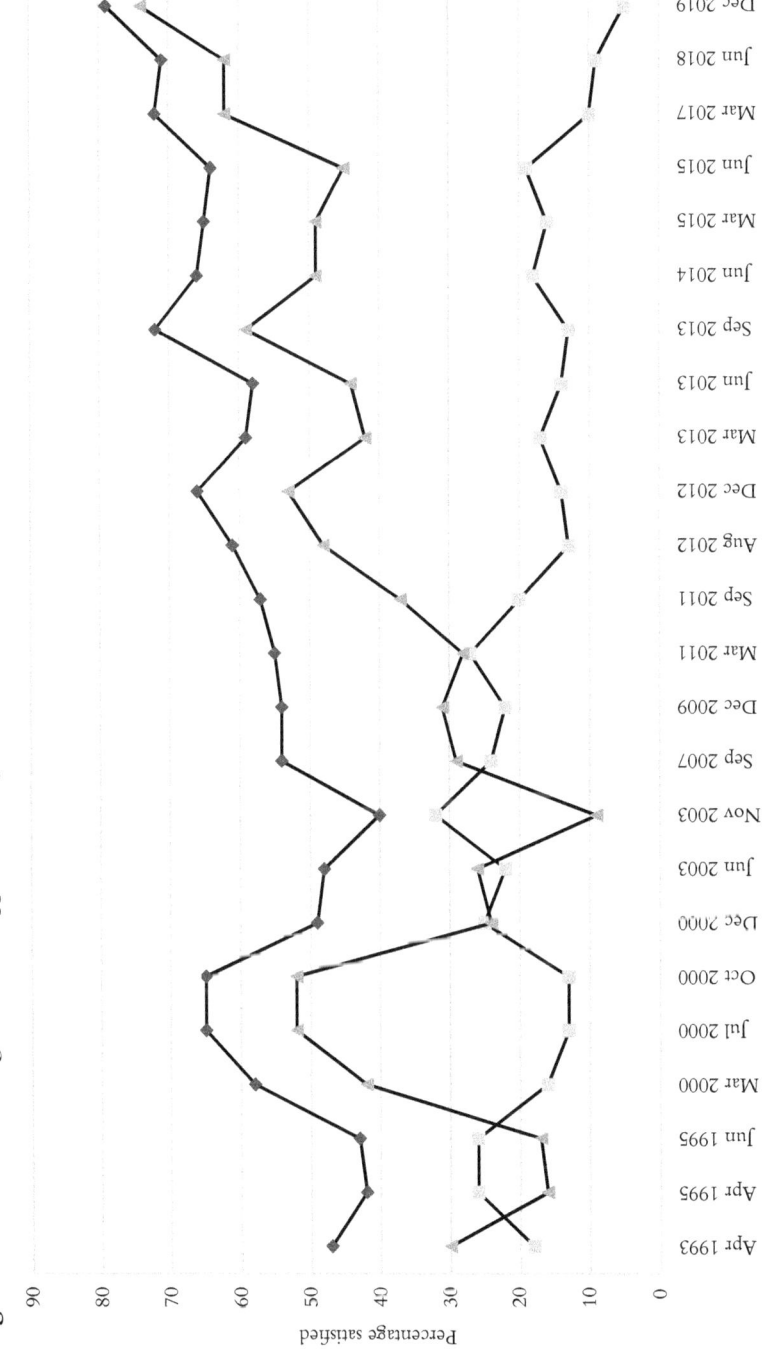

Figure 4.2: Net trust ratings of the Philippine military, 1993–2019

Source: *Social Weather Stations* (2020) 'Fourth Quarter 2019 Social Weather Survey: 79% of Filipinos are satisfied with the performance of the AFP', 5 March, www.sws.org.ph/swsmain/artcldisppage/?artcsyscode=ART-20200305101015

administration has exhibited a steadfast resolve to address the Philippines' security challenges. One striking observation is its heavy dependence on the armed forces to accomplish security goals, albeit at great cost to the nation's democracy. Unseen since the martial law era, this military role expansion now includes leading the COVID-19 response.

Favouring military officers for their apparent efficiency and obedience, by 2017, Duterte had the greatest number of retired generals in any presidential cabinet in the post-dictatorship period (Gita, 2019). Although former military officials usually lead defence and security institutions (such as the Department of National Defence), the Duterte administration distinguished itself by also appointing them to head department portfolios dealing with the environment and social welfare, even the office in charge of the peace processes with various rebel groups. This has been severely criticized by the country's stalwarts of liberal democracy, such as the opposition, media and civil society. As more and more members of the military (active or retired) fused themselves with the administration, the more difficult it became to balance civil–military relations democratically.

This militarization of civilian structures was made possible by the sheer dominance of Duterte in Philippine politics. Never has there been a time in the country where the president had control over all branches of government given the administration's 'super-majority' in the legislature. The majority of the magistrates in the Supreme Court are Duterte appointees. His consolidation of power has attracted the military to embark on a partnership that defies a model of civil–military relations with democratic principles and norms, primarily civilian oversight and accountability.

Some ex-generals in top cabinet posts even replaced left-leaning officials endorsed by the country's communist movement, a complete reversal of the more accommodating stance of Duterte at the beginning of his presidency. Some see value in placing retired generals in political positions – they are seen as more efficient, strategic, quicker to respond and were socialized to obey their commander-in-chief. Anyone familiar with Philippine governance knows that delay, paralysis and bureaucratic politics are the policy process's maladies. As former military officials turned civilians, given their retirement from active service, many saw their experience as an asset to Duterte's government.

However, the 'civilianization' of the generals is at best only in form. Despite all efforts to portray themselves as civilians, soldiers retain what scholars of civil–military relations call 'the military mind'. Decades of socialization and practice formed a mental map with a different perspective on political affairs. This is also shaped by the country's specific historical experience where the military has intervened in domestic politics and decided the legitimacy of civilian governments.

Figure 4.3: Views on the role of retired generals in Duterte's cabinet

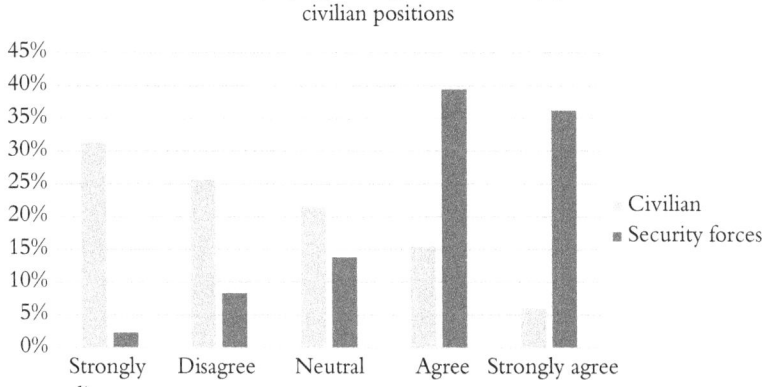

Source: Author's compilation based on data from Julio S. Amador III, Aries A. Arugay, Charmaine Misalucha-Willoughby and Justin Keith Baquisal (2020) 'National Security Agenda of the Philippines: Perceptions from the Filipino Strategic Community', Quezon City: Amador Research Services; www.amadorresearchservices.com/publications/national-security-priorities-and-agenda-in-the-philippines

Generals also do not lose their networks and connections within the military world. Every one of them brought other military officials (often fellow retirees who were their subordinates) into every government institution they led. This multiplier effect not only contributes to groupthink in decision-making but also exacts a toll on the development of civilian expertise in the government's already weakened bureaucracy.

How policy elites and members of the Filipino strategic community perceive this militarization depends on what grouping they identify with. On the question of whether the Duterte administration was more effective in promoting national security by appointing retired military generals to civilian positions, Figure 4.3 shows divergence within the Filipino security community. While respondents from the security sector agreed with the practice, civilian respondents were vehemently opposed.

It becomes problematic when civilian leaders invite and encourage the military's direct involvement in the formulation and implementation of security policies. Sources from inside the Duterte administration observed that there is a lack of diverse perspectives in peace and security policy circles and a complete absence of contentious debate (which is critical to arriving at a satisfactory policy outcome) because military officers are trained to focus on immediate responses to perceived crises and are not used to prolonged deliberation (Arugay, 2021). In a complex policy area such as peace and security, a government whose most dominant voice comes from the military might settle for quick fixes and lack a holistic appreciation of multifaceted realities.

A substitutive informal institution: military dominance in security policy

As Duterte assumed the role of the military's *padrino* (godfather), the guard rails normally maintained by the civilian government over the republic's guardians started to corrode. The military's top brass, both active and retired, began to shift their attention to its historical enemy – the communist movement. An executive decree signed by the president in 2018 sought to 'end local communist armed conflict' by the end of Duterte's term in 2022 (Ranada, 2018). The decree aligned with the military's enduring interest to score a final victory against their communist nemesis since it knows that future presidents might not share the same conviction.

Euphemistically called a 'whole of nation' approach, the heavily funded counter-insurgency strategy seeks to mobilize all relevant stakeholders within the government and even society through collaborative efforts. However, a closer look at its implementation reveals that this approach is dictated by elements of the military establishment. The approach has been distorted towards one wherein all of society must rally behind the military's leadership. The Duterte administration's inability to impose democratic civilian control has put the military in the driver seat of this anti-communist drive. With both retired and active generals at the helm of implementing the strategy, the military is determined to put a violent rather than a negotiated end to perhaps the longest running Maoist-inspired communist insurgency in the world.

Therefore, it is not surprising that the military went full-throttle in its McCarthy-like campaign against an insurgency that they believe has penetrated all sectors of society. Though historically seen as rebels with a cause, the communist movement is now labelled as a terrorist group, a term the government used to reserve for jihadists and other religious extremists. Amid a crippling pandemic, the government also passed a new draconian anti-terrorist law that further legally empowered the state to designate terrorists, conduct surveillance, freeze assets and detain those they believe are terrorists in a process that has jeopardized constitutionally guaranteed rights.

Academic freedom has become the latest casualty in this 'scorched earth' campaign to rid the country of communism – an ideology not banned by the 1987 Constitution – but the Duterte government has successfully linked it with lawless violence and crime. In doing so, it has not exercised caution in labelling dissidents and critics as communists themselves or as their sympathizers. This has a chilling effect on the nation's academic institutions' ability to critically think, study, and analyse important matters, which inevitably includes how the Duterte administration governed a country it promised to serve and protect.

The focus of the military toward internal security under the Duterte administration has veered it away from the external defence re-orientation. This sends confusing signals to the AFP since it has mostly adopted a re-orientation toward external defence capability-building since 2010 mainly due to civilian pressure. While changing military doctrine is a much slower process than modifications in strategy and tactics, the younger generation of AFP officials have sought to balance the internal and external security needs of the Philippines. Moreover, it seems that the leadership of the navy for example, has taken the position of asserting the crucial importance of defence from external threats, particularly to the country's maritime interests.

There is little doubt that a group of retired generals have dictated current peace and security policy in recent years. More than that, their placement in other agencies involved in rural development and public services delivery obscures the civil–military divide that is essential to maintaining civilian supremacy in governance structures and democratic civilian control over the military. This trend also potentially confounds the military's reformist stance and reorientation toward external defence that form the focus of its current doctrine and strategy. Therefore, strategic policy, especially one that focuses on the military's external mission, is affected by the civil–military relations imbalance.

One can argue that with the military possessing leverage to influence the civilian government, it can divert precious attention and mobilize scarce resources to more strategic concerns. However, the Philippine military seems to be more interested in quashing domestic enemies rather than focus on external security threats. The Filipino security community, however, seems to have more idealistic aspirations for a more outward looking military, as seen in Figure 4.4.

For the Filipino security community, there is consensus that a more professional military must be externally oriented (Amador et al, 2021).

Conclusion

This chapter analysed the developments in civil–military relations in the Philippines since 2010 with an emphasis on the erosion of democratic civilian control over the military in the Duterte administration. It argued that reform efforts and progress in the previous civilian governments were undermined by a populist-authoritarian and highly popular leader that has also eroded other norms and institutions of Philippine democracy. The Philippine case reveals that SSR, even if relatively successful, can be overturned by the presence of competing and substitutive informal institutions that undermine otherwise democratic civil–military relations.

Figure 4.4: Views on the appropriate mission of the Philippine military

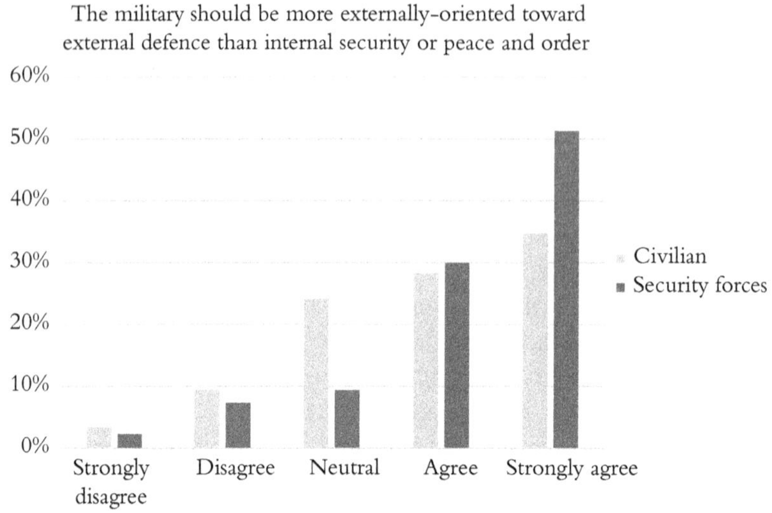

The military should be more externally-oriented toward external defence than internal security or peace and order

[Bar chart showing responses from Civilian and Security forces across categories: Strongly disagree, Disagree, Neutral, Agree, Strongly agree. Approximate values — Strongly disagree: ~2%/2%; Disagree: ~9%/7%; Neutral: ~24%/9%; Agree: ~28%/30%; Strongly agree: ~34%/50%.]

Source: Author's compilation based on data from Julio S. Amador III, Aries A. Arugay, Charmaine Misalucha-Willoughby and Justin Keith Baquisal (2020) 'National Security Agenda of the Philippines: Perceptions from the Filipino Strategic Community', Quezon City: Amador Research Services; www.amadorresearchservices.com/publications/national-security-priorities-and-agenda-in-the-philippines

Without regard for Philippine democracy's long-term welfare, the Duterte administration embraced the military as a political partner despite the constitutional principle of civilian supremacy. This relationship has blurred the critical boundaries between civilian authority and the military establishment. Duterte has given the military everything it wants in terms of perks, resources and political patronage. Without civilian supervision, he has allowed the military to lead the crafting and implementation of security policies. Finally, the populist president has tolerated a military to generally act with impunity as it wages its wars against its people, rather than defending the state against its enemies abroad.

Addressing the confounding and corrosive role of informal institutions and norms in the pursuit of more democratic civil–military relations is a challenge for the Philippines and other militaries in Asia. As reform initiatives tend to pursue a legal and institutional approach often using formal models, they tend to disregard deeper normative, cultural and sociological practices that predate these reforms. The Philippine case has shown that despite the reform of the military in the past decades, it remains to have undue political prerogatives in the realm of security policy and it can be re-invited by friendly politicians who do not necessarily have the discernment regarding the consequences of politicizing the military. This gradual role expansion of the military tips the civil–military balance in their favour despite operating in an otherwise democratic and constitutional framework.

The military reciprocated Duterte's favour by defending the authoritarian leader's rhetoric and policies. With very few exceptions, members of the armed forces have rallied around the administration, even if its policies in the long run can undermine military professionalism and modernization. This can also potentially harm the credibility it presently enjoys. By fusing itself with a president, failure to fulfil a government's promises and expectations might lead to damaging repercussions for the military's institutional reputation.

The negative legacies of the Duterte administration have far-reaching implications for the future of civil–military relations and democracy in the Philippines. It has already been a struggle to de-militarize politics and governance after the Marcos dictatorship and it seems that the country has regressed in democratizing civil–military relations. Moreover, there could be worse outcomes still than the present situation where the military allies with politicians with a similar mindset and vision for the country. If these politicians lose power to a leadership determined to assert civilian supremacy, it is possible that the military would choose to intervene in a more direct way and capture the Philippine state.

Notes

1. The author conducted an online non-random survey of Filipino members of the country's strategic community. They comprise scholars, researchers, members of the civilian bureaucracy, and officials and personnel of the security sector (military, police, coast guard and so on). The survey ran from 1 March until 11 April 2019 and received 228 unique responses. There is also a good balance between members of the security sector (55 per cent) and the civilian sector (45 per cent) that comprised the academe, civilian government officials and personnel, and members of the private sector.
2. Article XI, Section 12, 1987 Philippine Constitution. www.ombudsman.gov.ph/index.php?home=1&navId=MQ==&subNavId=Nzk=.
3. Section 15 of Republic Act No 6770: An Act Providing for the Functional and Structural Organization of the Office of the Ombudsman, and for other purposes.
4. 'Who We Serve.' Republic of the Philippines Commission on Human Rights official website. www.chr.gov.ph/MAIN%20PAGES/contact_us.htm.
5. Article VI in the 1987 Constitution of the Republic of the Philippines.
6. Article VI, Section 21 and Article VI, Section 18 in the 1987 Constitution of the Republic of the Philippines.
7. Article VI, Section 24 in the 1987 Constitution of the Republic of the Philippines.
8. Article VI, Section 21 in the 1987 Constitution of the Republic of the Philippines.
9. Section 1, Resolution No 5 in Rules of Procedure Governing Inquiries in Aid of Legislation of the Philippine Senate, 2010.
10. 2015 Country Assessment (The Philippines), Government Defence Anti-Corruption Index, Transparency International, http://government.defenceindex.org/countries/philippines/.

References

Amador, J. III, Arugay, A.A., Misalucha-Willoughby, C. and Baquisal, J.K. (2021) 'National security agenda of the Philippines: perceptions from the Filipino strategic community', *Amador Research Services*, [online], 21 December, Available from: www.amadorresearchservices.com/publications/national-security-priorities-and-agenda-in-the-philippines [Accessed 24 October 2021].

Arugay, A.A. (2011) 'The Philippine military: still politicized and increasingly autonomous' in M. Mietzner (ed) *The Political Resurgence of the Military in Southeast Asia: Conflict and Leadership*, London: Routledge, pp 85–106.

Arugay, A.A. (2019) 'Fall from grace, descent from power? Civil society after Philippine democracy's lost decade' in I. Deinla and B. Dressel (eds) *From Aquino II to Duterte (2010–2018): Change, Continuity, and Rupture*, Singapore: ISEAS–Yusof Ishak Institute, pp 285–308.

Arugay, A.A. (2021) 'The generals' gambit: the military and democratic erosion in Duterte's Philippines', *Heinrich Böll Stiftung Southeast Asia*, [online] 18 February, Available from: https://th.boell.org/en/2021/02/18/generals-gambit-military-and-democratic-erosion-dutertes-philippines [Accessed 23 October 2021].

Arugay, A.A. and Slater, D. (2019) 'Polarization without poles: Machiavellian conflicts and the Philippines' lost decade of democracy, 2000–2010', *The ANNALS of the American Academy of Political and Social Science*, 681(1): 122–36.

De Castro, R.C. (2014) 'Philippine strategic culture: continuity in the face of changing regional dynamics', *Contemporary Security Policy*, 35(2): 249–69.

Esguerra, C.V. (2019) 'Why Duterte surrounds himself with ex-soldiers', *ABS-CBN News*, [online] 21 August, Available from: https://news.abs-cbn.com/news/08/21/19/why-duterte-surrounds-himself-with-ex-soldiers [Accessed 24 October 2021].

Gita, R.A. (2019) 'Special report: A 'militarized' government', *Sunstar*, [online] 20 July, Available from: www.sunstar.com.ph/article/1815070/Manila/Local-News/Special-Report-A-militarized-government [Accessed 10 June 2021].

Greitens, S.C. (2016) *Dictators and Their Secret Police: Coercive Institutions and State Violence*, Cambridge: Cambridge University Press.

Hedman, E.L.E. (2001) 'The Philippines: not so military, not so civil', in M. Alagappa (ed) *Coercion and Governance: The Declining Political Role of the Military in Asia*, Stanford: Stanford University Press, pp 165–186.

Helmke, G. and Levitsky, S. (2006) 'Introduction', in G. Helmke and S. Levitsky (eds.) *Informal Institutions and Democracy: Lessons from Latin America*, Baltimore: Johns Hopkins University Press, pp 1–30.

Hernandez, C.G. (1979) *The Extent of Civilian Control of the Military in the Philippines* [Unpublished doctoral dissertation], Buffalo: State University of New York.

Hernandez, C.G. (1997) 'The military and constitutional change: problems and prospects in a redemocratized Philippines', *Public Policy*, 1(1): 42–61.

Hernandez, C.G. (2014) 'Security sector reform in Southeast Asia: from policy to practice', in F. Heiduk (ed.) *Security Sector Reform in Southeast Asia: From Policy to Practice*, London: Palgrave Macmillan, pp 23–53.

ISDS (Institute for Strategic and Development Studies) (2010) *Developing a Security Sector Reform Index (SSRI) in the Philippines: Towards Conflict Prevention and Peace-building*, Manila: United Nations Development Programme and the Office of the Presidential Adviser on the Peace Process.

Lee, T. (2020) 'The Philippines: civil–military relations, from Marcos to Duterte', in W.R. Thompson and H.B. Nassif (eds) *Oxford Research Encyclopaedia of Politics*, Oxford: Oxford University Press. DOI: https://doi.org/10.1093/acrefore/9780190228637.013.1845

Loveman, B. (2004) *For la Patria: Politics and the Armed Forces in Latin America*, Wilmington: Rowman & Littlefield.

Mangosing, F. (2020) 'SWS: AFP enjoys rising satisfaction rating, shedding bad image of the past', *Philippine Daily Inquirer*, [online] 4 March, Available from: https://newsinfo.inquirer.net/1236966/sws-afp-enjoys-rising-satisfaction-rating-shedding-bad-image-of-the-past#ixzz7A4omnMbQ [Accessed 24 October 2021].

McCoy, A.W. (2009) *Policing America's Empire: The United States, the Philippines, and the Rise of the Surveillance State*, Madison: University of Wisconsin Press.

Pion-Berlin, D. (2010) 'Informal civil–military relations in Latin America: why politicians and soldiers choose unofficial venues', *Armed Forces & Society*, 36(3): 526–44.

Ranada, P. (2018) 'Duterte creates task force to address causes of communist insurgency', *Rappler*, [online] 11 December, Available from: www.rappler.com/nation/218667-duterte-creates-task-force-address-communist-armed-conflict-causes/ [Accessed 25 October 2021].

The Fact-Finding Commission (to Investigate the Failed Coup of December 1989) (1990), *The Final Report*, Manila: Bookmark Publishers.

5

Mind the Gap: The Curious Case of Everyday Civil–Military Relations in Singapore

Jun Yan Chang and Shu Huang Ho

The SAF is arguably 'the most impressive military force in contemporary Southeast Asia' (Huxley, 2000, p 249). Yet, the threat of military intervention in Singapore's political system, what Feaver (1999, p 214) terms the 'civil–military problematique' – wherein the 'very institution created to protect the polity is given sufficient power to become a threat to the polity' – is unlikely (Tan, 2011, p 148). Scholars have contended that Singapore's civil–military relations transcend Feaver's problematique. Four decades earlier, Chan (1985, p 136) already noted 'the most striking feature of the Singapore scene is the undisputed predominance of the civilian sector over the military.' We broadly agree with Tan (2001, p 276), who explains that such control is achieved through 'civil–military fusion' whereby 'the military, both in leadership and in structural terms, functions as an integral part of a centralized, bureaucratic state'; and also with Chong and Chan (2016), who observed civilian society is arguably built in the likeness of a quintessential military force, with a seeming permeation of martial values. We, however, suggest an alternative for such integration. Rather than one world enfolding the other into a hyphenated whole, a 'civilianized military' or 'militarized civilian', we argue that the foundational cultural values of Singapore society and government, and its armed forces, are the same, precluding separate 'civilian' and 'military' worlds in the first place.

In Singapore's history, such ontologically distinct worlds never existed to a significant extent, nor did Singapore's development allow them to be created. Consequently, there is no civil–military gap – a key concern in civil–military relations scholarship – in Singapore, transcending the civil–military problematique. While the military naturally plays a different *role*, it does not occupy a different *world*. Singapore presents a curious case of how its military evolution has existed within the operational role of the SAF as opposed to a changing relationship between different worlds. While this edited volume has valuably highlighted Asian militaries can indeed slowly evolve to defuse disputes between themselves and civilian leaders within Asian democracies to achieve developmental and security goals more synergistically, Singapore is different from this novel conception of the study of civil–military relations. The SAF was already structured at its inception to minimize such disputes and maximize efficiency in reaching national goals. It was an institution designed to fit in with, and not stand apart from, civilian governance. Our study of Singapore thus further suggests civil–military relations scholarship would do well to explore the fundamental notions of the 'civilian' and 'military'.

The influence of Singapore's colonial legacy and how the SAF is embedded socially and politically, the nub of this volume's first two guiding questions, situates our argument. It is developed across three main sections. The first charts the theoretical development of civil–military relations, highlighting the traditional gaps between the two worlds that underpin the civil–military problematique. The second posits these gaps do not exist in Singapore through a historical examination of the country's political, social and security institutions since independence. The third focuses on the absence of a cultural gap, the wellspring for the lack of two ontologically distinct 'civilian' and 'military' worlds. The chapter concludes by emphasizing that Singapore's civil–military relations need to be understood in terms of the 'everyday' transition between military and civilian roles by members of the SAF.

Characterizing the relationship between distinct worlds

In order to understand the differences in Singapore, we start by looking at foundational civil–military relations theories. Huntington's *The Soldier and the State* is a natural starting point. To Huntington (1957, p 2), the military is apolitical and with its own values, an expert in its craft of defending the state as a tool of government. Attaining the goal of security is a function of the interaction between two imperatives: the 'functional imperative' of national security threats and the 'societal imperative' of the impact social values, ideologies and other institutions have on the military. Security is only achieved through 'objective civilian control' of the military where the functional imperative prevails, with Huntington (1957, p 464) even calling for 'a shift in basic American values from liberalism to conservatism' to minimize a liberal imperative which could impinge on the military's effectiveness. Huntington's construction of the relationship between the military and non-military is dichotomous and oppositional, although he fails to offer exact definitions of the 'military' and 'civilian'.

In contrast, Janowitz (1971, p ix) questions Huntington's civil–military separation, seeing national security as contingent on the greater, though not complete, 'civilianization' of the military since 'the interpenetration of the civilian and the military is required' as the scale and scope of war expand. Janowitz (1971, pp 8–11) hypothesized that the military was becoming more civilian in five areas: (1) a civilian style of management by 'persuasion, explanation and expertise' replacing the military's conservative disciplinarian tradition of blind obedience; (2) a 'narrowing skill differential between military and civilian elites'; (3) the outlook of military officers becoming 'democratized'; (4) the varied career patterns of military officers; and (5) the military having to become more politically attuned to discharge its duties well. Janowitz's sociological approach to civil–military relations therefore recognizes the 'military' as a group within wider society. Civilian control is achieved by bringing the military into the fold of societal relations (Janowitz, 1971, p 421; Rukavishnikov and Pugh, 2006, p 133). Yet, as much as he argues that the worlds are growing closer together, Janowitz always contrasts the 'military' and the 'civilian' (Feaver, 2003, p 8). Significantly, Janowitz (1971, pp x–xv) himself acknowledges limits to civilianization, since the 'military' remains the 'specialist in violence'.

As much as the Janowitzian sociological approach broadened it, civil–military relations studies would largely reside in political science with military scholars continuing down the path Huntington had first paved, focusing on Feaver's problematique. Crucially, the assumption of distinct 'civilian' and 'military' spheres prevailed. Contemporary civil–military relations theories can subsequently be categorized by the variable employed to explain the civil–military problematique: agency-centric, structural or a mix of these two (Kuehn and Lorenz, 2011, pp 232–4).

Regarding agency, Feaver (2003, pp 2–4) developed his understanding of civil–military relations in a significantly different post-Cold War context. The range of non-warfighting roles the military had to undertake, from humanitarian relief to counterterrorism, required military and civilian elites to work closer together than ever before. Such complex missions, however, amplified the differences between these elites. Relations between both were thus the 'stormiest' in decades, with the military vigorously challenging civilians in policy making, questioning civilian supremacy. Conceived earlier, Huntingtonian and Janowitzian macro civil–military relations theories are less helpful in understanding the micro-level challenges in daily interaction. Feaver thereby applies a principal-agent model to explain how civilians attempt to control the military, especially 'day-to-day'. Civilians, the principal, decide how to control the military based on their assessment of its compliance. On the other hand, the military, the agent, decides if it will obey based on whether their 'shirking' will be noticed by civilian political leaders and incur a cost.

In contrast to agency-centric theories, structural civil–military relations theories posit structures determine outcomes. These may include ideational factors like norms of military professionalism (Huntington, 1957) or levels of political culture (Finer, 2002); institutional variables such as the set of relations and controls between the ruling party of a state and its armed forces (Perlmutter and LeoGrande, 1982); or larger environmental variables such as societal pressures, the geopolitical environment or the threat environment (Lasswell, 1941; Moskos, Williams and Segal, 2000). Desch's structural civil–military relations theory is archetypical. Desch (1999, pp 1–17) starts with the premise that the US and Russia, 'have both experienced a weakening of civilian control' post-Cold War. He therefore contends that civilian control of the military is predicated on the threat environment: (1) the location of the threat, whether internal or external; and (2) its intensity, high or low. If internal threat is low but external threat high, civilians are content to rely on objective control of the military, with the military focused outward, leaving civilian control of the military at the optimal level. The worst level of civilian control happens when internal threat is high but external threat low: civilian attention is distracted while the military is free to look at domestic issues rather than focus on external defence, inviting political interference by the military.

Yet another approach is to marry agential and structural variables, bypassing the agent–structure duality. For instance, Schiff (1995; 2009), examining civil–military relations in relation to nation-building splits the 'civilian' into two separate entities: 'citizens' and the 'political leadership', both defined in terms of function. The latter governs the state and the former is the broader society interacting with the 'military'. Consequently, subservience of the military is contingent upon 'concordance' between these three spheres, indicated by: '(1) the social composition of the officer corps; (2) the political decision-making process; (3) the military recruitment method; and (4) the military style', by which Schiff (2009, p 44 and p 47) means 'the external manifestations and inner mental constructions associated with the military'. Notwithstanding the various critiques of concordance theory (Wells, 1996), such as the applicability of the theory (Zulfiqar, 2014; 2016) or the methodology involved,[1] concordance's insight is that the civilian and military spheres need not be separated with one sphere dominant over the other. On the contrary, they can coexist through 'dialogue, accommodation, and shared values or objectives' (Schiff, 1995, p 12).

This brief review of the literature has shown that the theories explaining civil–military relations are many and varied. All of them, however, assume the 'military' is ontologically different from the 'civilian'. Civil–military relations theories are ultimately concerned with the problems arising from a 'civil–military gap' stemming from differences between the two worlds. Rahbek-Clemmensen et al. (2012) identified four areas where gaps could be present: (1) policy preferences where the two worlds have different objectives, (2) the relationship between the civilian and military institutions, (3) a demographic gap in the societal representation within the military and (4) a cultural gap with the two differentiated by values. The wider the gap, the more difficult it will be to control the military. Using these four categories, the next section shows how their absence in Singapore broadly explains the fusionist nature of civil–military relations in the country.

What gap? Observations of integrated civil–military relations in Singapore

Past Singapore civil–military relations scholarship suggests the lack of a civil–military gap because Singapore's peculiar nature fuses the 'military' and 'civilian'. Chan (1975, p 51) already notes Singapore's political system as different from Western democracies, describing Singapore as an 'administrative state' where 'the meaningful political arena' is the bureaucracy. Commenting on civil–military relations in Singapore, Huxley (1993) further expands this arrangement to a 'military–administrative state' to include an SAF co-opted into the bureaucracy. For these reasons, Tan (2001) highlights the difficulty in applying traditional civil–military relations approaches to Singapore, suggesting 'fusion' replace 'relations' in understanding how the 'civilian' and 'military' relate to each other in Singapore, and not Huntington's 'objective civilian control'. Tan's (2001, p 278) civil–military fusion notes the military does not function 'as an independent or dysfunctional component outside the civilian polity', suggesting a civilianization of the military. Chong and Chan (2016) agree with his observation that the 'military' and 'civilian' worlds are integrated, though they contend it manifests as the militarization of civilians. They, however, stress their conception of militarization focuses on the entrenchment of national defence being paramount, and is not akin to militarism, which Chan (1985, p 136) had also convincingly rejected.

A process of mutual influence between the functional 'military' and 'civilian' policy worlds united in objectives precludes the development of a policy preference gap, a cornerstone of integrationist observations of civil–military relations in Singapore. This is due to the privileging of a 'vulnerability' narrative that prioritizes national defence as the first among other equal national objectives (Chong and Chan, 2016; Loo, 2004; Tan, 2001; Tan, 2011). At independence in 1965, Singapore faced internal and external political, economic, environmental and societal vulnerabilities, including perceived unfriendly neighbours, the lack of natural resources and strategic depth, as well as communalism demonstrated by earlier racial riots. These led Singapore's political elites to securitize vulnerability itself, with an ever-present security fear and the consequent need to mitigate vulnerabilities (Chang, 2019). As Lee Kuan Yew (cited in Ng, 2018b) emphasizes: 'Without security … there can be no economic or even social progress.' Policy preferences between existing 'military' and 'civilian' worlds were thus melded together by common and arguably sacrosanct vulnerabilities right from Singapore's independence.

At the elite-level, there is therefore an integration of the management of external and internal security resources. It initially began at independence out of necessity: resources were limited. The military had to serve both internal and external national security functions as part of a 'whole-of-government' approach towards safeguarding the island-state. Lee (2000, pp 22–3) recalls he was relieved that Goh Keng Swee, an economist by training, was 'willing and eager' to handle both an external and internal security portfolio as the first Minister of Interior and Defence (MID). That the military played a crucial internal security role then suggested a remarkable level of trust given to it by Singapore's leadership since the domestic deployment of the military typically sits uncomfortably with mainstream civil–military relations models of civilian supremacy. Although the MID was eventually separated into two ministries for 'defence' and 'home affairs' in 1970, a unified 'whole-of-government' approach to security still exists. While there is a clear functional division of labour among each of these ministries, high-level decisions are reached from a common position. This is a key pillar of the fusion model. In Tan's (2011, p 149) words, 'the military is not an independent or oppositional component outside the civilian polity, but forms an integral part of the administrative structure'. It is a 'creation' of the ruling People's Action Party (PAP), which has formed the civilian government of Singapore since self-rule in 1959 (Tan, 2001, p 279).

The sharing of human capital between the SAF and public service is also institutionalized, further minimizing any distinctively civilian or military policy preferences among individuals within an already integrated structure. Tan (2001, p 282) describes the SAF as 'virtually a "civil service in uniform" whose officers functioned not so much as an autonomous set of military professionals but as civil servants who were obediently carrying out the policies of the political leadership'. The movement of 'soldier scholars', regular officers whose higher education was paid for by the SAF, into non-military public service roles typifies this (Huxley, 1993; Tan, 2001; Tan, 2011). Such movements involve both recently retired military officers, as well as, significantly, those still in uniformed service seconded to non-military appointments in the civil service. Singapore's current cabinet comprises three retired SAF generals turned politicians, most noticcably Prime Minister Lee Hsien Loong and Senior Minister Teo Chee Hean. A former Chief of Navy (CNV), Lai Chung Han, is the highest-ranked civil servant in the education ministry. Former Chief of Defence Force (CDF) Neo Kian Hong was one of the highest-ranked civil servants in the defence ministry before he became the

Group Chief Executive Officer (CEO) of the Singapore Mass Rapid Transit Corporation. Other retired generals have headed companies in strategic industries in the private sector. Neo, for example, succeeded Desmond Kuek, a retired CDF himself. Yet another former CDF, Ng Yat Chung, served as CEO of the national media company, Singapore Press Holdings, until 2022, and prior to that, as CEO of a Singaporean shipping company, Neptune-Orient Lines. Additionally, Colonel David Neo was the group chief of the Silver Generation Office, a government agency in charge of elderly welfare from April to July 2018 before returning to uniformed service, having been promoted to brigadier-general and placed in command of one of the SAF's three combined-arms divisions. The current CDF, Mervyn Ong, was similarly seconded to a civil service appointment as the Deputy CEO of the Early Childhood Development Agency (ECDA) between 2013 and 2014. Brigadier-general Tan Chee Wee was subsequently seconded as the chief executive of the ECDA in 2021. Many more non-soldier scholars have also transited from a full military career into a second one in the civil service because of the SAF's comparatively early retirement age.

Convergence remains true even at the societal level. All Singaporeans are absorbed into a broad security strategy, 'Total Defence', introduced in 1984. Under Total Defence, military defence is only one of the six pillars safeguarding Singapore's total security, externally and internally. The other five pillars are: (1) psychological defence, the resilience of the citizens; (2) economic defence, the strength of the state's economy; (3) social defence, the harmony and unity of the citizens; (4) civil defence to deal with emergencies; and (5) digital defence in cyberspace. As Ho and Chan (2015, p 12) put it: 'Total Defence suggests a democratisation of defence, where every Singaporean' plays a part. All parties have to work synergistically together to defend Singapore, naturally dissipating policy preference gaps between the civilian and military spheres at all levels when it comes to national security.

Integration also bears out when one surveys the relationship between military and civilian institutions in Singapore. Rahbek-Clemmensen et al (2012, p 673) cite the relationship between military and civilian institutions like 'the media, the courts and the education system' as another category where a civil–military relations gap can exist. Institutional partisanship is absent in Singapore, with the military sharing a cooperative relationship with civilian institutions. For instance, the *Ah Boys to Men* movie tetralogy about SAF military service was the biggest earner among locally produced movies (Yip, 2017). While previous movies by director Jack Neo have also been subtle critiques of social issues in Singapore, the first *Ah Boys to Men* movie was produced 'in conjunction with the 45th anniversary of National Service [compulsory military service] in Singapore' in 2012 (Loh, 2012), with all in the series presenting National Service (NS) and the SAF favourably. Additionally, the SAF does not have its own judges – those who preside over court-martials are civilian judges serving their NS as citizen-soldiers. In secondary schools, the National Cadet Corps (NCC), an extra-curricular activity for students, is closely affiliated with the SAF, focusing on character-building and familiarizing youth with NS, although by itself it is not a through-train into the SAF. Such civil–military synergy among institutions demonstrates the absence of an institutional civil–military gap.

Furthermore, NS amplifies integration by blurring the lines between the 'military' and 'civilian' across all of Singapore society, diminishing the demographic civil–military gap, as Tan (2001; 2011) and Chong and Chan (2016) detail. All Singaporean males and second-generation permanent residents serve two years full-time and another ten years part-time thereafter, in the Singapore Police Force, the Singapore Civil Defence Force or the SAF. All in, National Servicemen (NSmen) are liable for service up to at least age 40, making NS a significant feature in one's life. Roughly half of Singapore's residential population serves NS, and Singapore's military-participation ratio is one of the highest in the world. NS has reflexively established a military that has to broadly represent Singapore as the policy recruits without discrimination towards political or religious belief, socio-economic standing or geographical residence. Its key principles of meeting a critical security need, universality and equity are strenuously upheld (Ng, 2018a). NS is more rigorously implemented than the US draft ever was, with service deferments, let alone exemptions, rarely granted (Ng, 2018a; Teo, 2006). Those who are not liable for NS – female family members and friends, as well as employers – are invariably also involved in supporting the policy because of the large number of men who do serve. NS has resulted in a high level of societal ownership of a familiar military that does not exist in a separate world because it draws its strength from 'all sectors of society' as the 'SAF Declaration' emphasizes (Singapore Monitor, 1984). Additionally, Singapore's physical smallness prevents the geographic concentration of military activities and infrastructure, which could widen a demographic gap (Chong and Chan, 2016, p 374). The next section elaborates our novel explanation according to which these absences of civil–military gaps identified by previous scholars are due to the non-existence of different worlds in the first place.

Neither the civilianized military nor the militarized civilian

In explaining the absence of a gap in the policy preference, institutional and demographic categories, prior scholarship is premised upon integrating two separate 'civilian' and 'military' worlds into a single one; there is no gap because the different worlds are conjoined with permeable boundaries. However, in the first place, the undergirding logic of a civil–military gap is not questioned. Must the 'civilian' and the 'military' be ontologically different? We suggest they do not have to be and go beyond the integrationist logic by contending a gap does not exist simply because there are no separate 'civilian' and 'military' cultural worlds in the first place. The idea of discrete 'civilian' and 'military' worlds is inapplicable in Singapore. While the military plays a unique *role*, and like any organization may privilege certain traits, it is not a different *world* of its own that plainly stands apart from civilians.

This is admittedly counter-intuitive. *Prima facie*, the military should have a distinct culture from civilians given it is one of the few institutions that can legitimately employ violence. Moskos (1977, p 42) further contrasts the self-sacrificial institutional perspective with the occupational one of economic motivation, noting the former has been traditionally associated with the military profession. Military culture has three key traits thus; 'communal life', hierarchy and discipline, all of which seemingly go against the Western liberal societal norms Huntington identified. Yet, a universal military culture does not exist even though civil–military relations scholarship typically describes military culture in opposition to a seemingly universal civilian one (Soeters et al, 2006, pp 238–41). Instead, military culture reflects and varies with national culture, crucially suggesting a military may not necessarily possess a distinct culture from wider society.

Although previous scholarship has implied as much, it has not been sufficiently clear and at times even contradictory. For instance, Tan (2001, p 278) observes Singapore's military 'does not possess its own independent political or ideological ambitions but instead identifies fully with the values, interests, and national goals set by the civilian government'. The SAF has thus 'never developed a distinct corporate culture', according to Tan (2011, p 158 and p 162), yet he subsequently ambiguously suggests that the 'military' and 'civilians' have different mindsets, 'subculture, jargon, and values'. Huxley (1993; 1995) similarly suggests that a 'military mindset' could result in security concerns unduly influencing government policy. While Chong and Chan (2016, p 367 and p 381) argue that 'military and civilian values are perfectly interchangeable', they assert the 'militarization of the civilian' is done by 'creating an institutionally schizophrenic dual personality'. Likewise, Chan (1985, p 144 and p 150) contends the SAF's 'ideology … was formulated by the politicians in keeping with the armed forces' professional role', while concurrently observing that Singapore society 'embraced civilian values' and held the military in poor esteem.

In contrast, we argue one must make a distinction between 'military' tasks and values, when relating them to the 'civilian'. Acknowledging the subtle yet significant difference between function and values reconciles the apparent contradictions in previous scholarship. SAF personnel may approach tasks in a particular way given their professional training and experience, as other professionals like an engineer or a doctor might, but the SAF is still culturally indistinct from civilians, just like engineers or doctors are. The differential is thus in expertise, not values. While the military function contrasts against any civilian one given the uniqueness of defence and warfighting, there has been no fundamental delineation between a 'civilian' or 'military' culture in Singapore from independence onwards and therefore no cultural civil–military gap. No process of 'civilianizing' the 'military' nor 'militarizing' the 'civilian' has occurred.

The former did not occur as there was no substantive 'military' world to convert at independence. The establishment of the SAF occurred in the halls of government rather than the fields of battle; a bureaucratic challenge of a new state rather than an existential one in war (Chan, 1985, p 149). With a lack of military veterans and no significant military tradition in Singapore since its defence had been provided by the colonial British and subsequent Malaysian governments, many in the early SAF's senior leadership were civil servants who were rapidly promoted with only proximate skills. For example, Kirpa Ram Vij was appointed the first Commandant of the SAF Training Institute (SAFTI) in 1965 from his post as an administrative officer with the Land Office and Ministry of Finance. Just five years later, he was promoted to lead the Singapore Army as director of the general staff. MID civil servants not only gave the orders that shaped the SAF, but their colleagues seconded to a uniformed role in the SAF carried them out as well (Peled, 1998, pp 115–16; Tan, 2001, p 282). Furthermore, they would lead an SAF dominated by citizen-soldiers, not an all-volunteer professional force.

This sizeable body of civilians and absence of a military tradition, however, did not make for a liberal SAF either, what Cohen (2006, p 771) describes as a 'coup in reverse'. In fact, the Western-centric conception of a conservative 'military' and liberal 'civilians' was inapplicable because Singapore's early political leadership had conservative values by Western standards despite most of its leaders' Western-styled education.[7] At independence, the government was concerned that some of Singapore's de facto national values were too liberal, identifying bad traits stemming from the city-state's 'migrant and parvenu trading origins' as a colonial outpost (Goh, 1977, p 233). Goh further observed: 'Some of the valuable and indispensable qualities such as social discipline and moral values have unfortunately not been instilled in our education system', with the result being 'a generation of young people who are largely amoral' (Parliament of Singapore, 1967). Values with a seemingly martial bent, such as self-sacrifice, discipline, hard work and obedience, would be entrenched in society to correct these perceived flaws. Such conservatism by Singapore's early political leaders would culminate in the 'Asian values' debate against Western/universal liberal values in the 1990s.

Yet the adoption of these national values was not because of a militarization of the 'civilian'. Singapore had no prior significant military tradition to initiate such a process. These values were adopted for mainly pragmatic reasons. They were deemed necessary to promote speedy and efficient national development. Pragmatism was itself a key national value, with Lee (Lee K.Y., 2015) later acknowledging that Singapore is 'not enamoured with any ideology'. Noting that raising an all-volunteer SAF would be fiscally imprudent for newly independent Singapore as much as defence and security was prioritized, he quickly decided a conscript-based military led by a far smaller group of regulars was the best way forward (Chan, 1985, p 140). Lee (1967) did not want an SAF of 'professional soldiers', declaring Singaporeans 'must learn to live and work for a living. And if you are only a [professional] soldier, you do not contribute to the productivity of the place'.

Pragmatism featured prominently in the development of the SAF's organization culture. Though the fledgling SAF had advisors from Israel, the United States and the United Kingdom, countries with very strong military traditions, the focus was on the practical acquisition of warfighting skills rather than adopting their military values. The Israeli 'fast and compressed' approach to training was particularly appreciated (Chan, 1985, p 141). Israeli advisors did not take command but primarily focused on imparting functional military skills to a cadre of local instructors; a system of training the trainers. Practical-minded instructors, not the transient foreign advisors who might have inculcated a distinct military culture in a fledgling SAF had they more time, would subsequently raise the SAF. The priority was to build up a technically competent SAF that could raise, train and sustain itself in practical terms, not a culturally distinct one with a professional military ethos markedly different from wider society. The SAF would pragmatically develop the functional role it was to play, rather than create a distinct world for it to occupy.

The SAF's 'Code of Conduct', introduced by Goh in 1967, is instructive here. First, the specific substance of the Code was derived pragmatically. 'Perplexed' by what it should contain, Goh (1967) asked a Jesuit priest, and not the military, to draft the Code. SAF officers only provided feedback on the completed draft, unusual for a crucial military document, as Chan (1985, p 150) notes. In contrast, the US 'Military Code of Conduct' was authored by a senior career US military officer who was a veteran of World War II and the Korean War (Schudel, 2006).

Second, Goh (1967) advocated a 'social reason' for the Code; it was a practical way to correct negative perceptions of the military in Singapore by raising 'professional efficiency of the armed forces', thereby leading to 'high standards of behaviour' that would 'ensure that a sense of dignity and purpose prevails throughout the army'. Goh's intention for introducing a code of conduct was therefore not to initiate the creation of a separate 'military' world, but to pragmatically list what was expected of military personnel and organize a fledgling military into a disciplined force. Moreover, the SAF would have values similar to those of newly independent Singapore.

In fact, it was the government's 'duty' to discern and support these values for the benefit of the people in the long run (Goh, 1967). Goh (quoted in Tan and Lew, 2017, p 10) also pointed out that SAF personnel upholding these standards would be 'an example of good citizenship', role models for those outside the SAF to emulate. The point Goh (1967) alluded to was thus that the SAF would be a tool of the government to influence 'the minds of men in the mass', a nation-building role to propagate new national – not necessarily traditionally martial – values crucial for Singapore's wider success that were implicit in the Code. The SAF has consistently played this role because of its reach and administrative capacity (Tan and Lew, 2017; Tan, 2001, p 287). Even the agency in charge of 'strategic planning, direction and coordinating NE [National Education] initiatives at the national level' (NEXUS, 2016), resides in the Ministry of Defence and is headed by an SAF officer.

Third, the Code's expectations, such as 'we take pride in our unit, our uniform, our discipline, our work, our training, and ourselves', 'we must be exemplary in our conduct' and 'we are devoted to duty but not to ourselves' (Singapore Army, 2006, pp 14–15), are premised on principles equally applicable to any civilian organization in Singapore, just contextualized for the military. The subsequent SAF Declaration, an expansion of the Code, would also contain corporate speak such as 'people-oriented management, leadership by example and discipline', 'commitment and confidence, pride in service and team spirit' (Singapore Monitor, 1984).

In 'the absence of a professional military caste' (Chan, 1985, p 150), 'military' and 'civilian' values in Singapore were therefore undifferentiated. In 1991, in a speech to newly commissioned officers, then-CDF Winston Choo (1992, p 6) reminded them to embrace and commit to 'values and norms as typified in a sense of purpose that transcends individual self-interest in favour of a higher good'. Earlier in the year, a similar principle of 'placing society above self' had already been introduced as a key 'shared value' of the official national ideology (Singapore National Library Board, nd). More recently in 2013, 'safety' was added as a 'SAF Core Value' following a series of fatal military training accidents the previous year (Chow, 2013). This was an awkward addition, arguably the antithesis to the dangerous task of warfighting, though one already promulgated in many civilian workplaces. The other existing 'Core Values' – loyalty to the country, leadership, discipline, professionalism, fighting spirit, ethics and care for soldiers – were already not unique to, or only desirable in, the military. The values of the Singapore public service – people, integrity, service and excellence – are also broadly similar in substance (Public Service Division, nd).

This has led to some questioning if the SAF was becoming too 'civilian'. Noting that 'armies are raised and trained to fight wars, the values which are respected differ from civilian values', Goh (1977, pp 229–34) himself lamented that the SAF had adopted some 'soft' civilian values and had become lax and complacent. Others similarly saw military recruits as being increasingly motivated by the monetary incentives characterizing civilian occupations rather than seeing the military as a 'noble calling' (Lim, 2002; Tan, 2011).

These perceptions, however, stemmed from concerns that peace would undercut the commitment and motivation of SAF personnel, thereby undermining the SAF's competence in fulfilling its vital role as the protector of Singapore, not a harkening back to a treasured military world that was slowly being eroded. It was hoped that a traditional martial culture of self-sacrifice and sense of duty would perhaps inherently motivate those in the military to do better even if there was no immediate threat faced. Hence, when then Brigadier-General Lee Hsien Loong declared in 1984 that the 'SAF is an armed force: it is not a civilian corporation', he was reiterating the SAF's mission 'to defeat its enemies, ruthlessly and completely', and not making a statement on cultural difference (Lee, 1984a). The crux of apparent suggestions for the need for a distinct military world was actually a pragmatic concern of military (in)competence in relation to Singapore's defence.

Moreover, attaining Huntingtonian objective control, with a clear separation of the military from civilians so that the former can competently fulfil its role, would be challenging given the absence of an existential clear and present danger to Singapore. Huntington's model emerged from the existential threat of the Cold War. In fact, the SAF has to employ 'occupationalist' market approaches to attract, retain and motivate talent (Chan, 1985, pp 144–8; Tan, 2011, p 159), instead of relying on institutional commitment. Most tellingly, a 'holistic human capital strategy' for recruiting for the Republic of Singapore Air Force (RSAF) suggested by a group of officers in 2016 was exclusively built on overtly 'occupationalist' human resource concepts such as 'career branding', 'rightsizing' and developing a 'high performance culture' (Tee et al., 2016). These human resource challenges and suggested approaches are similar to the ones faced by the public service (Teo, 2016), again reflecting a lack of distinct 'military' and 'civilian' worlds.

Besides the ironic problem of peace, NS also inhibits the SAF from developing its own separate cultural identity. The sizeable number of NSmen across most ranks and vocations spend considerably more time outside the SAF than in it. The SAF had to define its 'norms, value system, and doctrines' around civilians temporarily in uniform (Tan, 2001, p 289), as opposed to developing into a traditional military institution strictly characterized by communal life, hierarchy and discipline. Where operationally required, these characteristics are negotiated and explained, and not imposed as a matter of course. Such was the SAF's reality by the mid-1980s. Brigadier-General Lee (1984b, p 1) already noted traditional conceptions of military 'professionalism' to be a 'natural problem' for the SAF since it predominantly comprised conscripts and reservists, many of whom were key appointment holders. He similarly described measures of professionalism in the SAF in starkly functional terms of individual proficiency, systems discipline and macro-competence. The NSman's transient service thereby prioritized excelling in his military functional role as the main marker of the military professionalism in Singapore and not a complete identification with a unique military culture (Tan, 2001, p 288). The case in Singapore is thus neither the civilianized military nor the militarized civilian since neither world exists separately.

Conclusion: The roles, not worlds of everyday civil–military relations in Singapore

Traditional civil–military relations theories such as Huntington's objective control, Janowitz's civilianization, Feaver's agency, Desch's structural theory or Schiff's concordance examine the domestic problem of the civil–military problematique. In so doing, they posit the existence of a civil–military gap, whether this gap is in terms of policy preference, institutional, demographical or cultural. This chapter has demonstrated the absence of such a civil–military gap in Singapore by repositioning, as well as updating, existing observations of civil–military relations in the country. The internalization of the discourse of vulnerability establishes a common policy preference of both the military and civilians. This is further strengthened by the sharing of human capital between them, as well as other policies such as Total Defence. The 'military' and the 'civilian' institutions share good relations with the latter often supporting the former. Demographically, NS makes the SAF representative of broader society, further enabling the military's nation-building role. Tan (2011, p 161) hence highlights the 'porosity between the military and the state' as 'a manifestation of the almost symbiotic relationship that has always existed between the civil and military leadership', arising 'from the convergence of interests among the Singaporean elite, both inside and outside the military'.

Nonetheless, in spite of the 'fusion' or integration of the 'civilian' and the 'military' due to the close alignment between the SAF, politicians and the bureaucracy, prior scholarship on Singapore civil–military relations has also wondered about the applicability of the civil–military problematique in Singapore should the ruling PAP lose power. Even though the SAF itself was created by the PAP, they conclude that a scenario of military intervention on its behalf to be highly improbable as the SAF and the PAP are 'neither structurally nor ideologically' linked (Huxley, 1993, p 17; Tan, 2011, p 149 and p 164). We go further in contending that a civil–military gap does not exist simply because there were no separate 'civilian' and 'military' cultural worlds in the first place at Singapore's independence, going beyond the earlier observations of the absence of a gap stemming from a close integration of two worlds. The other three gaps cannot exist because a cultural one does not. While the roles of the civilian and the military in Singapore certainly differ, the core of the Singaporean's identity is the same, with the same mindset, values and culture. Without separate worlds, the civil–military problematique is not even a 'question in Singapore, much less a paradox. After all, civil–military relations is a question of politics. However, when there is no politics, as in the curious case of Singapore as an 'administrative state' wherein the decisions and discussions about the allocation of resources are made bureaucratically rather than politically (Chan, 1975; Huxley, 1993), the civil–military problematique does not exist.

The widely held notion of civil–military relations therefore has to be reframed in Singapore's context. With the civil–military problematique a non-issue, neither the 'citizen-soldier' nor the 'militarized civilian' quite describes civil–military relations in Singapore. Rather, Singapore civil–military relations consists of the 'everyday': a process of shuttling between 'military' and 'civilian' roles daily. While SAF personnel, be they regulars, full-time NSmen or Operationally Ready NSmen, fulfil the 'military' function of defending the state, they too fulfil 'civilian' roles outside the military in their families, social communities and in the case of NSmen, their civilian workplace. Given that the SAF comprises mainly NSmen, the ability to 'seamlessly switch' from civilian and military roles and effectively do both, is the hallmark of the model NSman (Tan, 2012).

Similarly, as an organization, the SAF has to also balance and switch between 'military' and 'civilian' roles. Its decision to be a 'full-spectrum' force has similarly seen it being tugged in multiple directions by a disparate range of tasks, including non-military ones, it is expected to undertake. While its core focus is on warfighting, the SAF is also involved in co-organizing civilian events, including annual occurrences, such as the National Day Parade, or one-off occasions, such as the 2010 Youth Olympic Games and 2015 Southeast Asian Games. At both the individual and organizational levels, 'everyday' civil–military relations is thus the management of a relationship of roles rather than of two worlds with different identities and values.

Notes

[1] Our criticism: Schiff (2016, p 231) argues that the theory is 'grounded in deductive causation', but it seems rather more inductive given the lack of deductive reasoning behind the four indicators posited.

[2] Lee Kuan Yew studied law at Cambridge University, Goh Keng Swee was conferred a doctorate in economics by the London School of Economics and S. Rajaratnam's law studies at King's College London were disrupted by World War Two.

References

Chan, H.C. (1975) 'Politics in an administrative state: where has the politics gone?', in C.M. Seah (ed) *Trends in Singapore: Proceedings and Background Paper*, Singapore: Singapore University Press for ISEAS, pp 51–68.

Chan, H.C. (1985) 'Singapore', in Z.H. Ahmad and H. Crouch (eds) *Military–Civilian Relations in South-East Asia*, Singapore: Oxford University Press, pp 136–56.

Chang, J.Y. (2019) 'Conscripting the audience: Singapore's successful securitisation of vulnerability', in S.H. Ho and G. Ong-Webb (eds) *National Service in Singapore*, Singapore: World Scientific, pp 83–103.

Chong, A. and Chan, S. (2016) 'Militarizing civilians in Singapore: preparing for a "crisis" within a calibrated nationalism', *The Pacific Review*, 30(3): 365–84.

Choo, W. (1992) 'The challenge of leadership in the military profession: address by the Chief of Defence Force, Lt-Gen Winston W.L. Choo, at the Appointment Certificate Ceremony for OCC 3/91 on 27 Dec 91', *Pointer: Journal of the Singapore Armed Forces*, 18(1): 5–8.

Chow, J. (2013) 'SAF adds "safety" to its list of core values', *The Straits Times*, [online] 16 April, Available from: https://str.sg/UGLm [Accessed 8 April 2022].

Cohen, S.A. (2006) 'Changing civil–military relations in Israel: towards an over-subordinate IDF?', *Israel Affairs*, 12(4): 769–88.

Desch, M.C. (1999) *Civilian Control of the Military: The Changing Security Environment*, Baltimore: Johns Hopkins University Press.

Feaver, P.D. (1999) 'Civil–military relations', *Annual Review of Political Science*, 2: 211–41.

Feaver, P.D. (2003) *Armed Servants: Agency, Oversight, and Civil–Military Relations*, Cambridge, MA: Harvard University Press.

Finer, S.E. (2002) *The Man on Horseback: The Role of the Military in Politics*, New Brunswick: Transaction Publishers.

Goh, K.S. (1967) 'Speech by Dr Goh Keng Swee, Minister of Defence and Chairman of the Army Board, for the Promulgation Ceremony of the Code of Conduct for the Singapore Armed Forces on Friday, 14th July, 1967' *National Archives of Singapore*, [online] 14 July, Available from: www.nas.gov.sg/archivesonline/data/pdfdoc/PressR19670714.pdf [Accessed 2 November 2018].

Goh, K.S. (1977) *The Practice of Economic Growth*, Singapore: Federal Publications.

Ho, S.H. and Chan, S. (2015) *Singapore Chronicles: Defence*, Singapore: Institute of Policy Studies and Straits Times Press Pte Ltd.

Huntington, S.P. (1957) *The Soldier and the State: The Theory and Politics of Civil–Military Relations*, Cambridge, MA: The Belknap Press of Harvard University Press.

Huxley, T. (1993) 'The political role of the Singapore Armed Forces: towards a military-administrative state?' *SDSC Working Papers*, 279.

Huxley, T. (1995) 'Singapore's soldier scholars', *The Asian Wall Street Journal*.

Huxley, T. (2000) *Defending the Lion City: The Armed Forces of Singapore*, St Leonards, Australia: Allen & Unwin.

Janowitz, M. (1971) *The Professional Soldier: A Social and Political Portrait*, New York: Free Press.

Kuehn, D. and Lorenz, P. (2011) 'Explaining civil–military relations in new democracies: structure, agency and theory development', *Asian Journal of Political Science*, 19(3): 231–49.

Lasswell, H.D. (1941) 'The garrison state', *American Journal of Sociology*, 46(4): 455–68.

Lee, H.L. (1984a) 'BG Lee Hsien Loong's farewell speech', *Pointer: Journal of the Singapore Armed Forces*, 10(4): 39–41.

Lee, H.L. (1984b) 'Professionalism in the SAF', *SAF Professional Reading List: Tri-Service Warfighter Course*, [online] 28 June, Available from: www.mindef.gov.sg/oms/content/imindef/publications/pointer/supplements/saf_prl2008/_jcr_content/imindefPars/0010/file.res/PRLTSWCunclassed.pdf [Accessed 8 April 2022].

Lee, K.Y. (1967) 'Transcript of speech by the Prime Minister at a celebration in the Toa Payoh Community Centre on 21st February, 1967, held in connection with the conferment of Public Service Star Awards on Tan Tong Meng and Inche Buang B. Siraj. National Archives of Singapore', *National Archives of Singapore*, [online] 21 February, Available from: www.nas.gov.sg/archivesonline/data/pdfdoc/lky19670221.pdf [Accessed 2 November 2018].

Lee, K.Y. (2000) *From Third World to First: The Singapore Story: 1965–2000*, Singapore: Times Media Private Limited.

Lee, K.Y. (2015) 'In quotes: Lee Kuan Yew', *BBC*, [online] 22 March, Available from: www.bbc.com/news/world-asia-31582842 [Accessed 8 April 2022].

Lim, A.N. (2002) 'The professional soldier', *Pointer: Journal of the Singapore Armed Forces*, 28(3): 83–93.

Loh, G. (2012) 'Three to see: turning boys into men', *Today*, 12 September.

Loo, B.F.W. (2004) 'Explaining changes in Singapore's military doctrines: material and ideational perspectives', in A. Acharya and L.T. Lee (eds) *Asia in the New Millennium*, Singapore: Marshall Cavendish, pp 352–79.

Moskos, C.C. (1977) 'From institution to occupation: trends in military organization', *Armed Forces & Society*, 4(1): 41–50.

Moskos, C.C., Williams J.A. and Segal D.R. (2000) 'Armed forces after the Cold War', in C.C. Moskos, J.A. Williams and D.R. Segal (eds) *The Postmodern Military: Armed Forces after the Cold War*, Oxford: Oxford University Press, pp 1–13.

NEXUS (2016) 'Our milestones', *Singapore Ministry of Defence*, [online] nd, Available from: www.mindef.gov.sg/oms/nexus/ [Accessed 2 November 2018].

Ng, E.H. (2018a) 'Oral reply by Minister for Defence Dr Ng Eng Hen, to parliamentary questions on national service deferment for parliamentary sitting on 6 August 2018', *MINDEF Singapore*, [online] 6 August, Available from: www.mindef.gov.sg/web/portal/mindef/news-and-eve nts/latest-releases/article-detail/2018/august/06aug18_pq [Accessed 3 September 2018].

Ng, E.H. (2018b) 'Speech by Minister for Defence, Dr Ng Eng Hen, for the 49th Goh Keng Swee Command and staff college graduation ceremony and dinner', *MINDEF Singapore*, [online] 27 October, Available from: www. mindef.gov.sg/web/portal/mindef/news-and-events/latest-releases/arti cle-detail/2018/october/27oct18_speech [Accessed 2 November 2018].

Parliament of Singapore (1967) 'National Service (Amendment) Bill: official reports', *Singapore Statutes online*, [online] 1 March, Available from: https:// sso.agc.gov.sg/Bills-Supp/3-1967/Published/19670301?DocDate=19670 301 [Accessed 29 April 2022].

Peled, A. (1998) *A Question of Loyalty: Military Manpower Policy in Multiethnic States*, New York: Cornell University Press.

Perlmutter, A. and LeoGrande, W.M. (1982) 'The party in uniform: toward a theory of civil–military relations in communist political systems', *American Political Science Review*, 76(4): 778–89.

Public Service Division (nd) 'Our vision, mission and core values: Singapore Prime Minister's Office', *Public Service Division*, [online] nd, Available from: www.psd.gov.sg/who-we-are/our-vision-mission-and-core-values [Accessed 2 November 2018].

Rahbek-Clemmensen, J., Archer, E.M., Barr, J., Belkin, A., Guerrero, M., Hall, C. and Swain, K.E.O. (2012) 'Conceptualizing the civil–military gap: a research note', *Armed Forces & Society*, 38(4): 669–78.

Rukavishnikov, V.O. and Pugh, M. (2006) 'Civil–military relations', in G. Caforio (ed) *Handbook of the Sociology of the Military*, New York: Springer, pp 13–49.

Schiff, R.L. (1995) 'Civil–military relations reconsidered: a theory of concordance', *Armed Forces & Society*, 22(1): 7–24.

Schiff, R.L. (2009) *The Military and Domestic Politics: A Concordance Theory of Civil–Military Relations*, Abingdon, Oxon: Routledge.

Schiff, R.L. (2016) 'Concordance theory in Pakistan: response to Zulfiqar Ali', *Armed Forces & Society*, 42(1): 226–34.

Schudel, M. (2006) 'Marine Col F. Brooke Nihart', *Washington Post*, [online] 30 September, Available from: www.washingtonpost.com/archive/local/2006/09/30/marine-col-f-brooke-nihart/ef8bdab0-e8ee-42ab-afde-649be0f277b0/ [Accessed 29 April 2022].

Singapore Army (2006) *Our Army Customs and Traditions: Understanding Why We Do What We Do*, Singapore: Singapore Army.

Singapore Monitor (1984) 'A statement of ideals', *Singapore Monitor*, [online] 1 July, Available from: https://eresources.nlb.gov.sg/newspapers/digitised/issue/singmonitor19840701-1 [Accessed 29 April 2022].

Singapore National Library Board (nd) 'Shared values are adopted, 15th Jan 1991', *Singapore National Library Board*, [online] nd, Available from: https://eresources.nlb.gov.sg/history/events/62f98f76-d54d-415d-93a1-4561c776ab97 [Accessed 2 November 2018].

Soeters, J.L., Winslow, D.J. and Weibull, A. (2006) 'Military culture', in G. Caforio (ed.) *Handbook of the Sociology of the Military*, New York: Springer, pp 237–54.

Tan, F.W.S. and Lew, P.B.C. (2017) 'The role of the Singapore Armed Forces in forging national values, image, and identity', *Military Review*, 97(2): 8–16.

Tan, G.W. (2012) 'Graduating as better commanders', *Pioneer*, [online] 26 October, Available from: www.mindef.gov.sg/web/portal/pioneer/article/regular-article-detail/milestones/2018-dm/26Oct2012_01761 [Accessed 2 November 2018].

Tan, T.Y. (2001) 'Singapore: civil–military fusion', in M. Alagappa (ed) *Coercion and Governance: The Declining Political Role of the Military in Asia*, Stanford: Stanford University Press, pp 276–93.

Tan, T.Y. (2011) 'The armed forces and politics in Singapore: the persistence of civil–military fusion', in M Mietzner (ed) *The Political Resurgence of the Military in Southeast Asia: Conflict and Leadership*, Abingdon, Oxon: Routledge, pp 148–66.

Tee, P.L., Tjong, W.C. and Wong, C.W. (2016) 'Human capital challenges for the RSAF', *Pointer: Journal of the Singapore Armed Forces (Beyond the Horizon: Forging the Future RSAF)*, [online] nd, Available from: www.mindef.gov.sg/oms/content/dam/imindef_media_library/graphics/pointer/PDF/2016/af-supp2016/af-supp2016_full.pdf [Accessed 29 April 2022].

Teo, C.H. (2006) 'Ministerial statement on national service defaulters by Minister for Defence Teo Chee Hean in Parliament, 16 Jan 2006', *Singapore Government Media Release*, [online], 16 January, Available from: www.nas.gov.sg/archivesonline/data/pdfdoc/20060116991.htm [Accessed 2 November 2018].

Teo, C.H. (2016) 'Speech by Deputy Prime Minister Teo Chee Hean at Committee of Supply 2016', *Singapore Public Service Division*, [online,] 13 April, Available from: www.psd.gov.sg/press-room/speeches/speech-by-deputy-prime-minister-teo-chee-hean-at-committee-of-supply-2016 [Accessed 2 November 2018].

Wells, R.S. (1996) 'The theory of concordance in civil–military relations: a commentary', *Armed Forces & Society*, 23(2): 269–75.

Yip, W.Y. (2017) 'Ah Boys to Men 4 opens big at the local box office', *The Straits Times*, [online], 10 November, Available from: https://str.sg/3Rnw [Accessed 29 April 2022].

Zulfiqar, A. (2014) 'Contradiction of concordance theory: failure to understand military intervention in Pakistan', *Armed Forces & Society*, 40(3): 544–67.

Zulfiqar, A. (2016) 'Pakistan, military coup, and concordance: four objections to Schiff', *Armed Forces & Society*, 42(2): 463–69.

6

The Role of the Malaysian Armed Forces in Defence Diplomacy: A Foreign Policy Outworking of Civil–Military Relations in Malaysia

David Han

In contrast to most countries in the Asia-Pacific in which threats and occurrences of military coups are not uncommon, Malaysia's civil–military relations have remained non-turbulent and uneventful, such that scholarly studies on this topic have gained little traction. Moreover, due to its partially democratic and soft-authoritarian political system, Malaysia has been a peculiar case where the civilian government has been able to exert considerable control over the military over a long period in a manner resembling civil–military relations in Western democracies (Liew, 2019; Matsuura, 2002, pp 1–2).

A handful of studies on Malaysia's civil–military relations have sought to account for the stability in the Malaysian Armed Forces' (MAF) subordination to the former Barisan Nasional (BN) government. Some scholars opine that the MAF's lack of involvement in political affairs can be explained by both constitutional restraints which prevent the military from participating in politics, and the MAF's adherence to the democratic principle of a civilian-military divide and professionalism inherited from British colonialism (Ahmad, 1985, pp 127–29; Jeshurun, 1989, p 92; Jeshurun, 1994, pp 200–3; Matsuura, 2002, p 5). As Bellamy and Beeson (2008) have highlighted, the MAF has been playing only a secondary role in the BN's political survival, whereas the police have performed a far more politicized function in preserving the BN regime (pp 88–9). Other scholars argue that given the military's strong professionalism and subordination to civilian authority, the military would most likely engage in a coup or political intervention only if there were to be major political upheavals in the country (Nathan and Govindasamy, 2001, p 274). Overall, then, these studies reflect what Feaver describes as the tendency of civil–military relations studies to focus on the occurrence or non-occurrence of coups (Feaver, 2003, pp 10–11). As Bellamy and Beeson (2008) have noted, the relatively constant and stable civil–military relations in Malaysia could hardly warrant a fresh study of this topic (pp 88–9).

A new study is justifiable, however, given that the external security environment, not just domestic factors, condition Malaysian civil–military relations which have a bearing on Malaysia's defence diplomacy in MOOTW. Indeed, external security challenges may constitute a major rationale for the Malaysian government to steer the MAF towards addressing such challenges, thereby reifying the apolitical nature of the military. Hence, this chapter seeks to explore the external arena of foreign policy in which the Malaysian government has been employing defence diplomacy to reinforce the military's subordination to the civilian government.

Towards this objective, this chapter addresses the following questions: if modernization has been attained, especially in the economic realm, does the Malaysian military retrench itself towards a guardianship role vis-à-vis the maintenance of a status quo of authoritarian prosperity or does it support democratic prosperity? Is Malaysia's civil–military relations a strength in handling defence diplomacy *qua* HADR and peacekeeping, and in what way? Is Malaysian defence diplomacy a means of ensuring that international security in the Indo-Pacific operates on two 'synergistic' tracks: mostly civilian roles in fronting formal security discussions while military representatives in and out of uniform float trial balloons in Track II fora? By examining the impact of civil–military relations in the context of external security challenges, the chapter thus sheds new insights on how the considerable stability in civil–military relations has been conducive to Malaysia's efforts in defence diplomacy.

The chapter utilizes Huntingtonian and Janowitzean perspectives to understand the effect of civil–military relations on Malaysia's defence diplomacy under the former BN regime from the end of the Cold War to the collapse of the Pakatan Harapan (PH) government in 2020. It argues that the stability and continuity in civil–military relations, as undergirded by an evolutionary process of translating civilian leadership over the military in addressing domestic challenges and adapting this relationship for external purposes, have been conducive and advantageous to Malaysia's participation in peacekeeping and HADR efforts. During the Cold War, given the MAF's professionalism coupled with socio-cultural conditioning through the state's Malay-centric communalism, the civilian government was able to direct the military to support the wider strategy of socio-economic development rather than a heavy reliance on hard military power for achieving domestic security. Subsequently, the BN government dovetailed the military's domestic counter-insurgency role, which supported the civilian-driven, socio-economic development with a Malaysian foreign policy that favoured diplomacy rather than overt military means as the key to achieve Malaysia's external security. Hence, as the counterinsurgency against communist threats ended in the late 1980s, the government externalized the MAF's supportive role in national development within the domestic context towards a constabulary function in defence diplomacy, especially in peacekeeping and HADR activities. Thus, Malaysia could draw upon its military's operational expertise to project leadership at ASEAN Track II fora to enhance cooperation in HADR and peacekeeping. Even though these Track II fora are arenas for floating 'trial balloons', the insights promulgated by Malaysian defence officials in these platforms have been derived from actual operational experiences. The subsequent but short-lived PH government largely preserved the MAF's efforts in peacekeeping and HADR, and its engagements in Track II platforms, while placing more emphasis on the military's war-fighting capacity. The stability in civil–military relations even after the collapse of the PH government during the COVID-19 pandemic would ensure the continuity of Malaysia's existing approach to MOOTW efforts in peacekeeping and HADR.

This chapter is divided into seven parts. The first section discusses the theoretical perspective for analysing Malaysia's civil–military relations. Their development during the Cold War and its subsequent impact on peacekeeping and HADR efforts in the post-Cold War era under the BN regime are examined in the second and third sections, respectively. The fourth section covers civil–military relations under the PH government, followed by the fifth section on defence diplomacy in this period. The sixth section looks at the development of civil–military relations during the COVID-19 pandemic, before concluding with an assessment of Malaysia's civil–military relations and its impact on defence diplomacy in the future.

Analysing Malaysia's civil–military relations

The pre-dominant theoretical perspectives on civil–military relations have focused mainly on Western democracies. Samuel Huntington's seminal work, *Soldiers and the State*, postulates that as a democratic civilian government seeks objective civilian control over its military to secure the state against an external threat, the civilian government and society at large would have to downplay liberal principles and support the conservatism of the military so that it can function properly to defend against such a threat (Huntington, 1957, pp 83–4). To forestall a military coup, a democratic civilian government exerts control over a powerful military through institutional means and professionalization of the state's armed forces to render it largely apolitical

(Huntington, 1957, pp 83–4). Morris Janowitz's (1970) perspectives on civil–military relations emphasize the sociological influences that underlie civilian control over the military by relying on civic society's liberal democratic values. Thus, the sociological norms of democracy would bring about the military's subordination to civilian authority while remaining focused on its core military functions (Janowitz, 1970). Through this subordination to civilian supremacy, the military becomes 'a constabulary force when it is continuously prepared to act, committed to the minimum use of force, and seeks viable international relations rather than victory' (Janowitz, 1970, p 418).

Both Huntington and Janowitz's theoretical viewpoints suggest that the military's submission to civilian authority according to domestic institutional and socio-cultural conditions is necessary for achieving the state's external security on the global stage. Since defence diplomacy centres on peaceful cooperation among militaries to forestall the possibility of conflict, Janowitz's characterization of the military as having a constabulary role in international affairs to deal with external security challenges is appropriate to examine a country's defence diplomacy and, by implication, its foreign policy as well. As such, a constabulary role could entail a military performing a 'policing' function, in order for a state to preserve a preferable status quo in international security matters, rather than aiming for an outright victory in war.

Studies on civil–military relations have highlighted that the notion of a military's professionalism with its purported apolitical nature in Western democracies is too glamourized (Sarkesian, 1981; Brooks, 2020). Ideally, professionalism should entail that the military is solely focused on fulfilling defensive functions in warfighting and peacetime operations, without involvement in political affairs. However, a sharp bifurcation between the military's professionalism and domestic politics, whereby the former is unaffected by the latter, may not be realistic (Sarkesian, 1981). As such, military professionalism does not connote complete neutrality and non-involvement vis-a-vis domestic politics. A military's professionalism may involve subordination to civilian supremacy, but it does not preclude the military from being influenced by civilian governments for political purposes, as both agencies interact in shaping defence and security policies (Brooks, 2020, pp 17–24). Therefore, despite the MAF's claims to strict professionalism, it may not be completely free of political machinations from the civilian leadership.

The Huntingtonian and Janowitzean perspectives are analytically valuable in highlighting how the MAF's professionalism, as manifested in its continuous subordination to the civilian leadership on the domestic front, has enabled the military to fulfil a constabulary role on the international stage, especially in peacekeeping and HADR. This chapter contends that the concept of Asian military evolution entails an adaptive process through which civil–military relations change gradually not only according to local needs and developmentally driven issues but also in response to external security challenges. For Malaysia, the evolutionary process refers to the civilian government's adaptation of efforts in directing the military to support policies which eschew overly militarized solutions to address changing security challenges in the domestic and international domains, thereby reinforcing the military's professionalism for apolitical objectives. This can be gleaned from a qualitative case study of the impact of civil–military relations on defence diplomacy from the 1990s onwards under the BN regime until the collapse of the PH government in 2020. This period marks the MAF's transition from a highly domestic role towards a significant focus on HADR and peacekeeping in the post-Cold War era. Moreover, the military's subordination to the democratically oriented PH coalition after the fall of the BN regime demonstrates the stability of civil–military relations. This shaped the PH's policies in defence diplomacy. Through the insights from this case study, this chapter seeks to understand future developments in civil–military relations in the context of the COVID-19 pandemic.

The origins of the MAF's constabulary role on the international stage

The constabulary nature of the MAF on the international stage in peacekeeping and HADR efforts can be traced to the military's domestic functions during the Cold War. The MAF undertook the development of capabilities in counter-insurgency warfare (CIW) to combat a communist insurgency. The government had channelled the military's professional capabilities towards supporting socio-economic development, for this was viewed as the primary means of achieving national security (Nathan and Govindasamy, 2001, pp 262, 270 and 271). Under the strategy of '*Keselamatan dan Pembangunan*' (KESBAN) as articulated by the first prime minister of Malaysia, Tunku Abdul Rahman, the military's task in performing CIW against the communist insurgency was subsumed under an overarching and holistic anthropological strategy in winning hearts and minds through socio-economic development, without recourse to an overtly military solution to supress the insurgents (Yadi, 2004, pp 2–4). Subsequently, the MAF's role in KESBAN contributed to socio-economic conditions that facilitated Mahathir Mohamad's nationalistic, developmental state policies aimed at shifting Malaysia's agriculture-centric economy towards significant industrialization, infrastructural development and export-oriented liberalization in the 1980s (Beeson, 2000, pp 339–43; Jomo, 2003).

Although the military was never heavily manipulated by the civilian leaders to sustain regime legitimacy and survival, the MAF's subordination to and support for the BN government's KESBAN policies were achievable due to the military's socio-cultural conditioning under Malaysia's ethnocentric communalism that embedded the military's professional ethos on the necessity of Malay supremacy and leadership (Matsuura, 2002, pp 39–40; Jeshurun, 1994, pp 200–3; Jeshurun, 1989, p 92; Ahmad, 1985, pp 127–9). Under Malaysia's ethnocentric communalism, since Malays are '*bumiputera*' ('sons of the soil'), they are entitled to dominate the defence establishment. This guaranteed that Malay interests within the military were favoured and the loyalty of its Malay personnel towards the civilian government assured (Ahmad, 1985, p 131).

With the end of the communist insurgency in the late 1980s, the government started to shift the main focus of the military away from domestic security issues towards addressing external challenges arising from the uncertainties of the post-Cold War (Storey, 2020, pp 2–3). The highly authoritarian government of the first Mahathir premiership asserted strong civilian control over the military, such that defence policies were subsumed under Mahathir's foreign policy thrust that sought to amplify Malaysia's influence in global affairs (Saravanamuttu, 1996; Saravanamuttu, 2003, p 307). Thus, the post-Cold War period paved the way for a foreign policy outworking of the MAF's security functions in the government's KESBAN policy onto the international context in MOOTW activities in the realm of defence diplomacy. Indeed, Malaysia's foreign policy elites depended on a combination of bilateral and multilateral diplomacy in Southeast Asia and beyond as part of an overall strategy to attain security without relying on a strong military build-up to mitigate external security threats (Andrew, 2019, p 3; Daud, 2019, pp 57–8).

Defence diplomacy from the post-Cold War period to the Najib premiership

As Malaysia's defence diplomacy has been a foreign policy manifestation of domestic KESBAN efforts, the MAF converged largely with the government's preferences for the military to perform major roles in MOOTW. Since the 1990s, beginning from the first Mahathir premiership to the end of the Najib premiership in 2018, the military actively participated in non-combat, UN peacekeeping and HADR operations. To be sure, the military's peacekeeping role did not originate in the 1990s (see also Jenne in this volume). As early as the 1960s, the MAF was involved in peacekeeping, such as the contributions of the Malay Special Forces as part of the UN peacekeeping contingent in the Republic of Congo. From the 1990s onwards, this commitment to peacekeeping efforts was further increased as the MAF began to extend its peacekeeping operations to places such as Namibia, Cambodia, Somalia, Kuwait, Iran–Iraq, Bosnia, East Timor and Afghanistan. As peacekeeping has been a prominent feature of Malaysia's contribution in safeguarding international security, it is not surprising that regarding its non-permanent membership in the UN Security Council from 2015 to 2016, the government brandished the country's credentials by highlighting its contributions to missions around the world (Ministry of Foreign Affairs of Malaysia, 2021).

Malaysia's commitment to peacekeeping was further concretized when the Malaysian Peacekeeping Centre (later renamed as the Malaysian Peace Training Centre [MPTC] in 2006) was formed in 1996 to highlight the military's core strength in peacekeeping operations. In this regard, strong civilian oversight in steering the military in developing its expertise in peacekeeping was evident after it was first mooted by then Defence Minister Najib Razak in 1994. Since its inception, the MPTC has been the premier MAF institute to train personnel from the MAF, the Royal Malaysian Police and NGOs in peacekeeping.

Likewise, the MAF's HADR activities in Southeast Asia were becoming more prominent. For example, in the aftermath of the December 2004 Boxing Day Tsunami that hit the Indonesian island of Sumatra, Malaysia despatched the military's medical personnel upon Indonesia's request to set up a relief centre in Aceh and a makeshift field hospital to provide medical treatment for locals (Reliefweb, 2005a). Similarly, the town of Tacloban in the Philippines received humanitarian assistance from the MAF's medical team in the aftermath of Typhoon Haiyan in November 2013 (Ahmad, 2013). In 2017, the Rohingya crisis presented an occasion for the MAF to aid Bangladesh in handling the influx of Rohingya refugees from Myanmar. The MAF Health Services provided medical aid to Rohingya refugees, including the setting up of a makeshift medical hospital at Cox Bazaar (Soon, 2018).

These HADR efforts highlighted Malaysian civilian leaders' position that the military serves as an effective instrument in enhancing diplomatic relations with countries receiving humanitarian assistance from Malaysia. For example, the MAF's practice of involvement in HADR solely for humanitarian purposes had enabled Malaysia to possess the credibility to engage in defence diplomacy without arousing regional sensitivities, particularly the principle of non-interference within ASEAN. A case in point was Malaysia's efforts to offer humanitarian aid to people in Myanmar affected by Cyclone Nargis. Then Deputy Prime Minister Najib Razak articulated at the Shangri-La Dialogue in 2008 that the MAF's presence in Myanmar reflected previous endeavours in humanitarian activities in other countries with no other agendas, adding that the militaries of ASEAN member states would provide the best response to those affected by Cyclone Nargis (Simon, 2010, p 47; Cook and Yogendran, 2019, p 46). Malaysia's objective of improving regional ties through the military's HADR endeavours appeared to have paid off, as the Philippines, Indonesia and Bangladesh showed appreciation for such efforts (Reliefweb, 2005b; Department of

Foreign Affairs of the Republic of the Philippines, 2013; The Daily Star, 2021). Additionally, the Najib administration's gesture of sending a medical team from the military to Afghanistan also contributed to the improvement of security ties with the United States (The Star, 2010; The White House, Office of the Press Secretary, 2014).

Given that the MAF's defence diplomacy was subsumed under foreign policy objectives, it is not surprising that Malaysia's civilian leaders would front the overarching security discussions in the region while its defence officials would be accorded opportunities to present their expertise in peacekeeping and HADR at Track II platforms. While the ASEAN Regional Forum (ARF) has been helmed primarily by foreign policy elites of participating states such that there appeared to be some resentment among defence officials about their secondary status in the forum (Tan, 2012, p 236), this arrangement fitted with Malaysia's civilian leaders' avoidance of a full-blown military posture, while preserving the primacy of diplomacy to achieve regional security and peace. However, it would be a caricature to portray the MAF's contributions in defence diplomacy at Track II fora as merely amounting to novel ideas in the form of 'trial balloons'. As several scholars of ASEAN multilateralism have observed, due to the slow pace of key ASEAN platforms (for example, the ARF) for developing concrete measures for security matters, this has prompted the development of the ADMM, ADMM-plus, and other follow-up Track II fora to foster practical security cooperation among ASEAN militaries (Haacke, 2009, pp 427–429; Emmers and Tan, 2011, pp 44–60; Tan, 2017, p 282).

Indeed, the MAF's activism in ASEAN Track II forums has been exhibiting a degree of leadership in initiating policy ideas on HADR and peacekeeping operations among civilian agencies and militaries. For example, Malaysia's initiative in pushing for HADR matters in the ADMM was visible in its proposal for the ASEAN Military Ready Group (AMRG) on HADR during the ADMM meeting hosted in Langkawi in 2015. The Terms of Reference on the AMRG on HADR that were crafted in this meeting was subsequently adopted by ASEAN member states in Vientiane, Laos in 2016. It indicated that this AMRG on HADR will serve 'as a collective and solid intent to establish an ASEAN military team for quick deployment to support humanitarian assistance and disaster relief in a coordinated manner' (ASEAN, 2016).

Additionally, the policy ideas on HADR and peacekeeping presented by Malaysia's defence practitioners at ASEAN Track II fora were derived from actual operational experiences. One example is the MAF's participation in the Network of ASEAN Defence and Security Initiative (NADI). NADI serves as an informal Track II workshop for analysts and defence officials to discuss perspectives on security matters raised at ASEAN summits and the ADMM, so that these discussions would eventually translate into practical policies on security cooperation among ASEAN member states (S. Rajaratnam School of International Studies, nd). For instance, during the Track II NADI Workshop on Peacekeeping Operations held in October 2010, Lt Col Kamal Idris Johari from the National Defence University Malaysia shared his personal peacekeeping experience in Somalia to rescue US forces trapped at the Bakhara Market. From this experience, he emphasized the importance of practical UN mandates, strong partnerships among peacekeeping forces, effective mission planning backed up by sufficient logistical support as well as strong command, control and communication structures. He added that a peacekeeping force should be sent to conflict zones where there is a lack of political will for affected parties to resolve the conflict (Tan and Tsjeng, 2017, p 78). In another NADI workshop on defence diplomacy, Colonel Johnny Lim who was the Director Policy Research, Malaysian Institute of Defence and Security (MiDAS), explained the importance of defence diplomacy in fostering engagement with regional and global partners as well as cooperation among the militaries of ASEAN to tackle non-traditional security threats (Tan and Tsjeng, 2017, p 333). He noted that Malaysia's experience with peacekeeping and HADR missions can help to build trust leading to the practice of 'one good turn deserves another' to promote reciprocity in meeting complex, non-traditional security challenges (Tan and Tsjeng, 2017, p 334).

Admittedly, the perspectives promulgated during ASEAN Track II fora might not have translated immediately into practical policies. Yet, the track record of the MAF in HADR and peacekeeping has provided valuable inputs into cultivating regional cooperation in MOOTW activities among ASEAN militaries. This display of leadership in peacekeeping and HADR matters at the ASEAN level can be attributed to the transformation of the MAF from its domestic function in supporting the government's KESBAN strategy in the Cold War into a foreign policy instrument from the 1990s onwards. As such, the MAF's role in defence diplomacy conducted at Track II fora also reflected subordination to domestic civilian primacy.

However, civilian leadership over the military did not necessarily result in efficient and effective coordination between civilian and military agencies in handling challenging search and rescue operations. A case in point was the search for Malaysian Airlines flight MH370, which disappeared on 8 March 2014 after departing Kuala Lumpur International Airport en route to Beijing. The BN government, in tandem with the military and other civilian agencies, sought to project leadership and control over Malaysia's response to the tragic situation. However, statements by the Malaysian authorities during press conferences and media briefings on search and rescue efforts were confusing (The Straits Times, 2014; Loh, 2016, pp 560–563). For example, according to local media Malaysian Air Force Chief General Rodzali Daud remarked that the MH370 had turned back on its original flight and reached the Malacca Straits, but this was later refuted by Daud himself (Al-Jazeera,

2014). As a Malaysian defence official admitted, the confusing messages represented shortcomings in organizational and bureaucratic coordination among the civilian and military agencies in coping with this unprecedented and complex search and rescue operation (Grudgings, 2014). Thus, while the search and rescue efforts for the MH370 were haphazardly conducted, this did not represent a significant change in the military's subordination to civilian leadership. Rather, it highlighted bureaucratic and organizational deficiencies that hampered Malaysia's capacity in responding optimally to the MH370 incident.

Democratic transition to PH governance

Despite the unexpected fall of the BN regime in the May 2018 general elections, the MAF showed few signs of posing a significant threat of military coup to undermine the new PH government. As discussed later, the spectre of a coup had not only materialized due to the PH government's continuation of existing civil–military arrangements but also because of democratic reforms to further concretize the professional and apolitical nature of the military.

The likelihood of a coup or other kinds of MAF intervention to preserve the BN regime was never a straightforward and foregone conclusion, due to split positions within the military on domestic politics. According to conventional wisdom, civil servants and military personnel have a tendency to vote for the incumbent government. A study on Malaysia's civil–military relations has claimed that since military personnel are not allowed to visit polling stations to cast their vote but do so through submission of voting forms in the sight of their commanders, they are pressured to vote naturally for the incumbent (Matsuura, 2002, p 29). In March 2018, it was reported that during a function with top leaders in Malaysia's military and security establishments, Prime Minister Najib Razak warned that if the 'wrong leadership' came into power, Malaysian police and troops may lose their jobs, and the Royal Malay Regiment could be disbanded if that new government pushed for a 'Malaysian Malaysia' (Kamarulzaman, 2018a). Ostensibly, Najib was referring to the Mahathir-led PH opposition coalition. Adding to Najib's remarks, the Chief of the Armed Forces reportedly urged the military and police to remain loyal to Najib and his government, since Najib had paid special interests to the security forces (Kamarulzaman, 2018b). However, other senior officers within the military and police had sounded a more neutral tone with regards to whether the security forces should be loyal to Najib's BN government. When former Prime Minister Mahathir Mohamad as the leader of the PH opposition urged the military to help ensure that Malaysians can vote freely without hindrance, for the first time in Malaysia's political history the Chief of Royal Malaysian Navy and the Chief of Police made an unusual gesture of openly calling out their service personnel to vote freely and wisely without interference from external influence (Chew, 2018). These signals from the military seemed to be contrary to the aforementioned study which claims that military personnel are pressured to show endorsement for the incumbent regime. The sentiments of high-ranking officers could be an indicator that at least in the upper echelons of the military, there was no definitive or overwhelming support for the incumbent BN regime.

Although it is debatable whether the military had been under an obligation to endorse the authoritarian BN regime in general elections, or that the military had sympathies towards the opposition coalition, a plausible inference is that the MAF's ideals of being highly professional and apolitical by focusing solely on military and security functions did not prevent civilian attempts to exploit the military for political purposes. As noted previously, existing studies have alluded to the fact that the MAF has had to face some degree of manipulation by civilian leaders through personal linkages and ethnic-based privileges associated with the Malay-oriented leadership of the civilian government, thereby suggesting that civilian leaders had sought to maintain the military's loyalty to the government. Consequently, it is not surprising that there were elements within the MAF's top brass who were strongly against external influence that could lure the MAF to lend support to political groups including opposition parties, as this could undermine the apolitical nature and professionalism of the military (New Straits Times, 2018).

In the aftermath of the general elections in May 2018, the MAF's strong adherence to autonomy from political affairs and professionalism in military roles with minimal involvement in politics was further strengthened under the more democratically oriented PH government. The PH coalition largely preserved the existing civil–military arrangement, while adding on democratic reforms in national defence policies. These reforms sought to introduce transparency and accountability into the dynamics of civil–military relations. As stated in Malaysia's first ever DWP published by the PH government:

> Legitimacy is about government authority, a central element in internal resilience. The DWP, having been deliberated and prepared after extensive consultation across civil–military lines with considerable input from academics, think-tanks, industry representatives, civil society organisations, all components of the government and private sector, reflects a broad spectrum of viewpoints about Malaysian defence including the required functions of the armed forces. Inclusively engaging the public and a wide range of stakeholders in the policy-making process is a fundamental exercise in democracy. It confers a great procedural legitimacy on the DWP and related policies. (Ministry of Defence Malaysia, 2020, p 17)

Overall, the PH government did not overturn the core features of Malaysia's civil–military relations. The brief democratic interlude under the PH coalition did not completely repudiate the *bumiputera* communalism undergirding the socio-cultural ethos of the military. In fact, the PH government was itself a coalition containing elements of Malaysia's longstanding race-based politics that is deeply entrenched in Malay supremacy. Hence, the MAF's support of the PH coalition was still considerably grounded in the continuation of institutional and sociological structures inherited from the era of the preceding BN regime, notwithstanding that there was a degree of democratic augmentation to these internal arrangements.

Malaysia's defence policy in peacekeeping and HADR under the PH government

Under the PH government, the impact of civil–military relations on the MAF's involvement in peacekeeping and HADR possessed both continuities and differences when contrasted with the previous BN regime's approach to defence diplomacy. Specifically, the PH coalition continued to endorse a strong focus on Malaysia's longstanding participation in defence diplomacy in terms of HADR and peacekeeping activities and activism in Track II ASEAN forums. As the PH's Deputy Defence Minister Liew Chin Tong had articulated, the MAF must continue to uphold its strong capacity in HADR functions and peacekeeping to strengthen inter-operability and coordination with other ASEAN states in responding to humanitarian disasters (Liew 2019). Defence Minister Mat Sabu, in his speech at a conference organized by MiDAS on responses to humanitarian disasters, reiterated Malaysia's tradition in peacekeeping and its military's cooperation with civilian agencies in supporting HADR functions in the region (Yusien and Nordin, 2019, pp 3–4). Moreover, Mat Sabu expressed his government's support for ASEAN platforms (for example, ADMM, ADMM-Plus), and the setting up of the ADMM-Plus Experts' Working Groups (EWGs) to strengthen shared inter-operability and coordination among countries for more effective responses in HADR (Yusien and Nordin, 2019, pp 3–4).

Indeed, this continuation in the MAF's defence diplomacy was clearly affirmed in the DWP, which vowed:

> To conduct Military Operations Other Than War (MOOTW) including Humanitarian Assistance and Disaster Relief (HADR), Search and Rescue (SAR) and Non-Combatant Evacuation Operations (NEO) among others, assisting the civil authorities in enforcement, nation building and supporting world peace efforts through the United Nations (UN) Peacekeeping Operations (PKOs). (Ministry of Defence Malaysia, 2020, p 44)

Similar to the emphasis on defence diplomacy through ASEAN multilateral platforms as it had been during the BN era, the DWP made it clear that ASEAN forums promoting regional cooperation in HADR will be a mainstay on how the MAF would offer humanitarian assistance through regional coordination. In particular, the DWP acknowledged Malaysia's role in AMRG on HADR that 'aims to prepare ASEAN military teams for deployment to areas of crises in a quick and coordinated manner', and the EWGs for supporting 'areas of practical cooperation which are maritime security, counterterrorism, HADR, PKOs, military medicine, humanitarian mine action and cyber security' (Ministry of Defence Malaysia, 2020, p 71).

However, while preserving the military's functions in HADR and peacekeeping, the PH government sought to accentuate the military's primary task of protecting 'national interests, particularly to defend national sovereignty and territorial integrity from traditional and non-traditional threats by conducting maritime, air, land and cyber electromagnetic operations' (Ministry of Defence Malaysia, 2020, p 44). Although the MAF's ability to respond to humanitarian disasters and engage in peacekeeping is to be lauded, the military should not be seen as the first resort in response to humanitarian issues (Liew, 2019). This re-prioritization in the MAF's purpose was attributable to the existing external environment which has become more uncertain, not least due to growing tensions in Southeast Asia arising from the increasing China–US rivalry, the South China Sea disputes, rising extremism and the increasing frequency of non-traditional security threats, among others. Not surprisingly, Malaysia's defence posture under the PH government emphasized that the military should be further strengthened in its doctrines and capabilities as part of the overall defence strategy in the midst of these uncertainties.

Yet, the DWP also stated that Malaysia would avoid a full military solution for achieving national security, opting instead for bilateral, regional, and multilateral diplomacy alongside an enhanced Malaysian military to attain this objective. Thus, not unlike the BN regime, the PH government had intended for the MAF's external security role to be subsumed under and remain deferential to the civilian leadership's preference for foreign policy means through diplomatic channels to obtain external security.

Post-PH era: Malaysia's civil–military relations in the COVID-19 world

Although the PH government abruptly collapsed in February 2020, resulting in the formation of the Perikatan Nasional (PN) government helmed by Muhyiddin Yassin, it did not significantly alter the MAF's relationship with the civilian government during political uncertainties and the COVID-19 pandemic. The MAF's domestic presence became more prominent during the pandemic as the PN coalition mobilized the military to provide additional manpower to assist in enforcing the Movement Control Order (MCO) in order to contain the spread of COVID-19. This mobilization triggered local concerns that the MAF could exert undue force and influence to enforce the MCO (The Straits Times, 2020). However, such speculation fails to consider that the increased presence of the military in domestic law enforcement during peacetime is not a novel phenomenon. Instead, the MAF's increased presence in the COVID-19 pandemic appeared to underscore the military's longstanding role in supporting the civilian government's policies to cope with national crises, as can be observed in the military's past efforts in tackling the communist insurgency and enforcing security in the aftermath of the 1969 racial riots. In an allusion to this domestic function, the Chief of Malaysia's Defence Force General Affendi Buang reportedly said that the military's cooperation with the police to enforce the MCO is a secondary duty in peacetime (The Straits Times, 2020).

If this development signals a status quo in the military's subordination to civilian oversight in pursuit of a broader agenda of socio-cultural and economic policies in achieving national security, the deference to civilian authority could remain a fundamental principle underlying the military's functions in peacekeeping and HADR efforts. Even the military's greater emphasis on its war-fighting capacity in recent times should not be interpreted as a turn towards a more military-centric strategy for regional peace and stability. Instead, given the government's penchant for foreign policy to drive regional diplomacy, and if foreign policy decision-making continues to reside firmly in the hands of top civilian leaders, the military's constabulary stance in this diplomacy-driven strategy will remain largely unchanged for the foreseeable future.

Conclusion

This chapter sought to explain how the considerable stability and continuity in the MAF's subordination to civilian leadership have been positively enabling Malaysia to engage actively in defence diplomacy in the areas of HADR and peacekeeping. The military's internal counter-insurgency operations in supporting the government's socio-economic development plans to achieve national security without heavy reliance on military means during the Cold War was highly compatible with Malaysia's foreign policy in the 1990s, which favoured diplomacy over military capacity to obtain external security.

After the end of the counter-insurgency operations against communism in the late 1980s, the civilian government was able to externalize the MAF's domestic security role and transformed the military to perform a constabulary function under foreign policy objectives towards the Southeast Asian region.

Thus, Malaysia's strategic interests and viewpoints at major ASEAN security forums have been largely fronted by civilian leaders who prefer diplomatic means to build regional security cooperation amicably, not least because of the dominance of foreign policy elites in Malaysia's international security outlook. Given the military's experiences and expertise in peacekeeping and HADR efforts, such expertise has been an asset in Malaysia's attempts at leadership during defence diplomacy at Track II fora. During the brief democratic rule of the PH government, there were reforms towards a higher degree of democratic transparency and accountability in defence policy making. There was a re-orientation of the MAF towards strengthening its primary war-fighting objectives in the face of new emerging security challenges in the region. Nevertheless, the PH government's management of the MAF continued to recognize the importance of the military's competence in peacekeeping and HADR efforts.

Although the stability and continuity of the MAF's subordination to the civilian leadership has been instrumental in allowing Malaysia to project leadership in defence diplomacy through peacekeeping and HADR, the frequent domestic political changes in recent times could undermine such a status. The fall of the BN, PH and the PN governments allude to the inherent instability in present-day Malaysian politics and society. Moreover, increasing regional uncertainty could trigger concerns for Malaysia's defence planners. Should there be more drastic political and societal alterations, or serious external security threats and uncertainties leading to the reconfiguration of civil–military relations, it cannot be ruled out that these scenarios could significantly alter Malaysia's approach to defence diplomacy. Even if there were to be no military coups in the future, civil–military relations would still be part and parcel of Malaysia's evolving defence diplomacy.

References

Ahmad, R. (2013) 'Malaysia offers aid to Philippines in wake of Haiyan', *The Star*, [online] 12 November. Available from: www.thestar.com.my/news/nation/2013/11/12/malaysia-ready-to-help-nation-offers-aid-to-philippines-in-wake-of-haiyan [Accessed 8 May 2021].

Ahmad, Z.H. (1985) 'Malaysia', in Z.H. Ahmad and H.A. Crouch (eds.) *Military-Civilian Relations in South-East Asia*, Singapore: Oxford University Press, pp 118–135.

Al-Jazeera (2014) 'Confusion, contradictions mount in search for Flight MH370', Al-Jazeera, [online] 11 March, Available from: http://america.aljazeera.com/articles/2014/3/11/search-for-malaysiaairlinesflighttargetslandhtml [Accessed 25 October 2021].

Andrew, I.M. (2019) 'Capability Management in Defence', *The Journal of Defence and Security*, 10(1): 1–13.

ASEAN (Association of Southeast Asian Nations) (2016) 'Terms of reference ASEAN militaries ready group on humanitarian assistance and disaster relief (AMRG on HADR)', [online] 22 April, Available from: http://mod.gov.la/10thADMM/assets/4.7.1-tor-on-amrg-as-of-20160422.pdf [Accessed 3 April 2021].

Beeson, M. (2000) 'Mahathir and the markets: globalisation and the pursuit of economic autonomy in Malaysia', *Pacific Affairs*, 73(3): 339–43.

Beeson, M. and Bellamy, A. (2008) *Securing Southeast Asia: The Politics of Security Sector Reform*, London and New York: Routledge.

Brooks, R. (2020) 'Paradoxes of professionalism: rethinking civil–military relations in the United States', *International Security,* 44(4): 7–44.

Chew, A. (2018) 'Malaysia's navy, police tell staff free to vote for party of their choice in polls', *Today*, [online] 5 May, Available from: www.channelnewsasia.com/news/asia/malaysia-election-navy-police-tell-staff-free-to-vote-ge14-10205024 [Accessed 18 February 2021].

Cook, A.D.B. and Yogendran, S. (2020) 'Conceptualising humanitarian civil–military partnerships in the Asia-Pacific: (re-)ordering cooperation', *Australian Journal of International Affairs*, 74(1): 35–53.

Daud, M. K. B. (2019) 'Spread of Violent Extremism Ideology in Malaysia: The Islamic State in Iraq and Syria (ISIS) Threat', *The Journal of Defence and Security*, 10(1): 51–63.

Department of Foreign Affairs of the Republic of the Philippines (2013) 'PHL embassy expresses gratitude for assistance from Malaysian government, general public for Yolanda victims', *Department of Foreign Affairs of the Republic of the Philippines*, [online] 14 November, Available from: https://dfa.gov.ph/authentication-functions/148-typhoon-yolanda/1281-phl-embassy-expresses-gratitude-for-assistance-from-malaysian-government-general-public-for-yolanda-victims [Accessed 8 May 2021].

Emmers, R. and Tan, S.S. (2011) 'The ASEAN regional forum and preventive diplomacy: built to fail?', *Asian Security*, 7(1): 44–60.

Feaver, P.D. (2003) *Agency, Oversight, and Civil–Military Relations*, Cambridge, MA, and London: Harvard University Press.

Grudgings, S. (2014) 'Corrected – Malaysia failing credibility test as flight confusion deepens', *Reuters*, [online] 13 March, Available from: www.reuters.com/article/malaysia-airlines-confusion-pictures-gra-idUSL2N0M90JN20140313 [Accessed 23 October 2021].

Haacke, J. (2009) 'The ASEAN regional forum: from dialogue to practical security cooperation?', *Cambridge Review of International Affairs*, 22(3): 427–49.

Huntington, S.P. (1957) *The Soldier and the State: The Theory and Politics of Civil–Military Relations*, Cambridge, MA: Belknap Press of Harvard University Press.

Janowitz, M. (1970) *The Professional Soldier: A Social and Political Portrait: A Social and Political Portrait*, Glencoe, IL: The Free Press.

Jeshurun, C. (1989) 'Civil–military relations and national security in ASEAN', *Pacific Focus*, 4(2): 75–98.

Jeshurun, C. (1994) 'Malaysian defence policy revisited: modernization and rationalization in the post-Cold War era', Southeast Asian Affairs, 1994: 194–206.

Jomo, K.S. (2003) 'Mahathir's economic legacy', *Kyoto Review of Southeast Asia*, [online] nd, Available from: https://kyotoreview.org/issue-4/mahathirs-economic-legacy/ [Accessed 8 April 2021].

Kamarulzaman, Z. (2018a) 'PM: 'Malaysian Malaysia' might spell end of the Malay regiment', *Malaysiakini*, [online] 30 March, Available from: www.malaysiakini.com/news/417805 [Accessed 25 March 2021].

Kamarulzaman, Z. (2018b) 'Be loyal to gov't and PM, Armed Forces chief tells troops and police', *Malaysiakini*, [online] 31 March, Available from: www.malaysiakini.com/news/417824 [Accessed: 25 March 2021].

Liew, C.T. (2019) 'Armed forces the last resort', *New Straits Times*, [online] 7 July, Available from: www.nst.com.my/opinion/columnists/2019/07/502361/armed-forces-last-resort [Accessed 8 May 2021].

Loh, D.M.H. (2016) 'ASEAN's norm adherence and its unintended consequences in HADR and SAR operations', *The Pacific Review*, 29(4): 549–572.

Matsuura, Y. (2002) *Civil Military Relations in Southeast Asia*, MSc Dissertation, Nanyang Technological University.

Ministry of Defence Malaysia (2020) 'Defence White Paper: a secure, sovereign and prosperous Malaysia', *Ministry of Defence Malaysia*, [online] nd, Available from: www.mod.gov.my/images/mindef/article/kpp/DWP-3rd-Edition-02112020.pdf [Accessed 13 May 2020].

Ministry of Foreign Affairs of Malaysia (no date) 'Strengthening the UN peacekeeping operations', *Ministry of Foreign Affairs of Malaysia*, [online] nd, Available from: http://malaysiaunsc.kln.gov.my/index.php/malaysia-at-the-unsc/malaysia-s-commitment/strengthening-the-un-peacekeeping-operations [Accessed 25 March 2021].

Nathan, K.S. and Govindasamy, G. (2001) 'Malaysia: a congruence of interests', in M. Alagappa (ed) *The Declining Political Role of the Military in Asia*, Stanford, CA: Stanford University Press, pp 275–95.

New Straits Times (2018) 'Malaysia's navy, police tell staff free to vote for party of their choice in polls', *New Straits Times*, [online] 4 May, Available from: www.nst.com.my/news/politics/2018/05/365676/my-statement-has-been-twisted-navy-chief-call-vote-remarks [Accessed 18 February 2021].

Reliefweb (2005a) 'Malaysia to proceed with humanitarian aid in Aceh', *Reliefweb*, [online] 17 January, Available from: https://reliefweb.int/report/indonesia/malaysia-proceed-humanitarian-aid-aceh [Accessed 8 May 2021].

Reliefweb (2005b) 'Indonesia says troops from ASEAN countries welcome in Aceh', *Reliefweb*, [online] 17 January, Available from: https://reliefweb.int/report/indonesia/indonesia-says-troops-asean-countries-welcome-aceh [Accessed 8 May 2021].

Saravanamuttu, J. (1996) 'Malaysia's foreign policy in the Mahathir Period, 1981–1995: an iconoclast come to rule', *Asian Journal of Political Science*, 4(1): 1–16.

Saravanamuttu, J. (2003) 'Iconoclasm and foreign policy – the Mahathir years', in B. Welsh (ed) *Reflections: The Mahathir Years*, Washington DC: Southeast Asia Studies Program, Johns Hopkins University-SAIS, pp 307–17.

Sarkesian, S.C. (1981) 'Military professionalism and civil–military relations in the West', *International Political Science Review/ Revue Internationale de Science Politique*, 2(3): 283–97.

Simon, S.W. (2010) 'Southeast Asian international relations: is there institutional traction?' in N. Ganesan and R. Amer (eds) *International Relations in Southeast Asia: Between Bilateralism and Multilateralism*, Singapore: ISEAS–Yusof Ishak Institute, pp 37–68.

Soon, R. (2018) 'Refuge for the refugees: a military pharmacist on serving the Rohingya of Cox's Bazar, Bangladesh', *MIMS*, [online] 12 December, Available from: https://specialty.mims.com/topic/refuge-for-the-refugees-manvikram-singh-gill [Accessed 8 May 2021].

S. Rajaratnam School of International Studies (nd) 'NADI: Track II network of ASEAN defence and security institutions', *S. Rajaratnam School of International Studies* [online] nd, Available from: www.rsis.edu.sg/nadi/ [Accessed 8 May 2021].

Storey, I. (2020) 'Malaysia and the South China Sea dispute: policy continuity amid domestic political change', *ISEAS Perspective*, 2020(18): 1–10.

Tan, S.S. (2012) '"Talking their walk"? The evolution of defense regionalism in Southeast Asia', *Asian Security*, 8(3): 232–50.

Tan, S.S. (2017) 'Providing for the other: rethinking sovereignty and responsibility in Southeast Asia', *Critical Studies on Security*, 5(3): 270–86.

Tan, S.C. and Tsjeng, Z.Z. (eds) (2017) *Track II Network of ASEAN Defence and Security Institutions (NADI): Commemorating 10 Years of NADI*, Singapore: S. Rajaratnam School of International Studies.

The Daily Star (2021) 'Rohingya crisis: Bangladesh hopes Malaysia will play instrumental role in ASEAN summit', *The Daily Star*, [online] 13 April, Available from: www.thedailystar.net/rohingya-crisis/news/rohingya-crisis-bangladesh-hopes-malaysia-will-play-instrumental-role-asean-summit-2077149 [Accessed 8 May 2021].

The Star (2010) 'Malaysia to send military personnel to Afghanistan', *The Star*, [online] 15 July, Available from: www.thestar.com.my/news/nation/2010/07/15/malaysia-to-send-military-personnel-to-afghanistan [Accessed 1 April 2021].

The Straits Times (2014) 'Lost: untold stories of MH370: Chapter three: Controlling the chaos', *The Straits Times*, [online] nd, Available from: https://graphics.straitstimes.com/STI/STIMEDIA/2014/mh370-special/chapter3.html [Accessed 23 October 2021].

The Straits Times (2020) 'Coronavirus: army patrols Malaysian streets as cases spike', *The Straits Times*, [online] 22 March, Available from: www.straitstimes.com/asia/se-asia/coronavirus-malaysian-soldiers-on-streets-to-assist-cops-in-enforcing-movement-curbs [Accessed 23 October 2021].

The White House, Office of the Press Secretary (2014) 'Joint statement by President Obama and Prime Minister Najib of Malaysia', *The White House*, [online] 27 April, Available from: www.whitehouse.gov/the-press-office/2014/04/27/joint-statement-president-obama-and-prime-minister-najib-malaysia-0 [Accessed 31 March 2021].

Yadi, M.Z. (2004) *Malaysia Emergencies: Anthropological Factors in the Success of Malaysia's Counterinsurgency*, MSc thesis, Monterey, CA: Naval Post Graduate School.

Yusien, M.A.A. and Nordin, N.A.B.M. (2019) 'Humanitarian assistance and disaster relief: a shared responsibility', *MiDAS-KAS Conference 2019, Kuala Lumpur, Malaysia, August 27–28*, [online] nd, Available from: www.kas.de/documents/272088/272137/MiDAS-KAS+conference+report+2019.pdf/c3a9dad4-8874-d94c-f87e-f73ab5df1e7a?version=1.0&t=1580887852215 [Accessed 23 February 2021].

7

The Architecture and Evolution of Civil–Military Relations in Vietnam

Alexander L. Vuving

States have to rely on military force as their *ultima ratio*, but how does the state ensure the loyalty of the 'ultimate arbiter of power'? The overwhelming answer in the literature is civilian control of the military. Yet Vietnam's solution is different. Organized as a Leninist state, it keeps its armed forces loyal through political control. Unlike civilian control, which implies a zero-sum game between the state and its military, political control is a reciprocal mechanism based on the mutual embeddedness of the armed forces in the Communist Party and of the Party in the armed forces. This architecture characterizes the relationship between Vietnam's ruling Communist Party (VCP) and its armed forces, which include the military and the police.

The mutual embeddedness of the state and its military manifests itself in a host of organizational devices such as the institution of the political commissar in every military unit, the mechanisms of political–ideological work in the military and the representation of the military in key policy making bodies, giving rise to both the politicization of the military and the involvement of the military in policy making. These aspects have evolved significantly and yet, mutual embeddedness has remained constant throughout the history of Communist Vietnam. This constant – political control of the military through mutual embeddedness of the military and the ruling party – is probably the architectural kernel of the Leninist state.

With these main arguments, this chapter will outline the architecture of civil–military relations in Vietnam and trace the evolution of its constituents since the country was reunified in 1975. After a brief discussion of the origins of civil–military relations in Communist Vietnam, I will examine how the state controls the military and how the military influences politics. Finally, I will address the evolution of the military's missions and the military's attitude toward modernization and democratization.

Origins

The military in today's Vietnam – the Vietnam People's Army (VPA) – traces its roots to the armed teams that operated under the guidance of the Communist Party in the struggle against French colonialism and Japanese occupation during World War Two (Ministry of National Defence, 2019, p 72). Although they engaged in battles soon after their formation, their main mission was propaganda, not armed combat. Indeed, their name was 'Vietnam Propaganda Unit of the Liberation Army' (*Doi Viet Nam Tuyen truyen Giai phong Quan*). Under direct supervision of the Party, these armed teams followed the Party's philosophy of revolutionary struggle, which, bearing the mark of Mao Zedong's ideology, was articulated by Party leader Ho Chi Minh as follows: 'Political action is more important than military action; propaganda is more important than fighting' (Pike, 1986, p 31).

The Propaganda Unit was soon merged with other armed groups to form the main military force of the Vietnam Independence League (*Viet Minh*), the front organization of the Communist Party that would seize power in Vietnam at the end of World War Two. These rural groups were the initial cells from which the new state's military was organized. With the new state's presence in the urban centres, urban youth joined the new military, bringing with them new knowledge and organizational skills. One of the skills brought in by the urban youth that had a significant impact on the new military is that of the Boy Scouts. By the end of 1945, the new state was able to raise a military – the Vietnam National Army – of about 50,000 troops, organized into 40 units. In 1950, as the Viet Minh-ruled state openly took the Communist side in the global conflict against the West, its military was renamed the Vietnam People's Army. It is in the early 1950s that the first divisions of the VPA were established. The military continued to wage both guerrilla and conventional warfare under the general concept of a 'people's war'. When the VPA defeated French troops at Dien Bien Phu (1954), its military leadership did not work separately from the Party's political leadership. The Vietnamese victory owed much to the superb logistics led and mobilized by the party-state and carried out by civilians, including women and children. Dien Bien Phu was the result, to use the parlance of today, of a 'whole-of-government' and 'whole-of-society' approach.

In the subsequent decades, the VPA underwent tremendous changes. One author argued that the nature of civil–military relations in Communist Vietnam evolved from 'fused' (1944–54) to 'symbiotic' (1954–82) to 'coalitional' (1983–93) within the overarching ethos of the Revolutionary

Professional Soldier (Walker, 1994). According to Perlmutter and LeoGrande (1982, pp 778–89), this Revolutionary Professional Soldier is the ethos of civil–military relations in states organized in the Leninist way, which presupposes a hegemonic Marxist–Leninist party that views itself as the vanguard of society. The VPA has evolved enormously under the influence of changing circumstances and the people that joined and led it, but one big thing remained constant. As Pike (1986, p 145) noted: 'Within the People's Army of Vietnam [PAVN] is, as there has been, the party. Known by various names over the years, the Vietnamese Communist Party inside PAVN is the steel rod in a ferro-concrete building, the ever-present goading conscience, an eternal looming specter.' This constant – the Communist Party's dominance in the military – is only one side of a larger coin; the other side of the same coin is the military's involvement in politics. It is this mutual embeddedness and not solely the dominance of the Party in the military that characterizes the architecture of civil–military relations in Vietnam.

How the party controls the military

Politics in Vietnam is organized along Leninist lines and the military works within the confines of the Communist political system. Central among these parameters is the principle of the Communist Party's vanguard role that produces in practice a political system in which the Party is the absolute sovereign (Perlmutter and LeoGrande, 1982, pp 779, 786). Although the Party formally acknowledges that all powers should come from the people, it claims to be the only group that is able to represent, articulate, protect and advance the true interests and aspirations of the people. As Perlmutter and LeoGrande (1982, pp 781, 788) have noted: 'The primacy of party authority is the norm within which virtually all military participation in politics takes place.' When the military 'intervenes' in politics, 'it intervenes on behalf of the party, upholding the hegemony of one party faction over the other'.[1]

In Communist political systems civil–military relations are therefore not a zero-sum game as the concept of civilian control implies. The zero-sum perspective is either implicit or explicit in most of the literature on civil–military relations, whose normative foundations are derived from the ideological premises of liberal democracy.[2] The concept of civilian control as generated by this literature is not useful and often misleading when applied to the case of Vietnam. In Vietnam the military's political role is both legitimate and important for the survival of the Communist Party's hegemony. The military is the guardian and saviour of the Party; it fights for the Party's supremacy, not for its own supremacy. Its politicization, political influence and involvement are the *sine qua non* for upholding the Party's power.

This does not mean, however, that the core issue underlying civil–military relations ceases to exist in Communist states. On the contrary, that issue continues to inform civil–military interactions under Communist Party rule, and the military's political influence and 'interference' are just some of the major manifestations of the way the Party copes with that issue. The core issue underlying civil–military relations is how to create a military strong enough to protect its civilian master but at the same time loyal enough to civilian authority.[3] The democratic solution is a professional and apolitical military that refrains from interfering in politics. The Communist – or more precisely, Leninist – solution is, contrarily, a highly politicized and indoctrinated military.[4] 'Party control' and 'political control' are better terms than 'civilian control' in characterizing the way the military in a Communist political system is controlled by its master.

Vietnam's Leninist state controls its soldiers through ideological indoctrination and a host of organizational devices. First, it imbues the military with an ideology that worships the Communist Party as the absolute sovereign. Reflecting this ideology, for example, the main conference room of the National Defence Ministry in Hanoi is decorated with portraits of the former Communist Party chiefs, not the former heads of state (see the pictures in Tran Thuong, 2020). The indoctrination is one of the central tasks of political work, which is the main job of the political commissars and the military's General Political Directorate but carried out by all military officers. Political commissars and their line organization in the military, the General Political Directorate, are responsible for educational, ideological, organizational and personnel matters in the military. Second, the military elite is a dual elite – all military officers of consequence are concurrently members of the Communist Party. This dual role of the military elite ensures that military officers also take command from higher echelons in the Party hierarchy and are subject to Party inspection and discipline. Third, the political penetration of the military is built in the military organization through key structures such as the Party committee and the political commissar system. All these devices are to bring into practice the idea of subordination of the military to the political, which is central to the Communist Party's relations with its armed forces. In an article explaining Party policy, then Lieutenant General Ngo Xuan Lich, head of the General Political Directorate, who would later become Minister of Defence, noted that throughout the history of the VPA, the VCP has always emphasized the primacy of politics over military affairs. He quoted President Ho Chi Minh as saying 'politics is more important than military affairs' and 'military tasks should be subordinated to political tasks' in all activities of the VPA (Ngo Xuan Lich, 2011). In a more recent interview with the Party's central newspaper, Le Kha Phieu, who was the chief political commissar of the military prior to becoming VCP General Secretary, emphasized:

the Party's absolute, direct, and comprehensive leadership of the armed forces is an unchanging and consistent principle throughout the development of Vietnam's revolution and the decisive factor of all successes, which ensures that the armed forces are increasingly mature and strong and successfully complete its historical mission for the nation. (Le Kha Phieu, 2019)

The primacy of politics is reflected in the fact that the political commissar and the commander are two paramount officers in a military unit. A 'two-boss system' (*che do hai thu truong*) with the commander and the political commissar equally supreme in a military unit was replaced in the late 1970s by a 'one-commander system' (*che do mot nguoi chi huy*), in which the political commissar system was abolished and the unit commander became the single top officer (Vasavakul, 2001, pp 342–4). However, the political commissar system was restored in the mid–1990s, with the political commissar being the deputy commander in charge of political affairs. In 2005, the VCP Politburo issued Resolution No 51 endorsing a hybrid regime that amalgamated the one-commander system with the political commissar system. In this regime, the political commissar is responsible for political affairs, while the commander is responsible for professional matters. More importantly, both are equal in rank and their relationship is defined as one of coordination, not subordination (Nguyen Van Nghien, 2010). Party control is further ensured by the subordination of both chief officers as well as the entire unit to a higher command of the unit's Party committee, which is usually led by the political commissar but works according to the principle of collective leadership.

Political control of the military in Vietnam is characterized by the mutual embeddedness of the Party and the military. This pattern exists at all levels of both military and state organization. At the highest level, the entire armed forces are placed under the supreme command of the Central Military Commission (CMC), which is an organ of the Communist Party rather than of the state administration. The head ('Secretary') of the CMC is by statute the VCP General Secretary, while his deputy is the Minister of Defence. The 'standing commissioners' (*uy vien thuong vu*) include the State President, the Prime Minister, the Head of the VPA General Political Directorate, the Chief of the VPA General Staff and a Deputy Minister of Defence. At the local (provincial and district) levels, the military is placed under the command of the local Party committee, while the local military commander is a member of the local government and the local Party committee. These are the main formal channels through which the Party controls its armed forces at the local levels.

The backbone of this mutual embeddedness is the dual elite between Party and military, which, as Perlmutter and LeoGrande (1982, p 782) have noted, 'is both the source of the military's politicization and the guarantor of party supremacy'. This dual elite acts both as the Party's agent in the military and the military's agent in the Party. Contrary to the perspective of the 'civilian control' discourse of the dominant civil–military relations paradigm, military involvement in politics under the Communist political system is neither illegal nor unusual; rather, it is a routine activity and a prerequisite of 'normal politics'. The 'party in uniform', as Perlmutter and LeoGrande call the military in the Communist political system, is *obliged* to participate in politics. The military constantly plays a role in politics not just because it wants to but primarily because it ought to. The question is not whether the military is involved in politics but rather how it is involved, to what extent and for what purpose. Another implication of political control and mutual embeddedness as the architecture of civil–military relations in Vietnam's Leninist state is that, as will be shown in the next sections, the military is not a self-interested actor but rather a strategic resource. The military is not a unified faction in Party politics. Rather, it is a strategic resource that various Party factions in and outside the military may employ in their struggle for power.

Military representation in policy making

The military's involvement in policy making is formally channelled via the representation of the military in the country's policy making bodies. The highest-level policy making bodies in Vietnam include the Politburo, the Secretariat and the Central Committee of the VCP. Members of these bodies have the final word on all major decisions and policies involving all facets of life in the country. These also include decisions and policies regarding the selection and placement of the elites themselves. As a key branch of the Party, the military is reserved a number of seats on the Politburo, the Secretariat and the Central Committee. The size of military representation is, however, not predetermined and is subject to decision by the Party leadership. As a result, while military representation in policy making bodies is guaranteed, its actual size is a matter of intense bargaining among the Party elites.

Military representation in the VCP's leadership since the end of the Vietnam War in 1975 exhibits several interesting trends (see Table 7.1). The share of the military in the Central Committee dropped sharply from 16.5 per cent at the 4th Party Congress in 1976 to 11.8 per cent at the 5th Congress in 1982 and remained between 9.3 per cent and 12.4 per cent throughout the decades that followed. During these years, the military possessed on average 10.5 per cent of the seats on the Central Committee, which is in some sense equivalent to the parliament in a democracy.

The 4th Party Congress was the first after three decades of war (1946–75), which dominated the history of modern Vietnam. The larger number of military members in the 4th Central Committee can be explained by the

Table 7.1: Military representation on the VCP Politburo and Central Committee, 1976–2021

Period	Congress	Politburo		Central Committee**	
		Mil rep/Total	%	Mil rep/Total	%
1976–1982	4th	3/14	21.4	22/133	16.5
1982–1986	5th	3/14	21.4	18/152	11.8
1986–1991	6th	1+1*/12	16.7	19/173	11.0
1991–1994	7th	1+1*/13	15.4	14/146	9.6
1994–1996	Mid-term Conference	2+1*/17	17.6	15/161	9.3
1996–2001	8th	3+1*/19-1†	22.2	21/170-1†	12.4
2001–2006	9th	1/15	6.7	14/150	9.3
2006–2011	10th	1/14+1†	(7.1; 6.7) 6.9	18/181	9.9
2011–2016	11th	1/14+2†	(7.1; 6.3) 6.8	21/200	10.5
2016–2021	12th	1/19-3†	(5.3; 6.3) 5.9	22/200	11.0
2021–2026	13th	2/18	11.1	23/200	11.5
Average	1976–1986		21.4		14.2
Average	1991–2001		19.2		10.9
Average	1986–2021		11.6		10.5
Average	1976–2021		13.8		11.3

Notes:
* Retired VPA general
† Politburo members elected *post mortem* at a Party Congress or not serving full tenure
** Including full and alternate members (alternate membership was abolished from the 7th until the 9th Congress)
Sources: Author's database and Nguyen Huu Tri and Nguyen Thi Phuong Hong, 2004, p 121

hot legacies of the war that had just ended a year before, while the lower share of the military afterward reflects the new strategic priorities that Vietnam adopted in a time of peace. These numbers also indicate that in the post-war era the VCP has managed to keep the military share of its Central Committee relatively stable and at a relatively reasonable level (Thayer, 2011). The military share peaked with the 8th Central Committee (1996–2001) at 12.4 per cent, a figure higher than even that of the 5th Central Committee (1982–86), which presided over two concurrent wars, one in Cambodia and another along the Sino-Vietnamese border. With 10 per cent higher than the average level of the post-war period (11.3 per cent), this figure clearly indicates the rise of military influence in the 1990s.

The ascent of military representation in policy making can be seen clearer still in the makeup of the top Party leadership, the Politburo. For one decade after the Vietnam War the VPA was accorded three of the 14 seats on the Politburo. When the 6th Party Congress launched *doi moi* in 1986, it created a new, informal rule that the VPA is represented by a single Politburo member and this person is the Minister of Defence. The reform programme introduced a radically new economic and foreign policy that shifted the strategic orientation from international confrontation to international integration. Economic development received the highest priority in this reform programme (Nguyen Co Thach, 1990). Still, the military managed to gain more influence than what the new norm suggested. On the 6th Politburo, beside the Minister of Defence (General Le Duc Anh), there was a retired general (Dong Si Nguyen), whose networks, power base and career lay mainly in the military. Nguyen served on the Politburo as a Deputy Prime Minister. The pattern of an active duty and a retired general as two Politburo members with primarily military backgrounds not only survived the 7th Party Congress in 1991 but was even augmented at the Mid-Term Party Conference in 1994, where the number of active duty military officers in the Politburo was lifted to two. From 1991 until 1997 the retired general in the Politburo (Le Duc Anh) assumed the post of State President. In 1996, the 8th Party Congress increased the number of Politburo members who were active duty military officers to three. It also enlarged the size of the Politburo to 19 members. Significantly, as many as four military men sat on the Politburo (three in active duty and one retired) during 1996–98 with a retired general, Le Kha Phieu, being the top leader of the VCP from 1997 until 2001. With the fall of Phieu at the 9th Party Congress in 2001 the number of military members in the Politburo returned to one and remained so until the end of the 12th Central Committee's term. The Central Committee elected at the 13th Congress in 2021 broke this informal rule and placed two active duty military officers on the Politburo. At the same time, it refused to promote the hero of Vietnam's battle against COVID-19, Deputy Prime Minister Vu Duc Dam, to the Politburo. This indicates that the Party prefers to rely on coercion rather than legitimacy to maintain power.

It is worth noting two contradictory trends in post-unification Vietnam. During 1979–89, when Vietnam was waging two wars, in Cambodia and along the Sino-Vietnamese border, military representation in the principal policy making bodies experienced a steady decrease. Equally counterintuitively, military influence made a rapid rise during 1989–2001, when the country no longer had any armed conflicts with foreign countries. What explains the military's ascendency in the 1990s? This rise appears to have resulted from the combination of two major factors interacting in the context of the architecture of civil–military relations in a Leninist state.

The first factor is the quest for power of a military faction led by General Le Duc Anh, who entered the Politburo at the 5th Party Congress as the commander of the Vietnamese expeditionary force in Cambodia.

Significantly, his Politburo membership broke the rule that the military bloc is represented on the Politburo by its three most senior officers – the Minister of Defence, the Head of the General Political Department (the military's chief political commissar) and the Chief of the General Staff. Were the rule respected, General Le Trong Tan, then Chief of the General Staff, would be a Politburo member.[5] The clue for this irregularity can be found in the biographies of key leaders. The person in charge of recommending candidates for the Politburo was Le Duc Tho, the powerful head of the VCP Organization Department. Tho and Anh had worked closely in Cambodia and Anh was Tho's successor as head of the Vietnamese Advisory Corps there. Anh succeeded Tan as Chief of the General Staff and then became Minister of Defence after the sudden and mysterious deaths in 1986 of Tan and Hoang Van Thai, two widely respected generals who ranked higher than Anh in the military hierarchy. Both General Thai and General Tan died shortly after they were picked as the next Minister of Defence (Huy Duc, 2012a, pp 360–62). Thai and Tan had worked closely with General Vo Nguyen Giap throughout their career and the three were known as 'intellectual generals' as opposed to 'political generals' in the VPA. However, Giap's disadvantage was that both VCP General Secretary Le Duan and Le Duc Tho considered him their main rival in the Party (Huy Duc, 2012b, pp 135–80). Although not a 'political general' himself, Anh sided with the regime conservatives, of which Tho was a leading figure, against the 'intellectuals' in the military and the modernizers in the Party at large.

The second factor leading to the rise of the military is the psychological effect of the collapse of Communist regimes in Eastern Europe. During 1989 popular protests brought down four decades of Communist Party rule in Eastern European countries one after another. Earlier in the year, large-scale protests were also held in China but met with a bloody crackdown by the army. Anti-Westerners in the VCP thought that these protests were incited by Western propaganda and spies. Interpreting the changes in Eastern Europe as a 'peaceful evolution' directed by 'imperialists' led by the United States to eliminate Communist Party rule, anti-Westerners believed that the Communist regime was fatally threatened by the West. The collapse of Communism in Eastern Europe helped redefine Vietnam's political landscape. A new cleavage emerged between anti-Westerners and modernizers. By late 1989 VCP General Secretary Nguyen Van Linh, who was regarded by most as the lead reformer in the previous period, became a premier figure of the anti-Western camp. The other leading anti-Western voice was Defence Minister Le Duc Anh, who had emerged as a main critic of the new foreign and security policy adopted by reformers two years before (Tran Quang Co, 2003). The leading modernizers included Foreign Minister Nguyen Co Thach, Deputy Prime Minister Vo Van Kiet, who would become prime minister in 1991, and senior Politburo member Tran

Xuan Bach. Like Thach and Kiet, General Vo Nguyen Giap was also a deputy prime minister and a prominent modernizer (Vuving, 2013). Intriguingly, however, both Thach and Bach were initially Tho's protégés.

Led by Anh, anti-Westerners in the military played a crucial role in the campaign against modernizers, who were sympathetic with modernization, democratization, and international opening. At the 8th Plenum of the 6th Central Committee in March 1990 Bach was dismissed from the Politburo and the Central Committee for his advocacy of 'political pluralism' while anti-Westerners prevailed over modernizers. In the run-up to the 7th Party Congress scheduled for 1991, General Giap emerged as a possible candidate for a prominent role in the Party's next leadership. He was respected by both China and the West. With his wide popularity in the military, the population and internationally, his background in the military and expertise gained from his tenure as vice-premier in charge of science and technology, he was seen by many in the Party as the ideal candidate for the next general secretary in a time when economic development, national defence and international peace were the highest priorities. A few months before the 7th Party Congress, however, Giap fell victim to a plot made by a group of military intelligence officers with close ties to Anh. The conspiracy was later revealed and known as the 'Sau Su Affair'. They fabricated testimonies by an agent named 'Sau Su' slandering Giap, Senior Lieutenant General Tran Van Tra, and some other senior military officers to deceive the Central Committee, making Giap a suspect person and eliminating his chances of remaining in the leadership (Huy Duc, 2012b, pp 135–41).

The two years from 1989 to 1991 was a time of hot debates within the Party over ideology, international friends and foes as well as grand strategy. It was also a period of intense power struggle between factions and leaders within the VCP (Huy Duc, 2012b; Vuving, 2013). Anh and Prime Minister Do Muoi forged an alliance against the reformers and, with the critical support of incumbent Party chief Nguyen Van Linh, emerged victorious at the 7th Party Congress. The Congress set up a new leadership configuration in which Muoi was the Party general secretary, Anh the state president, and Kiet the prime minister. Unprecedentedly, Anh assumed the authority of a Politburo member in charge of defence, security and foreign affairs, which oversaw these areas in the entire political system. During his tenure as state president (1992–97), Anh was able to promote his close associates to leading positions in the military and the Party. Most significantly, Lieutenant General Le Kha Phieu, who had worked under Anh in Cambodia, rose rapidly to general secretary of the VCP within four years in the Politburo, a record speed.[6] Lieutenant General Pham Van Tra, who had been Anh's subordinate for many years in the 9th Military Region and in Cambodia, became minister of defence, a post he held from 1997 until 2006, after only two years as chief of the general staff, also a record tempo.

The fall of Phieu at the 9th Party Congress in 2001 exhibits a similar pattern of how the military gains and loses influence. As Phieu was appointed general secretary of the VCP, Anh, Muoi and Kiet were promoted to senior advisors of the Central Committee, a post that allowed them to participate in the Politburo meetings and thus interfere with their work. In an attempt to consolidate his power, Phieu ordered the VPA General Department for Defence Intelligence (widely known as General Department II) to spy on the senior advisors and other Politburo members. As soon as Anh and Muoi knew of the intrigue, they started an intraparty campaign to unseat Phieu – and succeeded (Koh, 2001; Huy Duc, 2012b, pp 328–59; Thayer, 2003). Ironically, Anh and Muoi's successful coup against Phieu also marked the crumbling of their factions and put an end to the rise of the military.

As shown in this section, while formally accorded bloc representation on the Party leadership, the military is not a cohesive group that acts on the basis of its common interests and corporate identity. Given General Giap's immense prestige and the presence of modernizers within the military establishment, it is hard to say that the Le Duc Anh faction represented the military. Given the nature of civil–military relations in the party-state, the VPA is far from a unitary actor. Rather, it is available as a strategic coercive resource for different Party factions and leaders in and outside the military to mobilize for their own purposes. In the post-Cold War period, a network of officers led by General Anh was able to dominate the military's political engagement. This network gave rise to a powerful faction within the Party, which brought Phieu to the top post in the Party. After this faction broke up with the fall of Phieu in 2001, the military continued to be a mighty power base for some Party factions. During General Phung Quang Thanh's two terms as minister of defence (2006–16), he was able to build a network of officers that engaged deeply in rent-seeking activities. Empowered by a conducive environment in Vietnam's 'market Leninist' system, these rent-seeking activities commercialize the military's privileges for personal benefits. By 2016, Thanh's network was one of the biggest rent-seeking networks in the country, comparable with those led by then Prime Minister Nguyen Tan Dung and Ho Chi Minh City Party boss Le Thanh Hai (Vuving, 2019).

Military involvement in politics

Although military representation in policy making bodies is the formal channel of military involvement in Vietnam's politics, the scope of the involvement does not reflect the size of the representation. During the pre-1989 period, when Vietnamese politics was dominated by the First, Second, and Third Indochina Wars, the military played a role mainly on the frontline of the wars. Its role and involvement enlarged significantly in the post-1989 period when Vietnam no longer engaged in warfare. Behind this enlargement is the argument that the Communist regime faces an existential threat in the form of a 'peaceful evolution' from all kinds of 'reactionary forces' ranging from the United States and the West to Vietnamese dissidents, democracy activists, and even liberals within the regime. However, it was the quest for power (and resources) of the Le Duc Anh faction that gave the military an extensive role in both external relations and domestic politics. As seen in the previous section, this faction helped to secure the prevalence of anti-Westerners over modernizers during the pivotal time following the Cold War's end. The dominance of anti-Westernism in turn helped leaders of this faction to occupy powerful positions in the party-state.

Military influence was most extensive during Le Duc Anh's presidency (1991–97) and Le Kha Phieu's time as Party chief (1997–2000). It was an unprecedented period when this faction was able to shape Vietnam's foreign policy to a large extent and to assume a large role in domestic spying. Minister of Defence Le Duc Anh's secret meeting with the Chinese ambassador to Hanoi in June 1990 marked the first time when the military took a leading role in steering Vietnamese foreign policy (Tran Quang Co, 2003). Consistently with Party control but contrarily to normal procedures, it was conducted with the support of Party chief Nguyen Van Linh while sidelining the Foreign Ministry. Subsequently, Anh played a key role in the renormalization of Sino-Vietnamese relations. When he was in charge of foreign affairs, he used the VCP External Affairs Department to sideline the state-to-state channels of the Ministry of Foreign Affairs, including the Vietnamese Embassy in Beijing, to communicate with China. Under Anh's presidency the political core of Sino-Vietnamese relations was largely reduced to a party-to-party, at times even person-to-person relationships. After Anh's retirement, Phieu and General Department II continued to prefer informal and personalized ways in relations with China. Their manners and messages in communicating with China certainly gained them special treatment by Beijing. They became the senior officials who could work with China most easily, and this has enhanced their value in Vietnam's relations with the giant neighbour. While military involvement through the Anh faction facilitated much of Sino-Vietnamese relations, it presented a major obstacle to Vietnam's regional integration and cooperation with the West. For example, Anh and Phieu played a key role in delaying Vietnam's accession to ASEAN and a landmark Bilateral Trade Agreement with the United States during the 1990s (Huy Duc, 2012b, pp 270–7, 334–50). Today, the military remains a bulwark against the West within the Vietnamese party-state. The military's domestic spying was justified by the threat of peaceful evolution. The arrest of Nguyen Thai Nguyen, an aide to Prime Minister Phan Van Khai, revealed that General Department II (the military intelligence agency) had obtained the prerogatives to place their agents in state agencies deemed relevant to national security.

Partly due to the rise of military influence and the efforts of the Anh faction, the VPA's mission in the post-Cold War era was extended to include areas traditionally reserved for domestic security agencies. The military's primary role was redefined in the aftermath of the fall of communism in Eastern Europe to include the defence of the regime in addition to the defence of the country (Thayer, 2011, p 68). In fact, defence of the regime was given highest priority by anti-Westerners who dominated the VPA, and this has effectively shifted much of the military's focus to domestic security. After the 'peak time' of the Anh faction (1991–2000), the VPA's role in domestic security continues to be most extensive in ideological–political work and riot control.

The military takes the lead in designing and conducting the national programme of defence and security education for high school and university students, government officials, community leaders and religious dignities (Thayer, 2011, pp 78–9; Thuy Linh, 2011). The VPA also tries to influence society through the mass media (Thayer, 2011, pp 78–9). Defence and security education has become compulsory to large segments in the society including high school and college students and government employees. Completing a course of defence and security education provided by the National Defence Academy is a prerequisite for promotion of upper middle- and high-ranking government officials.

In dealing with unrests, as Thayer (2011, p 74) notes: 'The VPA has been very circumspect [...] about involving itself in direct confrontation with the public, preferring to see the Minister of Public Security's armed police to take the lead role in dealing with public protests, riots and violent demonstrations.' However, troops were reportedly sent to quell all major riots such as the Thai Binh unrests during 1997, the Montagnard uprisings in the Central Highlands during the late 1990s and early 2000s, and the Muong Nhe Hmong mass protests in 2011. Army troops were also involved in pacification projects after execution of security operations (Thayer, 2011, pp 74–5). The unprecedented deployment of the military to help maintain law and order during a COVID-19 lock-down in Ho Chi Minh City in the fall of 2021 was reportedly to prevent riots.

While the aforementioned troops were deployed by the central government, the subordination of local military units to local Party bosses in the provincial government has sometimes led to abuse of military force and troops by local authorities. In one prominent instance, local military troops, militia, and even border guards, alongside the police, were deployed to crush farmers' resistance to land grabs by provincial and district authorities in Tien Lang, Hai Phong. The incident sparked outrage nationwide, with former State President Le Duc Anh and retired Lieutenant General Nguyen Quoc Thuoc weighing in against the use of troops for such purposes. Echoing the popular sentiment, General Anh argued that 'troops have the only mission of defending the Fatherland, fighting invaders, and protecting sovereignty and territory; deploying troops to force citizens in land issues is not allowed' (Ngoc Quang, 2012). As troops' loyalty to Party leadership was of utmost importance to the party-state, no public punishment of the local authorities for the abuse of the troops was announced.

The missions of the military

Like other parts of Vietnam's political system, the military is assigned, in the jargon of the VCP, 'two strategic tasks: building and protecting the socialist Fatherland', which constitute the long-term mission of the party-state. The military is expected to contribute to both because the two are closely intertwined, but as the ultimate coercive resource, it is a key tool of the state in 'protecting the socialist Fatherland'. The concept of 'Fatherland protection' has evolved in the post-Cold War period to include a wide spectrum of objectives ranging from 'firmly safeguarding the country's independence, security, sovereignty, and territorial integrity, protecting the people, the Party, and the socialist regime' to the 'protection of the cause of renovation, industrialization and modernization' and the 'protection of national culture' (Vuving, 2016, p 96). The all-inclusive nature of this concept reflects less the adoption of the internationally popular concept of comprehensive security than the jockeying for importance of different sectors and factions within the party-state. For the military, its particular role is defined within the confines of the 'two strategic tasks' through the channels of Party control. Thus, it is often time-specific and circumstance-specific, depending on what the Party leadership, in which the military is represented, emphasizes at a given time. The effectiveness of the military then refers to how well it contributes to the parts of the 'two strategic tasks' that the Party assigns to it.

Five tasks stand out in recent years as the main missions of the military. Besides the ever-important task of national defence and safeguarding territorial integrity, which no other than the military can fulfil, there is the central task of protecting the Party, the state and the socialist regime, which places the military, together with the police, as the armed forces of the party-state, squarely at the centre of domestic security. China and the United States are perceived as posing the biggest challenges to Vietnam's territorial integrity and regime security, respectively. As Vietnam is aware that its military can be overwhelmed in war by either great power, it puts a premium on '*giu nuoc tu xa*', a Vietnamese concept of 'forward defence' that means to defend the country ahead of time when the danger is still from afar, which entails weaving a network of interlocking strategic relationships with several major powers (Vuving, 2023). For the military, the best defence is deemed maintaining a peaceful international environment, and engaging the enemy in war is the last resort. This requires a wide-range defence diplomacy and a credible deterrence. While Vietnam's military deterrence is not highly credible, the military actively participates in defence diplomacy both bilaterally with major regional and global powers and multilaterally within the framework of the ASEAN Defence Ministers' Meeting Plus (ADMM-Plus) with the ultimate mission of maintaining a peaceful international environment conducive to the construction and protection of the socialist Fatherland.

After the VCP adopted 'comprehensive international integration' as a long-term national policy in 2011, it amended Vietnam's Constitution and other legal frameworks to reflect the new policy. Article 65 of the 2013 Constitution stipulates that the armed forces shall be 'absolutely loyal to the Fatherland, the People, the Party and the State', and their missions include 'protecting the Fatherland's independence, sovereignty, unity, and territorial integrity, national security and social order and safety; protecting the People, the Party, the State, and the socialist regime; building the country together with the entire people and fulfilling international obligation'. The added clause on 'international obligation' was meant to provide the legal basis for Vietnam's participation in the United Nations' peacekeeping operations, which Vietnam started in 2014 (see also Chapter 9), and other possible overseas deployment of the military as required by Vietnam's 'comprehensive international integration' policy.

Recent years also saw Vietnam's military embrace the concept of non-traditional security. The military takes a leading role in search and rescue and a key role in disaster relief. The National Search and Rescue Commission (VINASARCOM) is led by a deputy minister of defence and staffed mainly by the military. The military also played a key role in providing shelter and food to quarantined people during the COVID-19 pandemic. The military earned popularity and respect for its service and sacrifice in search and rescue and disaster response.[7] A mission that has been assigned to the military from the start is the production of armament. The indigenous defence industry is playing an increasing role in defence modernization. Significantly, the President of Viettel, the military's telecommunications company and defence industry group, had a seat on the 12th VCP Central Committee. He and the presidents of two other state-owned enterprises, Vietnam Airlines and Vietcombank, constituted a bloc of state-owned enterprises in the Central Committee. He would become minister of information and communication in 2018 after the incumbent was dismissed for a corruption charge.

The tight Party control ensures that the military will assist the Party in anything within the wide spectrum of 'building and protecting the socialist Fatherland' when called out by the Party leadership. Despite the Party's monolithic façade, factional struggles always exist in the Party and the military is always involved in this internal politicking as a strategic resource. How the military behaves in domestic politics depends in large part on the particular faction that dominates the military leadership. However, military leaders tend to side with 'regime firsters' as opposed to 'country firsters' because Party control is a reciprocal relationship that gives military leaders more say and more privileges than they would have under more democratic conditions. Any faction that puts the country above the regime is massively disadvantaged in the military not only due to the pre-existing indoctrination of the military but also due to the prospects of depoliticizing the military. Ever since the start of the reform era in 1986, the leadership of the Ministry of Defence has always sided with the conservative wing in the VCP. More recently, military leaders formed a united front with regime conservatives against the idea of depoliticizing the military, which is based on the thought that the military must be loyal to the nation above any party. For many military leaders, a depoliticized military will have no say in politics, cannot capitalize on its critical weight to reap benefits in the domestic struggle among factions and will lose the massive privileges they enjoy under Communist Party rule. Vietnam's military will likely be the last Leninist bulwark on the country's road to modernization.

Conclusion

The nature of the Communist state blurs the distinction between those within the state apparatus who carry arms and those who do not. They all are cadres working for the same party and subject to a single party leadership. Whether in uniform or not, what they are supposed to do is carry out the Communist Party's directions, lines and policies. 'Civil–military relations' seems to refer to a false distinction when applied to the reality in Communist political systems. Yet, this distinction is not as false as it first appears. The core issue that lies at the heart of civil–military relations continues to exist in Communist political systems. Furthermore, if politics is the exercise of power in pursuit of ends, the underlying tension in civil–military relations cuts to the core of politics. This is the question of how to put power into the service of ends (Feaver, 1999). Communist political systems' answer to this question is, as has become a political slogan in Vietnam, the Communist Party's absolute, comprehensive and direct leadership of the political system. However, this leadership is based on reciprocity, not one-way imposition. It gives military leaders more say and more privileges than they would have under more democratic conditions. This reciprocity, between the Party and the administration and between the Party and the armed forces, explains both the system's resilience and its internal stability.

Vietnam's civil–military relations have evolved enormously since the inception of the Communist state after World War Two. Different models of the command system of the military and different sizes of the military representation in policy making, for instance, have been experimented. The military's political influence and involvement in politics have also ebbed and flowed throughout the decades. Yet, the architecture of Vietnam's civil–military relations is the single most important thing that withstood all changes in the external and internal environment. This architecture, which I characterize as 'mutual embeddedness', is typically inherent in the Leninist state. Through the dual-role elites, ideological inculcation processes that preach Communist Party supremacy, and organizational devices such as the Party committee, the political commissar and permanent political work, the military is embedded into the Party in a mutual way. These mechanisms ensure that the military is unable to act as a self-interested actor. As a result, the military becomes a coercive resource of strategic importance for factions and individuals within the Party to mobilize for their own purposes.

Two major studies of the military's role in Vietnam's politics have identified some trends toward commercialism (Vasavakul, 2001) and professionalism (Thayer, 2011) in the VPA. The earlier analysis suggests that neither trend is likely to become the mainstream in the foreseeable future because both erode Party control of the military. The VPA is deeply politicized and the political control of the military serves the interests of both the Party and the military leadership. Barring a major political reform in the VCP itself, the VPA will remain more political than professional and commercial.

Notes

1. This refers to military behaviour under 'normal' conditions, not in crises.
2. For a summary of the literature, see Feaver (1999). For a recent development of the concept of civilian control, which continues to conceive civil–military relations in zero-sum terms, see Croissant et al (2010).
3. For slightly different formulations of the civil–military core issue, see Feaver (1999, pp 214–16); Alagappa (2001, pp xv, 6–8).
4. The two correspond in some sense with Samuel Huntington's seminal distinction between objective and subjective control in Huntington (1957).
5. According to Senior Lieutenant General Hoang Minh Thao, the leading military strategy expert in the VPA and Director of the Advanced Military Academy and the Military Strategy Institute, Tan is after Vo Nguyen Giap the best general that the VPA has ever had. Ranked third is General Hoang Van Thai, the first chief of the VPA General Staff. See Hoang Minh Thao (2007).
6. All other general secretaries of the VCP in the post-unification period have been to date appointed general secretary after at least nine years on the Politburo.
7. For a review of the military's missions in recent years by a VPA leader, see Nguyen Chi Vinh (2020).

References

Alagappa, M. (2001) 'Preface' and 'Introduction', in M. Alagappa (ed) *Coercion and Governance: The Declining Political Role of the Military in Asia*, Stanford: Stanford University Press, pp xv–xviii; 1–26.

Croissant, A., Kuehn, D., Chambers, P. and Wolf, S.O. (2010) 'Beyond the fallacy of coup-ism: conceptualizing civilian control of military in emerging democracies', *Democratization*, 17(5): 950–75.

Feaver, P.D. (1999) 'Civil–military relations', *Annual Review of Political Science*, 2: 211–41.

Hoang Minh Thao (2007) 'Thuong tuong Hoang Minh Thao: Van nguyen ven nguoi linh thoi binh lua', *Dien dan Doanh nghiep*, [online] 6 September, Available from: http://cpd.vn/Default.aspx?tabid=723&doctorid=60&articlecatid=720&articleid=30 [Accessed 9 May 2022].

Huntington, S. (1957) *The Soldier and the State: The Theory and Politics of Civil–Military Relations*, Cambridge: Harvard University Press.

Huy Duc (2012a) *Ben Thang Cuoc (The Winning Side), vol. 1: Giai phong (Liberation)*, Los Angeles: OsinBook.

Huy Duc (2012b) *Ben Thang Cuoc (The Winning Side), vol. 2: Quyen binh (Power)*, Los Angeles: OsinBook.

Koh, D. (2001) 'The politics of a divided party and Parkinson's state in Vietnam', *Contemporary Southeast Asia*, 23(3): 533–51.

Le Kha Phieu (2019) 'Giu vung nguyen tac Dang lanh dao tuyet doi, truc tiep ve moi mat doi voi luc luong vu trang' [Maintain the principle of the party's absolute, comprehensive, and direct leadership of the armed forces], *Nhan Dan*, [online] 29 November, Available from: https://nhandan.com.vn/tin-tuc-su-kien/giu-vung-nguyen-tac-dang-lanh-dao-tuyet-doi-truc-tiep-ve-moi-mat-doi-voi-luc-luong-vu-trang-378395/ [Accessed 9 May 2022].

Ministry of National Defence, Socialist Republic of Viet Nam (2019) *2019 Viet Nam National Defence*, Hanoi: National Political Publishing House.

Ngo Xuan Lich (2011) 'Quan triet Nghi quyet Dai hoi XI cua Dang, tiep tuc xay dung quan doi vung manh ve chinh tri' [Understand the resolution of the 11th Party Congress, further build the military to be politically strong], *Quoc phong Toan dan*, [online] 6 October, Available from: http://tapchiqptd.vn/vi/quan-triet-thuc-hien-nghi-quyet/quan-triet-nghi-quyet-dai-hoi-xi-cua-dang-tiep-tuc-xay-dung-quan-doi-vung-manh-ve-chinh-tri/812.html [Accessed 9 May 2022].

Ngoc Quang (2012) 'Dai tuong Le Duc Anh: Su dung bo doi de cuong che la tuyet doi sai' [Using troops for domestic enforcement is absolutely wrong], *Giao duc Viet Nam*, [online] 9 February, Available from: https://giaoduc.net.vn/tieu-diem/dai-tuong-le-duc-anh-su-dung-bo-doi-de-cuong-che-la-tuyet-doi-sai-post35580.gd [Accessed 9 May 2022].

Nguyen Chi Vinh (2020) 'Thuong tuong Nguyen Chi Vinh noi ve chien luoc quoc phong trong tinh hinh moi' [Senior Lieutenant General Nguyen Chi Vinh talking about military strategy in the new situation], *VietNamNet*, [online] 22 December, Available from: https://vietnamnet.vn/vn/tuanvietnam/tieudiem/thuong-tuong-nguyen-chi-vinh-noi-ve-chien-luoc-quoc-phong-699197.html [Accessed 9 May 2022].

Nguyen Co Thach (1990) 'Nhung chuyen bien moi tren the gioi va tu duy moi cua chung ta' [New changes in the world and our new thinking], *Quan he Quoc te*, 3: 2–7.

Nguyen Huu Tri and Nguyen Thi Phuong Hong (2004) *Mot so van de doi moi to chuc bo may Dang Cong san Viet Nam* (Some issues in renovating the organization of the Vietnam Communist Party), Hanoi: Chinh tri Quoc gia.

Nguyen Van Nghien (2010) 'Giai quyet moi quan he giua chinh tri vien va nguoi chi huy o phan doi phong khong-khong quan' [Resolving the relationship between political commissar and commander in air force-air defense units], *Xay dung Dang*, [online] 26 October, Available from: www.xaydungdang.org.vn/Home/Lyluan-Thuctien-Kinhnghiem/2010/2962/Giai-quyet-moi-quan-he-giua-chinh-tri-vien-va-nguoi-chi.aspx [Accessed 9 May 2022].

Perlmutter, A. and LeoGrande, W.M. (1982) 'The party in uniform: toward a theory of civil–military relations in communist political systems', *American Political Science Review*, 76(4): 778–89.

Pike, D. (1986) *PAVN: People's Army of Vietnam*, New York: Presidio Press.

Thayer, C.A. (2003) 'Political developments in Vietnam: the rise and demise of Le Kha Phieu', in L.B.W. Drummond and M. Thomas (eds) *Consuming Urban Culture in Contemporary Vietnam*, London: RoutledgeCurzon, pp 21–34.

Thayer, C.A. (2011) 'Military politics in contemporary Vietnam: political engagement, corporate interests, and professionalism', in M. Mietzner (ed) *The Political Resurgence of the Military in Southeast Asia: Conflict and Leadership*, London: Routledge, pp 65–86.

Thuy Linh (2011) '10 nam nhin lai cong tac giao duc quoc phong-an ninh' [A 10-year review of the national defense and security education], *Tap chi Cong san*, [online] 8 September, Available from: https://tapchicongsan.org.vn/hoat-ong-cua-lanh-ao-ang-nha-nuoc/-/2018/12852/10-nam-nhin-lai-cong-tac-giao-duc-quoc-phong---an-ninh.aspx [Accessed 9 May 2022].

Tran Quang Co (2003) *Hoi uc va Suy nghi*, Reminiscence and Reflection, Unpublished.

Tran Thuong (2020) 'Tang cuong su lanh dao tuyet doi, moi mat cua Dang doi voi Quan doi' [Strengthening the party's absolute and comprehensive leadership of the military] *VietNamNet*, [online] 30 November, Available from: https://vietnamnet.vn/vn/thoi-su/chinh-tri/tang-cuong-su-lanh-dao-tuyet-doi-moi-mat-cua-dang-doi-voi-quan-doi-693638.html [Accessed 9 May 2022].

Vasavakul, T. (2001) 'Vietnam: from revolutionary heroes to red entrepreneurs', in M. Alagappa (ed) *Coercion and Governance: The Declining Political Role of the Military in Asia*, Stanford: Stanford University Press, pp 336–56.

Vuving, A.L. (2013) 'How experience and identity shape Vietnam's relations with China and the United States', in J.-W., Park, G-W., Shin and D.W. Keyser (eds) *Asia's Middle Powers? The Identity and Regional Policy of South Korea and Vietnam*, Stanford: Walter H. Shorenstein Asia-Pacific Research Center Books, pp 53–71.

Vuving, A.L. (2016) 'ASEAN and Vietnam's security', in L. Dittmer and C.B. Ngeow (eds) *Southeast Asia and China: A Contest in Mutual Socialization*, Singapore: World Scientific, pp 93–112.

Vuving, A.L. (2019) 'Vietnam in 2018: a rent-seeking state on correction course', in D. Singh and M. Cook (eds) *Southeast Asian Affairs 2019*, Singapore: Institute of Southeast Asian Studies, pp 375–94.

Vuving, A.L. (2023) 'The evolution of Vietnamese foreign policy in the *Doi Moi* era' in B. Ljunggren and D.H. Perkins (eds) *Vietnam: Navigating a Rapidly Changing Economy, Society, and Political Order*, Cambridge: Harvard University Press, pp 347–369.

Walker, G.R. (1994) *The Evolution of Civil–Military Relations in Vietnam*, Master's thesis, Naval Postgraduate School, Monterey.

8

The Stubborn Illiberalism and Trialectical Dynamics of Thailand's Civil–Military Relations

Gregory V. Raymond

When former Thai general, coup-maker and junta leader Prayuth Chan-ocha swore an oath of loyalty to Thailand's monarch following the 26 March 2019 election, he and his cabinet omitted a pledge to 'uphold and observe the Constitution of the Kingdom of Thailand in every respect' ('Ombudsman refers oath blunder to Constitutional Court', Bangkok Post, 27 August 2019). To this date, the omission has not been rectified and the Constitutional Court refused to accept a case on its unconstitutionality. If it were needed, after 18 coups producing 19 constitutions (Harding and Leyland, 2011, p xxx), the absent oath eloquently conveyed the uncertain place of constitutional law in the governance of Thailand, particularly in the eyes of its two most important institutions, the military and the monarchy.

Western civil–military relations, and especially the principle of civilian control of the military, reside in a framework in which rule of law is fundamental. It is law that defines the relations between civilian and military leaders. So what kind of rule of law applies in Thailand? While Thailand formally adopted a Western criminal code in 1908, and established a Constitutional Court in 1997, Thailand's practice of law remains far from that of Western states (Wise, 2019). This applies at the top echelons of the legal system, with judges demonstrably unable to truly accept the constitution as the highest law. It also applies in civil matters, with northern Thais preferring Buddhist ethics and karmic justice to courts and litigation for dealing with the wrongdoings encountered in their daily lives. This is not to say that Thai rule of law is unchanging. The reforms of 1997, including the establishing of independent organizations such as anti-corruption and electoral commissions, and indeed the constitutional court, have brought the law into new spheres and established new norms.

The relative weakness of rule of law and especially constitutionalism, however, reflects the enduring coexistence of modern and traditional notions of legitimacy in governance. Some observe that Thailand's history, as a polity never formally colonized, has provided greater scope for continuity with its pre-colonial past (Wise, 2019, p xvi). It is true that powerful elites have mined Thailand's past to promote traditional ideologies that resonate with the Buddhist cosmology shared by the vast majority. These ideologies reinforce traditional social hierarchies. The Thai moral universe, especially but not only in elite circles, remains informed by Buddhist principles of merit and theories of kingship (Jory, 2016). These theories tend to ascribe the position of those at the top of the social order to their accumulated merit, with the monarch at the apex reflecting vast reserves of merit. Since people at the bottom are of low merit, a leader elected by the people has less legitimacy than a leader with the imprimatur of the monarch, who has greater merit.

Thai civil–military relations are inseparable from these concepts of governance. The importance of this is difficult to overstate. While Thailand's constitutions formally vest sovereignty in the people, since 1932 Thailand has spent seven out of every ten years under military rule.[1] Moreover, the Thai military has largely remained a no-go zone for rule of law. A comprehensive examination of the activity of Thailand's anti-corruption commission in examining unexplained wealth, for example, found that investigations were rarely pursued against Thai military officers (Pathmanand and Connors, 2019).

That is not to suggest that Thai civil–military relations have remained static. The period between 1992 and 2006 saw Thailand edge closer to a Western model of civil–military relations. But the momentum that produced those reforms has long since dissipated, and in the years since the coup of 2006, Thailand's democracy has regressed, as has rule of law. Instead, the power shared by the military and the monarchy, always latent, has become more nakedly exercised. The dissolution of opposition political parties before and after the March 2019 elections, are powerful examples. At a symbolic level, the weakening commitment to democracy has also been evident in ways beyond Prayuth's missing oath. Others include the stealthy removal of monuments and memorials devoted to the 1932 revolution that ended the absolute monarchy (Lawattanatrakul, 2019).

In this article, I propose a 'trialectical' construct for understanding the forces shaping Thailand's civil–military relations. This construct reaches beyond the churn of day-to-day politics and comprises the push-pull dynamics between three principal forces. First, the interests and ideologies of elites and oligarchies, including monarchical networks, the military and most recently, Sino-Thai business elites. Second, the aspirations for liberal and egalitarian forms of government from disenfranchised groups whose demands for participation in Thai governance have increased over time. Third, the effects of the international environment, including pressures for democratization and modernization, and the reverse, tolerance for authoritarianism. This dynamic resembles a dialectical process, in which there is 'the potential for alternative forms of development arising from the confrontation of opposed social forces' (Cox, 1981, p 215). But as there are clearly three forces at work here, I will use the term 'trialectic' or 'trialectical' and argue that Thailand's three-cornered 'trialectical' dynamic has underpinned the most important attribute of its civil–military relations, the extent of Thai military involvement in politics. As a matter of course, the greater the military involvement in politics the less the potential for civilian governments to control the military organization in matters of policy, budget, procurement and personnel appointments.

To an extent, this approach to understanding the evolutionary processes of Thai civil–military relations has affinities with Marxist analyses of historical change, which see political arrangements as emerging from struggle between socio-political forces. Applied to Southeast Asian states, this method has been prominent in the work of the so-called Murdoch school (see for example Carroll et al, 2020; for a specifically Thai example applying a similar approach to understanding Thai constitutions, see Nidhi, 2003). But because my trialectical model also emphasizes the role of the transmission of ideas and capital across borders in explaining historical change, it also draws on the wider lens used in the work of scholars working in the field known as Global Historical Sociology (for a summary of key precepts in GHS see Go and Lawson, 2017). By employing an approach informed by these methods, I contribute to the study of Thai civil–military relations in a way that differs from previous studies, particularly those which emphasize specific factors such as the monarchy–military partnership (Chambers and Napisa, 2016) or factionalism (Lissak, 1976; Surachart, 1999; Lee, 2006). This trialectical, evolutionary approach also allows a view over the *longue durée*, distinguishing it from work that analyses Thai civil–military relations in shorter periods (Surachart, 1999; Surin, 2003).

The trialectical dynamic thus derived, I examine its workings in three periods. I begin with the 19th century to the 1932 revolution, as Thailand modernized and established a modern professional military. Here I consider why a factor that has shaped military and civil–military evolutions elsewhere, frequent war, was absent in Thailand's case. I then move to the mid-20th century and Cold War period. I describe the events and trends that led to the toppling of the absolute monarchy, and the unleashing of the military as a political force from 1932. In this section I also appraise the effects of the enmeshment with the United States during the Cold War. Finally, I analyse the post-Cold War period, where despite the opening of government to wider participation, the monarchy–military complex has survived pressures for modernization and democratization. While tracing this evolution, I explain the relative lack of utility of the classic Western literature for conceptualizing Thai civil–military relations, address the role of the military in national development projects, and set out some of the implications for the characteristics and behaviours of the military. I also reflect on the legacy of Thailand's avoidance of colonization, and the circumstances of the founding of the modern Thai military as a palace guard, crucial aspects of Thai civil–military relations. In sum, this chapter addresses three of this book's key themes: (1) How colonial legacies influence the evolution of civil–military relations and the military's self-definition of vital roles; (2) how Asian militaries can be socially, politically and economically embedded; and (3) the relationship between Asian militaries and state developmental and modernization goals.

Beginnings: The modern Thai state and the professional Thai military

In 1979 Kenneth Waltz, observing a form of survival of the fittest in the behaviour of markets, saw structure in international affairs as exercised through selection:

> Where selection according to behaviour occurs, no enforced standard of behaviour is required for the system to operate ... Internationally, the environment of states' action, or the structure of their system, is set by the fact that some states prefer survival over other ends obtainable in the short run and act with relative efficiency to achieve that end. (Waltz, 1979a, pp 92–3)

Similarly, historian George Modelski (1978, p 231) wrote that 'states competing in the global power game developed similar organizational forms and similar hardiness: they too become nation-states – in a defensive reaction, because [they are] forced to take action with or to confront a global power'. To a limited extent, this realist view encompassed the development of militaries. While this was not an abiding concern of Waltz, he did proffer that states will generally choose the most efficient military practices: 'Contending states imitate the military innovations contrived by the country of greatest capability and ingenuity' (Waltz, 1979b, p 128).

Theorists of state-making also subscribed to the notion that selection, in the form of frequent war, significantly shapes the characteristics of states, including their militaries. Charles Tilly's (1985) succinct formulation 'War made the state and the state made war', and his argument that states began as 'protection rackets', applied mainly to the development of European states.

But Francis Fukuyama (2011, pp 110–15) saw similar forces in China having led to the strong Chinese state. In a 294-year period of the Zhou dynasty (770–256 BC), there were 1,211 wars and only 38 years of peace. As well as forcing military innovation, frequent war propelled the development of a bureaucracy to administer taxes and fund armies. It also encouraged merit-based promotion. As nobles were felled in battle, commoners were promoted based on ability, and that idea eventually, argues Fukuyama, found its way into bureaucracies.

The fiscal state process in the case of Thailand was different. The establishment of the modern Thai state in the form of an absolute monarchy was driven by the incorporation of Thailand into the Western system of global free trade, rather than by experience of war (Kullada, 2004). Thailand's astute monarchs Rama IV (1851–68) and Rama V (1868–1910) used the pressure of Western demands for trade opening as a pretext for rearranging economic relations, away from labour as the primary source of value that it had been hitherto, and towards property (Puangchon, 2020). By abolishing slavery and corvee labour, and instituting tax on trade as a preferred source of revenue, the monarchy enriched itself while reducing the power of the noble class.

Where was war and the military in this transition? War had been a frequent occurrence in mainland Southeast Asia up until the 19th century. Battye (1974, p 1) found that the Siamese kings of Ayutthaya, the pre-colonial city-state precursor of modern Thailand, fought 70 wars in 417 years, an average of one war every six years. Puangthong (2018) has recently revealed that Siam under Rama III engaged in significant depopulation raids over the Mekong in today's Laos and Cambodia, to bring back war slaves in order to build Siam's strength.

The arrival of European colonial powers from the early 19th century changed attitudes towards the utility of military force. Rama II (1809–24) was told by his Chinese interlocutors to be wary, that the British would begin by asking for increased trade and would finish by seizing the country (Vella, 1960, p 116). The British conquest of the hitherto much-feared Burmese forces in the first Anglo-Burmese war of 1824–26, and the humbling of China in the Opium War of 1839–42 each made a profound impression. This was such that the Thai monarch Rama IV wrote in 1868 that: 'The only weapons that will be of real use to us in the future will be our mouths and our hearts, constituted so as to be full of sense and wisdom for the better protection of ourselves' (Battye, 1974, p 260).

The circumstances of the founding of a professional Thai military in the reign of Mongkut's son and successor Chulalongkorn Rama V were therefore unlike those of Europe's. While Chulalongkorn thought that military forces *could* offer a deterrent to European colonizers, he had other strong imperatives, other than defence of the realm, for undertaking military reform. The first was protection of the throne from his rivals, other nobles.

These potential rivals had, on Chulalongkorn's ascent to the throne, significant control of military forces. This was because the military system followed an economic and social system in which control of labour was paramount. Called the *sakdina* system, every member of Siamese society was assigned a numerical score, indicating their rank and power. The king possessed the greatest *sakdina*, while the nobles possessed somewhat less, but more than the *phrae* (commoners) or slaves who possessed the least. Unlike in medieval Europe, nobles were not landed, and their power was based on their *sakdina*, which conferred control of a certain quantity of followers and labourers. There was no professional caste of soldier. Instead, in times of war, nobles became generals and their followers became soldiers; in effect 'the social hierarchy itself was fundamentally an organisation for external security' (Battye, 1974, p 24). This dispersal of force carried risks. Nobles attempted coups with regularity, especially after a disputed succession, and distrust was such that some kings preferred to employ foreign mercenaries as personal guards (Baker and Pasuk, 2017, pp 150–72).

When Chulalongkorn took the throne as a sickly adolescent, his tenure was not assured. The regent Sisuryawong was from a powerful noble family, the Bunnags, who controlled several ministries as well the trade in weapons and munitions. Chulalongkorn's uncle Phra Phin Klao was in charge of the kingdom's largest private army, a personal force of some 2,700 personnel (Battye, 1974, p 100). There was also a so-called 'second king', Prince Wichaichan, who was Chulalongkorn's anointed successor should anything befall him. Tensions between the second king and Chulalongkorn reached serious levels in the 1875 Front Palace incident, with Chulalongkorn fearing a coup. After resolving the crisis in his favour, Chulalongkorn saw an opportunity to reduce the risk from the noble class by incorporating military reform into his larger modernization programme. As described previously, he had already shifted the economic and taxation base of his monarchy in response to external pressure, in a way that advantaged himself vis-à-vis the noble class; now military reform along European lines would further strengthen his reign.

Chulalongkorn accelerated the military modernization that had commenced with the founding of the Bodyguard Regiment five years earlier. Here he had consciously sought to establish a modernized army under his patronage, complete with regiments and companies, social cohesion and common traditions. By 1873, this regiment was 500 strong and organized as an English infantry regiment with six companies. Chulalongkorn worked on fostering the ethos and character of a professional military. He built barracks and a club-house for the officers. A disciplinary code of 40 regulations was implemented, both to acculturate to Western military ways and to instil discipline. With the abolition of slavery in 1874, military service based on hereditary and personal service bonds was transformed into a system based on paid employment. This denied the nobles access to their own forces. The model was gradually exported to military units beyond the Royal Bodyguard Regiment. Chulalongkorn also unified the fragmented command and control of the remaining pre-modern military formations. By 1892 he was able to place all forces under a single Ministry of Defence, as one of 12 new ministries (Directorate of Education and Research, 1982, pp 110–12).

Apart from protecting his rule from rivals, establishing a modern military offered other advantages. It strengthened his rule against the predation of foreign military powers in two ways. First, it provided a constabulary force that, in providing a capacity to quell unrest, removed the pretext for intervention. Second, it later offered a deterrent to raise the cost of foreign adventurism. With respect to the former, Chulalongkorn learnt quickly that either ambiguity regarding territorial boundaries, or disorder in the administration of his kingdom endangering the lives and property of foreign expatriates resident in Siam, could provide a case for annexation by France and England. British officials warned Chulalongkorn that recognition of Siam as a sovereign state depended on its capacity to maintain internal order. In 1872 the British Consul delivered a blunt message on the unregulated and overlapping sovereignty of the frontier provinces: 'Give up uncontrolled territory or take immediate steps to drive out intruders' (Battye, 1974, p 116).

Later, after his personal experience of brute coercion at the hands of the French navy in the 1893 Pak Nam crisis, he added deterrence of imperialists to the missions of the modern Thai military. He was guided by his trusted adviser, the Belgian-born Gustav Rolin-Jaequemins, who saw in Thailand's situation parallels with the experiences of smaller European states, including his own Belgium:

> You are between England and France like we are between France and Germany. We in Belgium are quite persuaded that the greatest forces which we could levy could not resist for long [against] a German or French invasion, but we are equally persuaded that we must nevertheless do what we can, if not to make an invasion impossible, at least to render it more difficult, more costly and more dangerous for the invaders. We consider this as an absolute necessity to back our diplomacy. (Tips, 1996, pp 52–62)

The expansion of the Thai army to ten divisions each comprising ten thousand soldiers, via the 1902 conscription law, was the concretization of this policy.

In summary, the modern Thai military came about through a confluence of circumstances. A monarch needing to protect his reign with a loyal force, found a necessary rationale in the external pressures compelling modernization. The implications for Thai civil–military relations were of both short and long-term importance. While the absolute monarchy lasted, the relationship between the military and the monarchical institution was direct, mediated only by those close family members whom Chulalongkorn and his two successors appointed as ministers and generals. No parliament or civilian bureaucracy interceded. In the longer term, the memory of the Thai military's first mission, of protecting the monarchy, was burnished and embellished as the monarchical restoration proceeded from the depths of the Cold War.

The circumstances of the founding of the military also had implications for the military's development and internal security role. While there was a break from the past in the establishment of a permanent paid professional force, there was continuity in retaining an internal role. Battye (1974, p 240) records that the 1st Foot, the second unit to be professionalized (after the Royal Bodyguard Regiment), had a multitude of diverse responsibilities:

> As police, they patrolled the streets of Bangkok; as coolie labourers, they erected the ephemeral architecture of state and religious ceremony; as troops, they put down the tax-resisting Chinese bootleggers in Ratburi and Nakhon Pathom. The Siamese soldier did not idly await or single-mindedly rehearse for war, a rather remote concern; rather he earned his keep by police and public works, his steady employ.

This duality of roles continues until the present day.

Civil–military relations from 1932 to 1973

The 1932 revolution overthrew the absolute monarchy but also allowed the military to become a political actor, with profound consequences for Thai civil–military relations thereafter. If the founding of the professional military was the first critical juncture arising from the convergence of external and internal pressures, the 1932 revolution was the second time the trialectic of international trends, egalitarian aspiration and noble privilege collided with visible result.

External influence came in the form of global trends away from absolute monarchy. In Thailand the reverberations of the overthrowing of the Chinese and Russian monarchies in 1911 and 1917 were heard loudly, especially by the unpopular Rama VI (1910–25), who had taken the throne in 1910. He was profligate in his personal spending, and by creating a private paramilitary force, alienated the military. In 1912 a military plot was uncovered. The participants in the so-called *Ror Sor 130* rebellion incident had an average age of 20 and wanted to turn Thailand into a 'modern nation' or a 'democracy' (Charnvit, 2009, p 20). Rama VI responded with an intense effort to establish a royalist–nationalist ideology, the remnants of which are still visible. His formula of *chat satsasna phramaha kasat* – nation religion and monarchy – is still widely cited today as representing the pillars of the Thai state (Dressel, 2018).

But undercurrents of dissatisfaction remained, and under another unpopular monarch, Prajadhipok Rama VII (1925–35), grew. Prajadhipok was a strong supporter of the military and believed that Thailand needed a force for external security. But he came to the throne on the cusp of a global economic downturn. He cut military spending as a proportion of the total budget, from 25 per cent in 1925 to 17 per cent in 1932 (Jittraporn, 1978, p 85). Additionally, because he believed that the military was a tool to protect the monarchy, Prajadhipok placed family relatives and nobles back in key positions, many of whom had been removed during Vajiravudh's rule (Jittraporn, 1978, p 64). At the same time commoners who tried to express their views on the nation's future were put in jail, as in the case of the intellectual Thienwan (Sulak, 2002, p 36).

These issues generated a cadre of disenchanted military officers, which together with more general dissatisfaction with the system of absolute monarchy, culminated in the revolution of 1932. A group of students including three military officers returned from Europe wanting to modernize Thailand. Over a brief period, they built a one-hundred-member People's Party and on the morning of 24 June 1932, successfully staged a revolution. Phibun Songkhram, one of the two strong leaders who emerged from the revolution, led the military group within the People's Party.

The 1932 revolution marked a profound turning point. An organization that had been an obedient tool of the monarchy, dominated by members of the royal family, now became a self-interested political actor. Nonetheless because the revolution produced a constitution with room for the monarch and aristocratic class to manoeuvre, the military was embattled. Its solution to disputes or dissatisfaction was inevitably to resort to further coups. Thus, the following year the military conducted another coup, ejecting the conservative leaning Prime Minister Mano and installing Phahon (Chambers, 2013a, pp 122–3). Underscoring the fragility of the new regime, royalists attempted a comeback in 1933 but were defeated. In 1935, lower-ranking military officers dissatisfied with their conditions and payment attempted a coup but failed. In 1938, the 1932 revolutionary leader and army officer Phibun took power after the resignation of the civilian prime minister. He was to remain the military strongman leader either proximate or in power, save for a brief period from 1944 to 1947, until 1957. He was followed by a further series of military strongmen, first Sarit Thanarat (1958–63) and then Thanom Kittikachorn (1963–73). Constitutions and democratic process were either fig leaves or entirely missing; coups and other unconstitutional transfers of power were regular occurrences.

In the 1932 to 1957 period, the military and monarchy were competitors. While formally retaining a monarchy bound by a constitution, in practice Phibun Songkram emulated the secular nationalism of fascist Italy, Japan and Germany. Under the 1932 Constitution, Phibun deprived the monarchy of immunity from litigation, and reduced its control of the Royal Household, Privy Purse, Royal Guards and Privy Council. He banned the teaching of the royal language (*Rajasap*), and successfully sued King Prajadhipok for transferring his money to private accounts overseas (Handley, 2006, pp 61, 150–52). The anniversary of the 1932 revolution replaced the monarch's birthday as the premier national day. After Prajadhipok abdicated in 1935, Thailand had no resident reigning monarch for the next 16 years (Thak, 2007, p 204).

This competition was, however, in the end, temporary. Instead, a more comfortable and symbiotic relationship between the two institutions emerged. Here, the trialectic was again in action. Under Phibun, Thailand had begun an alliance with the United States, undertaken as much for reasons of regime security as national security (Fineman, 1997, p 66). As the Cold War progressed, the increasingly influential United States and the Thai military concurred on the restoration of the monarchy as a hedge against communism. Field Marshal Sarit Thanarat, who had taken power via a coup in 1957 had little interest in democracy but realized his coup group lacked legitimacy. Royal support would provide a more solid foundation for military rule (Thak, 2007, p 205). For its part, the United States supported promoting the monarchy as a unifying force capable of firewalling the loyalty of the predominantly rural populace against Marxist influence at a time of growing popularity of communism throughout Southeast Asia. With the restoration of prominent public rituals, the popularity of the monarch Bhumipol Adulyadej grew throughout the 1960s.

The military and the monarchy, now in partnership, commenced an interest in developmentalism. Sarit introduced Thailand's first National Economic Development Plan in 1961 and gave a bigger role to economists such as Dr Puey Ungphakorn, Governor of the Bank of Thailand, and other experts. After Sarit died in 1963, this policy was maintained until at least 1971, with economic services averaging 26 per cent of government spending, compared with 16 per cent each for defence and education (Chai-anan, 1971, p 45, 50). 'Developmental democracy' became an ideology (Connors, 2007, p 66) entailing 'the gradual immersion of thinking about democracy in terms of how to relate "Thai characteristics" to democratic rule, and plans toward developing the population such that it was fit for democracy'. Some projects were carried out under the auspices of the military, but increasingly they were royal projects, carried out with either the authorship or imprimatur of the monarch. The royal projects conveyed an image of Bhumiphol as a development monarch (*kasat nakphattana*) who was concerned for the welfare of his people (Puangthong, 2017, p 10). The projects served the psychological warfare objectives of the regime and the United States in lessening the appeal of communism.

Civil–military relations from the 1973 revolution until the present

Sarit's rule left in its place a royalist–nationalist ideology and a Thai-style of democracy that at its deepest levels, entrenched monarchical, military and bureaucratic dominance over elected politicians (Hewisson and Kengkij, 2010). The system was, however, subject to increasing demands for popular participation, first in the 1973 revolution but then in later political crises spurred by dissatisfaction with military rule. Consequently, nominally civilian rule began to occur more frequently. The military itself decided that visible democratic process would be an effective brake on the communist insurgency (Surachart, 1999). In toto this meant the raw exercise of military power became less acceptable and Thai democracy began to take on hybrid characteristics; elections took place regularly while the military exercised influence behind the scenes, such as in the guise of senators. The monarchy's ascent continued. As the final decades of the 20th century wore on, the monarchy began to assume a double mantle: a sometimes advocate for democracy, while retaining a role as a senior partner and protector of the military. In doing so, Handley (2006, p 8) notes that coups and bloody incidents:

> took place in the throne's name with the palace's quiet nod, always under the rubric of nation, religion and king. As long as the generals paid more respect and attention to the throne than to the constitution or parliament, and as long as the kingdom was orderly under their direction, Bhumipol accepted their hold on power.

As the contours of this unofficial quid pro quo became clearer, the military became ever more fervent in its promulgation of royalist ideology and more religious in their personal devotion. Pervasive use of ritual helped in inculcating this level of royalism. For example, every senior military officer would periodically be relieved from their normal duties to *khao fao*; greet, guard or accompany a royal family member on their travels (Raymond, 2018, p 76). Immediate family members of military personnel were entitled to a Buddhist cremation ceremony in which the pyre was lit with a flame taken from a royal temple. The royalism, increasingly of an intensity described as hyper-royalism (Thongchai, 2016) was also manifested in reverence for the military's founding-father, Chulalongkorn. Every day officer cadets at the Royal Thai Army's Chulachomklao Royal Military Academy pledge loyalty before a statue of Chulalongkorn, promising to maintain his heritage with their blood (Wasana, 2009, p 32). Many cadets prayed before the equestrian Chulalongkorn statue in Bangkok's Lumpini Park every Tuesday and Thursday.

For outsiders, post-Cold War and especially after 2006, Thai politics was confused and unstable. The Thai state appeared to exist in a condition of ambivalence as to its fundamental orientation, with competition between supporters of different regime types ranging from liberal to statist to plutocratic (Connors, 2009). All were willing to resort to authoritarian and extra-constitutional mechanisms – including coups – to pursue their preferred political visions.

Within this flux, for the military, civil–military relations was relatively simple. It was summed up in Prem Tinsulanonda's horse analogy. In 2006 the former prime minister, trusted adviser to the king and army general described the military as a horse, the monarch as its owner and the government as its jockey ('Bad leaders doomed to failure', *The Nation*, 1 September 2006). Civilian control of the military was transient, in other words, while the monarchy's control was permanent. General Prem's statement exposed a vision of a Thai-style democracy in which the monarch's role is far less constrained by law than in Western-style constitutional democracies. Even where laws did exist, these gave limited power to civilian governments to control the military. For example, under the 2008 Defence Administration Act, movement or promotion of officers above brigadier general was approved by a committee of seven comprising the four military service chiefs, the permanent secretary, the prime minister or deputy defence minister and the defence minister. Elected officials had only two of the seven positions (Chambers, 2013a, p 340).

The monarchy maintained its hold on the military via the Privy Council. In the Bhumipol era, the monarchy's control of the military was exercised through intermediaries, principally Prem Tinasulanond, then President of the Privy Council (Handley, 2006, p 422). Prem vetted the promotional lists each year to ensure officers of the right calibre and political persuasions were given the top spots. A key reason for the coup of 2006 was popular Prime Minister Thaksin Shinawatra's attempt to control the military promotions process (Ockey, 2007, p 110).

The royal transition to Bhumiphol's son Vajiralongkorn Rama X in 2016 has seen the modification of the 'horse' model of civil–military relations, with the new king, a professional soldier since his teens, managing the affairs of the military more directly (Macan-Markar, 2019). Displaying his more substantive interest in military affairs compared to Bhumiphol, he has established a personal force, the Royal Security Command, directly under his command. This unit is no mere bodyguard but comprising six battalions, each of between 300 to 800 soldiers, amounts to a force of several thousand soldiers (Nanuam, 2014) He is also interfering more directly in the military, issuing directions on matters such as training (Itthipongmaetee, 2018). He has personalized control over some prestigious King's Guard units that previously existed within the mainstream chain of command (Government Gazette, 2019). This may reflect a degree of insecurity, as Vajiralongkorn is a less popular monarch than his father. It is certainly moving civilian control of the military further away.

In the 21st century, two of the opposing forces of the 'trialectic', elite interest and popular aspiration, have reached an uneasy stalemate. Thailand's junta has embraced autocratic innovation, in which authoritarian governments use a menu of clever methods to maintain power while adhering to a facade of democracy and rule of law. The political system is in effect 'designed to mimic the presence of horizontal and vertical accountability, but also prevent the actual practice of it' (Morgenbesser, 2020, p 2). Hence although Thailand held elections in 2019, these were under a constitution that allowed an unelected senate comprising a high proportion of former and serving military officers to participate in the selection of the new prime minister. It produced a government that allowed May 2014 coup makers to remain in office. Meanwhile, the courts have been used more frequently to remove opponents who have become too vocal or too influential (O'Connor, J., 2019).

The stability of this arrangement, and the royalist ideology which justifies it, is for the time being enhanced by an oligarchical concentration of wealth. Thailand's monarchy, the world's wealthiest at an estimated USD$43 billion in 2019 (Pek, 2019) maintains investments in many sectors of the Thai economy. A small group of Sino-Thai families dominate the Thai economy and maintain close links with both the military and the monarchy (Crispin, 2019). Their suspicion of democracy and fears of unrest from below were amplified after the 2010 Red Shirt riots paralysed Bangkok. Since then, their mentality has tended towards a 'protection pact' (Slater, 2010; Raymond, 2019), in which freedoms are less important and where there is support for the military's role in internal security, including the expansion of the Internal Security Operational Command.

This stalemate is nonetheless becoming precarious. On the one hand, the third leg of the 'trialectic', the international environment, is becoming less conducive to democracy and more hospitable to authoritarianism. Thailand's democratic regression has occurred in parallel with a global retreat from democracy that started in the mid-2000s (Diamond and Croissant, 2020, pp 12–13). The increasing global influence of Russia and China has provided Thai anti-liberal forces with ideological support and practical alternatives. After the United States took a hardline following the 2014 coup, some were quick to point out that if the United States chose to withdraw its support from the totemic Cobra Gold multilateral exercise, there was always the potential to establish an equivalent 'Panda Gold' with China ('Panda Gold versus Cobra Gold!', *Thai Post*, 2 June 2014, p 4). While this has not occurred, it did communicate the dangers of US pressure driving Thailand closer to China. Meanwhile, Thai elites in the political, military and banking circles have become more positive towards the idea of Thailand adopting the China model of "market Leninism" (Zawacki, 2017, pp 297–99). Thailand also shares with Russia some suspicion of globalization and democracy promotion. Its former ambassador to Russia wrote, in a volume celebrating Russian and Thai diplomatic ties, that:

> The threat toward the independence of and sovereignty of small countries nowadays no longer has to do with defending territory such as during the age of imperialism. Rather, the threat comes in the form of political, economic and social exploitation in the name of globalization. *Western-style democracy which fuels ideological struggle and economic competition as well as the race for economic supremacy represents real challenges and tests whether Thailand can withstand the force of changes in the globalized world with pride and dignity in the same impressive way that past Thai monarchs has pursued shrewd foreign policies during the era of colonialism* [emphasis added]. (Royal Thai Embassy Moscow, 2007, p v)

On the other hand, Thailand's younger generation are becoming increasingly impatient with both the monarchy and the military's continued hold on power. Thai youth overwhelmingly voted for democratic change in the form of the Future Forward Party in the March 2019 elections (Thai Enquirer, 2020). Following the dissolution of the party, they commenced a series of university-based demonstrations that in 2020 became large public demonstrations, that in an unprecedented move, demanded monarchical reform.

Still, increasingly and for the foreseeable future, Thai military modernization and civil–military relations will not equal Westernization (Rachman, 2016). Nor will professionalization bring civilian control of the military. While Huntington (1957) famously hypothesized that increasing focus on the development of professional skills and capabilities would tend to produce a military increasingly disinterested in politics, empirical survey data suggests that such causality is for the Thai military absent. Sirivunnabood and Ricks (2016, p 28) surveyed 569 Thai military officers and did not find professionalism, defined as comprising expertise, responsibility and corporateness, to be a good predictor of whether a military officer was inclined to be apolitical. Neither has the Thai military's exposure to Western norms of military behaviour, through overseas training and education, had any significant impact. Thousands of Thai military officers have participated in the United States International Military Education and Training Program (IMET), but many IMET alumni have participated in coups against elected governments (Chambers, 2013b, p 24).

In addition to the deleterious consequences for Thai democracy, the absence of independent strong control and accountability for the Thai military also impedes military reform, reduces operational capability and fosters corruption. The Thai military has not attempted any substantial reform since the failed attempt by civilian Prime Minister Chuan Leekpai in the 1990s. There is little joint operational doctrine and materiel acquisition occurs according to the individual preferences of service chiefs and not according to joint operational and capability plans (Raymond, 2018, pp 213–44). The operational performance of the Thai military in its last serious security crisis, Vietnam's occupation of Cambodia 1979–89, was less than stellar (Raymond, 2020).

Thai society also suffers, most grievously with respect to the military conscription system, which applies to all males over 21 years of age. This has become prone to abuse. Conscripts are used as personal servants or their salaries diverted to commanders (Amnesty, 2020, p 27). Serious physical and sexual abuse is rife (Amnesty, 2020). Unsurprisingly, conscription became an election issue in the 2019 election; however, the party which promised its abolition was subsequently dissolved ('FFP bill seeks to end conscription', *Bangkok Post*, 15 Nov 2019; 'FFP dissolved, executives banned for 10 years', *Bangkok Post*, 21 Feb 2020). Pervasive exploitation of junior ranks by commanders was made hideously visible in Thailand's first ever mass shooting, when Sergeant-Major Jakrapanth Thomma killed 30 civilians in the north-eastern city of Nakhon Ratchasima in February 2020 (Charuvastra, 2020; 'Mass shooting by Jakrapanth Thomma puts Thai army officers' side deals under scrutiny' (2020) [no author], *The Straits Times*). The commander had been running a side-business involving a government loan system for soldiers to acquire housing, and had owed the assailant about USD$13,000 (Picard, 2020). Tragically, any longer-term momentum for military reform provoked by the slaughter may have been eliminated by the subsequent onset of the coronavirus pandemic.

At the same time, in the post-Cold War era the military continues to do good work in the community, especially in support of royal projects, partly offsetting the damage done to its reputation through issues such as corruption and conscription. In the 1990s projects under army commander and later Prime Minister Chaovalit Yongchaiyudh include the Green Isaan project in the Northeast and the Tung Mountain project in the upper North (Surachart, 1999, p 143). The Green Isaan project began with the King's initiative to truck water to the people of the Northeast in 1987 and became a model for other military development projects in the North and South. It also assisted Chaovalit's campaign for prime minister at a later stage (Surachart, 1999, p 144). In other public relations innovations, the new monarch established his own volunteer force, the *jit arsa* ('Volunteer Spirit'), in 2017. There are now a reported 4 million members, across the country and social strata (Wongcha-um and Thepgumpanat, 2018). The *jit arsa* perform community work, such as cleaning streets and rivers, as well as disaster relief, and commence each task by saluting a portrait of the king. In July 2019 all 1,798 staff and executives of the Siam Commercial Bank pledged loyalty to the scheme, citing the importance of the 'four major institutions of the country: Nation, Religion, Monarchy, and People' (Siam Commercial Bank, 2019).

Conclusion

Thailand's civil–military relations remain and will remain for the foreseeable future starkly unlike the Western model in which a professional military acts under the control of elected politicians. Thailand's status as the only Southeast Asian polity to have remained uncolonized may have contributed to the survival of an ideology of Buddhist kingship, which coexists uneasily with constitutionalism and a bureaucratic-legal model of modern governance. When it considers its raison d'être from within this worldview, the Thai military is inclined to see in the circumstances of its founding as a royal bodyguard, historical continuity, as well as justification for its modern-day royalism and anti-liberalism. This viewpoint is, however, historically inaccurate and ignores critical junctures, such as in the aftermath of the 1932 revolution and during the Cold War, when the choices of leaders could have taken Thailand either towards republicanism or a more genuine constitutionally constrained monarchy. Instead, Thai civil–military relations have remained stubbornly illiberal. They continue to protect elite privilege, repress egalitarian aspiration and defy pressures from beyond Thailand's borders.

Note
[1] Based on Chambers (2013).

References
Amnesty International (2020) *'We Were Just Toys To Them' Physical, Mental And Sexual Abuse Of Conscripts In Thailand's Military*, London: Amnesty International Ltd.
'Bad leaders doomed to failure' [no author], *The Nation*, 1 September 2006.
Baker, C. and Pasuk, P. (2017) *A History of Ayutthaya: Siam in the Early Modern World*, Cambridge: Cambridge University Press.

Battye, N. (1974) *The Military, Government and Society in Siam, 1868–1910: Politics and Military Reform During the Reign of King Chulalongkorn*, PhD Thesis, Cornell University.

Carroll, T., Hameiri, S. and Jones, L. (2020) *Political Economy of Southeast Asia: Politics and Uneven Development Under Hyperglobalisation*, Cham: Palgrave Macmillan.

Chai Anan, S. (1971) *The Politics and Administration of the Thai Budgetary Process*, PhD thesis, University of Wisconsin, Wisconsin.

Chambers, P. (2013a) *Knights of the Realm: Thailand's Military and Police, Then and Now*, Bangkok: White Lotus.

Chambers, P. (2013b) 'Unruly boots: military power and security sector reform efforts in Thailand', PRIF Report No 121, Peace Research Institute Frankfurt (PRIF).

Chambers, P. and Napisa, W. (2016) 'The resilience of monarchised military in Thailand', *Journal of Contemporary Asia*, 46(3): 425–44.

Charnvit, K. (2009) *Siamese/Thai Nationalism and Cambodia: A Case Study of the Preah Vihear Temple*, Bangkok: Toyota Thailand Foundation/Foundation for the Promotion of Social Science and Humanities Text Books.

Charuvastra, T. (2020) Korat mass shooter shot dead, death tolls rose to 30, Khao Sod English, 9 February.

Connors, M. (2007) *Democracy and National Identity in Thailand*, Copenhagen: NIAS Press.

Connors, M. (2009) 'Liberalism, authoritarianism and the politics of decisionism in Thailand', *The Pacific Review*, 22(3): 355–73.

Cox, R. (1981) 'Social forces, states and world orders', in R. Keohane (ed) *Neorealism and its Critics*, New York: Colombia University Press, pp 204–54.

Crispin, S. (2019) Thailand's 'five families' prop and imperil Prayut, *Asia Times*, 13 December.

Diamond, L. and Croissant, A. (2020) 'Introduction: reflections on democratic backsliding in Asia', *Global Asia*, 15(1): 8–13.

Directorate of Education and Research (1982) ประวัติกองทัพไทยในรอบ๒๐๐ปี พ.ศ.๒๓๒๕-๒๕๒๕ Royal Thai Armed Forces, History of the Royal Thai Armed Forces in 200 Years BE 2325–2525 [AD 1882–1982], Bangkok: Supreme Command Headquarters.

Dressel, B. (2018) 'Thailand's traditional trinity and the rule of law: can they coexist?', *Asian Studies Review*, 42(2): 268–85.

'FFP bill seeks to end conscription' (2019) [no author], *Bangkok Post*, 15 November.

'FFP dissolved, executives banned for 10 years' (2020), *Bangkok Post*, 21 February.

Fineman, D. (1997) *A Special Relationship: The United States and Military Government in Thailand, 1947–1958*, Honolulu: University of Hawaii Press.

Fukuyama, F. (2011) *The Origins of Political Order*, New York: Farrar, Straus and Giroux.

Go, J. and Lawson, G. (2017) 'Introduction: for a global historical sociology' in J. Go and G. Lawson (eds) *Global Historical Sociology*, Cambridge: Cambridge University Press, pp 1–34.

Government Gazette (2019), Royal Order Transferring Personnel and Budget from the Army and Ministry of Defence to the Royal Security Command 136/103, 30 September.

Handley, P. (2006) *The King Never Smiles: A Biography of Thailand's Bumiphol Adulyadej*, New Haven: Yale University Press.

Harding, A. and Leyland, P. (2011) *The Constitutional System of Thailand: A Contextual Analysis*, Oxford and Portland, OR: Hart Publishing.

Hewison, K. and Kengkij, K. (2010) '"Thai-style democracy": the royalist struggle for Thailand's politics', in S. Ivarsson and L. Isager (eds) *Saying the Unsayable: Monarchy and Democracy in Thailand*, Copenhagen: NIAS Press, pp 179–202.

Huntington, S. (1957) *The Soldier and the State*, Cambridge, MA: Belknap Press.

Itthipongmaetee, C. (2018) 'King orders military training in cave rescue', *Khaosod English*, 4 July.

Jittraporn, C. (1978), การจัดราชการทหารในรัชสมัยพระบาทสมเด็จพระปกเกล้าเจ้าอยู่หัว (พ.ศ.๒๔๖๘ – ๒๔๗๗), *The Organization of the Royal Thai Armed Forces in the Reign of King Rama VII 1925–1935*, MA thesis, Chulalongkorn University.

Jory, P. (2016) *Thailand's Theory of Monarchy: The Vessantara Jataka and the Idea of the Perfect Man*, Albany: State University of New York Press.

Kullada M. (2004) *The Rise and Decline of Thai Absolutism*, London: Routledge Curzon.

Lawattanatrakul, A. (2019) 'Uprooting democracy: the war of memory and the lost legacy of the People's Party', *Prachatai English*, [online] 19 December, Available from: https://prachatai.com/english/node/8312 [Accessed 22 April 2022].

Lee, T.C. (2006) *The Causes of Military Insubordination: Explaining Military Organizational Behaviour in China, Indonesia, the Philippines and Thailand*, PhD thesis, University of Washington, Washington.

Lissak, M (1976) *Military Roles in Modernization: Civil–Military Relations in Thailand and Burma*, London: Sage Publications.

Macan-Markar, M. (2019) All the king's men: Thai military power shifts away from Prayuth', *Nikkei Asian Review*, 2 July

'Mass shooting by Jakrapanth Thomma puts Thai army officers' side deals under scrutiny' (2020), The Straits Times, 12 February

Modelski, G. (1978) 'The long cycle of global politics and the nation state', *Comparative Studies in Society and History*, 20(2): 214–35.

Morgenbesser, L. (2020) 'The menu of autocratic innovation', *Democratization*, 27(6): 1053–72.

Nanuam, W. (2014) 'Elite royal guards go on Defence Ministry payroll', *Bangkok Post*, 13 February.

Nidhi, E. (2003) 'The Thai culture constitution', *Kyoto Review of Southeast Asia*, 3, Available from: https://kyotoreview.org/issue-3-nations-and-stories/the-thai-cultural-constitution/ [Accessed 22 April 2022].

Ockey, J. (2007) 'Thailand's 'professional soldiers' and coup-making: the coup of 2006', *Crossroads: An Interdisciplinary Journal of Southeast Asian Studies*, 19(1): 95–127.

O'Connor, J. (2019) 'Future Forward leader Thanathorn removed as MP by the Constitutional Court over prohibited media link', Thai Examiner, 20 November.

'Panda Gold versus Cobra Gold!' (2014), *Thai Post*, 2 June.

Pathmanand, U. and Connors M (2019) 'Thailand's public secret: military wealth and the state', *Journal of Contemporary Asia*, 51(2): 278–302.

Pek, C. (2019) 'Who are the richest royals in the world and how much are they worth?', *Singapore Tatler*, [online] 14 October, Available from: https://sg.asiatatler.com/society/the-richest-royals-in-the-world-2019 [Accessed 11 April 2022].

Picard, M. (2020) 'Commentary: the troubling trends underlying Thailand's mass shooting', *Channel News Asia*, [online] 17 February, Available from: www.channelnewsasia.com/news/commentary/thailand-shooting-mass-terminal-21-mall-army-chief-camp-12436010 [Accessed 11 April 2022].

Puangchon, U. (2020) *Royal Capitalism: Wealth, Class, and Monarchy in Thailand*, Wisconsin: University of Wisconsin Press.

Puangthong, P. (2017) *The Central Role of Thailand's Internal Security Operations Command in the Post-Counter-insurgency Period*, Trends in Southeast Asia, ISEAS, Singapore: Yusof Ishak Institute.

Puangthong, P. (2018) 'Warfare and depopulation of the Trans-Mekong Basin and the revival of Siam's economy', in M. Charney and K. Wellen (eds) *Warring Societies of Pre-colonial Southeast Asia: Local Cultures of Conflict Within a Regional Context*, Copenhagen: NIAS Press, pp 21–46.

Rachman, G. (2016) *Easternization: Asia's Rise and America's Decline: From Obama to Trump and Beyond*, New York: Other Press.

Raymond, G. (2018) *Thai Military Power: A Culture of Strategic Accommodation*, Copenhagen: NIAS Press.

Raymond, G. (2019) 'Competing logics: between Thai sovereignty and the China model in 2018', *Southeast Asian Affairs 2019*, ISEAS-Yusof Ishak Institute, pp 341–58.

Raymond, G. (2020) 'Strategic culture and Thailand's response to Vietnam's occupation of Cambodia, 1979–1989', *Journal of Cold War Studies*, 22(1): 4–45.

Royal Thai Embassy Moscow (2007) *From Your Friend: 110 Years of relations between Thailand and Russia*, Bangkok: Boon Rawd Trading International.

Siam Commercial Bank (2019) 'SCB executives and staff pledge loyalty and commitment to Royal Volunteer Spirit Program 904 VorPorRor', Siam Commercial Bank Webpage, Available from: www.scb.co.th/en/about-us/news/jul-2019/csr-nws-royalvolunteer-2562.html [Accessed 18 October 2022].

Sirivunnabood, P., and Ricks, J. (2016) Professionals and Soldiers: Measuring Professionalism in the Thai Military. *Pacific Affairs*, 89(1): 7–30.

Slater, D. (2010) *Ordering Power: Contentious Politics and Authoritarian Leviathans in Southeast Asia*, New York: Cambridge University Press.

Sulak, S. (2002) 'The crisis of Thai identity', in C. Reynolds (2002), *National Identity and Its Defenders: Thailand Today*, Chiang Mai: Silkworm Books, pp 33–48.

Surachart, B. (1999) *From Dominance to Power Sharing: The Military and Politics in Thailand, 1973–1992*, PhD thesis, Columbia University, New York.

Surin, M. (2003) 'The Thai military: from domination to alienation to separation to cooperation' in C. Hogue (ed) *The Development of Thai Democracy Since 1973*, Canberra: ANU, pp 55–66.

Thai Enquirer (2020) Opinion: 'Is Thailand's political future with the Future Forward Party or the military?', Thai Enquirer, 20 Feb.

Thak, C. (2007) *Thailand: The Politics of Despotic Paternalism*, New York: Cornell University Press.

Thongchai, W. (2016) *Thailand's Hyper-Royalism: Its Past Success And Present Predicament*, Trends in Southeast Asia No. 7, ISEAS, Singapore: Yusof Ishak Institute.

Tilly, C. (1985) 'War making and state making as organized crime', in P.B. Evans, D. Rueschemeyer and T. Skocpol (eds) *Bringing the State Back In*, Cambridge: Cambridge University Press, pp 169–91.

Tips, W. (1996) *Gustav Rolin-Jaequemins and the Making of Modern Siam: The Diaries and Letters of King Chulalongkorn's General Advisor*, Bangkok: White Lotus.

Vella, W. (1960) *Siam Under Rama III: 1824–1851*, Locust Valley, New York: J.J. Augustin Incorporated Publisher.

Waltz, K. (1979a) 'Political structures', in R. Keohane, *Neorealism and Its Critics*, New York: Colombia University Press, pp 70–97.

Waltz, K. (1979b) 'Anarchic Orders and Balance of Power', in R. Keohane, *Neorealism and its Critics*, New York: Colombia University Press.

Wasana, N. (2009) ลับลวงพรางภาคพิสดาร *Secrets Deception Disguises: The Improbable Phenomenon*, Bangkok: Post It Books.

Wise, J. (2019). *Thailand: History, Politics and the Rule of Law,* Singapore: Marshall Cavendish.
Wongcha-um, P and Thepgumpanat, P. (2018) 'Thai king's yellow and blue volunteers boost his support, visibility', Reuters, 4 September.
Zawacki, B. (2017) *Thailand Shifting Ground between the US and a Rising China*, London: Zed Books.

9

Peacekeeping: An Emerging Area of Southeast Asia's Defence and Security Cooperation?

Nicole Jenne

The practice of international peacekeeping has experienced considerable change over the past decades. For the purpose of this chapter, peacekeeping is defined as:

> the expeditionary use of uniformed personnel (police and/or military) with or without UN authorization, with a mandate or programme to (1) assist in the prevention of armed conflict by supporting a peace process; (2) serve as an instrument to assist in the implementation of ceasefire or peace agreements; or (3) enforce ceasefires, peace agreements or the will of the UN Security Council in order to build stable peace. (Bellamy and Williams, 2010, p 18)

Since the end of the Cold War, peacekeeping has come to incorporate a growing number of military, civilian and police functions aimed at creating long-term stability in the host country. At the same time, it underwent a shift with regards to personnel contributing countries, with increasingly higher numbers of peacekeepers coming from the global south. In this regard, Southeast Asia is no exception. Singapore, Thailand and the tiny sultanate of Brunei began to participate in peacekeeping under the aegis of the United Nations after the Cold War ended. Cambodia became part of the group of contributing countries in 2005 and Vietnam in 2014. Indonesia and Malaysia, the regional countries with the longest history of contributing to UN peacekeeping, have significantly broadened their engagement in the past two decades. Indonesia has even ranked among the top ten contributors to UN peace operations in recent years. To some extent, the Philippines also broadened its peacekeeping engagement. Myanmar, which had adopted an internationally isolationist stance in the 1960s, reversed its peacekeeping policy in 2015, during a democratization period, and for a few years sent a handful of peacekeepers to different missions. Thus, of the ten countries of ASEAN, to date only Laos has no direct experience in peacekeeping.

At the same time as peacekeeping became more prominent in the region, it also turned into 'a growing focus for defence cooperation' between the ASEAN states themselves and with external partners (Capie, 2015, p 120). The ASEAN states had begun experimenting with turning different MOOTW into activities of defence diplomacy already in the 1970s as a civil–military evolution towards keeping external peace in order to facilitate state and nation-building. Peacekeeping was added to this agenda with security officials from across Southeast Asia, including Laos, participating in a series of multilateral activities organized to promote exchange of information and best practices around peacekeeping. These include international summits and regular meetings under regional frameworks such as the ARF and the ASEAN Defence Ministers Meeting (ADMM). Although the individual motives for participating in peace operations vary and are typically mixed (Blum, 2000; Bove and Elia, 2011), clearly there has been one common rationale to Southeast Asia's recent interest. Peacekeeping, as Cambodia's 2006 Defence White Paper officially stated, is expected to contribute to regional peace and security (Cambodia, 2006, p 84) through forging an international society of states. As such, it is seen as part of ASEAN's proclaimed Political-Security Community (APSC).

The APSC aims at bringing 'ASEAN's political and security cooperation to a higher plane' (ASEAN, 2016b, p 1). As the roadmap for the years 2016 to 2025 specifies, '[t]he APSC will ensure that the peoples and Member States of ASEAN live in peace with one another', and to this end, '[i]t shall be a means by which ASEAN Member States can pursue closer interaction and cooperation to forge shared norms and create common mechanisms to achieve ASEAN's goals and objectives in the political and security fields' (ASEAN, 2016b, pp 1–2). In this context, peacekeeping is supposed to fulfil at least two functions. First, the creation of local Southeast Asian peacekeeping capacity can help in managing intraregional conflicts while avoiding outside involvement. Thus, the APSC Blueprint 2025 lists ASEAN members' active participation in peacekeeping as one of the 'key elements of the peaceful, secure and stable region' (ASEAN, 2016b, pp 11, 24). The strife for autonomy from external actors reflects Southeast Asia's longstanding diplomatic principle of saving face as states seek to be seen as taking care of their own region. This thinking was clearly expressed by Indonesia's President Habibie in 1999 when he called upon ASEAN to send more troops to the international mission in East Timor to have '"brown-faces [sic]" assuming control over security there' (Anwar, 2014, p 196).

The second expected benefit from peacekeeping is its potential to create social capital. Social capital is necessary to allow for ASEAN's existence as a 'no-war community' in which states cooperate to uphold its fundamental principles and institutions (Jenne, 2021). In the process of consolidating the ASEAN community, peacekeeping, considered to be a 'soft' security issue, 'stands to facilitate a slow deepening of "hard" security cooperation at the ASEAN level' (Borchers, 2014, p 6) since it employs force in a non-offensive way. Being it an international exercise, peacekeeping creates contacts between security officials that may lead to positive attitudes towards each other and can eventually be used to ease tensions in potential conflict situations. Moreover, peacekeeping is believed to lead to convergence in defence policies, missions and values, thus bringing states closer together (Thayer, 2014, p 220). In sum, peacekeeping is assumed to have transformative effects on a state's security and defence sector with positive implications for relations with other states (Caballero-Anthony, 2005; Capie, 2015, pp 122–23), which in turn is a key element in the Southeast Asian development model.

Whether these expectations actually rest on a sound basis is far from clear. ASEAN's security and defence cooperation has often been criticized as little more than a talk-shop susceptible to shifts in political preferences. Has peacekeeping created social interaction capacity – common frames of reference, shared knowledge and particular habits – that strengthened the APSC? Given that Southeast Asian countries committed to increase their participation in UN peacekeeping (ASEAN, 2016b, p 24), can we expect peacekeeping to play a role for the future development of the ASEAN community of states?

By addressing these questions, the chapter speaks broadly to three of the central themes of this book. First is the meaning of effectiveness in civil–military relations. To what extent is military effectiveness understood as a means to achieve developmental and modernization goals in the ASEAN states rather than a measure related to peacekeeping performance or outcomes? The second theme is the role of civil–military relations in the context of defence diplomacy, which Southeast Asian states have strongly geared towards constructing a regional international society, at least in discourse. Do activities around peacekeeping have the potential to change the military's mindset about their relationships with civilian authorities, society at large and with foreign militaries? Third, the chapter will shed light on the engagement of civilian versus military personnel in peacekeeping and its related activities. Does the expanding mission of peacekeeping provide new ground for the military to become an active player, or is it mainly civilians that broaden their range of activity?

The remainder of the chapter is divided into five parts. The following section explains why peacekeeping is relevant for Southeast Asian foreign and security policies individually and collectively. In this same section I also discuss the existing literature and show the need for a more nuanced assessment of the potential benefits peacekeeping is supposed to bring about. In order to provide such an assessment, I examine three aspects relevant to the consolidation of an ASEAN community of states that cooperates for the benefit of a common public good. The subsequent section compares the relevance peacekeeping has historically occupied in different Southeast Asian countries to establish whether there is convergence in the relative importance attributed to peacekeeping. Next, I take stock of the regional and international initiatives around peacekeeping the ASEAN members take part in. The fifth section discusses to what extent we can speak of regional cooperation considering states' participation in peace operations. The concluding section brings the findings together and relates them to some of the central questions posed in the introduction of this book.

Peace operations and regional cooperation: expectations and limits

Peace operations as an evolution of military means to keep the peace without resorting to kinetic measures fit neatly with ASEAN's aspirations from the 1970s when states began to develop defence diplomacy as a tool to provide for domestic stability and development. Still, peacekeeping is a comparatively new policy area in Southeast Asia and clearly secondary to others such as maritime security or terrorism. Nevertheless, both supply and demand side factors merit a closer look at peacekeeping and its potential future in regional security cooperation. With regards to supply side factors, as the APSC Blueprint 2025 indicates (ASEAN, 2016b, pp 24–5), there is a trend towards enhancing Southeast Asia's national and regional peacekeeping capacities. Indonesia, Malaysia, the Philippines and more recently also Cambodia and Vietnam have clearly expressed their preference for enhanced cooperation in this area. Demand exists at both the regional and global levels. Southeast Asia is not free from disputes and regional capacities for peacekeeping can have advantages over UN-led missions if a conflict escalates (Kamarulzaman, 2005). At the global level, despite predictions that future UN peace operations might become smaller in size, it is to be expected that the demand for peacekeepers and particularly specialized capacities will keep up. The UN has repeatedly called upon regional organizations to take on responsibility in accordance with Chapter VIII of the UN Charter. Based on these provisions, mainly the European Union and the African Union have carried out so-called hybrid missions in which regional organizations work together with the UN to stem the political, financial, logistical and military responsibilities of a mission. Since ASEAN is generally considered to be one of the most successful regional organizations, it is worth asking whether the organization will be willing to meet the global expectation of burden sharing such as indicated in a concept note from Vietnam for the Security Council on cooperation between the UN and ASEAN (UN Security Council, 2020).

So far, little has been written on Southeast Asia's participation in peace operations. While there is now a considerable number of studies dealing with peacekeeping in Europe and Africa, scholars of Southeast Asian security regionalism deal with the topic in passing. Pointing out that encounters in and around peacekeeping have increased the already 'impressive number of ASEAN defence-related meetings, conferences and activities' (Singh and Tan, 2011, p 9), these studies raise the question whether peacekeeping activism actually led to the creation of social capital within the APSC. In a previous study together with Jun Yan Chang, I have argued that peacekeeping-related defence diplomacy activities have at times even undermined moralistic trust, defined as 'the belief about the good intentions of others' (Chang and Jenne, 2020, p 333).

Some ASEAN scholars have expressed almost blind faith in the joint exercise of peacekeeping yielding transformative effects. Tang (2015), for instance, states that '[c]orralling a multinational military force under the ASEAN banner would deepen confidence-building and engender strategic trust among the ASEAN militaries'. Occasional talk about an integrated ASEAN peacekeeping force notwithstanding, it is highly unlikely that such will be created in the foreseeable future (see SIPRI, 2014). Even if Southeast Asian countries participate in the same peace operation, interaction between the national contingents is usually limited to encounters between a comparatively small number of individuals during preparatory training.

Considering exchanges of information and education programmes around peacekeeping, these appear to be global as much as regional in scope with the US being the largest provider of bilateral peacekeeping capacity assistance. This type of triangulated defence cooperation in which the US (and other extra-regional states) bring the ASEAN countries together has a longstanding tradition in Southeast Asia and may serve to increase the social interaction capacity between the local states. Yet, if extra-regional partners are equally or even more sought after as compared to regional peers, it is debatable whether activities related to peacekeeping can realistically be expected to make a distinctive contribution to the APSC. In this regard, Vietnam's officially cited motivation to break with its historic reticence in 2014 and set new legal bases to send peacekeepers abroad is illustrative. As the Deputy Minister of Foreign Affairs wrote in the official National Defence

Journal, '[p]articipating in UN's peacekeeping operations [constituted] a breakthrough in Vietnam's integration process […], contributing to the completion of its panorama of multilateral diplomacy in particular and of the country's international integration in general' (Ha Kim Ngoc, 2016). Neither this nor similar statements made at the occasion referred to the regional level.

Lastly, the claim that greater activity as a result of participating in peacekeeping leads to positive outcomes internationally can be questioned on the theoretical basis that cooperation in 'soft' security issues leads to the deepening of international ties. First, contemporary peacekeeping reflects a broad security agenda including both 'hard' and 'soft' issues. Missions typically combine 'robust military forces capable of limited peace enforcement tasks, should a ceasefire break down, with a strong civilian component that often includes civil administration, humanitarian agencies and police and justice officers' (Bellamy and Williams, 2010, pp 279–80). The 'hard', military component may be considered less sensitive in the context of peacekeeping where the contributing states have no stake in the conflict where they deploy, at least theoretically. Above all, however, it is the 'soft', civilian and humanitarian activities of peacekeeping that have been considered as potential catalysts of deeper security cooperation (Borchers, 2014). However, as Chong and Chang (2016) have convincingly shown, humanitarian assistance and disaster relief has functioned as an area of security competition 'by proxy' between Southeast Asian states. According to the authors, such 'soft' security issues provide 'the perfect political cover for geopolitical rivalry without the consequences of dealing with combat-induced casualties and nationalist umbrage over territorial acquisitions and surrenders, allowing militaries to compete under the veneer of "cooperating" to do "good"' (Chong and Chang, 2016, p 78). Thus, in line with Chang and Jenne, activities around peacekeeping have been motivated not only by benevolent considerations but also competitive ones in Southeast Asia (2020).

To what extent, then, can it be said that peacekeeping has furthered security cooperation between the ASEAN states? To assess the role of peacekeeping and its related activities in the context of the APSC, the following sections discuss three aspects. First is the relative importance different states attach to peacekeeping domestically to assess whether there is compatibility or even convergence. Second, I examine the success of regional cooperation in relation to peacekeeping, specifically the initiatives under Southeast Asia's track I and track II defence diplomacy. Third, I deal with Southeast Asian countries' cooperation in specific peacekeeping operations. In none of these areas, I will argue, is there a clear, discernible trend towards a quality shift in ASEAN security and defence cooperation based on activities revolving around peacekeeping. The secondary importance attached to peacekeeping and limited cooperation in concrete peacekeeping initiatives indicates that it is little more than another issue area that broadens security cooperation without significant potential to deepen it.

National peacekeeping trajectories

If peacekeeping is to deepen Southeast Asian regional cooperation, we should see convergence towards a strengthened commitment to prepare for and participate in peace operations. As this section will show, it is possible to identify a general, though not homogeneous trend to increase Southeast Asia's participation in UN peace operations such as it is envisaged in the APSC Blueprint 2025 (ASEAN, 2016b, p 24). Nevertheless, none of the ASEAN countries has a clear foreign policy strategy to foster peacekeeping as a priority area.

Within ASEAN, Indonesia, Malaysia and the Philippines have the longest history of sending peacekeeping personnel abroad. Their status as contributing countries dates back almost to the beginnings of the UN (see Table 9.1). Indonesia participated in the first armed UN mission to address the Suez Crisis in 1956. Earlier, the Philippines and Thailand had contributed troops to the United Nations Command (UNC) in the Korean

Table 9.1: Participation in UN peacekeeping by Southeast Asian countries

Country	First UN mission	Personnel deployed in April 2022 (troops, experts on mission and staff officers)	Active armed forces
Brunei	1992: UNTAC (Cambodia)	30	7,200
Cambodia	2005: UNMIS (Sudan)	781	124,300
Indonesia	1956: UNEF (Egypt)	2,521	395,500
Laos	–	–	29,100
Malaysia	1960: ONUC (Congo)	848	113,000
Myanmar	1965–1966 (Congo)	–	406,000
Philippines	1963: ONUC (Congo)	10	143,100
Singapore	1989: UNTAG (Namibia)	0	51,000
Thailand	1991: UNIKOM (Iraq/Kuwait)	285	360,850
Vietnam	2014: MINUSCA (CAR)	81	482,000

Source: Author's compilation based on multiple UN sources and International Institute of Strategic Studies (2021)

War (1950–53). The UNC was an example of collective security authorized by the Security Council to use the UN flag during the Soviet Union's absence in the Council. The UNC was not a peacekeeping mission proper but is commonly referred to in works dealing with peacekeeping as an example of peace enforcement, which has become more frequent since the Cold War ended (see, for example, Bellamy and Williams, 2010, p 83).

Neither Thailand nor the Philippines referred to their participation in the UNC as a peacekeeping mission at that time. Their ultimate goal for joining the war was a formal security commitment by the United States (Roehrig, 2011). However, as an official South Korean account shows, the 7,420 Philippine and 6,326 Thai troops on the Korean peninsula experienced a situation not unlike a peace operation (Ch'oe, 2010, pp 211–12):

> Those sixteen countries, which formed the UN forces, had different cultural and historical experiences, different eating habits, and different religious taboos. Therefore, food supply based on American or European standard dissatisfied non-American, non-European forces. […] The UN forces also had difficulty in commanding troops because not only the situations of home countries but also the cultural and historical backgrounds of component soldiers were different from each other. It was not an easy task for a UN commander to combine different forces from different nations into combat teams and to carry out combined operations in an effective way.

According to the same source, the UNC produced learning effects: 'These problems were gradually settled when soldiers from different countries came to understand each other. Besides, measures were also taken to respect different customs and cultures' (Ch'oe, 2010, p 211).

Against the backdrop of this experience, a decade after the Korean War the Philippines, together with Malaysia and Myanmar, joined the United Nations Operation in the Congo (ONUC, 1960–64). Myanmar, which was then in the early years of Ne Win's dictatorship, subsequently retreated from peacekeeping as it shifted towards an isolationist, even 'xenophobic' foreign policy (Egreteau and Jagan, 2013, p 72). This was reversed during a period of gradual liberalization between 2011 and 2021. In 2015, a decade after the country had sent civilian personnel to support the UN's political missions in Afghanistan (UNAMA) and Iraq (UNAMI), Myanmar temporarily re-joined the group of troop contributing states.

During the Cold War, the UN only carried out a limited number of peace operations. With the end of bipolarity came important changes for peacekeeping generally and its relevance to Southeast Asia in particular as more states began to deploy peacekeepers to an increasing number of missions around the globe. Brunei, Singapore and Thailand began to participate in UN peace operations. Their decision reflected a worldwide upsurge in the number of peacekeeping personnel deployed and coincided with specific regional and national interests. At the regional level, two UN missions deployed to Southeast Asia provided a strong motivation for states to contribute to stabilize their immediate neighbourhood. UNTAC in Cambodia saw troops and police contributions by all six of ASEAN's members at the time. The different missions in East Timor (UNAMET, INTERFET, UNTAET, UNMISET) counted with military, police and civilian personnel from Malaysia, the Philippines, Singapore and Thailand, and each country held the position of Force Commander for one year on a rotational basis (see Table 9.2). Brunei signalled its commitment with the region by sending a company of British Ghurkhas (Ismail, 2005, p 6). For obvious reasons, only Indonesia did not take part in East Timor.

The domestic push-factors for participation in UN peace operations have varied across time and space. Singapore, for instance, has justified peacekeeping 'in the context of how globalization has affected its security interests' (Heng and Ong, 2014). Since the mission in East Timor came to an end, this meant that Singapore has not been involved in UN peace operations but participated in other multilateral missions alongside the US such as the UN-mandated International Security Assistance Force (ISAF) in Afghanistan, the multinational anti-piracy mission CTF-151 in the Arabian Gulf and in the international coalition to fight the Islamic State in Iraq. These missions have been explained with reference to Singapore's national defence strategy, which builds on a close relation with Washington and a strong US presence in the Asia Pacific (Hussain, 2017).

In Indonesia and intermittently in Thailand, democratization processes triggered greater involvement in peacekeeping. In post-*reformasi* Indonesia, considerations of democratizing and civilianizing the armed forces through their engagement in international operations opened the way for peacekeeping participation on an unprecedented scale. Although the country's *Vision 4,000 peacekeepers 2015–2019* failed to materialize, in recent years Indonesia has continuously featured among the ten top contributing countries to UN missions.

In Thailand, it was during a democratic period when Prime Minister Chuan Leekpai (1997–2001) and his Foreign Minister, Surin Pitsuwan, promoted peacekeeping as a possibility to foster the country's international engagement and to better relations with their regional neighbours. Yet, they had to fight hard to convince the military to participate.[1] Until today, the Royal Thai Army (RTA) has remained reticent to accept peacekeeping as a mission of the armed forces with many considering it as a second-order mercenary activity below the RTA's standard. Interestingly, the authoritarian regime under retired Army General Prayuth Chan-Ocha appeared to see

Table 9.2: Senior appointments in UN peacekeeping by Southeast Asian countries

Country	Appointment[+]
Brunei	–
Cambodia	–
Indonesia	Maj Gen Rais Abin: UNEF II Force Commander (Egypt/Israel, 1976–79)
	Brgd-Gen Susilo Bambang Yudhoyono: UNPROFOR Chief Military Observer (Bosnia, 1995)
	Maj Gen Imam Edy Mulyono: MINURSO Force Commander (Western Sahara, 2013)
Laos	–
Malaysia	Col Mazlan Bahamuddin: UNASOG Chief Military Observer (Chad/Libya, 1994)
	Lt Gen Aboo Samah Bin Aboo Bakar: UNOSOM II Force Commander (Somalia, 1994–95)
	Brgd-Gen Tengku Ariffin bin Mohammed: UNMOT Chief Military Observer (Tajikistan, 1998–99)
	Lt Gen Khairuddin Mat Yusof: UNMISET Force Commander (East Timor, 2003–05)
Myanmar	–
Philippines	Maj Gen Jaime De Los Santos: UNTAET Force Commander (East Timor, 2000)
	Rodolfo Tor: UNMIT Police Commissioner (East Timor, 2006–08)
	Maj Gen Natalio C. Ecarma: UNDOF Head of Mission and Force Commander (Golan Heights, 2010–12)
Singapore	Maj Gen Eric Tan Huck Gim: UNMISET Force Commander (East Timor, 2002–2003)
Thailand	Maj Gen Songkitti Jaggabatara: INTERFED Dep. Force Commander (East Timor, 1999)
	Lt Gen Winai Phattiyakul: UNMISET Force Commander (East Timor, 1999–2002)
	Gen Boonsrang Niumpradit: UNTAET Force Commander (East Timor, 2000)
	Lt Gen Winai Phattiyakul: UNTAET Force Commander (East Timor, 2002)
Vietnam	–

Note: + The following senior appointments are considered: Special Representative of the UN Secretary General, Head of Mission, Force Commander, Deputy Force Commander, Chief of Staff, Police Commissioner, Chief Military Observer

Source: Author's compilation based on Jenne (2022). (Jenne 2022 is a short article, a so-called data feature, which presents the database from which the data used for Table 9.2 were taken.)

peacekeeping as a possibility of international legitimization. As one official website stated not long after the 2014 coup: 'Thailand under the Prayuth administration has a clear policy to contribute as much as possible to the UN peace operation [sic]. Thai troops have been under training to increase their capacity to support the UN peace operation [sic] around the world' (Thailand, 2015). While the years following the coup saw fewer than 30 Thai peacekeeping personnel deployed, since 2019 Thailand has again increased its contributions to close to 300.

The trend towards greater participation is illustrated by the case of Cambodia. The country's participation in UN peacekeeping dates back to 2005 and has steadily increased since. In particular, the Royal Cambodian Armed Forces (RCAF) have carried out demining and explosive ordnance disposal operations in support of peace operations around the world. The latest ASEAN member to join the group of contributing states is Vietnam. In 2014, Vietnam amended its constitution to lay the legal basis for the military to engage in peacekeeping. In the same year, a specialized peacekeeping training centre was created. Interestingly, in broadening their participation in peacekeeping, Cambodia and Vietnam also diversified their deployments by including the highest share of female peacekeepers among the ASEAN countries, with 15 per cent and 9.7 per cent as of April 2022, respectively (United Nations Peacekeeping, 2022). Apart from these countries, Indonesia and Malaysia have also increased the number of female peacekeepers over the past years in keeping with the pledges made in the Security Council Resolution 1325 on Women, Peace and Security. While so far only Indonesia and the Philippines have developed a National Action Plan to implement Resolution 1325, Vietnam made the Women, Peace and Security agenda a priority of its ASEAN Chairmanship in 2020 and its term as a non-permanent member of the UN Security Council in 2020–21.

Based on this overview, it is possible to conclude that there has been some convergence on identifying peacekeeping as an important, although not a primary policy area among the ASEAN states. Several observers have even suggested that states have come to converge on the increased acceptance of the contemporary, robust UN missions of peace enforcement (Caballero-Anthony, 2005; Capie, 2015). How significant are these developments for ASEAN's Political-Security Community?

The historical peacekeeping experiences constitute a joint resource for the creation of social capital. Through their participation in peacekeeping, most ASEAN member states have developed at least some expertise in international security cooperation within the framework of the UN. The growing importance most states have attached to this new mission indicates common interests that may serve as a basis for closer cooperation. Yet, no state has singled out peacekeeping as a primary mission. Malaysia is probably closest to including peacekeeping among its priorities, but like Indonesia and Vietnam, enhancing maritime security has taken precedence over other missions. In Singapore, the military is overwhelmingly concentrated on national defence against a potential external aggressor. On the other extreme, the security forces of Cambodia, Myanmar, the Philippines and Thailand are committed domestically either because they play a major political role or because they are engaged in internal armed conflict.

The secondary role of peacekeeping is reflected in the fact that only Indonesia appears to have valued positively the possibility to occupy senior positions in UN peacekeeping missions. As Table 9.2 shows, only Indonesia, Malaysia and the Philippines, not coincidentally the three countries with the longest history of UN peacekeeping, have occupied senior positions in missions other than those in East Timor. Malaysia had a notable presence of four top-level representatives in peace operations on different continents, but it needs to be stressed that the missions were concentrated within the time frame of a single decade. Beyond, seemingly little attention was paid to the possibility to promote nationals in senior peacekeeping appointments.

The apparent lack of efforts to increase the national peacekeeping profiles of the ASEAN states through leading positions in the UN is corroborated when considering the role of peacekeeping for military promotion. Anecdotal evidence suggests that the different national armed forces' promotion systems fail to provide special incentives for their best troops to serve as peacekeepers. In Singapore, overseas missions are rated positively in the annual performance reviews without the type of mission being accounted for. Similarly, in Malaysia, no consideration is given to peacekeeping in the standard rules of promotion that are applicable up to the rank of brigadier general. At the top level of the MAF, peacekeeping experiences are unlikely to serve as a distinctive career asset since promotion is political. Likewise, Indonesia's promotion commissions lack established rules and in Cambodia, the formal promotion system is not being implemented.

Neither differences in peacekeeping trajectories nor the fact that peacekeeping is a secondary military mission are necessarily an obstacle to successful regional cooperation in peacekeeping as long as states perceive a mutual benefit in cooperating. Thayer (2014, p 219) identifies such a benefit when he suggests that ASEAN's newer contributing states can learn from their more experienced peers through socialization in peace operations and training exercises. In the following sections, I assess whether the necessary conditions for the expected socialization effects and the creation of social interaction capacity effectively exist.

Regional cooperation around peacekeeping: defence diplomacy

When one looks at peacekeeping as an evolutionary military practice, defence diplomacy as the 'peacetime cooperative use of the armed forces and related infrastructure [primarily defence ministries] as a tool of foreign and security policy' (Cottey and Forster, 2004, p 6), becomes a major item on the post-Cold War international security agenda. Southeast Asia is no exception in this regard, and over the past two decades, peacekeeping has become an integral part to the region's defence diplomacy involving both state officials (track I) and non-state actors (track II). This section takes stock of regional cooperation around peacekeeping, which includes preparation, training and education activities in the area of peacekeeping but exempts taking part in a peace operation. The relevance of peacekeeping activities taking place among the ASEAN states is then compared to bilateral cooperation schemes between individual Southeast Asian countries and their extra-regional partners, which illustrate ASEAN's mode of expanding MOOTW to nurture a regional international society. Activities with extra-regional partners increase the APSC's potential for social interaction capital by creating basic capacities that can facilitate further cooperation within ASEAN. However, cooperation with external partners on its own falls short of contributing to the consolidation of a regional society of states. For the APSC to strengthen, 'the ground rules of regional society must go beyond those of international society to give the concept its distinguishing mark as well as greater normative content' (Ayoob, 1999, p 248).

Cooperation around peacekeeping began under the Asia Pacific-wide ARF in 1996. At the first Inter-Sessional Meeting on Peacekeeping Operations, '[p]articipants agreed that the discussion on the subject of peacekeeping in the ARF context promotes greater understanding in the Asia Pacific region' (ARF Intersessional Meeting, 1996). Following two peacekeeping training-related workshops during 1997, however, the ARF concluded that it was no longer necessary to hold on to a formal mechanism and suspended the Inter-Sessional Meeting. On part of the ASEAN states, the lukewarm commitment to enhance peacekeeping multilateralism reflected at least in part the unease of some with the liberal peace model. During the 1990s, liberal peace principles such as human rights and transitional justice became central peacekeeping activities in direct opposition to the authoritarian policies of many ASEAN states. Nevertheless, between 1998 and 2005, two peacekeeping training courses, four seminars and one workshop were held in different ARF member countries. In 2007, a new Peacekeeping Experts' Meeting was institutionalized and convened six times until 2013. It is likely not a coincidence that after several years of discontinuity, it was revived in 2019 in China, which had only recently turned into a top troop contributing country and the only permanent member of the UN Security Council with a significant number of blue helmets taking part in UN missions.

The ARF had kick-started talks on the possibility to create a regional peacekeeping centre. In 2009, the ASEAN states moved ahead with the idea and established an ASEAN Peacekeeping Centre Association. Two years later, the Association became an official network between the then existing five peacekeeping training centres (Vietnam was the sixth to join in 2014; see Table 9.3). The network was to promote information sharing, joint planning and training in order to 'promote and enhance cooperation among defence and armed forces [sic] within ASEAN' (ADMM, 2011). In the long term, states pledged to enhance interoperability and create a regional standby arrangement.

The network's first meeting in 2012 was co-hosted by Thailand and Indonesia, the two more liberal and progressive ASEAN members at the time. Participation was gradually extended to include all national peacekeeping centres as listed in Table 9.3, plus the military representatives from the four ASEAN states with no specialized training centre. The centres have received a limited number of foreign trainees, which has provided an additional venue of exchange. Yet, concrete plans to achieve interoperability have yet to be presented, let alone the creation of a joint ASEAN force as envisioned in the network's Concept Paper.

Peacekeeping-related activities have also been carried out in the framework of the ADMM-Plus. This forum brings together the defence ministers of the ten ASEAN states plus the eight countries of Australia, China, India, Japan, New Zealand, ROK, Russia and the US. The ADMM-Plus convenes Experts Working Groups in five areas, including peacekeeping. Within this framework, two exercises have been organized in the Philippines (2014) and in India (2016).

Table 9.3: Southeast Asian peacekeeping centres

Country	Creation
Cambodia	2005: National Centre for Peacekeeping Forces, Mine and ERW Clearance
Indonesia	2014: Indonesia National Defence Forces Peacekeeping Centre (PMPP TNI)
Malaysia	1995: Malaysian Peacekeeping Training Centre
Philippines	2002: Peacekeeping Operations Centre
Thailand	2006: Peace Operations Centre (RTArF-POC)
Vietnam	2014: Vietnam Peacekeeping Centre

Source: Author's compilation

Apart from the instances described previously, capacity-building activities have taken place mostly through bilateral mechanisms between the ASEAN states and their extra-regional partners. In this context, the US's engagement is of special relevance. Cobra Gold, the US-led annual theatre security exercise in Thailand that brings together up to 30 countries involved peace support and civilian evacuation operations. The US also held bilateral peacekeeping exercises with Indonesia (Garuda Shield) and Cambodia (Angkor Sentinel) (Capie, 2015, p 121). Additional programmes aimed at improving peacekeeping education and training infrastructures in Southeast Asia have been funded through the US State Department's Global Peace Operations Initiative (GPOI).

Other important ASEAN partners in cooperation around peacekeeping are Australia and the countries of the G8, most notably Canada, France, Japan and the UK.[2] These initiatives comprise a wide range of activities such as a cooperation scheme by the British Council to improve the English language skills of prospective peacekeepers in Thailand and Vietnam. China, which is increasingly becoming involved in all aspects of UN peacekeeping, is likely to expand its cooperation in this area further. A first step in this direction was a Memorandum of Understanding on UN Peacekeeping Operations signed with Vietnam in 2015.

Taken together, peacekeeping has become another area of defence diplomacy with possibilities to build personal contacts and develop shared security outlooks. Defence diplomacy's tangible results are notoriously difficult to measure, but if one is to judge where the largest benefits from peacekeeping capacity building originate, it is clear that the important resources come from outside the region rather than from within.

Regional cooperation in peacekeeping operations

The relatively high level of activity *around* peacekeeping in Southeast Asia contrasts with comparatively fewer possibilities for transformative effects to arise from cooperation in the actual exercise of peacekeeping. In this section I discuss the potential for an integrated ASEAN peacekeeping force as well as ASEAN states' cooperation in individual peacekeeping operations. Both areas provide only limited opportunities for encounters and joint learning experiences that could consolidate a regional society of states. The absence of closer cooperation in peacekeeping missions indicates that peacekeeping is seen as a type of neo-combat experience more than a new military mission of a different, non-competitive character, as proponents of the transformative effects-thesis propose. Thus, a logic of strategic competition prevails over the desire to promote a regional public good in the form of peacekeeping capacity.[3]

The idea of an integrated Southeast Asian force dates back to the 1980s (Acharya, 1991, p 161). Indonesia was the first country to present a formal proposal in its role as the ASEAN chair in 2003 (Capie, 2016, pp 17–18). Around this time, regional peacekeeping capacities were developed in Europe and Africa. The Indonesian proposal was part of the country's initiative to establish a regional community to allow ASEAN a greater role in Southeast Asian security matters. Yet, the idea was quickly silenced with Singapore's Minister of Foreign Affairs saying that ASEAN was 'the wrong entity to play a peacekeeping role' (Kuah, 2004, p 2). Thailand saw no need for a peacekeeping force either, claiming that the region had 'no conflict' to take care of. Vietnam declared that it was too early to consider such a form of cooperation (Kuah, 2004, p 2).

For Tay and Choo, the fact that ASEAN even expressed 'such thinking [was] a considerable step forward for the group' (2013, p 229). Yet, when the issue was brought up again in 2015, ASEAN was still not prepared to discuss a joint force. This time, Malaysia pitched the idea during official visits to other ASEAN countries while it held the annual ASEAN Chairmanship, which also coincided with Malaysia's term as a non-permanent member of the UN Security Council. Other than tacit support from Cambodia and the Philippines, however, the proposal fell on deaf ears.

Some have attributed the failure to agree on a joint peacekeeping force to divergent views on the principle of the Responsibility to Protect (R2P) (Tang, 2015). This claim is hardly convincing considering that the Malaysian proposal foresaw a dedicated force of specialists in disaster relief and military medicine that would be dispatched upon the request of the host country only (Parameswaran, 2015). Instead, it must be concluded that ASEAN's reticence to build joint peacekeeping capacities has more to do with the fact that peacekeeping serves as a substitute of the traditional mission of defence against external opponents. Maintaining the same line of competitive thinking, states engage in peacekeeping to show off their capacities and gain operative experience rather than to overcome international rivalries while, simultaneously, maintaining rival relations largely free of violence through the construction of a non-combat common language across the region by engaging in peacekeeping-related defence diplomacy activities.

The perhaps most significant attempt to build an ASEAN peacekeeping record dates from 2011 when Indonesia, as the yearly chair of ASEAN, brokered an agreement to station an observer mission along the Thai–Cambodian border. The mission was sanctioned by the UN and the International Court of Justice to prevent the recurrence of violent clashes along a disputed border stretch (see Jenne, 2017). However, although the Thai government had previously approved of the agreement, the Army refused to accept foreign observers on Thai soil. None of the ASEAN states spoke up to defend what had been presented as an example of collective action. Indonesia, too, chose not to push the competitive element, which clearly prevailed in the perception of the Thai Army that found it could well take care of its own business.

In a conference organized by SIPRI in 2014, Southeast Asian participants agreed that the creation of an ASEAN force was unrealistic at least for the foreseeable future (SIPRI, 2014). While such a force would reflect a deeper commitment to security and defence cooperation that could facilitate the creation of social interaction capacity, ASEAN's alternative way of peacekeeping cooperation remained flexible and non-binding. Thus, the ADMM adopted the foundations for an ASEAN Militaries Ready Group on Humanitarian Assistance and Disaster Relief with voluntary participation and separate command structure (ASEAN, 2016a). Similarly, the measures foreseen in the APSC Blueprint 2025 lowered expectations as the ASEAN members, far from creating regional capacities, agreed once again on the purpose of their defence diplomacy activities and merely planned to '[t]ake stock and explore the possibility of establishing a database on peacekeeping and post-conflict peacebuilding capabilities' (ASEAN, 2016b, p 24).

While there are no opportunities for direct, regional cooperation within a Southeast Asian peacekeeping structure, such possibilities are limited also in the context of UN peace operations. A review of Southeast Asian states' deployment strategies reveals no preference for a specific type of mission or geographic area where peacekeepers deploy. Thus, within the past decade, there was no single one UN mission in which even half of all ASEAN members participated. Even if the national contingents deploy in the same mission, however, it is questionable whether the common experience leads to more contact or even a common security outlook. National contingents are answerable to both the mission's force commander and to their national authorities and generally operate in different areas. Apart from UN training sessions at the beginning of each deployment, there are few possibilities for direct encounters to build social capital.

Two notable exceptions provided Southeast Asian militaries with a possibility to closer cooperation. The first is Singapore, which participated in the UN's Timor mission with an infantry company as part of a Thai battalion. However, this specific example is more a deployment strategy of Singapore as a small state rather than one of cooperation driven by the desire for further cooperation in the future. Due to operational considerations, Singapore has embedded medical teams and troops in other instances in which its partners were either more experienced or large, professionalized armies from outside the region (Heng, 2012, p 134).

The second exception is Brunei's engagement in the UN Interim Force in Lebanon (UNIFIL), where Bruneian troops deployed as part of a Malaysian battalion (Ministry of Defence Brunei Darussalam, 2011). This cooperation built on previous experience in the International Monitoring Team (IMT) in Mindanao in the Philippines (to be discussed later). The fact that Brunei's armed forces are simply too small to rival the Malaysian military helps to explain this peculiarity, and the cultural and historical closeness between the two militaries suggests that the absence of strategic competition in peacekeeping was a precondition rather than the result of cooperation between the two states.

The type of cooperation in peacekeeping that has come closest to a regional security arrangement took place in two missions outside the framework of the UN. In the European Union's 2005 observer mission to Aceh (AMM), Indonesia, civilian personnel from five ASEAN states (Brunei, Malaysia, Philippines, Singapore, Thailand) represented about 40 per cent of the 200–50 unarmed peacekeepers tasked to supervise the disarmament of rebels and the withdrawal of Indonesian troops. Notably, the ASEAN states praised the mission as a 'model for cooperation between ASEAN Member Countries in conflict resolution as provided for in the ASEAN Security Community' (ASEAN, 2005).

In the second mission in Mindanao in the southern Philippines, the involvement of Southeast Asian peacekeepers was again not related to ASEAN but in this case to the Organisation of Islamic Cooperation (OIC). The OIC, which counts Indonesia and Malaysia among its members, has been involved in the conflict between the Manila government and Muslim separatists since the 1970s. During 1995–96, the OIC sent an observer mission to oversee the implementation of a largely Indonesia-brokered peace agreement (Hopmann and Zartman, 2011, p 5). After the agreement broke down, peace talks resumed in 2004 with Malaysia in the role as facilitator and later as the mediator of another peace deal concluded in 2012. To monitor the 2004 cease-fire agreement, the OIC established a renewable one-year IMT with personnel from Malaysia, Brunei and Libya. Japan, Norway, Indonesia and the EU joined the mission subsequently. Brunei's contingents were variedly integrated with Malaysia and Indonesia (Hayat, 2016), the two states that have provided the bulk of peacekeeping personnel in Mindanao. While the experience will most likely have fostered a set of common peacekeeping understandings between the three states, their reference is not ASEAN but Islamic cooperation. Nevertheless, considering the lack of advances towards an integrated ASEAN force and the limited range of opportunities for joint action and learning in UN peace operations as described in this section, Southeast Asia's non-UN missions stand out as significant experiences where joint learning and socialization were possible.

Conclusion

This chapter situated peacekeeping within ASEAN's security and defence cooperation. The following summarizes the conclusions drawn from this specific case of a MOOTW and relates these insights to the book's general theme of Asian civil–military relations and their variety of civil–military fusions.

Considering the supposedly positive effects that have been ascribed to participating in activities around peace operations, notably its potential to improve relations between states, the conclusions reached here caution against too much enthusiasm. The coming into being of a regional international society in which force is seen as non-offensive requires social capital, but for such to develop peacekeeping has so far offered limited possibilities. The ASEAN members have varying traditions of participating in UN-led peace operations and none has included peacekeeping among the primary missions of its armed forces. There is no integrated, regional peacekeeping capacity to foster a common peacekeeping culture. Capacity-building activities and joint training and education appear to be at least as important in cooperation with extra-regional partners as they are with states from inside the region.

Peacekeeping shows at once the limitations of common security in Southeast Asia *and* the strong consent on the quintessential elements of ASEAN cooperation, the latter of which has historically been driven by the idea of creating a stable external environment to facilitate internal development. Intramural sensitivities about saving face, respecting sovereignty and not least persisting mistrust between states all stand in the way of concrete steps to consolidate the APSC through joint activities going beyond consultative meetings. Peacekeeping in the form of defence diplomacy has therefore been only a cautious way forward in ASEAN cooperation. As in other areas, the ASEAN members have sought to balance the preference for non-integration with the need to render the organization capable of acting, often to the detriment of the latter. However, since military effectiveness here is understood in terms of creating an environment conducive to state and nation-building, the lack of tangible deliverables has not been perceived as a problem. Given that ASEAN itself has associated the strengthening of its international role with closer cooperation in peacekeeping (Shoji, 2013, p 8), however, it would be well advised to take tangible steps to enhance its capacities in this area. In other words, the consideration of effectiveness, which this book shows to be mostly subordinate to ideas of the military's nation and state building roles in the Asian civil–military relations model, should be given greater consideration. Enhancing Southeast Asia's regional peacekeeping capacities need not go all the way to implement a liberal peace-type standing force but could take the form of a rapid reaction group drawing on national contingents. This way, states would maintain control over where and when peacekeepers are deployed.

What does peacekeeping cooperation tell us about the civil–military relations equilibria in the ASEAN member states? Troops deployed in peace operations are subordinated to civilian orders and are hard pressed to comply with UN standards of human rights, protecting civilians and cooperating with civilian actors. These standards are transmitted in UN-certified national peacekeeping education and training facilities as well as in international fora such as the International Association of Peacekeeping Training Centres (IAPTC), in which the ASEAN centres take part. For those exposed to peacekeeping experiences on the ground or through institutional channels, these constitute a common resource for the creation of social capital that could boost potential transformative effects on national civil–military relations. In order for peacekeeping to produce such transnationally supported, transformative effects, however, it likely requires a critical mass of individuals with exposure to peacekeeping which Southeast Asia is yet to acquire. Moreover, there is little reason to believe that peacekeeping will affect civil–military relations independent of any broader reform processes under way. The latter, as demonstrated in the Southeast Asian case studies in this book, is currently not taking place anywhere.

Who stands to gain more from peacekeeping as a field of activity where the civilian and military spheres are fudged? While civilians are an integral part of peacekeeping in all its phases including decision-making, planning and execution, the overview provided in this chapter shows that clearly the military has a role to play in peacekeeping, both nationally and in defence diplomacy.

Taken together, peacekeeping has evolved as a new foreign and security policy in Southeast Asia, although to uneven degrees. Measured against ASEAN's aspirations proper, however, the potential of peacekeeping cooperation is veritably an incremental but consistent contribution to the consolidation of the APSC. Such a process would occur in the hybridized mode of Asian civil–military relations described in this book where the military has its legitimate role to play in constructing a Political-Security Community, not only executing policies but potentially also participating in their design and overview in the case of Asia's authoritarian regimes.

Notes

[1] Personal conversation with Panitan Wattanayagorn, then at the prime minister's office, Bangkok, June 2014.
[2] In 2004, the G8 adopted the Action Plan *Expanding Global Capability for Peace Support Operations*.
[3] This section draws in part on Chang and Jenne (2020).

References

Acharya, A. (1991) 'The Association of Southeast Asian Nations: "security community" or "defence community"?', *Pacific Affairs*, 64(2): 159–78.

ADMM (2011) 'Concept paper on the establishment of ASEAN Peacekeeping Centres Network', ASEAN Defence Ministers' Meeting (ADMM), [online] nd, Available from: https://asean.org/wp-content/uploads/images/archive/document/18471-j.pdf [Accessed 10 July 2022].

Anwar, D.F. (2014) 'Indonesia's peacekeeping operations: history, practice, and future trend', in C. Aoi and Y.-K. Heng (eds) *Asia-Pacific Nations in International Peace Support and Stability Operations*, New York: Palgrave Macmillan US (*Asia Today*), pp 189–210.

ARF Intersessional Meeting (1996) *Summary Report of the ARF Inter-Sessional Meeting on Peacekeeping Operations 1–3 APRIL 1996, Kuala Lumpur. Malaysia.*

ASEAN (2005) 'Chairman's statement of the 11th ASEAN summit. Kuala Lumpur', *ASEAN Association of Southeast Asian Nations*, [online] 12 December, Available from: http://asean.org/?static_post=eleventh-asean-summit-kuala-lumpur-12-14-december-2005 [Accessed 10 July 2022].

ASEAN (2016a) 'Terms of reference', *AMRG on HADR*, [online] 22 April, Available from: http://mod.gov.la/10thADMM/assets/4.7.1-tor-on-amrg-as-of-20160422.pdf [Accessed 10 July 2022].

ASEAN (2016b) *ASEAN Political-Security Community Blueprint 2025*, Jakarta: ASEAN Secretariat, *ASEAN Association of Southeast Asian Nations*, [online] nd, Available from: www.asean.org/wp-content/uploads/2012/05/ASEAN-APSC-Blueprint-2025.pdf [Accessed 10 July 2022].

Ayoob, M. (1999) 'From regional system to regional society: exploring key variables in the construction of regional order', *Australian Journal of International Affairs*, 53(3): 247–60.

Bellamy, A. and Williams, P. (2010) *Understanding Peacekeeping*, 2nd edn, Cambridge, UK; Malden MA: Polity.

Blum, A. (2000) 'Blue helmets from the south: accounting for the participation of weaker states in United Nations peacekeeping operations', *Journal of Conflict Studies*, 20(1), Available from: https://journals.lib.unb.ca/index.php/JCS/article/view/4334 [Accessed 16 April 2017].

Borchers, H. (2014) 'ASEAN's environmental challenges and non-traditional security cooperation: towards a regional peacekeeping force?', *ASEAS – Österreichische Zeitschrift für Südostasienwissenschaften*, 7(1): 5–20.

Bove, V. and Elia, L. (2011) 'Supplying peace: participation in and troop contribution to peacekeeping missions', *Journal of Peace Research*, 48(6): 699–714.

Caballero-Anthony, M. (2005) 'UN peace operations and Asian security', *International Peacekeeping*, 12(1): 1–17.

Cambodia (2006) *Defending the Kingdom of Cambodia: Defense White Paper*, Phnom Penh: Government Publication.

Capie, D. (2015) 'Evolving attitudes to peacekeeping in ASEAN', in K. Tsukamoto (ed) *New Trends in Peacekeeping: In Search of a New Direction*, Tokyo: National Institute for Defence Studies, pp 111–25.

Capie, D. (2016) 'Indonesia as an emerging peacekeeping power: norm revisionist or pragmatic provider?', *Contemporary Southeast Asia: A Journal of International and Strategic Affairs*, 38(1): 1–27.

Chang, J.Y. and Jenne, N. (2020) 'Velvet fists: the paradox of defence diplomacy in Southeast Asia', *European Journal of International Security*, 5(3): 332–49.

Chong, A. and Chang, J.Y. (2016) 'Security competition by proxy: Asia Pacific interstate rivalry in the aftermath of the MH370 incident', *Global Change, Peace & Security*, 28(1): 75–98.

Ch'oe, Kyŏng-sik (2010) *The Eternal Partnership, Thailand and Korea: A History of the Participation of the Thai Forces in the Korean War*, Seoul: Ministry of Patriots and Veterans Affairs, Republic of Korea.

Cottey, A. and Forster, A. (2004) *Reshaping Defence Diplomacy: New Roles for Military Cooperation and Assistance*, Oxford: Oxford University Press for the International Institute for Strategic Studies.

Egreteau, R. and Jagan, L. (2013) *Soldiers and Diplomacy in Burma: Understanding the Foreign Relations of the Burmese Praetorian State*, Singapore: NUS Press in association with IRASEC.

Ha Kim Ngoc (2016) 'Participating in UN's peacekeeping operations, a breakthrough in Vietnam's integration process', *National Defence Journal*, [online] 17 October, Available from: http://tapchiqptd.vn/en/theory-and-practice/participating-in-uns-peacekeeping-operations-a-breakthrough-in-vietnams-integration-process/9412.html [Accessed 10 July 2022].

Hayat, H. (2016) 'Brunei sends new peacekeeping contingent to Mindanao', *Borneo Bulletin*, [online] 14 September, Available from: https://borneo363.rssing.com/chan-61976226/all_p58.html [Accessed 10 July 2022].

Heng, Y.K. (2012) 'Confessions of a small state: Singapore's evolving approach to peace operations', *Journal of International Peacekeeping*, 16: 119–51.

Heng, Y.K. and Ong, W. (2014) 'The quest for relevance in times of peace: operations other than war and the third-generation Singapore Armed Forces', in C. Aoi and Y.-K. Heng (eds) *Asia-Pacific Nations in International Peace Support and Stability Operations*, New York: Palgrave Macmillan US (*Asia Today*), pp 141–63.

Hopmann, T. and Zartman, W. (eds) (2011) 'Mindanao: understanding conflict 2011', *Conflict Management Program: Student Field Trip to Mindanao*, John Hopkins University, School for Advanced International Studies.

Hussain, Z. (2017) 'Singapore–US relationship is deep, very sound: PM Lee', *The Straits Times*, [online] 21 October, Available from: www.straitstimes.com/singapore/singapore-us-relationship-is-deep-very-sound-pm-lee [Accessed 10 July 2022].

International Institute of Strategic Studies (2021) 'Chapter six: Asia', *The Military Balance*, 121(1): 218–313.

Ismail, R. (2005) Peacekeeping: should Brunei jump onto the bandwagon?, *Canadian Force College (Exercise New Horizons)*, [online] 29 April, Available from: www.cfc.forces.gc.ca/259/290/291/287/ismail.pdf [Accessed 10 July 2022].

Jenne, N. (2017) 'The Thai–Cambodian border dispute: an agency-centred perspective on the management of interstate conflict', *Contemporary Southeast Asia*, 39(2): 315–47.

Jenne, N. (2021) 'The domestic origins of no-war communities', *Journal of International Relations and Development*, 24(1): 196–225.

Jenne, N. (2022) 'Who leads peace operations? A new dataset on leadership positions in UN peace operations, 1948–2019', *Journal of Peace Research*, pp 1–13.

Kamarulzaman, A.A. (2005) 'A regional perspective of UN peace operations in Southeast Asia', *International Peacekeeping*, 12(1): 34–48.

Kuah, A. (2004) 'The ASEAN security community: struggling with the details', *Singapore: Institute of Defence and Strategic Studies, NTY (IDSS Commentaries)*, [online] 15 June, Available from: www.rsis.edu.sg/wp-content/uploads/2014/07/CO04021.pdf [Accessed 10 July 2022].

Ministry of Defence Brunei Darussalam (2011) 'RBAF deploys 5th UNIFIL contingent', *Ministry of Defence Brunei Darussalam*, [online] 12 January, Available from: https://mindef.gov.bn/Theme/Home.aspx [Accessed 10 July 2022].

Parameswaran, P. (2015) 'ASEAN peacekeeping meeting concludes in Cambodia', *The Diplomat*, [online] 9 October, Available from: https://thediplomat.com/2015/10/asean-peacekeeping-meeting-concludes-in-cambodia/ [Accessed 10 July 2022].

Roehrig, T. (2011) 'Coming to South Korea's aid: the contributions of the UNC coalition', *International Journal of Korean Studies*, 15(1): 63–97.

Shoji, T. (2013) 'ASEAN Defense Ministers' Meeting (ADMM) and ADMM Plus: a Japanese perspective', *NIDS Journal of Defense and Security*, 14: 3–17.

Singh, B. and Tan, S.S. (eds) (2011) *From 'Boots' to 'Brogues': The Rise of Defence Diplomacy in Southeast Asia*, Singapore: S. Rajaratnam School of International Studies.

SIPRI (2014) 'New geopolitics of peace operations: emerging powers', *SIPRI Stockholm International Peace Research*, [online] nd, Available from: www.sipri.org/research/conflicts-and-peace/peace-operations-and-conflict-management/new-geopolitics-of-peace-operations-emerging-powers [Accessed 3 June 2017].

Tang, S.M. (2015) 'Asean peacekeeping force? Points to ponder', *The Straits Times*, [online] 28 May, Available from: www.straitstimes.com/opinion/asean-peacekeeping-force-points-to-ponder [Accessed 3 June 2017].

Tay, S. and Choo, A. (2013) 'Peacekeeping, peacebuilding, and preventive diplomacy', in R. Sukma and Y. Soeya (eds) *Beyond 2015: ASEAN-Japan Strategic Partnership for Democracy, Peace, and Prosperity in Southeast Asia*, Tokyo: Japan Center for International Exchange, pp 228–40.

Thailand (2015) *ASEAN peacekeeping forces and Thailand, ASEAN Information Center*, [online] Available at: www.aseanthai.net/english/ewt_news.php?nid=434&filename=index [Accessed 4 June 2017].

Thayer, C.A. (2014) 'The contrasting cases of Cambodia and Vietnam: active engagement and considering engagement in United Nations peacekeeping operations', in C. Aoi and Y.-K. Heng (eds) *Asia-Pacific Nations in International Peace Support and Stability Operations*, New York: Palgrave Macmillan US (Asia Today), pp 211–44.

UN Security Council (2020) 'Vietnam: concept note for the Security Council briefing on the theme "Cooperation between the United Nations and the Association of Southeast Asian Nations"', *UN Security Council*, [online] 10 January, Available from: https://digitallibrary.un.org/record/3847743?ln=es [Accessed 10 July 2022].

United Nations Peacekeeping (2022) *Gender*, [online] 30 April 2022, Available from https://peacekeeping.un.org/en/gender [Accessed 21 July 2022].

PART II
Northeast Asia

10

Subjective Conditional Control: Return of the Strongman in China's Party–Army Relations

James Char

China's four decades of economic development have invariably coincided with a profound transformation of the PLA; nowhere has that change been more apparent than in the period following the 18th Party Congress of the CCP. With Xi Jinping's assumption of the trifecta of Party–state–military power coinciding with the structural growth in China's comprehensive strength, the PLA's status in Beijing's domestic and international calculus has become more pronounced. Since arriving at the top, the incumbent has shown considerably greater interest than his immediate predecessor in harnessing the Party's coercive forces as his own domestic powerbase as well as foreign policy instrument to complement hard Chinese economic power. To be sure, Xi's meddling in PLA affairs reflects his aspiration to reshape the Party–army into a force commensurate with Beijing's global stature in conformity with his 'China Dream' – that is, a strong country needs to possess an equally powerful military (Xinhua, 2017). Notwithstanding the increased time and resources devoted by Xi to managing his country's military affairs[1] – suggestive of the growing clout of the armed forces in the PRC – the PLA's rising stature has nevertheless been accompanied by the conundrum of concurrent efforts by its commander-in-chief to destabilize it. These have come in the form of purges against PLA elites on graft charges and Xi's push for the latest iteration of Chinese military modernization to streamline the PLA and its operations.

Not unlike previous eras of civilian paramountcy over the CCP's armed servants under the regime's revolutionary forebears, Xi's emergence as China's strongman leader would not have been possible without first gaining control of the Party's gun.² What accounts for the return to this manifestly politicized nature of authority more commonly associated with Mao Zedong – and to a lesser extent, Deng Xiaoping? Has Maoist absolute control of the Party's army returned to the fore? And what is its significance for the trajectory of CCP–PLA interactions in the medium to long term? Whereas more proximate factors of the PRC's recent past – particularly those emerging during the administrations of Jiang Zemin and Hu Jintao – have had a bearing on civil–military relations in the post-reform period, it is equally important to acknowledge *why* the seemingly outmoded methods of Maoist control have made a comeback, and *how* those means have been adapted within the present context.

While a number of notable contemporary studies into the civil–military relations of post-reform China mostly revolve around the 'conditional compliance' (Mulvenon, 2001) and 'state control' (Shambaugh, 2002; Scobell, 2005) models, politico-military developments in the period hitherto have since demonstrated the temporary utility of these analyses. Similarly, in spite of the rejection by a previous generation of PLA watchers (Joffe, 1987; Godwin, 1988) of the Huntingtonian framework (1957) on the account that the Chinese military can be both professional and politicized all at once, their works fail to consider key milestones in the CCP's history in shaping Party–army dynamics. Indeed, how the twin legacies in the development of the PRC – Mao's political insurrection, and Deng's economic revolution – influence Chinese domestic politics and concomitantly, the role of the PLA in China's elite politics, remains a lacuna in the literature. This chapter is an attempt to address this gap. To a large degree, it describes and assesses Xi Jinping's attempts at imposing civilian authority over the CCP's armed servants especially given the 'reign without overt rule' of his immediate predecessors – Hu Jintao, and before Hu, Jiang Zemin (You, 2015, p 156) – both considered 'first among equals' and certainly no paramount leader à la Mao and Deng. Against the backdrop of the ongoing military reforms in China and the PLA anti-corruption campaign, this chapter will show how the ideas that have guided Xi's *modus operandi* are informed by methods previously utilized by the Party's original strongman.

Overall, this chapter will answer three questions this edited volume seeks to address. First, it considers how the revolutionary legacy of the PRC's founding leader continues to influence CCP–PLA relations in contemporary China, in which the regime maintains as the raison d'être of its armed servants *first and foremost* the continuation of authoritarian rule.³ Second, it describes the trajectory of civil–military dynamics following Mao's passing and China's economic liberalization in 1978, and explicates on those conditions leading to the present state of affairs. Indeed, how did Maoist and Dengist 'absolute' control evolve into the PLA's 'conditional' compliance under Jiang and Hu – before paving the groundwork for the present 'subjective conditional' control

Xi has adopted to redress the unprecedented degree of PLA autonomy in Party–army relations? This will then be followed by a discussion of the incumbent leader's operationalization of subjective conditional control. Finally, and despite the increasing degree of politicization, this chapter argues against the traditional Western logic of civil–military relations and concludes that Xi's emphasis on 'politics-in-command' in governing the civil–military relations of China will in all likelihood preserve the *status quo* of authoritarian prosperity.

The Chinese Civil War and civil–military relations in Maoist China

As per Perlmutter and LeoGrande's assertion that 'the military is a normal participant in [the] politics' of Communist systems (1982), PLA involvement in Chinese politics therefore ought to be regarded as the norm – rather than the exception. With every Chinese leader since Mao Zedong having drawn power from his control of the Party's armed wing, the PLA's political entanglements could not be clearer. Especially given its Leninist foundations and the permeation of its political commissar (PC) system throughout PLA units down to the company level, the CCP's principle that the Party commands the gun has been practised since its earliest beginnings. Since the inauguration of the Chinese Workers' and Peasants' Red Army on 1 August 1927, CCP leaders have steadfastly adhered to the principle that 'the Party commands the gun'.[4] In its struggle against the former Kuomintang (KMT, or Nationalist) government that ruled China proper until 1949, armed insurrection was thus initiated when the CCP's leaders realized their political ends could only be accomplished through military means. Initially small and weak, the PLA had to withstand the onslaught of the stronger Nationalists until it became strong enough towards the final phase of the Chinese Civil War to defeat the KMT forces.[5] Following from the successful exploits of his armies, Mao could go on to proclaim the founding of the PRC in October 1949. Seen in this light, Xi Jinping's assiduous efforts at consolidating control over the PLA is therefore no coincidence.

That Xi has cemented his status as China's new paramount leader since Deng Xiaoping is not in doubt. Media and academe alike have portrayed him as 'a very confident and strong leader' (Landler, 2014). Analyses of the 19th Party Congress variously point to the incorporation of his eponymous governance philosophy 'Xi Jinping Thought on Socialism with Chinese Characteristics for a New Era' into the CCP constitution – a privilege denied to both his post-reform predecessors – as well as his rejection of the succession norms established by Deng, as conclusive evidence of his dominant position within China's political system. While Xi clearly dominates his colleagues at the apex Politburo Standing Committee (PBSC), his pre-eminent political status is also patently reflected in his command of the regime's armed forces in his capacity as CMC chairman. Indeed, on the occasion of the 19th Congress, Xi was able to monopolize yet greater military authority by reducing the number of generals in the PLA's top decision-making body while making sure they all came from his own camp.

With factional politics considered taboo in Communist China given the regime's aversion to intra-party strife, it is no surprise that previous studies of the CCP's internal dynamics have alluded to aphorisms such as 'five lakes and four seas' ('五湖四海'), as in the PLA's case, that officers must be drawn from 'all corners of the country' (Mulvenon, 2001, p 324). Contrary to those assertions, however, it would be remiss to overlook how the PRC's founding leader himself had conceded 'how peculiar it would be were there *no* factions in the Party' (Mao, 1968).[6] Veritably, Mao Zedong further saw to it that his own followers constituted the largest grouping in the Party-state, with this proclivity extending to the PLA. Despite expressing his opposition to 'mountaintop-ism' ('山头主义'), when the time came to share the spoils of war and bestow ranks to his officers after their successful revolution, those who were promoted to the uppermost echelons mostly came from the Maoist camp. Chiefly, these were men from the Chairman's First Front Army during the Long March from late 1934 to 1936.[7] Conversely, fewer generals from the at one time stronger Fourth Front Army and the smaller Second Front Army – despite having contributed their fair share to the Communist victory – were given such lofty appointments.

Moreover, at the risk of antagonizing those men responsible for the CCP's survival and his own personal safety, Mao scarcely shied away from humiliating professional soldiers for the purpose of imposing his authority on his generals. One such example came as the Nationalist forces were hot in pursuit of the former insurgents across the southwestern provinces of Guizhou, Sichuan and Yunnan during the Long March. Concerned that their troops were unduly exhausted from longer, tortuous treks instead of retreating along shorter, less winding routes, the legendary Communist general, Lin Biao, began to question Mao's judgement. As soon as the Red Army had extricated itself from the enemy's interdictions, the Chairman wasted no time in lambasting Lin – going as far as calling Lin 'a child' who 'knew nothing' (cited in Cao and Wu, 2014, p 130). Later, in the final phase of the Chinese Civil War in the late 1940s, Mao would once again excoriate Lin and his other generals for showing hesitancy in carrying out a risky attack on the city of Jinzhou during the Liao-Shen Campaign (Tanner, 2015, p 197). In making an example out of one of his most illustrious commanders, Mao succeeded not only in making an example out of Lin but also made clear to the rest who was in charge.

Following the PRC's founding, the former leader would also utilize institutional measures to tighten his grip over the PLA. In the wake of a purported coup d'état by Lin towards the end of Mao's reign, the Chairman neither hesitated to move against generals whose political allegiances to himself were suspect. With respect to those officers one level below the CMC in the military hierarchy overseeing China's regional commands, Mao was to approve of Deng Xiaoping's recommendation to curb their authority for fear that these military elites might establish independent fiefdoms. To weaken their powerbases, Mao reshuffled these commanders before effecting their lateral transfers 'without their staff' to avert the formation of powerful patron–client networks in their new posts (Vogel, 2013, pp 79–81). To minimize the potential for organized dissent among them, each re-assigned officer could bring with him only 'a doctor, a nurse, a personal secretary, a bodyguard, a driver, and a cook' to his new post (Li, 2015).

Emphatically, just as Mao Zedong had asserted his authority over his generals via a combination of personnel appointments, reshuffles and psychological intimidation, his current successor has turned to similar methods to impose himself on the PLA. As will be discussed later, even if civil–military relations in the PRC seemingly conforms with the politicization–professionalism spectrum described by Huntington (1957) and Janowitz (1960), the CCP–PLA dynamic is uniquely distinguished by considerable civilian intrusion since the PLA's founding. Under Xi Jinping, a model of civil–military relations based on the country's past – a culturally centred Maoist 'strongman' approach inspired by the Party-state's founding dictator – has emerged. Notwithstanding its inherent contradictions with the *modus operandi* alluded to in the Huntingtonian dialectic described in the introduction of this volume, a more politicized PLA under Xi, as the following sections will argue, is an inevitable outcome as the CCP's revolutionary old guard – Mao in 1976, and then Deng in 1997 – passed from the scene.

Growing PLA autonomy: post-Deng to pre-Xi

Reform and opening-up

Whereas any distinction in the functional responsibilities of the regime's elites were barely distinguishable during the Maoist and Dengist eras[8] – with dual-role leaders sharing civilian–military duties while the Party's uniformed elites also sat at the apex of Chinese politics[9] – the period after Deng Xiaoping's demise has been marked by civil–military bifurcation epitomized by Joffe's (2006) observation of 'two centres' of power: Between 2002 and 2004, the PLA found itself in the unusual situation of having to answer *separately* to the then CCP general secretary, Hu Jintao, and Hu's predecessor, Jiang Zemin, who had clung on to the CMC chair.[10] If the ascension of these two technocratic Chinese leaders did mark an important generational shift and 'led to an effective separation of military and civilian elites' (Mulvenon, 2001, p 318), it was actually the economic policies of China's last revolutionary leader that was exercising greater salience on civil–military relations in the contemporary period.

In that regard, three decades after Mao had 'emancipated' China, Deng's own liberation of the Chinese economy via Reform and Opening-up was to result in a Party–army no longer insulated from society. As the former paramount leader decided that economic development was to be prioritized as the Cold War was drawing to a close, the PLA leadership was forced to accept Deng's rationale that military reforms had to be pushed to the backburner in favour of first enriching the civilian economic base. As such, the Chinese military was thence authorized to generate its own income independent of the Party-state; for instance, through the leasing of PLA-held real estate to state-owned as well as private property developers in the country (Vogel, 2011, pp 548–51). Although that policy did make up for shortfalls in the national defence expenditure initially and helped the military improve its facilities and services, it was also only a matter of time before corruption within the ranks set in as the country's GDP growth began to soar.[11]

Partly motivated by Jiang Zemin's desire to 'maintain the PLA's conditional compliance to his authority' (Mulvenon, 2001, p 328) and especially since Jiang himself lacked the military credentials of Mao and Deng, the previous arrangement allowing the PLA to grow its commercial activities was thus permitted to continue for an extended period (Swaine, 2005). Indeed, it was not until the Party had instructed its military cadres more than once in the late 1990s to divest its business – and following a number of high-profile diplomatic exposés implicating the Chinese military (BBC, 2001) – that the former CMC chair announced the decision to dissolve the PLA's military–business complex. Then as it is now, there was considerable opposition and foot-dragging within the ranks. Evidence of the PLA's leverage over its civilian master during that period can be inferred when Jiang – likely concerned that the policy would be unpopular with the military establishment – instead pushed its implementation to Hu Jintao rather than take matters into his own hands.

Alongside its growing autonomy, malfeasance within the PLA also took a turn for the worse under Jiang's successor.[12] Most disturbingly, Hu Jintao even had to resort to relying on the civilian Central Discipline and Inspection Commission (CDIC) after the military's internal discipline body refused to do his bidding. As extant evidence suggests, despite ordering his uniformed subordinates to look into the activities of one blatantly corrupt senior PLA officer (Garnaut, 2012), Hu's CMC deputies simply ignored their chairman's legitimate command.[13] Such recalcitrance as well as the PLA's non-compliance with prohibitions first issued in the 1990s banning itself from pursuing its commercial interests would persist even as Hu handed over his Party and military portfolios to Xi Jinping at the 18th Party Congress.

As he relinquished his positions, Hu would make clear during the handover ceremony that the CCP's inability to deal with graft would deal a 'fatal' blow to the regime (China.org.cl, 2012) while also calling on its armed wing to maintain its 'glorious tradition' and 'fine work style'. On succeeding his predecessor, Xi would echo the same sentiments as he beseeched PLA leaders to 'make every effort to combat corruption and promote integrity in the army' (Xi, 2016). The matter of the PLA's image problem as perceived by Chinese society at large no doubt would have influenced the two men's calls for greater accountability since public anger over abuse of privileges by some military personnel had been simmering for some time (Xinhua, 2013). Moreover, negative perceptions of the CCP's armed wing were feeding into and reinforcing the image of an inherently corrupt regime.

Problems with conditional PLA compliance

Over time, limitations inherent in the 'conditional control' model also began to show. Although China's economy under Hu Jintao's administration saw a decade with near-double-digit growth, it also ushered in the buying and selling of ranks and the rampant misappropriation of national resources by Chinese military elites. A year before the 18th Party Congress, some media reports even suggested that as much as half of the PLA coffers had been siphoned off (Voice of America, 2014). It was also an open secret that prices had been set for billets at different levels of the PLA command (Phoenix Information, 2015; and Page, 2015). Given how some PLA leaders seemed more interested in acquiring personal financial gain than fulfilling their professional obligations, the Party's control over the military budget as a means of 'purchasing' its soldiers' compliance no longer seemed so certain.

Moreover, while the PLA was hurting the state internally as a parasitic institution with its misappropriation of valuable resources, China's national interests had also become global. Despite the military budget continuing to grow due to the country's expanding economic base, the scope and operational costs of overseas PLA activities – particularly its MOOTW – were experiencing exponential growth as Beijing took on more international obligations (Reuters, 2014; and Rajagopalan, 2014). With the rise in cost of operations amid the continued slowdown in Chinese economic growth, the need to 'improve management of military expenditures' was soon acutely felt (China Daily, 2013). Although in line with an ongoing trend to streamline the Chinese military, such prudent control of the purse also makes clear that the Party's economic leverage over its coercive forces cannot be sustained indefinitely.

At the same time, as well as undermining the reputation of the self-styled 'people's' military, it would have been equally, if not more, worrying that coteries of patron–client ties had formed within its ranks. But instead of being conjoined by loyalty and obedience to the CCP – with Xi Jinping at the core – such networks were congealed by corruption, with the implication that unmeritocratic practices over promotions was also having an adverse effect on troop morale. Under such circumstances, and against the backdrop that the Party's civilian and military elites concur that the greatest threat to their rule lies within PRC bounds (You, 2016), doomsday scenarios for the regime cannot be entirely ruled out if the PLA were to become so utterly vice-ridden that it would not be able to defend the regime. As revealed by the later indictments of some PLA generals, serious doubts about officers' political loyalty had indeed emerged – calling into question the Party's ideological penetration into its army.

From a strategic standpoint, the PLA's political reliability is also writ large in China's overall behaviour in its external environment. Economics aside, the Chinese security landscape had become fraught with challenges as Beijing began to draw unwanted attention as its global influence increased. With the Obama administration redirecting the United States' focus away from the War on Terror, the US military muscle was rebalanced to the Asia-Pacific under the aegis of freedom of navigation operations in response to PLA assertiveness and Chinese island reclamation operations in the South China Sea. As the military aspect of China's drive to realize Xi Jinping's ambitious 'China Dream' grows clearer, the need for the PLA to toe the Party line likewise has grown more pronounced (Xinhua, 2015b). But even if the PLA has contributed positively to realizing an international order conducive to the CCP's geopolitical and economic interests with image-building operations such as China's anti-piracy efforts in the Gulf of Aden, Xi would also have noted how his immediate predecessor had learned at his cost on those occasions when PLA elites did not comply with orders.[14] For Xi, therefore, the PLA's subordination – if still conditional – would at least need to be unambiguous if China is to successfully mitigate the geostrategic difficulties of becoming a global power. If 'conditional compliance' had indeed worked, the PLA accordingly could solely focus on the important matter of honing its martial prowess; that, however, was not the case.

Operationalizing subjective conditional control: putting Mao into practice

As would be expected of any new political leader, failure to appoint a team of trusted persons to key nodes of power could have disastrous consequences. Before Xi Jinping reached the top, the matter also weighed on his mind in the run-up to the 18th Party Congress.[15] Amid the fierce jockeying for power and the influence wielded by retired Party elders that has characterized the Chinese political system, Xi, then still the 6th ranked member on the PBSC, was unable to monopolize the selection of China's next generation of leaders.[16] However, significant changes have taken place in the period hitherto, and it is telling that he has since been able to dominate over personnel appointments at the more recent Party Congresses (Brookings Institution, nd).[17] This has largely come about as a result of Xi's consolidation of his own faction since his rise.[18] In that respect, he has promoted officials from his former political strongholds in Fujian and Zhejiang where he previously served as provincial governor and party secretary.

In its essence, the shift in CCP-PLA dynamics towards a 'subjective conditional control' model has much to do with the incumbent leader's attempts to borrow from Mao Zedong (Li, 2015). In the midst of soliciting the unquestioned obedience of Party and government apparatchiks,[19] an underlying principle behind Xi's *modus operandi* in asserting his authority concerns the use of compensatory tactics as he strives for Maoist 'absolute' control. Where the PLA is concerned, Xi has – despite his own lack of revolutionary credentials[20] – nevertheless curbed the post-reform excesses of senior military leaders with a combination of psychological intimidation and institutional mechanisms (Char, 2019). Given the economic and strategic changes that had occurred at the time of the leadership transition and how those developments had nullified the 'conditional control' paradigm under his immediate predecessors, Xi's rationale for restoring civilian paramountcy to the Party-state is clear. True to his 'Chairman of Everything' moniker (the Economist, 2016), he has since gone on to encroach on the PLA's internal affairs in a myriad of ways and left his personal imprint on the Chinese military establishment.

The PLA anti-corruption campaign

If the initial revelations of PLA corruption that first emerged a few months into Xi's tenure had caused concern (*Caixin*, 2013), the extent of malfeasance was made abundantly clear midway into his first term in July 2015. As the civilian anti-graft agency finally confirmed the downfall of a second vice-chairman from a previous CMC, suspicions over the pernicious growth in PLA autonomy reducing Hu Jintao to a mere figurehead were all but confirmed (Central Discipline and Inspection Commission, 2015). Although the PLA's top decision-making body was nominally beholden to Hu, it was effectively controlled by his subordinates.[21]

If anything, Hu's example was a powerful lesson for Xi how *not* to be commander-in-chief. Respectively nicknamed the 'Northwest Wolf' and the 'Northeast Tiger' in reference to the former Military Regions (MRs) they had risen from, the two CMC deputies, Generals Guo Boxiong and Xu Caihou, had run PLA affairs independently of the previous Chinese leader. As regards personnel appointments, potential candidates allegedly had to offer tens of millions of *renminbi* in bribes to vie for the approval of both Guo and Xu. As the identities of the deputy corps-level officers implicated in the anti-graft campaign since the 18th Party Congress indicate,[22] almost a dozen shared links with the two former top soldiers. Moving down the chain of command, a number of those deputy corps-level personnel netted had also formed their own patron–client networks with more junior colleagues (see Tables 10.1, 10.2 and 10.3).

Thus as well as eradicating Guo and Xu's networks, Xi therefore also had to guard against the coterie of officers the two generals and their associates had nurtured (Chan, 2018).[23] Foreshadowing the purges to come, the CMC chairman had earlier intimidated recalcitrant PLA elites by ordering them to reflect on their indiscretions (Xinhua, 2014). Prior to announcing the first batch of military 'tigers' in January 2015, a PLA political work conference was also organized in the township of Gutian in Fujian Province in October 2014 to warn the military of the dangers of a 'colour revolution' and to re-emphasize the Party's absolute control of the gun ('Strengthen and Improve the Political Work of the Military'). As they contemplated Xu Caihou and his fall from grace, many of those 'commanding officers especially senior officers' guilty of transgressions likely would have been overawed when Xi also pointed out how their actions had led to 'a lack of trust' in them by the rank-and-file. In a nod to Mao Zedong, PLA officers would have been keenly aware of the significance of Gutian and its origins as the site where the CCP's original strongman leader had established the principle that 'the Party commands the gun, the gun must never be allowed to command the Party' (Mao, 1965).

If there were initially doubts that Xi Jinping would 'refrain from a sustained campaign' on the grounds that it would reflect badly on the PLA (Perlez, 2012),[24] the series of austerity measures targeting the latter's culture of grandiose expenditure have proven otherwise. But before Xi had consolidated enough clout to address the structural flaws within the PLA's discipline and inspection processes (*The Paper*, 2014), he too had to turn to the civilian anti-corruption agency to bring down corrupt officers.[25] In wearing down his targets psychologically, Xi first leaned on the CDIC to build up its cases against targets.

Table 10.1: PLA senior officers under graft probe since the 18th Party Congress (patron–client ties with Xu Caihou)

No.	Client	Patron	Birthplace	Appointment	Rank	Grade	Branch	MR affiliation	Confirmed
1	ZHANG Gongxian	XU Caihou	Shandong	Director Political Department Jinan Military Region	MG	Corps leader	Army	General Political Department	2014.07.22
2	XU Caihou	JIANG Zemin	Liaoning	Vice Chairman Central Military Commission	G	CMC deputy leader	Army	Shenyang; 16th Group Army	2015.01.15
3	YANG Jinshan	XU Caihou	Henan	Deputy Commander Chengdu Military Region	LG	MR deputy leader	Army	Chengdu	2015.01.15
4	LIU Zheng	XU Caihou	Liaoning	Deputy Director General Logistics Department	LG	MR deputy leader	Army	General Logistics Department	2015.01.15
5	YU Daqing	XU Caihou	Liaoning	Deputy Political Commissar Second Artillery Corps	LG	MR deputy leader	Second Artillery Corps	General Political Department	2015.01.15
6	FANG Wenping	XU Caihou	Beijing	Commander Shanxi Military District	MG	Corps leader	Army	Beijing	2015.01.15
7	YE Wanyong	XU Caihou and YANG Jinshan	Hubei	Political Commissar Sichuan Military District (retired in 2012)	MG	Corps leader	Army	Chengdu	2015.01.15
8	WEI Jin	XU Caihou and YANG Jinshan	Shanxi	Deputy Political Commissar Tibet Military District	MG	Corps deputy leader	Army	Chengdu	2015.01.15
9	FU Linguo	XU Caihou and LIAO Xilong	Guizhou	Deputy Chief of Staff General Logistics Department	MG	Corps deputy leader	Army	General Logistics Department	2015.01.15

(continued)

Table 10.1: PLA senior officers under graft probe since the 18th Party Congress (patron–client ties with Xu Caihou) (continued)

No.	Client	Patron	Birthplace	Appointment	Rank	Grade	Branch	MR affiliation	Confirmed
10	ZHANG Daixin	XU Caihou		Deputy Commander Heilongjiang Military District	MG	Corps deputy leader	Army	Shenyang; 16th Group Army	2015.01.15
11	ZHANG Dongshui	XU Caihou	Shandong	Deputy Political Commissar Second Artillery Corps	MG	MR deputy leader	Second Artillery Corps	General Political Department	2015.03.03
12	WANG Xibin	XU Caihou	Heilongjiang	President PLA National Defence University (retired in 2013)	G	MR leader	Army	38th Group Army; 27th Group Army; Beijing	2017.02.24
13	WANG Jiurong	Xu Caihou	Beijing	Deputy Commander Second Artillery Corps (retired in 2014)	LG	MR Deputy leader	Second Artillery Corps	Second Artillery Corps; Base 54 (Luoyang); Base 56 (Xining)	2017.06.27

Notes:
[1] The General Political Department is now one of 15 functional departments/offices/commissions under the CMC.
[2] As part of the recent reforms, the former 18 Group Armies were reorganized into 13 new Group Armies (the 71st to the 83rd). 'Yi yuan 18 ge jituanjun wei jichu, tiaozheng zujian 13 ge jituanjun' [The original 18 Group Armies have been re-adjusted and organized into 13 Group Armies], *Ministry of National Defence of the People's Republic of China*, 27 April 2017.
[3] The General Logistics Department is now one of 15 functional departments/offices/commissions under the CMC.
[4] The Second Artillery Corps was renamed at the beginning 2016. See 'China inaugurates PLA Rocket Force as military reform deepens', Xinhuanet, 1 January 2016, available at: http://www.xinhuanet.com/english/2016-01/01/c_134970564.htm.

Sources: 中共十八大以来的反腐工作 (zh.wikipedia.org); 十八大以来反腐倡廉落马将领 (baike.baidu.com); various Chinese newspapers and Chinese official websites including the *PLA Daily*, *South China Morning Post* and China Military Online.

Table 10.2: PLA senior officers under graft probe since the 18th Party Congress (patron–client ties with Guo Boxiong)

No.	Client	Patron	Birthplace	Appointment	Rank	Grade	Branch	MR affiliation	Confirmed
1	FAN Changmi	GUO Boxiong and TIAN Xiusi	Shandong	Deputy Political Commissar Lanzhou Military Region	LG	MR deputy leader	Army	Lanzhou; 47th Group Army	2015.01.15
2	GUO Zhenggang	GUO Boxiong	Shaanxi	Deputy Political Commissar Zhejiang Military District	MG	Corps deputy leader	Army	Nanjing	2015.03.03
3	ZHAN Jun	GUO Boxiong	Hubei	Deputy Commander Hubei Military District	MG	Corps deputy leader	Army	Guangzhou	2015.04.26
4	ZHAN Guoqiao	GUO Boxiong	Zhejiang	Director Joint Logistics Department Lanzhou Military Region	MG	Corps leader	Army	Lanzhou; General Logistics Department	2015.04.26
5	DONG Mingxiang	GUO Boxiong	Anhui	Director Joint Logistics Department Beijing Military Region	MG	Corps leader	Army	Beijing; General Logistics Department	2015.04.26
6	FU Yi	GUO Boxiong	Shanxi	Commander Zhejiang Military District (retired in 2013)	MG	Corps leader	Army	Nanjing	2015.05.29
7	DENG Ruihua	GUO Boxiong	Gansu	Political Commissar, Joint Logistics Department Lanzhou Military Region	MG	Corps leader	Army	Lanzhou	2015.07.10

(continued)

Table 10.2: PLA senior officers under graft probe since the 18th Party Congress (patron–client ties with Guo Boxiong) (continued)

No.	Client	Patron	Birthplace	Appointment	Rank	Grade	Branch	MR affiliation	Confirmed
8	GUO Boxiong	JIANG Zemin	Shaanxi	Vice Chairman Central Military Commission	G	CMC deputy leader	Army	Lanzhou; 47th Group Army	2015.07.30
9	TIAN Xiusi	GUO Boxiong	Henan	Political Commissar PLA Air Force	G	MR leader	Air Force	Lanzhou; Chengdu	2016.07.09
10	FANG Fenghui	GUO Boxiong	Shaanxi	Member Central Military Commission	G	CMC member	Army	Xinjiang, Lanzhou, Guangzhou, Beijing; 21st Group Army	2018.01.09

Note: [1] Between 1965 and 1985, there were eleven military regions in China: Beijing, Chengdu, Fuzhou, Guangzhou, Jinan, Kunming, Lanzhou, Nanjing, Shenyang, Wuhan and Xinjiang. By 1985, the then Xinjiang Military Region had been incorporated into the former Lanzhou Military Region.

Sources: 中共十八大以来的反腐工作 (zh.wikipedia.org); 十八大以来反腐倡廉洛马将领 (baike.baidu.com); various Chinese newspapers and Chinese official websites including the *PLA Daily*, *South China Morning Post* and China Military Online.

Table 10.3: PLA senior officers under graft probe since the 18th Party Congress (patron–client ties with Xu Caihou and Guo Boxiong)

No.	Client	Patron	Birthplace	Appointment	Rank	Grade	Branch	MR affiliation	Confirmed
1	LIU Hongjie	XU Caihou and GUO Boxiong		Deputy Director Management and Support Department General Staff Department	MG	Corps deputy leader	Army	Central Military Commission	2015.03.03
2	ZHANG Yang	XU Caihou and GUO Boxiong	Hebei	Member Central Military Commission	G	CMC member	Army	Guangzhou; 63rd Group Army	2017.11.28

Sources: 中共十八大以来的反腐工作 (zh.wikipedia.org); 十八大以来反腐倡廉落马将领 (baike.baidu.com); various Chinese newspapers and Chinese official websites including the *PLA Daily*, *South China Morning Post* and China Military Online.

To gain leverage over the latter, the regime for a time also encouraged investigative reports by non-official Chinese media to generate speculation about who stood next in line. Towards that end, intentional leaks were supplied to news outlets affiliated with the Party-state such as *The Paper* and *Caixin*.[26] By opting against exposing the generals officially at the beginning,[27] mental strain would have weighed on those officers, their associates as well as their political patrons. After these personnel were finally outed, the arbitrariness with which punishments were meted out had the same intimidating effects on those who remained unscathed (*China Military Online*, 2014). Further, the commuting of death sentences in exchange for incriminating evidence against one's patron would have also encouraged defendants to cooperate with the inquests (Xinhua, 2015a).[28]

Amid the purges of the PLA's corrupt underpinnings, the commander-in-chief has at the same time replaced old loyalties with new allegiances to himself. Whereas the indictments of notable Jiang Zemin protégés no doubt would have cowed Jiang's other associates into submission, the arrests indubitably also provide fodder for Xi Jinping to censure the retired Party elder and remove Jiang's last vestiges of power. In fact, soon after General Guo Boxiong's indictment, one commentary in the CCP mouthpiece, the *People's Daily*, denounced the Party's former leaders for emplacing proxies in positions of power to retain influence – referring to the phenomenon as a destabilizing action that encouraged 'factionalism and mountaintop-ism', and prevented incumbents from ruling effectively. While the attack appeared to be directed at Guo, the message might well have been meant for Jiang (*People's Daily*, 2015). Whereas Mao Zedong had toppled his internal rivals on the basis of ideology during the Cultural Revolution, China's economic liberalization and widespread self-enrichment among the Party's elites meant there was utility to be had in fighting graft. In spite of its instrumental nature,[29] the anti-corruption campaign has paved the way for Mao's latest successor to overhaul the PLA's leadership to suit his own needs, and extend his political longevity.

PLA structural reforms and personnel appointments in the new CMC

Complementing his signature anti-corruption campaign, Xi Jinping also enshrined his civilian authority by revising the legal basis of the PLA's subordination to his CMC office (*PLA Daily*, 2016). Given the prevalence among some political officers to veto personnel decisions based on bribes and a proclivity by logisticians to embezzle funds, structural and procedural measures targeting the two vocations were promulgated in 2015. Of those that took aim at logisticians, new stipulations included 'Standards on Building and Renovating Military Barracks and Equipment' and 'Comprehensively

Implement Clean-up and Audit of Paid Services by the Military to External Parties'. Similarly, fresh directives to supervise political officers consisted of 'Opinions on Strengthening the Supervision of the Work of Selecting and Employing Personnel' and 'Opinions for Political Organs and Political Officers on Building Absolute Loyalty to the Party, Focusing on Combat Capabilities and Fine Work Style' (China Armed Forces, 2015).

While the mere codification of soldiers' behaviour and rules setting may not necessarily redress the erstwhile civil–military imbalance, Xi has since also increased civilian intrusion by introducing wholesale structural reforms of the PLA in November 2015. Starting from the CMC in which Xi had placed his most trusted military aides,[30] he went deeper still by effecting organizational reforms of the elite body. As a key aspect of the reorganization, the influential General Headquarters (GHQs) that previously oversaw staff, political work, logistics and armaments were all shaken up as they devolved part of their authority to 15 newly established departments under the CMC. Moreover, their defenestration was accompanied by official censure: Given how the former GHQs had accumulated such an outsized clout as to be able to indulge widespread corruption among their officeholders, one authoritative commentary in the *PLA Daily* made the rare move of criticizing these headquarters for their 'over concentrated powers' and 'independent command structure' – making it abundantly clear how their actions had impinged on 'the CMC's ability to exercise unified leadership' (Wu Ming, 2015).

By the start of 2016, the organizational changes had reached the PLA's regional commands. Reminiscent of Mao Zedong's response towards a potential resurgence of regional warlordism towards the end of his rule, the former Military Region (MR) system was demolished after the PLA regional commands were demonized as 'fiefdoms'.[31] This was then followed by their replacement with a modern US-style command structure comprising five Theatre Commands (TCs) (see Table 10.4). In line with Xi's re-emphasis on implementing the CMC Chairman Responsibility System (Kou, 2017), both the TCs and Services have unsurprisingly come under direct CMC supervision (Xianhua, 2015).[32] To further weaken PLA elites, the bureaucratic rank of the present incarnations of the four former GHQs were downgraded (*China Military Online*, 2016). Equally important, the CMC further incapacitated the former General Political and General Logistics departments by relieving them respectively of their internal discipline and auditing functions to enforce stronger oversight over the PLA's political and logistics officers.

The influence of Chairman Mao is again palpable in Xi's breaking up of tribal loyalties of corps-level units. As a means of 'curbing factionalism [...] and the pernicious influence' of Guo Boxiong and Xu Caihou given their connections with a number of senior officers, Xi outdid Mao's reshuffle in the 1970s by disbanding 5 out of the 18 former Group Armies (GAs) and reordering the remainder into 13 newly designated corps. Similar to how Mao had prevented his generals from bringing along their own retinue to their new postings, Xi reportedly gave the newly appointed commanding officers of the 13 GAs (71st to 83rd) only 24 hours to take up their posts. Purportedly, the commissar of 78th GA did not even have a chance to bid his former colleagues goodbye (*The Paper*, 2016). While there were certainly professional considerations behind Xi's reforms – with the renaming of the GAs seen as a 'necessary technical measure' to enhance PLA 'jointness' (Chan, 2017) – such a bold approach in disregarding the 'glorious record' of some of the GAs would no doubt have been perceived by some within the ranks as evidence of the civilian leader's egregious meddling.

Verily, at the nexus between the ongoing military reforms in China and the PLA's role in national security policy making, Xi Jinping has striven for enhanced civilian control – first, by subsuming the regime's top generals under the Central National Security Commission to subordinate military elites under civilian rule (Lampton, 2015);[33] and second, by cutting back on the number of key positions for senior PLA leaders. At the highest echelon for instance, the number of uniformed members on the CMC was reduced from ten to six at the 19th Party Congress (Bin, 2017).[34] Taking another leaf out of Mao's playbook, it is unsurprising that Xi made sure to stack the new CMC with his associates. In addition to his two deputies,[35] other members in the Chinese high command either served in the now-defunct Nanjing MR based in his former Fujian and Zhejiang strongholds or had been groomed for higher office by Xi himself.[36] The elevation of the PLA's internal discipline body, the CMC Discipline and Inspection Commission, to the top of the hierarchy following General Zhang Shengmin's appointment to the CMC is also noteworthy since every general is now answerable to Xi's proxy (Lo, 2018).

Limits and limitations of subjective control

In line with Xi Jinping's desire for the PLA to become a modern military by 2035 and a world-class force by 2050 (Zhao, 2017), the reorganization of its force structure to improve 'jointness' has gradually built up momentum since his announcement to make 300,000 personnel redundant (Chan, 2015).[37] But even as organizational changes have been forced upon it, the PLA has not been entirely acquiescent. One such example of the limitations of Xi's subjective control concerns the prolongation of ground troops' overwhelming clout. Even if the PLA has taken its first steps in transforming itself from a predominantly land-based power,[38] it remains the case that its Army – given its sheer size – will continue to dominate the PLA in the years ahead

Table 10.4: Group Army (GA) affiliations and leadership following the PLA reforms

Theatre command	Current GA (Former GA)	Appointment	Leader	Former Unit
Eastern TC	71st GA (12th GA)	Commander	Wang Yinfang	38th GA
		Commissar	Xu Deqing	47th GA
	72nd GA (1st GA)	Commander	Zhu Xiaohui	42nd GA
		Commissar	Wang Wenquan	27th GA
	73rd GA (31st GA)	Commander	Hu Zhongqiang	14th GA
		Commissar	Yang Cheng	21st GA
Southern TC	74th GA (42nd GA)	Commander	Xu Xianghua	65th GA
		Commissar	Liu Hongjun	21st GA
	75th GA (41st GA)	Commander	Gong Maodong	27th GA
		Commissar	Qin Shutong	1st GA
Western TC	76th GA (21st GA)	Commander	Fan Chengcai	Western TC Army
		Commissar	Zhang Hongbing	20th GA
	77th GA (13rd GA)	Commander	Lin Huomao	26th GA
		Commissar	Li Zehua	31st GA
Northern TC	78th GA (16th GA)	Commander	Wu Yanan	16th GA
		Commissar	Guo Xiaodong	26th GA
	79th GA (39th GA)	Commander	Xu Qiling	Central TC Army
		Commissar	Yu Yonghong	14th GA
	80th GA (26th GA)	Commander	Wang Xiubin	1st GA
		Commissar	Zhu Yuwu	39th GA

(continued)

Table 10.4: Group Army (GA) affiliations and leadership following the PLA reforms (continued)

Theatre command	Current GA (Former GA)	Appointment	Leader	Former Unit
Central TC	81st GA (65th GA)	Commander Commissar	Huang Ming Fang Yongxiang	41st GA Eastern TC Army
	82nd GA (38th GA)	Commander Commissar	Lin Xiangyang Zhang Mengbin	47th GA 42nd GA
	83rd GA (54th GA)	Commander Commissar	Xie Zenggang Lu Shaoping	21st GA 16th GA

Source: '13个新集团军主官人选均确定，原有的集团军主官全部换岗' [13 officers of the new group armies have been confirmed, officers of the original group armies redeployed], *The Paper*, 16 August 2016, available at: https://www.thepaper.cn/newsDetail_forward_1765430.

(Chan, 2016). While legacies such as 'Big Army' mentality require time to be undone, more recent plans to relocate the respective Services out of the Chinese capital to 'improve combat readiness and reduce cronyism' have likewise been met with disdain (Chan, 2019).

Then, there is also the concomitant matter of providing financial compensation for demobilized soldiers. As much as Xi himself has reassured the Party's armed servants that the regime would 'place emphasis on the employment of demobilized officers' (Xinhua, 2016), efforts hitherto have remained a contentious and problematic affair – raising doubts on the ability of local officialdom to provide for future batches of demobilized personnel (Char, 2016). The regime's uncharacteristic conciliatory tone towards protests by PLA veterans also reflects the inherent sensitivities in dealing with its former guardians – betraying yet again, the Party's deference to its coercive forces.[39] Although authoritative commentaries in the *PLA Daily* make clear the key source of resistance to the ongoing reforms 'comes from within, resulting from old mindsets and habits' (PLA Daily, 2015), any lapse in the handling of veteran affairs means that *outside* resentment could easily fuel resistance from *within* the Chinese military. As the military reforms move into the final phase focusing on adjusting military policies (*Duowei News*, 2019), the financial resources needed to smoothen out Party–army relations will be anything but cheap.

Conclusion

This chapter has expounded on the current state of CCP–PLA dynamics by tracing its evolution under the legacies of Maoist political revolution and Dengist economic restructuring. Such a traditional, culturally based approach focusing on the twin epochs of the PRC informs the characteristics inherent in the Chinese model and explains its divergence from traditional Western frameworks of civil–military relations. At the same time, how and why the 'conditional control' model under Jiang Zemin and Hu Jintao has been superseded by 'subjective conditional control' has also been contextualized and clarified. While the PLA's objective compliance as a standing army that is deferential to its civilian master on non-military matters continues unabated (Saunders and Scobell, 2016),[40] Xi Jinping's deeper intrusion into its institutional autonomy has imposed stronger subjective control on the Party's army. Driven by his personal desire to 'exert greater control', Xi has even done the unprecedented by donning combat fatigues during a televised inspection tour of the PLA Joint Command Centre in 2016 as he explicitly proclaimed himself 'commander-in-chief' (Sudworth, 2016).[41] But as Xi knows himself, old legacies will require time to be undone as he continues to impose himself on his subordinates.

The analytical value inherent in such a historically grounded approach is not unique to China, although it holds particular significance given the country's well-established political culture since China's imperial period to draw lessons from history. Noteworthily, despite his well-documented period of hardship under the Maoist excesses during the Cultural Revolution, China's current leader has nonetheless drawn inspiration from the regime's original strongman in tackling the problems confronting present-day Party–army ties. Just as the old guard was being replaced by post-revolutionary leaders who had never fought in battle, Reform and Opening-up and the PLA's partaking of the country's economic growth occurred at the same instance and compromised its allegiance to the polity it was sworn to uphold. Seen in this light, civil–military relations in the Xi era entails correcting the previous state of affairs.

This chapter has underlined that the civil–military relations of China do not adhere to the Huntingtonian model. Although the tenor of Party–army interactions has changed over time, the objective of every CCP leader remains unchanged: To dominate the regime by monopolizing control over the Party's gun. Particularly given Hu Jintao's weakly institutionalized control that resulted in the opportunistic power struggles exposed by the Bo Xilai affair (You, 2016, p 156), it was vital that Xi had the PLA's backing to prevail over his political rivals within the 'winner takes all' political environment in China. In the continued absence of political reforms, the incumbent has thus turned to subjective conditional control to do so.

But even as Xi has turned on the PLA with more intrusive interference, to assert that he now wields 'absolute' control over the military is premature, given how he continues to solicit its support.[42] Indeed, he has continued to observe the PLA's conditional compliance by catering to the latter's corporate interests and by being personally involved in the country's long overdue defence reforms to enhance the PLA's combat readiness. At the beginning of his CMC chairmanship, he did not hesitate to be perceived as being aligned with the military's hard-line positions[43] – while making sure that the latter's activities have not turned into an actual shooting war.[44] Moreover, by portraying the establishment as the defender *par excellence* of Chinese national interests, Xi also accorded the PLA pride of place in the Party-state. That said, Xi's great interest in PLA affairs could yet become a source of instability to civil–military relations in view of how his emphasis on 'CMC one-man rule' effectively leaves him as the only civilian leader overseeing the country's military issues (You, 2018, p 12). In a similar vein, the appointment of his own followers in managing the PLA's daily operations also means the professional weight of the corps regarding China's national security policy making may yet be compromised by groupthink.

Putting aside questions over the longer-term implications behind subjective civilian control, the centralization of power in a single person appears to have addressed the previous dearth of oversight over the PLA – in the near to medium term, at least. As long as the shared CCP–PLA interest in upholding regime stability and maintaining performance legitimacy can be preserved (Ren et al, 2013), there is no reason to doubt why the CCP's coercive forces will not continue to serve as the Party's last line of defence – as was the case when the PLA helped quell the Tiananmen protests in 1989, and more recently by supporting the medical services amid the lockdown of Wuhan due to COVID-19. In defying the Party's norms of political succession to prevent the excesses of having a Maoist 'strongman' leader (Buckley and Bradsher, 2018), Xi Jinping may find that letting go of power will not be easy. The bigger question in the civil–military relations of China then, perhaps, is that when the time comes for the incumbent to relinquish his post, his amassing of power would lead to challenges quite insurmountable by his successor.

Notes

[1] In addition to his other roles as CCP general secretary and leader of the PRC, Xi Jinping is known to spend at least half a day each week on military affairs in his capacity as chairman of the Central Military Commission (CMC) – China's highest military decision-making body.

[2] For scholarly assessments of the CCP–PLA dynamic during the Chinese Civil War, see Whitson and Huang (1973).

[3] Being a Party instrument, the PLA's conservatism means it can be counted on to remain acquiescent to the more militant aspect of the CCP's overall foreign and security policy making. Indeed, many PLA leaders have openly declared their ambitions to take Taiwan – forcibly, if necessary.

[4] See also Mao's speech at the 6th Plenary Session of the CCP 'Problems on War and Strategy' on 6 November 1938, *Selected Works of Mao Zedong*, Vol. II, pp 224–25 (1991).

[5] As much as the Party has emphasized the righteousness of its peasant-nationalist revolution, the condition *most* essential to its political victory in 1949 was armed struggle (Pepper, 2004, p 121).

[6] Mao's speech at the closing ceremony of the Eleventh Plenary Session of the 8th Central Committee on 12 August 1966, *Long Live Mao Zedong Thought*, available at: www.marxists.org/chinese/maozedong/1968/5-206.htm.

[7] Of the ten Marshal and ten Senior General ranks conferred in 1955, members of Mao's First Front Army from the Long March took up eight and seven places respectively. Among the ten top-ranked marshals, He Long and Xu Xiangqian were respectively of the Second Front Army and Fourth Front Army. For a study of the politics behind the Red Army during the period, see Yang (1990).

[8] After gaining pre-eminent military status during the Long March, Mao held on to military power until his death. Similarly, after Deng's political rehabilitation in the late 1970s, he would chair the CMC between 1981 and 1989 and was China's paramount leader until his passing. In 1989, Deng's dominance allowed him to direct the PLA in crushing the Tiananmen democracy movement; see Nathan and Link (2001).

[9] While it had been common for the PLA's top generals to enter the elite PBSC, no uniformed CCP cadre has gained membership since General Liu Huaqing stepped down in 1997.

10. When Jiang Zemin was scheduled to relinquish his Party and military leadership when his tenure ran out at the 16th Party Congress, he claimed he had to handhold his successor in military affairs and so remained as CMC chairman for two more years until 2004. That, despite Hu Jintao was due to succeed Jiang in 2002 having been anointed earlier in 1992 by Deng Xiaoping.
11. After the CCP approved the establishment of the Discipline and Inspection Commission (DIC) under the auspices of the former PLA General Political Department (GPD) following the 18th Party Congress, 174 major cases of corruption involving smuggling, bribery, embezzlement, fraud, speculation, illegal business activities and tax evasion were uncovered ('Qunian 15 ming jiang jun luoma Xu Caihou jia xianjin duiji rushan (quanwen)' [15 generals fell from grace last year; mountains of cash uncovered at Xu Caihou's home (Full Text)], *NetEase*, 28 January 2015, Available at: http://news.163.com/api/15/0128/06/AH1CF3BG0001124J_all.html#).
12. 'Military to study Hu Jintao's speech on anti-corruption', Xinhuanet, 1 July 2006, available at: www.gov.cn/english/2006-07/01/content_325175.htm
13. Under the PLA's previous organizational structure, its disciplinary body came under the former GPD controlled by Xu Caihou. The lack of institutional oversight within the establishment is laid bare by the fact that the anti-graft campaign only gained traction after General Liu Yuan – Xi Jinping's fellow Princeling – decided to become whistle-blower due to a personal grievance against Xu. As one of three CMC vice-chairmen under Hu Jintao from 2010 to 2012, Xi would have been aware how his predecessor's reign was compromised by such insubordination.
14. An oft-cited example is former US Defence Secretary Robert Gates' claim that the Chinese military had intentionally kept Hu Jintao in the dark about the launch of one of its new stealth fighters in 2011.
15. According to well-placed sources, the then heir-apparent was so upset over his lack of input in personnel decisions in the top CCP appointments that he threatened to abandon his anointment in a bid to convince Party elders to consult him.
16. It is obvious that some members of the 2012 iteration of the CMC were not associated with Xi given their subsequent indictments.
17. Of the six other members on the PBSC of the 19th CCP Congress, 3rd-ranked Li Zhanshu and 5th-ranked Wang Huning are considered members of Xi's faction. Of the wider Politburo, as many as half of the 18 non-Standing Committee members – including Generals Xu Qiliang and Zhang Youxia – also share connections with Xi. See 'China's new Politburo and Politburo Standing Committee', *Brookings*, nd, available at: www.brookings.edu/wp-content/uploads/2017/10/china_20171013_19thpartycongress_profiles.pdf.
18. Xi's swift consolidation of the trifecta of Party–state–military power was also helped by Hu Jintao's concurrent relinquishment of his CCP and CMC portfolios at the 18th Party Congress.
19. Of China's internal security apparatus, Xi relegated the bureaucratic rank of the once-powerful Central Political and Legal Affairs Commission previously helmed by Zhou Yongkang and purged the associates of the former domestic security czar. 'Former aide to Zhou Yongkang is latest target of graft buster', *Caixin*, 27 July 2015.
20. As a scion of a CCP revolutionary, Xi's personal connections with PLA elites gives him an advantage over Jiang Zemin and Hu Jintao. Earlier in his career, Xi served as personal secretary to China's then minister of defence, Geng Biao. Xi also held a variety of minor military appointments in the provinces he had been party secretary or governor before becoming heir-apparent in 2010. *China Vitae*, nd, available at: www.chinavitae.com/biography/Xi_Jinping.

21 Hu's authority over PLA was never strong to begin with given that for the first two years of his tenure following the 16th Party Congress, the CMC portfolio remained with Jiang.
22 For the significance of PLA grades and ranks, see Allen (2010).
23 Two leading Guo and Xu protégés to have been indicted on graft charges are the former CMC members: Generals Fang Fenghui and Zhang Yang. Zhang committed suicide while under probe ('Chinese general commits suicide as Xi's corruption crackdown grinds on', *Bloomberg News*, 28 November 2017).
24 Dismissing the anti-corruption campaign as mere rhetoric, one retired officer initially claimed Xi Jinping 'can't do too much, otherwise the party comes out too black.'
25 The synergistic relationship between the PRC's civilian and military discipline organs can be evinced from Xi's attendance at the Fifth Plenary Session of the CDIC – exactly one day before the unprecedented announcement of the initial list of 16 corrupt PLA officers in January 2015 ('Regiment-level and above cadres to be the focus of military anti-graft drive', *The Beijing News*, 15 January 2015).
26 The collaboration with *Caixin* is particularly noteworthy given the close links between the media outlet's founder and Wang Qishan, a noted Xi ally and former czar overseeing Party discipline.
27 For one, the official China Military Online quotes Hong Kong-based media instead of confirming the identities of graft suspects ('16 PLA officers on graft list', 16 January 2015).
28 The details of investigations into Gu Junshan's embezzlements and bribery before arriving at the verdict have never been fully disclosed. Despite authoritative reportage that Gu had misappropriated 600 million *renminbi*, the PLA procuratorate declared a sum of 600,000 *renminbi* only.
29 The endemic nature of rent-seeking and abuses of power in post-reform China means the fight against corruption has also been of a selective nature, targeting Xi Jinping's political rivals and their acolytes – as opposed to graft itself.
30 Alongside Xu Qiliang, Zhang Youxia as well as Wei Fenghe, another of Xi's trusted soldiers, Zhao Keshi, was director of the former GLD at the 18th Party Congress. Apart from Zhao – who reached retirement age at the 19th Party Congress – Xu, Zhang and Wei all retained their CMC membership at the 19th Party Congress.
31 Following the overhaul, the TCs are to undertake operational 'command' whereas the various Services are responsible for the administrative 'construction' of units. See 'President Xi announces establishment of five theatre commands', China Military Online (2016).
32 Or, according to Xi: 'the CMC takes charge of the overall administration of the PLA and the Chinese People's Armed Police; Theatre Commands to focus on combat; and the different Services to pursue their own construction.' See 'Xi Jinping: Fully implement the strategy of reforming and strengthening the military, and unswervingly follow the road of strengthening the military with Chinese characteristics', *People's Daily* (27 November 2015).
33 Xi has also circumvented other prominent Party institutions headed by his fellow CCP elites by making himself the chairman of a number of Central Leading Groups (CLGs), including Comprehensively Deepening Reforms; National Security; National Defence and Military Reforms, among others.
34 Previously, the Service chiefs from the Navy (PLAN), Air Force (PLAAF) and the former Second Artillery Corps – the latter since renamed the Rocket Force (PLARF) – were all represented on the CMC. With the recent force structure reforms started in April 2017, the change of the PLA's operational and tactical units from the corps- and division-levels to brigade-level and below means the opportunities for promotion from deputy corps-leader to corps-leader grade has been reduced.

35 Sources within the PLA attest to the role of Xu Qiliang and the PLAAF in providing Xi Jinping's security detail when the incumbent Chinese leader first assumed the top leadership. As well as being a fellow Princeling, Zhang Youxia is close to Xi on account of their fathers having served together in the Northwest Field Army during the Chinese Civil War.

36 Miao Hua, now the PLA's top-ranked political commissar, rose from the 31st Group Army in the former Nanjing Military Region.

37 Xi had in fact waited three years after the Third Plenary Session of the 18th Central Committee in 2012 before officially announcing the military reforms in November 2015.

38 For the first time in its history, the 1st-ranked CMC vice-chairman at the 19th Party Congress, General Xu Qiliang, is not an Army officer. The unprecedented appointments of Yuan Yubai (PLAN) and Yi Xiaoguang (PLAAF) respectively as commanders of the Southern and Central Theatre Commands a few years ago are also the first recorded instance of non-Army personnel heading the country's regional commands.

39 The regime's deference towards the military's interests can be gleaned from the dearth of MR-leader grade officers indicted on corrupt practices – possibly out of concerns that too many exposés would cause irreparable damage to the PLA's standing.

40 The PLA exercises its authority on military issues at the operational level but only has limited input at the strategic level.

41 Following the widely publicized commemoration of the 70th anniversary of Chinese victory in WWII, Xi enhanced his commander-in-chief persona further by presiding over even more large-scale military events, including the PLA's 90th anniversary parade at Zhurihe in July 2017; a televised PLA training mobilization in January 2018; and a naval parade in the South China Sea (SCS) later in April – in so doing, depriving the PLA of much needed time and resources that could have been better spent on training.

42 Two days following the CCP's announcement to scrap term limits on the presidency, the *PLA Daily* declared that 'officers and soldiers of the entire PLA and the People's Armed Police' had firmly stated they would 'resolutely uphold the CCP Central Committee's proposal to amend part of the country's constitution'. While this might be interpreted as the Chinese military's support for Xi, one could also argue it was absolutely crucial for him to secure the PLA's backing to overcome resistance from other Party elites ('The officers and men of the PLA and the PAP firmly stated that they resolutely support the proposal of the Central Committee of the CCP to amend the contents of the Constitution', 27 February 2018).

43 Pertinently, the PLA's proposal to declare an Air Defence Identification Zone (ADIZ) over the East China Sea promptly received Xi's blessings in 2013 despite the reservations of Chinese diplomats. Comments provided by a prominent PRC-based scholar at an RSIS conference, November 2014, Singapore.

44 Despite most Western media calling out the PLA for its aggressive manoeuvres in the SCS in September 2018, it may be argued on the other hand that the USS *Decatur* and *Lanzhou* managed to avert collision in September 2018 due to authoritative directives from the CMC to the Chinese destroyer.

References

Allen, K.W. (2010) 'Assessing the PLA's promotion ladder to CMC member based on grades vs ranks – Part 1', *China Brief*, 10(15): 6–8.

BBC (2001) 'China "flooding Philippines with drugs"', *BBC World Service* [online] 28 March, Available from: http://news.bbc.co.uk/2/hi/asia-pacific/1247253.stm [Accessed 1 May 2019].

Bin, H. (2017) 'China's military leadership undergoes reshuffle', *CGTN*, [online] 26 October, Available from: https://news.cgtn.com/news/33415 44e32597a6333566d54/index.html [Accessed 1 May 2019].

Brookings (nd) 'China's new Politburo and Politburo Standing Committee' *Brookings*, [online] nd, Available from: www.brookings.edu/wp-cont ent/uploads/2017/10/china_20171013_19thpartycongress_profiles.pdf [Accessed 1 May 2019].

Buckley, C. and Bradsher, K. (2018) 'China Moves to Let Xi Stay in Power by Abolishing Term Limit', *The New York Times*, [online] 25 February [Accessed 1 May 2019].

Caixin (2013) 'Graft probe of Gu Junshan has been confirmed, manhunt for his brother is underway', *Caixin*, [online] 2 August [Accessed 1 May 2019].

Cao, Zhi and Wu Xing. (2014) *Untold Story of Cao Xiangren: Chief Codebreaker of the Red Army*, Hong Kong SAR: Times Literature Publishing House.

Central Discipline and Inspection (2015) 'CCP Central Committee decides to expel Guo Boxiong from the Party, Guo's alleged crimes and evidence to be transferred to the judiciary to be dealt with according to law', *Central Discipline and Inspection*, [online] 30 July [Accessed 1 May 2019].

Chan, M. (2015) 'PLA officers in the line of fire as China's plan to axe 300,000 military personnel targets top brass over rank-and-file', *South China Morning Post*, [online] 4 September, Available from: https://www.scmp.com/news/china/policies-politics/article/1855451/tens-thousands-milit ary-officers-go-chinas-quest-leaner [Accessed 1 May 2019].

Chan, M. (2016) 'China's army keeps grip on top military jobs in 'compromise' reshuffle', [online] 6 January, Available from: https://www.scmp.com/news/china/diplomacy-defence/article/1898444/chinas-army-keeps-grip-top-military-jobs-compromise [Accessed 1 May 2019].

Chan, M. (2017) 'Why Xi Jinping is planning a historic move to rename China's army corps', *South China Morning Post*, [online] 24 April, Available from: https://www.scmp.com/news/china/diplomacy-defence/article/2089218/xi-jinping-plans-first-shake-chinese-army-corps-names [Accessed 1 May 2019].

Chan, M. (2018) 'Chinese military to prosecute former top general for graft', *South China Morning Post*, [online] 9 January, Available from: https://www.scmp.com/news/china/diplomacy-defence/article/2127513/chinese-milit ary-prosecute-former-top-general-graft [Accessed 1 May 2019].

Chan, M. (2019) 'Chinese military chiefs set to move PLA service branch headquarters out of Beijing', *South China Morning Post*, [online] 17 April, Available from: https://www.scmp.com/news/china/military/article/3006455/ chinese-military-chiefs-set-move-pla-service-branch [Accessed 1 May 2019].

Char, J. (2016) 'Demobilized and disaffected: another roadblock for China's military reforms', *Pacific Forum/CSIS*, [online] 20 October, Available from: https://pacforum.org/wp-content/uploads/2019/05/161020_PacN et_1677.pdf [Accessed 1 May 2019].

Char, J. (2019) 'Chinese civil–military relations: Xi Jinping's anti-corruption campaign and the People's Liberation Army', in R.A. Bitzinger and J. Char (eds) *Reshaping the Chinese Military: The PLA's Roles and Missions in the Xi Jinping Era*, Oxon: Routledge, pp 9–44.

China Armed Forces (2015) 'Beijing: Military Department of Xinhua News Agency', 32(2).

China Daily (2013) 'The Decision on Major Issues Concerning Comprehensively Deepening Reforms in brief', *China Daily*, [online] 16 November, Available from: www.china.org.cn/china/third_plenary_session/2013-11/16/content_30620736.htm [Accessed 1 May 2019].

China.org.cn (2012) 'Full text: Report of Hu Jintao to the 18th CPC National Congress', *China.org.cn*, [online] 16 November, Available from: www.china.org.cn/china/18th_cpc_congress/2012-11/16/content_27137540_12.htm [Accessed 1 May 2019].

China Military Online (2014) 'Military procuratorate answers questions about Xu Caihou's graft case', *China Military Online*, [online] 29 October [Accessed 1 May 2019].

China Military Online (2016) 'China's new Central Military Commission organ established', *China Military Online*, [online] 11 January [Accessed 1 May 2019].

China Vitae (nd) *China Vitae*, nd, Available from: http://www.chinavitae.com/biography/Xi_Jinping [Accessed: 1 May 2019].

Duowei News (2019) 'Tracing the Start of the Two Sessions: The Foundations for Determining China's 2019 Military Expenditure', *Duowei News*, [online] 3 March, [Accessed: 1 May 2019].

Garnaut, J. (2012) 'Rotting from within', *Foreign Policy*, [online] 16 April, Available from: https://foreignpolicy.com/2012/04/16/rotting-from-within/ [Accessed: 1 May 2019].

Godwin, H.B. (1988) *Development of the Chinese Armed Forces*, Maxwell Air Force Base, AL: Air University Press.

Han, B. (2017) 'China's military leadership undergoes reshuffle', *CGTN*, [online] 26 October, Available from: https://news.cgtn.com/news/3341544e32597a6333566d54/index.html [Accessed 1 May 2019].

Huntington, S.P. (1957) *The Soldier and the State: The Theory and Politics of Civil–Military Relations*, Cambridge, MA: Harvard UP.

Janowitz, M. (1960) *The Professional Soldier: A Social and Political Portrait*, Glencoe, IL: Free Press.

Joffe, E. (1987) *The Chinese Army After Mao*, Cambridge, MA: Harvard UP.

Joffe, E. (2006) 'The Chinese army in domestic politics: factors and phases' in Nan Li (ed.), *Chinese Civil-Military Relations: The Transformation of the People's Liberation Army*, Abingdon: Routledge, 17.

Kou, C-W. (2017) 'Xi Jinping in command: solving the principal–agent problem in CCP–PLA relations?', *The China Quarterly*, 232: 866–85.

Lampton, D.M. (2015) 'Xi Jinping and the National Security Commission: policy coordination and political power', *Journal of Contemporary China*, 24(95): 759–77.

Landler, M. (2014) 'Fruitful Visit by Obama Ends With a Lecture From Xi', *The New York Times*, [online] 12 November, Available from: www.nytimes.com/2014/11/13/world/asia/china-us-xi-jinping-obama-apec.html [Accessed 1 May 2019].

Li, C. (2015) 'Promoting "young guards": the recent high turnover in the PLA leadership (Part 1: Purges and reshuffles)', *China Leadership Monitor*, 48, [online] 9 September, Available from: www.brookings.edu/articles/promoting-young-guards-the-recent-high-turnover-in-the-pla-leadership-part-1-purges-and-reshuffles/ [Accessed: 1 May 2019].

Lo, K. (2018) 'China confirms anti-graft official's position on military's ruling body as war on corruption heats up', *South China Morning Post*, [online] 18 March, Available from: www.scmp.com/news/china/diplomacy-defence/article/2137732/china-confirms-anti-graft-officials-position-militarys [Accessed 1 May 2019].

Mao, Z. (1965) *Selected Works of Mao Tse-Tung* (1st edn), Peking: Foreign Languages Press.

Mao, Z. (1968) 'Zai ba jie shiyi zhong quanhui bimu shi shang de jianghua (Speech at the closing ceremony of the 11th Plenary Session of the 8th Central Committee on 12 August 1966])', *Long Live Mao Zedong Thought [Mao Zedong sixiang wansui]*, [online] no date, Available from: www.marxists.org/chinese/maozedong/1968/5-206.htm [Accessed: 1 May 2022].

Mao, Z. (1991) 'Problems of war and strategy', *Selected Works of Mao Zedong*, Vol 2, Beijing: Renmin chubanshe.

Mulvenon, J. (2001) 'China: conditional compliance', in M. Alagappa (ed) *Coercion and Governance: The Declining Political Role of the Military in Asia*, Stanford, CA: Stanford UP, pp 317–35.

Nathan, AJ. and Link P. (2001) *The Tiananmen Papers*, New York: Public Affairs.

Page, J. (2015) 'China's Antigraft Drive Exposes Military Risks', *The Wall Street Journal*, [online] 11 March, Available from: www.wsj.com/articles/china-antigraft-drive-exposes-military-risks-1426116777 [Accessed 1 May 2019]

People's Daily (2015) 'Renmin ribao sixiang zongheng: Bianzheng kandai "ren zou cha liang" [People's Daily ideological aspect: Scrutinising the phenomenon of "tea becomes cold after one has departed"]', *People's Daily*, [online], 10 August [Accessed 1 May 2019].

Pepper, S. (2004) 'The political odyssey of an intellectual construct: peasant nationalism and the study of China's revolutionary history: a review essay', *The Journal of Asian Studies*, 63(1): 105–25.

Perlez, J. (2012) 'Corruption in Military Poses a Test for China', *The New York Times*, [online] 14 November, Available from: www.nytimes.com/2012/11/15/world/asia/corruption-in-china-military-poses-test.html [Accessed 1 May 2019].

Perlmutter, A. and Leogrande, W.M. (1982) 'The party in uniform: toward a theory of civil–military relations in communist political systems', *The American Political Science Review*, 76(4): 778–89.

Phoenix Information (2015) 'Special planning of the Two Sessions: Major general reveals the inside story of Xu Caihou's selling of ranks', *Phoenix Information*, [online] 9 March [Accessed 1 May 2019].

PLA Daily (2015) 'Road to Winning Wars', *PLA Daily*, [online] 14 December [Accessed 1 May 2019].

PLA Daily (2016) 'Laoji shiming zhongtuo zhongshi lu zhi jinze' [Bear in mind the great undertaking and faithfully discharge duties], *PLA Daily*, [online] 6 February [Accessed 1 May 2019].

Rajagopalan, M. (2014) 'China to send elite army unit to help fight Ebola in Liberia', *Reuters*, [online] 31 October, Available from: www.reuters.com/article/us-health-ebola-china-idUSKBN0IK0N020141031 [Accessed 1 May 2019].

Ren, Tianyou, Zhao Zhouxian, and Liu Guangming. (2013) 'Zhongguo meng yinling qiang jun meng' Qiang jun men zhicheng Zhongguo meng' (China Dream marshals Strong Military Dream; Strong Military Dream supports China dream), *Communist Party of China News*, [online] 2 December, Available from: http://theory.people.com.cn/n/2013/1202/c40531-23717737-3.html [Accessed: 1 May 2019].

Reuters (2014) 'China to send 700 troops to South Sudan to assist UN mission', *Reuters*, [online] 25 September, Available from: https://reliefweb.int/report/sudan/china-send-700-troops-south-sudan-assist-un-mission [Accessed 1 May 2019].

Saunders, P. and Scobell, A. (2016) *PLA Influence on China's National Security Policymaking*, Stanford, CA: Stanford UP.

Scobell, A. (2005) 'China's evolving civil–military relations: creeping Guojiahua', *Armed Forces & Society*, 31(2): 227–44.

Shambaugh, D. (2002) *Modernizing China's Military: Progress, Problems, and Prospects*, Berkeley, CA: University of California Press.

Sudworth, J. (2016) 'China's Xi Jinping takes commander in chief military title', *BBC News*, [online] 21 April, Available from: www.bbc.com/news/world-asia-china-36101140 [Accessed 1 May 2019].

Swaine, M.D. (2005) 'Civil–military relations and domestic powers and policies', paper presented at the conference on 'Chinese Leadership, Politics, and Policy', *Carnegie Endowment for International Peace*, [online] 2 November, Available from: https://carnegieendowment.org/files/Swaine.pdf [Accessed: 1 May 2019].

Tanner, H.M. (2015) *Where Chiang Kai-shek Lost China: The Liao-Shen Campaign, 1948*, Bloomington, IN: Indiana University Press.

The Economist (2016) 'Chairman of everything', *The Economist*, [online] 2 April, Available from: www.economist.com/china/2016/04/02/chairman-of-everything [Accessed 1 May 2019].

The Paper (2014) 'Jundui shenji shu zai shengge qian lishu zhong houqin bu, shencha Gujunshan shi hen ganga' [Investigating Gu Junshan was awkward prior to the elevation of the military inspection organs (to the CMC)], *The Paper*, [online] 7 November [Accessed 1 May 2019].

The Paper (2016) '13 officers of the new group armies have been confirmed, officers of the original group armies redeployed', *The Paper*, [online] 16 August [Accessed 1 May 2019].

Vogel, E.F. (2011) *Deng Xiaoping: And the Transformation of China*, Cambridge, MA: Harvard University Press.

Voice of America (2014) 'Jiaodian duihua: Xucaihou fanchuan, Jiefangjun da zhenhan?' [Focus Dialogue: PLA shocked by Xu Caihou's removal?]', *Voice of America*, [online] 4 July [Accessed 1 May 2019].

Whitson, W.W. and Huang C-H. (1973) *The Chinese High Command: A History of Communist High Command: A History of Communist Military Politics, 1927–71*, New York: Praeger.

Wu Ming (2015) 'Reshaping our command and control structure is an inevitable choice to have a strong and powerful military', *PLA Daily*, [online] 30 November [Accessed 1 May 2019].

Xi, J. (2016) 'Build up Our National Defense and Armed Forces', Beijing: Foreign Languages Press Co. Ltd., nd [Accessed 1 May 2019].

Xinhua (2013) 'PLA launches anti-corruption drive', *Xinhuanet*, [online] 29 April, Available from: www.china.org.cn/china/2013-04/29/content_28691795.htm [Accessed 1 May 2019].

Xinhua (2014) 'Xi urges serious reflection on Xu Caihou's case', *Xinhuanet*, [online] 1 November, Available from: https://usa.chinadaily.com.cn/china/2014-11/01/content_18840748.htm [Accessed 1 May 2019].

Xinhua (2015a) 'Military procuratorate person-in-charge's media briefing on Gu Junshan's verdict after the first trial', *Xinhuanet*, [online] 10 August [Accessed 1 May 2019].

Xinhua (2015b) 'Xi Jinping: Fully implement the strategy of reforming and strengthening the army, unswervingly follow the road of strengthening the army with Chinese characteristics', *Xinhuanet*, [online] 26 November, Available from: http://www.xinhuanet.com//politics/2015-11/26/c_1117274869.htm [Accessed 1 May 2019].

Xinhua (2016) 'Xi stresses employment of demobilized military officers', *China Daily USA*, [online] 7 June, Available from: http://usa.chinadaily.com.cn/china/2016-06/07/content_25642947.htm [Accessed 1 May 2019].

Xinhua (2017) 'China needs strong military more than ever: Xi', *Xinhuanet*, [online] 30 July, Available from: http://www.xinhuanet.com/english/2017-07/30/c_136484692.html [Accessed 1 May 2019].

Yang, B. (1990) *From Revolution to Politics: Chinese Communists on the Long March*, Boulder, CO: Westview Press Inc.

You, J. (2015) 'Unravelling the myths about political commissars', in D.M. Finkelstein and K. Gunness (eds) *Civil–Military Relations in Today's China: Swimming in a New Sea*, Abingdon: Routledge, pp 146–70.

You, J. (2016) *China's Military Transformation*, Cambridge: Polity Press.

You, J. (2018) 'Xi Jinping and PLA transformation through reforms', *RSIS Working Paper* No 313, [online] 21 May, Available from: www.rsis.edu.sg/wp-content/uploads/2018/05/WP313.pdf [Accessed 1 May 2019].

Zhao, L. (2017) 'PLA to be world-class force by 2050', *Chinadaily*, [online] 27 October [Accessed 1 May 2019].

11

Military and Politics in Patrimonial North Korea

Jongseok Woo

North Korea remains the only communist state that has successfully completed three-generation hereditary successions, that is, Kim Il-sung (1948–94), to Kim Jong-il (1997–2011), and to Kim Jong-un (2011–current). Compared with other dictatorial regimes that suffered leadership succession dilemmas and political turmoil, the family successions in Pyongyang occurred without noticeable political unrest. Given that regime collapse in Pyongyang seems improbable through elite opposition, organized popular protests or intervention by foreign political forces, the KPA may be the only political force that possesses the means of physical violence to pose an immediate threat to the Kim-family regime (Jeon, 2000; Byman and Lind, 2010). One may wonder why the KPA demonstrates unwavering loyalty to the Kim family rule from the state-building years through to the current Kim Jong-un regime.

When Kim Jong-il promulgated his leadership with the slogan of *Songun* (military-first) politics in 1998, many North Korea watchers interpreted the *Songun* political system as one dominated by the KPA (Oh and Hassig, 2000; Suh, 2002; Kim, I., 2006). Kim Jong-il's *Songun* politics resulted in a massive increase in defence spending and adventurous foreign policies with the pursuit of nuclear weapons and Intercontinental Ballistic Missiles (ICBMs) in a time of economic distress and massive famine. The *Songun* system focused on Kim's regime survival at the expense of the national economy and ordinary people's well-being. A logical corollary was the assessment that Kim Jong-il's political survival was heavily dependent upon the KPA's political support; therefore, the military's political influence has been significantly expanded in recent decades. Moreover, a military coup might have been a possibility when the suspected power vacuum emerged after the death of Kim Jong-il (Saxonberg, 2013, pp 316–20). Contrary to such expectations, however, the hereditary power succession to his son Kim Jong-un has been smooth, as the current dictator has consolidated his undisputed leadership in the Korean Workers Party (KWP), the cabinet and the KPA.

Upon assuming power after his father's death in December 2011, Kim Jong-un carried out extensive institutional modifications that mostly targeted the once politically overgrown KPA during the *Songun* era. The reforms significantly curtailed KPA officers' presence in important political organizations, including the KWP Central Committee, the Politburo (Standing Committee), the Central Military Commission (CMC) and the National Defence Commission (NDC, currently renamed the State Affairs Commission [SAC]). Moreover, current Kim reforms have relocated management of numerous profit-generating businesses from the KPA to the KWP and the cabinet. Finally, such changes accompanied a personnel facelift through massive purges of KPA officers who occupied some of the most powerful positions in Pyongyang's political system (Woo, 2016). If *Songun* politics significantly augmented the armed forces' political influence, why has the KPA not even attempted to revolt (or even passively resist) Kim Jong-un's political overhaul that targeted KPA officers in key political positions? This is an intriguing question that is at odds with the mainstream Huntingtonian civil–military relations theories setting forth that politicization of the military for a civilian political purpose ultimately leads to political outgrowth of the armed forces and an eventual coup d'état (Huntington, 1957).

This chapter addresses two of the main puzzles presented in Chapter 1 of this volume. First, this chapter explores how the Japanese colonial rule until 1945 influenced the evolution of the military's self-definition of political roles from the early years of state-building to the present day. Second, it demonstrates that the historical evolution of civil–military relations in North Korea cannot be simply viewed as a gap between civilian and military elements. Indeed, North Korea has built the most militarized state in the world, but the army leadership has kept unwavering loyalty to the Kim family's hereditary rule. This chapter addresses the main reason for the coexistence of the KPA's political role and its continued loyalty to the Kim family. It argues that Pyongyang's political system is a patrimonial system in which the single dictator (called *Suryong*) is positioned above the partisan and ideological authorities and exercises unchecked political power. In Pyongyang, power and authority of major political institutions – including the KWP, KPA and cabinet – originate from *Suryong*. In particular, the KPA plays a role as the defender of the dictator and his family, that is, a mere servant to the Kim family rule. This chapter analyses how the KPA played the regime security role in three of the most critical historical junctures that defined North Korea's political paths: Kim Il-sung's power struggle and creation of patrimonial authority in the 1950s–60s, Kim Jong-il's *Songun* politics in the late 1990s and lastly, the family succession to Kim Jong-un and the KPA's political position since 2011.

The analysis in this chapter highlights how Japanese colonial rule and Kim Il-sung's leadership in the anti-Japanese guerrilla war shaped the core tenets of *Juche* ideology and the KPA's self-defined roles in politics. Moreover, contrary to the common findings from authoritarian rule experiences around the world, the analysis demonstrates that organizational expansion and politicization of the military does not always lead to its political domination, at least in the case of North Korea. A confluence of cultural and historical legacies – soldiers' socialization through guerrilla war experiences (both anti-Japanese and anti-US wars), personality cult of Kim Il-sung and his family together with a strong Confucian tradition of people's respect for political authority – has moulded a unique political system and the military's political roles in Pyongyang. The concept of Asian military evolutions helps in understanding the parallel existence of the KPA's political role and its political weaknesses.

The regime and the military in North Korea: conflicting assessments

From its inception until Kim Il-sung's death in 1994, North Korea specialists identified the KPA as the party's armed force, which honoured and carried out the party's political will. However, Kim Jong-il's *Songun* politics in 1998 engendered conflicting assessments among scholars about the changing influence and role of the KPA. Some scholars argue that Kim Jong-il's *Songun* politics fundamentally altered Pyongyang's political system from being party-centred to one dominated by the military (Wada, 1999; Oh and Hassig, 2000; Moon and Takesada, 2001; Suh 2002; Kim, I., 2006). This 'military rule' argument points to notable changes brought by the *Songun* system, including the KWP's loss of ideological and political authority during the political and economic crisis of the 1990s and resulting massive famine and the emergence of the KPA to overcome the crisis. During the *Songun* era, major party institutions stopped functioning, including the KWP Politburo (Standing Committee) and the CMC, since they never convened for political decisions. Instead, the NDC emerged as the highest decision-making authority. The 1998 constitution even designated the NDC chair as the leader of the nation. Moreover, Kim Jong-il prioritized the well-being of the top KPA leadership with massive promotions and appointment of senior officers in key positions (Horak, 2011). Finally, in a time of dire economic crisis, *Songun* politics brought about a massive increase in defence spending at the expense of the civilian economy and the people's well-being. Ultimately, the 'military rule' argument suggests that Kim Jong-il's *Songun* politics transformed Pyongyang's political system to a *de facto* military rule in which Kim's dependence on the military for political survival became more evident than ever.

An opposite argument is the 'totalitarian party-state' thesis, which suggests that *Songun* politics is nothing more than a political slogan for political survival and that the KWP's political supremacy over the military remains unchanged (Lee, 2003; Woo, 2014, 2016). The party–state argument points out that the 1998 constitution stated that 'all state activities must be conducted under the leadership of the KWP' and that the military as a loyal servant must perform its duties under the party's guidance (Woo, 2014, p 119). The totalitarian party–state thesis analyses the KPA's political role from Colton's participation model and Odom's interest congruence model, which were designed to study the Muscovite communist party–military relations (Colton, 1979; Odom, 1978). It argues that 'the party and military are inseparable but linked through inter-institutional penetrations and share the same ideology, political norms, and objectives' (Woo, 2018, p 231). Ultimately, *Songun* politics did not drastically change Pyongyang's political system, which had been installed by the Soviet military in the 1940s. In party–military relations, the KPA continues to be a mere servant that carries out the party's order.

The third assessment of the post-Kim Il-sung North Korea is the 'post-totalitarian state' thesis, which suggests that *Songun* politics transformed North Korea from a party-dominant totalitarian system to a post-totalitarian state (Scobell, 2005; Park, 2009; McEachern, 2009, 2010). North Korea under Kim Il-sung was ruled through the appeal of Kim's personal charisma and his *Juche* ideology as well as the KWP acting as the leading political organ that guided all sectors of the nation. However, Kim Jong-il was a different political character; he did not have political charisma like his father, nor did he have his own ruling ideology like *Juche*. Therefore, Kim Jong-il's ruling strategy adopted institutional separation across the party, the military and the cabinet and made them compete for his recognition and resource allocations. The outcome was increasing institutional (but not social) pluralism in which major political organs turned into bureaucratic institutions that prioritized institutional interests rather than *Juche* utopian propaganda. In post-totalitarian North Korea, the party and the military become equal peer institutions that compete for political and policy influence (McEachern, 2009, 2010).

Positioning the KPA's political place in Pyongyang will be vastly different depending on how one conceptualizes the country's political system. In the totalitarian party–state model, the KPA becomes a mere servant to the party and carries out the party's orders; in the military-rule model, the KPA replaces the party's role and becomes the ruler; and in the post-totalitarian state model, the KPA and the KWP are co-equal institutions that compete for resources and political power. As will become clear in this chapter, none of these conceptual models properly assess the KPA's political role. If one follows the totalitarian party-state model, North Korea's political system must have been highly unstable and prone to military coups since the 1990s, because the party stopped functioning, and, further, the party's control over the military was virtually non-existent throughout Kim Jong-il's rule. On the contrary, if Kim Jong-il's North Korea was under military rule, how could Kim Jong-un, a young and inexperienced political leader, conduct massive purges of senior KPA officers without backlash from the army's top brass? Similarly, if the KPA turned into a bureaucratic institution that pursues its own interest, why did the KPA remain loyal to the Kim Jong-un regime? If the KPA had been the ruler or interested in securing its own bureaucratic interest, it should have revolted or at least expressed complaints about Kim Jong-un's policy directions to curtail the military's political and economic influence (Woo, 2018).

A brief review of previous theoretical models about party–military relations in North Korea illustrates that one needs an alternative framework to correctly gauge the political role of the armed forces in post-Kim Il-sung North Korea. The following section conceptualizes North Korea as a patrimonial political system in which major political institutions – the party, the military and the cabinet – are mere servants to the Kim family; therefore, the KPA has never been a dominant political institution from its inception to the current Kim regime.

Patrimonial political system and the KPA

The political system in Pyongyang has taken the form of one-man dictatorships by Kim Il-sung (1948–94), Kim Jong-il (1998–2011) and Kim Jong un (2011–current). Kim Il-sung established his absolute authority after a decade-long power struggle in the 1950s in which he conducted massive purges of his rival factions. In this process, North Korea built a political system that was distinct from a party-centred totalitarian system in a typical communist state. In a communist state, the party, as the vanguard of the proletariat revolution, preserves the highest authority; the party envisions the state ideology and provides politico-ideological legitimacy to the dictator. In North Korea, however, the relationship is reversed, so that the Kim family is the origin of politico-ideological authority; without the leader, there is no party, the military or the people. The party and the military become legitimate institutions simply because they dutifully carry out the leader's instructions.

Although it preserves the major characteristics of a communist totalitarian state, Pyongyang's political system is distinct from that of a Muscovite regime. Kim Il-sung established a family-based one-man dictatorship in which 'traditional domination develops an administration and a military force which are purely personal instruments of the master' (Chehabi and Linz, 1998, p 4). Linz and Stepan used the term 'sultanism' to describe such a state when they illustrate that 'all individuals, groups, and institutions are permanently subject to the unpredictable and despotic intervention of the sultan' (Linz and Stepan, 1996, p 53). Due to the specific regional and historical connotations that sultanism entails, this chapter uses patrimonialism to describe Pyongyang's political system, which had been built based on the dynastic hereditary power successions transmitted through three generations.

The patrimonial tendencies in North Korea are prominent in three major areas. First, the ways that leadership establishment and power succession transpired were different from those of other communist states. In the communist Soviet Union and China, charismatic leadership by a single dictator (for example, Joseph Stalin and Mao Zedong) was followed by a more party-centred and bureaucratized system, that is, post-totalitarian state. In North Korea, however, a single dictator's power and authority did not fade away but were transmitted through family-based power succession that has been justified by the 'Baekdu bloodline'. As a result, political structure in Pyongyang remained unchanged, as it preserves a pure form of a patrimonial system.

Second, the hereditary successions became possible due to a strong family cult, which was reminiscent of the Confucian teaching of filial piety (called *hyo*) (French, 2014, p 60). Personality cult is a common occurrence in any totalitarian state, as political propaganda eulogizes the dictator's political brilliance and leadership quality. In North Korea, however, it goes beyond the cult of a single dictator to sanctify the entire family, including the leaders' ancestors and their wives. As Cumings illustrates, the three Kims in North Korea have been praised as the benevolent fathers and mothers who take care of the nation as one large family (Cumings, 1993, p 209). Therefore, the main source of legitimacy in North Korea is not the party, the military or the people but the Kim family and the ideology it creates.

Finally, political legitimacy in Pyongyang was built upon a strong sense of nationalism and patriotism drawn from a mythology of Kim Il-sung's heroic anti-Japanese guerrilla fighting in northeast China in the 1930s–40s. With this exaggerated narrative, Kim Il-sung justified his leadership and his guerrilla faction. At the same time, the fabricated history allowed Kim's guerrilla force to purge other competing factions in the country, including pro-Chinese and pro-Soviet faction members in the 1950s. Moreover, later in the 1990s, Kim Jong-il's *Songun* politics brought the descendants of the guerrilla members and their descendants to the forefront of his military-based rule.

What do these patrimonial tendencies in North Korea say about the KPA's political influence and role? More than anything else, the strength or weakness of the KWP's control over the KPA has little to do with the military's power position up to the point where it would challenge the Kim family rule. Rather, it is a mere reflection of the dictator's ruling method of choice for political expediency (Woo, 2018). Sometimes, the patrimonial dictator bypasses the partisan apparatus and mobilizes the KPA directly to secure his power, for example, what Kim Il-sung and Kim Jong-il did in the 1950s and 1990s, respectively. At other times, the dictator utilizes the partisan establishments for the same purpose, as Kim Il-sung did in the 1960s through 1994 and Kim Jong-un has been doing since 2011. Likewise, North Korea has had two distinct patterns of party–army relations: the dictator's personalistic control over the military (in the 1950s and 1998–2011) and control through the partisan apparatus (1960s–90s and since 2011). The historical analysis clearly illustrates that the different control methods have always been the patrimonial dictator's ruling method of choice, and that the KPA was never an autonomous political actor in North Korea.

Kim Il-sung's political rise and the KPA, 1948 to the 1960s

Pyongyang's patrimonial political system was created as a result of Kim Il-sung's power struggle with competing factions in the early years of state-building. Kim Il-sung's political rise from 1945 through the 1970s occurred in three distinctive historical stages. First, during the Soviet military occupation (1945–48), Kim Il-sung was not a dominant political figure in Pyongyang, although he quickly rose through the ranks with the Soviet Union's tutelage and support. The second stage entailed Kim's struggles with other competing factions in the party throughout the 1950s. Finally, Kim Il-sung declared undisputed patrimonial leadership after the massive purges of competing faction leaders and paved the way for hereditary succession to his son, Jong-il, in the early 1970s. Such political changes in Pyongyang occurred in parallel with changes in the KPA's self-defined missions, from the people's army (1948 to early 1950s), to the party's army (1950s to the 1960s) and to *Suryong's* army (since the 1970s).

When Japan surrendered to the allied forces and withdrew from the Korean peninsula in August 1945, it was not US troops that filled the power void on the Korean territory. Rather, the Soviet armed forces quickly occupied the northern half of the peninsula and consolidated their dominance in the occupied territory. Kim Il-sung, who led the anti-Japanese guerrilla force in northern China and later became a battalion commander of the 88th Brigade of the Soviet Army, returned to the port city of Wonsan in September 1945 as a captain of the Soviet Army, not as a national hero. In his mid-thirties, Kim was not a dominant political figure in post-liberation North Korea but just one of many who had fought for national liberation. Other prominent leadership figures included roughly three groups: those who led the indigenous communist independence movements in Korea, those who went to China and worked closely with the CCP, and those who had close connections with the Soviet Union. Political power struggles in Pyongyang happened among these factional groups.

However, for several reasons, Kim quickly rose to political prominence by the time of the inauguration of the Democratic People's Republic of Korea (DPRK) in September 1948. The first immediate reason was support from the Soviet occupation forces, which appointed Kim as First Secretary of the Korean Communist Party (KCP)-north branch and as the leader of the Provisional People's Committee (Woo, 2018, p 234). The latter position enabled Kim to align with the indigenous communist forces throughout northern Korea to counterbalance the communist leaders from China and the Soviet Union. Second, the KCP's political base was in Seoul, South Korea, which was under the US occupation; therefore, most of the notable communist leaders operated in the South. Furthermore, the southern communist leaders' influence became significantly weakened due to the US military government's and right-wing political groups' harsh crackdown on them (Oh and Hassig, 2000, p 83). Finally, Kim's guerrilla faction played a central role as his political support base. While the faction leaders were relatively weak in the KWP, they dominated the KPA hierarchy even before the inauguration of the DPRK. Prominent guerrilla leaders in the KPA included Choi Yong-gun (supreme commander of the KPA), Kim Il (commander of the Department of Culture), Moo Jeong (commander of the Artillery Department), Kang Geon (chief of general staff) and Kim Chaek (commander of the Second Army Corps), among others (Suh, 1988, pp 101–02; Ku et al, 2018, p 113).

Kim Il-sung's political position during the early years – weak leadership in the KWP and hegemonic leadership in the KPA – largely shaped the military's self-defined mission and political position. Specifically, until the outbreak of the Korean War (1950–53), the KPA was institutionally separated from the KWP; therefore, partisan control over the military was non-existent. Kim wanted the KPA to stay away from the partisan factional struggles and instead remain as his political stronghold. He blocked party leaders' penetration in the army hierarchy because it would further factionalize the military according to the party's internal fissures and ultimately weaken his political dominance in the military (Moon and Takesada, 2001, p 362). Although the party introduced the General Political Bureau for partisan control after the miserable defeat in the early stage of the Korean War, institutional separation between the KWP and KPA and the latter's institutional autonomy continued until the end of the 1950s.

The Korean War and the post-war reconstruction period brought about massive changes in Pyongyang's political structure in general and party–military relations, as well as the KPA's self-defined mission in particular. Immediately after the Korean War ended with an armistice agreement, power struggles in Pyongyang revolved around who would take responsibility for the war failure. Although Kim Il-sung was in the position of responsibility, he utilized the war failure to attack and purge his political competitors, including Pak Heon-yeong who was the leader of the KCP-south branch and Heo Ka-I, a Soviet faction leader. Pak, along with other prominent communists, was charged with 'allegedly aiding and abetting the enemy and plotting to replace the Kim regime' (Oh and Hassig, 2000, p 7). Moreover, the post-war power struggle centred on rebuilding the war-ravaged country and defining the KWP's political leadership and policy lines. In particular, the death of Josef Stalin and his successor Nikita Khrushchev's denouncement of him emboldened Kim's competitors to criticize Kim's monopoly of power and cult of personality. The Chinese and Soviet factions demanded a Soviet-style party-centred collective leadership (Lankov, 2015, p 14). The factional struggle reached its defining moment when the Soviet and Chinese factions tried to oust Kim Il-sung from power while Kim was on an extended trip to his Moscow and East European allies in the summer of 1956. In August, these faction leaders attempted a coup at the KWP Central Committee meeting by openly denouncing Kim's leadership and his policy lines. The failed coup attempt resulted in massive purges in the party and the military and ultimately consolidated Kim's personal dictatorship.

The so-called 'August incident' brought about notable changes in Kim Il-sung's political power and his relationship with the party and the military. The aborted coup had strengthened Kim's monopoly of power both in the party and the military, turning major political institutions into mere servants to the Kim leadership. *Juche* ideology played critical roles in justifying Kim's personalist dictatorship with two pillars of the policy line: anti-factionalism and anti-imperialism. *Juche*'s emphasis on anti-factionalism justified purges of competing faction leaders in the party and the military who had ties with Moscow and Beijing. Meanwhile, *Juche*'s anti-imperialism gave Kim political legitimacy by identifying North Koreans' arch enemies in Japan and the United States and capitalizing on his anti-Japanese guerrilla fighting in north-eastern China. *Juche* became an ideological tool for Kim and his guerrilla faction to establish hegemonic leadership in the party and the military. Moreover, *Juche* ideology turned Kim's personality cult into a cult of his family, including his ancestors, wives, son and grandson with the myth of 'Baekdu bloodline' (Yang 1994, p 255). Underscoring *Juche*'s family cult, Cumings classifies North Korea as an Asian version of the neo-socialist corporatist state, which was built based on hierarchy, organic connection and family (Cumings, 1993, p 209).

At the turn of the 1960s, Kim's guerrilla faction members filled all the seats in the KWP Central Committee; only one Soviet and three Chinese faction members kept their membership. The political rise of Kim and his guerrilla faction completely refashioned Pyongyang's political system from a Muscovite party-centred communist state into a personalized dictatorship. After the party and the military fell under Kim's tight control, he established the party machinery in the KPA for political control and indoctrination of officers with *Juche* ideology. Previously, the KPA maintained a monolithic command system from the dictator to the Ministry of National Defence and all the way down to the military units. Now, North Korea established the Military Committee within the KWP Central Committee and the General Political Bureau, which dispatched political commissars at all levels of the KPA hierarchy (Kim, S., 2006, pp 86–8). In 1962, the Kim regime created the Military Committee to direct the military's doctrines, leadership structure and policy making. These two organizations – Military Committee and the General Political Bureau – functioned as the pillars of the partisan control over the military until Kim Il-sung's death in 1994. Likewise, in the 1960s, the KPA transformed from the people's army into the party's army which strictly followed the party's political and ideological leadership. However, since the KWP became a mere servant to Kim Il-sung and his *Juche* ideology, the party's control over the military simply meant that the KPA grew into an armed servant for the Kim family.

Kim Jong-il's *Songun* politics and the KPA, 1998–2008

Although Kim Jong-il officially assumed political leadership in 1997, three years after his father's death, he had been the designated successor to his father since the early 1970s. Kim Jong-il began his political career in the KWP, as the head of the Organization and Guidance Department (OGD) and the Propaganda and Agitation Department (PAD), two of the most powerful institutions in the party. The hereditary succession became official at the 6th Party Congress held in 1980 in which Kim Jong-il was elected a member of the Politburo Standing Committee and the CMC, the highest military organization in the party (Woo, 2016, p 258). Likewise, Kim Jong-il's power succession transpired through the party organs. Through the PAD, Kim propagandized his father's *Juche* ideology and glorified the guerrilla fighters' heroic actions during the Japanese colonial rule; through the OGD that was often called 'the party within the party', he oversaw the appointment and monitoring of key officials in the party and the military (Jeon, 2009). In 1991, Kim Jong-il became supreme commander of the KPA; two years later, he was elected chair of the NDC (Kim I., 2006, p 60).

The three decades of hereditary succession process clearly illustrate that Kim Jong-il established his leadership in both the KWP and the KPA through the partisan institutions. One may wonder why Kim suddenly abandoned his partisan political base and quickly switched to the KPA with *Songun* politics. Did the KPA emerge as the most powerful institution in Pyongyang so that Kim had to rely on the military's support for his political survival? Was he vulnerable to the military's political influence? Numerous scholars interpreted *Songun* politics as a major political transition from a party-centred system to one dominated by the military (Wada, 1999; Oh and Hassig, 2000; Moon and Takesada, 2001; Kihl, 2006; Kim I., 2006; Horak, 2011; Jung, 2011). Such interpretation depends on a few notable political changes that occurred during Kim's rule. One immediate reason was the KWP's inability to cope with multiple challenges of the 1990s, including the demise of the socialist bloc and resulting diplomatic isolation, economic difficulties, frequent natural disasters that caused massive famine and the exodus of North Koreans to neighbouring countries. Faced with multiple crises, the KWP proved incompetent and 'plagued with bureaucratic indolence, arrogance, and rampant corruption' (Woo, 2018, p 118). The party's incompetence forced Kim to bring the KPA to the forefront of his rule to deal with the multiple crises that directly threatened security of the state and the Kim regime.

In the 1990s, major party organizations – the KWP Central Committee, the Politburo (Standing Committee) and the CMC – stopped functioning. The KWP Central Committee is the pillar of the party, which elects all important positions, including the Politburo and CMC members in the party, and supervises all party functionaries, among them the OGD and the PAD. It had been the central decision-making body of the party throughout Kim Il-sung's rule. Since the final meeting in December 1992, however, the Central Committee did not convene again until 2010. Similarly, the Politburo (Standing Committee) remained moribund under the *Songun* system. A body of a few-dozen highest-ranking party elites, the Politburo makes decisions while the Central Committee is not in session. Similar to the Central Committee, the Politburo did not have a meeting until the final year of Kim's rule and its seats remained vacant when the incumbent members retired or died. The third defunct party organ was the CMC. Originally, Kim Il-sung established the Military Committee in 1962 as a subcommittee under the KWP Central Committee. At the 6th Party Congress in 1980, in which Kim Jong-il was officially pronounced as the successor, the Military Committee was renamed CMC and elevated to be the highest military leadership organization in the party. Since then, the CMC became the central conduit through which Kim Jong-il entrenched his dominance over the KPA (Kim, S., 2006). However, the CMC also stopped functioning until 2010 (Jung, 2011, p 32).

The demise of major party organizations was followed by political ascendance of the NDC as the highest decision-making body and the symbol of *Songun* politics. The NDC was often misunderstood as a military and security decision-making institution due to its title and overlap with the *Songun* era. One observer even held that Kim Jong-il's rule through the NDC 'amounts to a military coup so that the military may rule the party' (Kim, I.,

2006, p 61). However, the NDC, until it was renamed as the State Affairs Commission (SAC) in 2016, functioned as the highest political decision-making body. Originally, the NDC was created in 1972 as a subcommittee of the Central People's Committee (SPC) and included a small number of top brass personalities from the army, including Kim Il-sung. Subsequently, the NDC's political rise paralleled Kim Jong-il's power succession; he was elected vice chair of the NDC in 1990 and chair in 1993. The 1992 constitution stipulated that the chair of the NDC was the second-highest political figure, next only to *Juseok* (the president and his father). The 1998 Constitution abolished the *Juseok* system by memorializing Kim Il-sung as the 'Eternal President', thereby making the NDC chair the highest political leader in North Korea (Woo, 2014, p 70). Likewise, the NDC emerged as the highest decision-making institution under *Songun* politics, in which many of the highest-ranking KPA generals participated.

Does *Songun* politics – demise of the KWP and rise of the NDC – reflect the KPA's political ascendance? It is argued here that *Songun* politics cannot be interpreted as the military's dominance in the Kim Jong-il regime, as it had always been a mere servant to the Kim family rule since the construction of the patrimonial political system in the 1960s and 1970s. Rather, *Songun* politics was Kim's choice of ruling method, switching his political tool from the party to the military. Realizing that Kim could not survive dire threats to the state and the regime through the party machine, he turned to the KPA and declared that the KPA was 'the most patriotic, creative, and effective institutions in society most capable of realizing the *juche* ideology' (Cho, 2005, p 95). Kim emphasized that 'the party is the very army and the army is the very party … without the army, there will be no party, no state, and no people' (Jeon, 2000, p 768). Ultimately, *Songun* politics was a declaration that Kim Jong-il would rule the country through the military – and not through the party. Institutionally, it brought about separation between the KWP and the KPA and the former's loss of control over the latter, something similar to the pre-1960s' party –military relations in which Kim Il-sung exercised direct control over the army.

However, this does not mean the political rise of the KPA under the *Songun* system; rather, it remained politically weak and under even tighter control than before. If the KPA was under partisan control and guidance, the *Songun* system separated the two, and Kim directly controlled the military with delicate inter-institutional and personal checks and balances and surveillance systems. North Korea under Kim Il-sung maintained a high level of interdepartmental coordination both within the party and the military, so that one person would be able to occupy multiple positions. For instance, O Jin-u, a loyal member of Kim Il-sung's guerrilla group and number-three political figure until his death, assumed various roles, including in the General Political Bureau, chief of general staff, KWP Central Committee member, and member of the Politburo (Woo, 2018, p 239). In contrast, Kim Jong-il's *Songun* politics compartmentalized institutions and personnel appointments with no possibility of horizontal communication, so that inter-institutional or interpersonal coordination and collusion for revolt were effectively thwarted. As a result, each political organization was engaged in competition for Kim's recognition and political influence, with Kim sitting at the hub of those disjointed institutions. At the same time, Kim's divide-and-rule tactic also applied to personnel management by appointing his father's guerrilla comrades as heads of government institutions and assigning younger and personally trusted officers to number-two (or -three) positions with real decision-making power (Jeon, 2000; Woo, 2014). Kim Jong-il received reports directly from, and gave orders to, the number-two (or -three) officers, while the top institution leaders remained political celebrities.

In sum, Kim Jong-il's *Songun* politics resulted in strengthening Kim's power and control over the entire party and military hierarchies through inter-institutional and interpersonal checks and balances. As a result, although the KPA was propagandized as the *Songun* revolutionary vanguard, the armed forces remained politically weak and under tight control. The political weakness of the military became evident when Kim Jong-un, a young and inexperienced leader, succeeded the leadership immediately after his father's death and conducted massive purges of KPA generals and sweeping institutional restructuring.

Kim Jong-un's hereditary rule and the KPA since 2011

The second hereditary succession from Kim Jong-il to Jong-un was a surprise to many observers of North Korea, largely because there was no such communist regime with three-generation hereditary successions to date and because Kim Jong-un was in his mid-twenties with no political career, which is atypical in a Confucian society where seniority matters. When the youngest Kim assumed power in December 2011, scholars offered varying projections for the fate of *Songun* politics and the new leadership. Focusing on his schooling and life experiences in Switzerland, some depicted Kim Jong-un as a reformer who would bring extensive policy overhaul from the *Songun* era (Rozman, 2011; Powell, 2012). Others were sceptical of his willingness and ability to come out of his father's shadow (Cha, 2009, 2012; Moynihan, 2013). Still, the most intriguing question was whether the young and inexperienced leader would be able to curb the politically influential military organization and safeguard political allegiance from it. However, the decade of political changes in Pyongyang clearly testifies that the KPA has never posed noticeable challenges to the Kim regime. Why, then, did the KPA not revolt or at least express its displeasure with massive purges of KPA officers by Kim Jong-un? One possible answer might be that top brass in the military shared the same interest in regime stability by keeping the young leader in power (Woo, 2018, p 240). If this is true, then the current Kim regime's political survival depends on the military's acquiescence; therefore, Pyongyang's political system may be highly unpredictable. This section demonstrates that this is not the case.

Upon taking over the leadership position a few weeks after his father's death, Kim Jong-un carried out extensive political institutional alterations and personnel changes that aimed at purging politically influential generals from his father's era. The youngest Kim's political overhaul focused on restoration of the KWP institutions, including the Central Committee, the Politburo and the CMC, as well as the party's supremacy over the KPA and the cabinet. Important decisions during the *Songun* era had come through the NDC. In contrast, Kim Jong-un's important political decisions have been made and announced through the partisan channel, especially the Politburo and the Central Committee. For instance, in a few weeks after his father's death, Kim Jong-un was proclaimed as supreme commander of the KPA through a Politburo decision – and not through the NDC. Another notable incident was the purge of Jang Song-taek, caretaker of the young leader as his uncle and the second-most-powerful leader in Pyongyang. The purge was pronounced at the KWP Central Committee and the Politburo extended meeting in 2013. Jang was arrested and executed for his 'anti-party, counter-revolutionary factional acts' (Mansourov, 2013). It has been rare for Kim Jong-un to make important decisions through the NDC; rather, it was the Politburo that made important decisions in politics, economy, military and foreign policy. The once omnipotent NDC under *Songun* politics was significantly weakened under the current Kim until the 13th Supreme People's Assembly (SPA) meeting in June 2016 formally replaced it with the SAC. Such institutional modification symbolically illustrates that Kim Jong-un has emerged from his father's *Songun* legacy and established his own brand of political leadership (Panda, 2016; Coduti, 2017).

Moreover, strengthening of the KWP accompanied swift personnel and policy changes that largely revolved around the purges of KPA leadership and the relocation of profit-generating business management from the military to the party and the cabinet. Depoliticization of the military in key political institutions has been consistent throughout the decade of Kim Jong-un's rule. For instance, the KWP Politburo includes 6 Standing Committee, 11 regular and 14 alternate members with no voting rights. The Standing Committee includes only one KPA officer, Choe Ryong-hae, a son of Choe Hyon who was one of the core members in Kim Il-sung's guerrilla faction. Choe Ryong-hae had begun his political career in the KWP and therefore did not have any military experience until 2010. However, he was bestowed the rank of KPA general in 2010 and promoted to vice marshal in 2012 (NK Leadership Watch, 2016). After the purge of Jang, Choe served as director of the General Political Bureau, the key partisan institution that controls the KPA hierarchy. The KPA's political influence vis-à-vis the KWP has weakened, as the KWP Politburo, Central Committee and CMC restored their pre-Kim Jong-il era political status and the KPA's representation in these institutions continued to wither.

Kim Jong-un's attempts to demote the KPA and restore political prominence of the KWP have not provoked any notable resistance from the military leadership. Indeed, political changes in Pyongyang in the past decade had focused on curtailing the KPA's presence in the party and the cabinet, including the purging and frequent reshuffling of the army leadership and relocating profitable businesses from the KPA to the party and the cabinet. Despite all these processes, top brass in the military continue to express their unwavering allegiance to the Kim family leadership.

Conclusion

Kim Jong-il's *Songun* politics served North Korea as an emergency measure for regime survival in a time of crisis and, therefore, could have not been a long-term solution for the country. The second hereditary succession in Pyongyang brought Kim's youngest son to the leadership position; thus, he inherited a politically influential military under *Songun* politics and a poverty-stricken economy suffering under severe sanctions from the international community. As the discussion from the previous section illustrates, Kim Jong-un's efforts as a leader have focused on curbing politically influential KPA officers, reinstating the once moribund party institutions and carrying out economic reforms. Many observers of Pyongyang have been puzzled by the KPA's lack of resistance to the young and inexperienced leader and his decisions to disenfranchise the military's vested interests in politics and businesses.

This chapter addressed the question of how the KPA's political outgrowth under *Songun* politics could go hand in hand with a deficiency of the military's political influence in North Korea. It analysed the KPA's political weaknesses in the light of a patrimonial political system, which was originally built by Kim Il-sung after political struggles with competing factions in the 1950s and which has remained unchanged till today. As the analysis of the three formative stages of party–military relations in North Korea illustrates, the rise and fall of the KPA's political role does not necessarily reflect its political power position. Rather, it merely reflects *Suryong*'s choice of ruling method – either ruling the country through the party institutions or through the military – which only resulted in strengthening the dictator's political power and regime security. This explains why the KPA has remained quiet and subservient to Kim Jong-un's rule, even though he was young, had no prior military leadership career and boldly curbed the KPA's role in politics and the economy.

What does this analysis tell us about theories of civil–military relations that explain civil–military dynamics in authoritarian dictatorial regimes, in general, and the nature and future of Pyongyang's political system, its (in) stability and policy directions, in particular? The trajectory of party–military relations in North Korea poses challenges to the existing theoretical models, which explain the military's political roles in authoritarian and communist totalitarian states. Huntington's concept of subjective control of the military, for instance, expects politicization of the top brass in the army and its political domination. However, the KPA's role expansion did not lead to a military-dominant system in North Korea, even during the *Songun* era. In North Korea, a notable paradox exists between the extensive roles played by the military and its political weakness. Meanwhile, some scholars continue to approach Pyongyang's party–military relations from theoretical frameworks that were designed to analyse the military's political roles in communist states like the Soviet Union, China, and other Muscovite regimes. As this chapter illustrates, however, these theories do not properly address the puzzle of the North Korean case, because weakening of the party's control mechanism did not necessarily result in the expansion of the military's political power.

Throughout the three-generation Kim family rule, Pyongyang's political system has sustained patrimonial rule, in which the ideology of *Juche* and political institutions (both the party and the military) have served the dictator. The analysis suggests that the current Kim Jong-un regime seems far more stable than most Pyongyang-watchers may realize, especially in terms of party–military relations. His father's *Songun* politics and pursuit of weapons of mass destruction did not augment the KPA's political clout; they were political tools for the Kim family's regime security. Moreover, Kim Jong-un has successfully curbed the KPA's political influence and completed institutional facelifts to restore the party's political authority. Between 2006 and 2017, North Korea conducted nuclear tests six times and developed the hydrogen bomb. In November 2017, the Kim regime successfully test-fired an intercontinental missile, which can allegedly reach North America. Today, North Korea has completed its two-decades-long journey of building weapons of mass destruction for state and regime security, as well as a diplomatic bargaining chip. With such capabilities in hand, Kim Jong-un offered to strike a deal with the United States in 2018. Such drastic changes in policy direction underscores that the KPA is under firm control by the Kim Jong-un leadership.

References

Byman, D. and Lind, J. (2010) 'Pyongyang's survival strategy: tools of authoritarian control in North Korea', *International Security*, 35(1): 44–74.

Cha, V. (2009) 'What do they really want? Obama's North Korea conundrum', *Washington Quarterly*, 32(4): 119–38.

Cha, V. (2012) 'Kim Jong Un is no reformer', *Foreign Policy*, [online] 21 August, Available from: foreignpolicy.com/2012/08/21/kim-jong-un-is-no-reformer/ [Accessed 16 July 2022].

Chehabi, H. and Linz, J. (1998) 'Theory of sultanism 1: a type of nondemocratic rule', in H. Chehabi and J. Linz (eds) *Sultanistic Regimes*, Baltimore: Johns Hopkins University Press, pp 3–25.

Cho, Y. (2005) 'The sources of regime stability in North Korea: insights from democratization theory', *Stanford Journal of East Asian Affairs*, 5(1): 90–9.

Coduti, M. (2017) 'The State Affairs Commission and the consolidation of Kim Jong Un's power', *NK NEWS.ORG*, [online] 21 September, Available from: https://www.nknews.org/2016/07/the-state-affairs-commission-and-the-consolidation-of-kim-jong-uns-power/ [Accessed 16 July 2022].

Colton, T. (1979) *Commissars, Commanders and Civilian Authority*, Cambridge: Harvard University Press.

Cumings, B.B. (1993) 'The corporate state in North Korea', in H. Koo (ed) *State and Society in Contemporary North Korea*, Ithaca: Cornell University Press, pp 197–230.

French, P. (2014) *North Korea: State of Paranoia*, New York: Zed Books.

Horak, S. (2011) 'Challenges to system stability in North Korea', *Asian Journal of Public Policy*, 4(1):121–27.

Huntington, S. (1957) *The Soldier and the State: The Theory and Politics of Civil–Military Relations*, Cambridge: Harvard University Press.

Jeon, J. (2000) 'North Korean leadership: Kim Jong Il's balancing act in the ruling circle', *Third World Quarterly*, 21(5): 761–79.

Jeon, M. (2009) 'The Kim Jong-il regime's "military-first politics": structure and strategy of discourse', *Review of North Korean Studies*, 12(4): 181–204.

Jung, S. (2011) *The Contemporary North Korean Politics: History, Ideology, and the Power Structure*, Seoul: Hanul.

Kihl, Y. (2006) 'Saying power of the socialist 'hermit kingdom', in Y. Kihl and H. Kim (eds) *North Korea: The Politics of Regime Survival*, New York: ME Sharpe, pp 3–33.

Kim, I. (2006) 'Kim Jong-il's military-first politics', in Y. Kihl and H. Kim (eds) *North Korea: The Politics of Regime Survival*, New York: ME Sharpe, pp 59–74.

Kim, S. (2006) *North Korea under Kim Jong Il: From Consolidation to Systemic Dissonance*, New York: SUNY Press.

Ku, Y., Lee, I. and Woo, J. (2018) *Politics in North and South Korea: Political Development, Economy, and Foreign Relations*, New York: Routledge.

Lankov, A. (2015) *The Real North Korea: Life and Politics in the Failed Stalinist Utopia*, New York: Oxford University Press.

Lee, D. (2003) *Why Doesn't the North Korean Military Make a Coup?*, Seoul: Hanul.

Linz, J. and Stepan, A. (1996) *Problems of Democratic Transition and Consolidation: Southern Europe, South America, and Post-communist Europe*, Baltimore: Johns Hopkins University Press.

Mansourov, A. (2013) 'North Korea: the dramatic fall of Jang Song take', *38 North*, [online] 9 December, Available from: http://www.38north.org/2013/12/amansourov120913/ [Accessed 16 July 2022].

McEachern, P. (2009) 'North Korea's policy process: assessing institutional policy preferences', *Asian Survey*, 49(3): 528–52.

McEachern, P. (2010) *Inside the Redbox: North Korea's Post-totalitarian Politics*, New York: Columbia University Press.

Moon, C. and Takesada, H. (2001) 'North Korea: institutionalized military intervention', in M. Alagappa (ed) *Coercion and Governance: The Declining Political Role of the Military in Asia*, Palo Alto: Stanford University Press, pp 357–82.

Moynihan, M. (2013) 'Kim Jong Un and the myth of the reformer dictator', *Daily Beast*, [online] 23 December, Available from: http://www.thedailybeast.com/kim-jong-un-and-the-myth-of-the-reformer-dictator [Available 16 July 2022].

North Korea Leadership Watch (2016) 'Choe Ryong Hae (Ch'oe Ryong-hae)', *38 North*, [online] 20 September, Available from: http://www.nkleadershipwatch.org/choe-ryong-hae/ [Available 16 July 2022].

Odom, W. (1978) 'The party-military connection: a critique', in D.R. Herspring and I. Volgyes (eds) *Civil–Military Relations in Communist Systems*, Boulder: Westview Press, pp 27–52.

Oh, K. and Hassig, R. (2000) *North Korea: Through the Looking Glass*, Washington DC: Brookings Institution.

Panda, A. (2016) 'North Korea gets rid of the all-powerful national defense commission. So what?', *The Diplomat*, [online] 4 July, Available from: http://thediplomat.com/2016/07/north-korea-gets-rid-of-the-all-powerful-national-defense-commission-so-what/ [Available 16 July 2022].

Park, P. (ed) (2009) *The Dynamics of Change in North Korea: An Institutionalist Perspective*, Seoul: Kyungnam University Press.

Powell, B. (2012) 'Is Kim Jong Un preparing to become North Korea's economic reformer?', *Time*, [online] 19 April, Available from: http://content.time.com/time/world/article/0,8599,2112567,00.html [Accessed 16 July 2022].

Rozman, G. (2011) 'Kim Jong-un, reformer? The promise and peril of North Korea's succession crisis', *New Republic*, [online] 20 December, Available from: https://newrepublic.com/article/98714/north-korea-kim-jong-il-succession [Accessed 16 July 2022].

Saxonberg, S. (2013) *Transitions and Non-transitions from Communism: Regime Survival in China, Cuba, North Korea, and Vietnam*, New York: Cambridge University Press.

Scobell, A. (2005) 'Making sense of North Korea: Pyongyang and comparative communism', *Asian Security*, 1(3): 245–66.

Suh, D. (1988) *Kim Il Sung: The North Korean Leader*, New York: Columbia University Press.

Suh, D. (2002) 'Military-first politics of Kim Jong-il', *Asian Perspective*, 26(3): 145–67.

Wada, H. (1999) 'The structure and political culture of the Kim Jong Il regime: its novelty and difficulty', in J. Park (ed) *North Korea in transition and policy choices: Domestic structure and external relations*, Seoul: Kyungnam University Press, pp 59–82.

Woo, J. (2014) 'Kim Jong-il's military-first politics and beyond: military control mechanisms and the problem of power succession', *Communist and Post-Communist Studies*, 47(2): 117–25.

Woo, J. (2016) 'Songun politics and the political weakness of the military in North Korea: An institutional account', *Problems of Post-Communism*, 63(4): 253–62.

Woo, J. (2018) 'Defining the nature and future of the party-military relations in North Korea', *Journal of Asian Security and International Affairs*, 5(3): 227–44.

Yang, S. (1994) *The North and South Korean Political Systems: A Comparative Analysis*, Boulder: Westview Press.

12

Curing National Insecurity through Developmental Authoritarianism in South Korea's Civil–Military Relations

Il Woo Lee and Alan Chong

The idea of a national security state that thrives on perpetuating a national climate of insecurity is often associated with the Global South. The military is geared to protect a nascent state that remains fallible despite years of experimentation with civilian control. More likely, having tasted and exercised power in the past, the military has entrenched for itself a reputation for being the indubitable guardian of normality and the security of the population, and even as the seeder of the correct formula for economic prosperity (Ahmad, 1985; Luckham, 1991). South Korea, also widely known by its formal name, Republic of Korea (ROK), is not completely distinct in its practice of civil–military relations from the rest of Asia. As we will argue in this chapter, the tussle over democracy in civil–military relations is more a symptom than a primary explanatory framework for South Korea. This is in view of the heavy social, psychological, and ideological burdens imposed by the legacies of Japanese colonialism, as well as the panicked improvisation of the South Korean economic growth strategies that started under General Park Chung-hee's direction between 1961 and 1979. In short, South Korea's current political stability was attained at a cost and its economic powerhouse status achieved through compromises arbitered by military rule and justified against a geopolitical environment of exaggerated insecurity.

The stereotypical Global South narrative about generals turning autocrats in pursuit of national salvation against civilian ineptitude and corruption is very much borne out by existing literature on South Korean civil–military relations. One distinct strand treats civil–military relations as the dramatic rise and fall of civilians pulling the puppet strings of military and paramilitary factions to stay in power (Cotton, 1991; Kim, 1998). Conversely, in the cases of the presidencies of Park Chung-hee, Chun Doo-hwan and Roh Tae-woo, elites within the military traded uniforms for civilian business suits to consolidate the appearance of civilian political supremacy (Cotton, 1991, pp 210–13; Croissant, et al, 2012, pp 19–20). The narrative of 'Generals and Presidents', to invoke the phrase coined by Carl Saxer's study of South Korea, is tied in with the mantra-like formula that anti-communist policy vis-à-vis the unfinished war with North Korea (the Democratic People's Republic of Korea, or DPRK) was best anchored to macroeconomic policies geared to deliver steady economic growth (Saxer, 2004). A middle class rooted to wealth and prosperity was therefore assumed to be the strongest bedrock for standing up to Pyongyang's propaganda and continuing military threats. A third stream in the current literature examines South Korean civil–military relations against the measure of how far the military presence in mainstream politics is curbed in favour of the exercise of democratic norms such as the rule of law, accepting the voice of public opinion and allowing elected civilians to exercise constitutional supremacy over institutions governing the monopoly of force (Kim, 1998; Croissant, et al, 2012; Adesnik, et al, 2013).

While no research is ever completely redundant, our contention is that pre-existing research mistreats South Korean civil–military relations within the framework of liberal democracy in the Western mould. The manipulative relationships between Generals and Presidents will always be important to some degree, along with considerations of South Korea's democratic progress. But it is also time to evaluate South Korean civil–military relations with reference to its deep social and historical contexts. In essence, this chapter poses inquiry into South Korean civil–military relations by asking if 'national insecurity' can only be existentially cured through developmental authoritarianism. 'National insecurity' is to be understood as a condition of permanent national siege, and in the case of South Korea, it translates as the absence of a definitive peace treaty ending the Korean War of 1950–53, compounded by the North's internecine plots to assassinate ROK politicians, kidnap exiles, infiltrate agents, and other acts of military sabotage. Additionally, since 2003, national insecurity has gained a nuclear dimension given the DPRK's demonstrated capability in short- and intermediate-range missile systems and nuclear tests. Developmental authoritarianism refers to *an ensemble of coercive and propaganda measures, coordinated to neutralize the South Korean public's susceptibility towards left wing ideologies by delivering middle class prosperity through an industrialized economy, fostering the creative industries, and pursuing export-oriented development*. It is authoritarianism in the sense that the political elites in charge communicate to the citizenry through a mixture of gentle persuasion and unsubtle coercion that the only route towards attaining a middle-class consumer lifestyle lies with a paternalistic government that does not necessarily conform to liberal democratic mores.

In the course of such an argument, we are therefore responding to two of the six questions raised by the editors in the Introduction to this volume: how do (Japanese) colonial legacies influence the evolution of civil–military relations (within South Korea) and the military's self-definition of vital roles? And second, is the Asian (or South Korean) military socially, politically, and economically embedded to the point that civil–military relations cannot be viewed as a gap between civilian and military elements? We respond to these questions with a three-stage argument. In the first stage, we will scrutinize the imperial roots of modern South Korea with expositions of the militaristic legacy of Japanese colonialism, its continuation into what we term 'social militarism' and the penchant for practices of political centralization as a sure-fire formula for national salvation. The second stage will treat developmental authoritarianism in its manifestation as a national security state, exemplified in particular by the institutionalized propagation of intermestic paranoia. The third and final stage of the argument will suggest that the South Korean state outwardly shows the trappings of a First World consumerist democracy, but beneath the surface we contend that the ROK polity has failed to fully civilianize (or liberalize) at least in the Western political sense.

The imperial roots of modern Korean civil–military relations: three stories

Japanese colonialism militarizes society and nationalism

Considering that the two Koreas were in essence national projects established and solidified by war, it would not be a stretch to imagine that the 'logic' for a persistent struggle is also deeply entrenched in the national system, both for North and South. While the machinery of a state, such as its elected officials, ministries and other so-called 'democratic' institutions have assigned roles to play and are routinely altered depending on the ruling regime or party, we posit that this 'rationale for persistent insecurity' remains consistent and expresses itself as a *modus operandi*, residing beneath the surface of South Korea's governing institutions. Likewise, we argue that it would be short sighted to trace such militant leanings and its particular Korean flavour as something that only began in 1950 with the advent of the Korean War. If anything, South Korea's special brand of martial governance can certainly find shadows of its current self when viewed from a wider lens, and in particular, its osmosis from colonial Japan.

First, the wealth of historical examination into Korea's subsumption under Japanese colonialism suggests that habits of invoking violent methods of political change were rife in the period between 1876 and 1945 (Uchida,

2011; Chae, 2013). Japanese settler colonists came as petty entrepreneurs, labourers, artisans, impecunious farmers and even prostitutes during the final years of Korean dynastic self-rule. The push to seek greener pastures on the nearby Korean peninsula came from Meiji Japan's own modernizing reforms that displaced many 'lower class Japanese' (Uchida, 2011, pp 37–43). Following gritty attempts to develop their socio-economic niches in Korean economy and society – though not always harmoniously – these settler colonists set themselves up as a lobby for Tokyo's intervention vis-à-vis local Korean rivals and Chinese entrepreneurs. These settlers viewed themselves as incipient stakeholders in Japan's ambition to prove itself a successful model of modernization and a first rate Asian power that advanced its people's well-being through territorial conquest and political guardianship of inferior peoples (Uchida, 2011, pp 46–70). The experiences of Koreans as a subject people echoed those found in the European colonies elsewhere in Asia (Uchida, 2011, pp 20–6). The Japanese settlers' and officialdom's attitudes vacillated between disdain and neglect of their Korean subjects with a sincere desire to tutor them to a level of social and intellectual sophistication in the image of modern Japan (Chae, 2013, pp 404–5). This consequently produced profound implications for Korean political culture.

Second, it is therefore objectively not possible to take a straightforward position on certain parts of the Korean population actively collaborating with the colonial authorities and their settlers while also rejecting the Japanese legacy as an unmitigated harsh, alien political and cultural influence (Akita and Palmer, 2015, pp 198–204; Palmer, 2013, pp 11–14). By the 1920s the use of military authoritarian methods gave way to softer modes of socializing Korean attitudes towards Japanese civilizational norms, and hence towards what the Japanese perceived to be modern and scientific mentalities that would amount to a Korean nationalism that could act in solidarity with Japanese visions of a new Asia. This 'cultural policy' was enacted in tandem with an administrative policy of opening civilian positions in the colonial government and Japanese military for the employment of Koreans. By the time the Pacific War (1937–45) broke out in full intensity, Japanese policy switched to total mobilization of Korean society in support of the wider Japanese war effort in penetrating and holding territory in China and elsewhere in Southeast Asia. It would be here that Japanese policy towards Korea became one of assimilation or *naisenitai*, roughly meaning 'Japan and Korea joined as one' (Lee, 2013, pp 4–6). Of course, one must bear in mind the possibility that this was little more than shrewd colonial manipulation of securing 'structural spaces' within an unshakeable colonial superstructure to ensure the latter's hegemony remained unquestioned (Ha, 2013, pp 46–9). On the other hand, it is acknowledged that when the Japanese provided public high schools for Koreans, they were also creating an 'imagined community' for young Koreans who now shared, albeit unevenly, aspirations, idealism, guilt or resentment against a common colonial authority represented in the classroom and its teachers (Ha, 2013, p 63). Regardless of these trends, it is worth noting that Japanese social engineering tended to neglect the village-bound 'poor Korean peasant'. Yong Chool Ha described the impact of deliberate colonial neglect in this way:

> [V]illage life during colonial rule probably looked like this: politically he [the villager] had to be silent, economically he had to suffer under tenancy, and socially he could not liberate himself from the village-wide clan order and close family obligations. While he might have heard or read about the outside world (if he received an education), in reality he was confined to his narrow village boundaries, feeling a great gap between the cognitive world and the world that he actually experienced because his travel radius was limited. (Ha, 2013, p 69)

We cite this at length to contrast against the systematic nation-building schooling system because when one scrutinizes the first coup-installed President of South Korea, Park Chung-hee, all these contradictory legacies of Japanese rule come to the fore in influencing his practice of civil–military relations. One of the final Japanese governors-general of Korea made it clear in 1945 that the Japanese instituted education system for Korean youths was meant to improve 'moral and mental training' for Koreans eligible for the military draft, except that it ought to have been more thorough, given the exigencies of Japan's military fortunes in the last year of the Pacific War (Palmer, 2013, p 95).

Third, it is suitable to treat the revelations of General-turned-President Park Chung-hee and of his experiences under Japanese rule as reasonably indicative of how the colonial legacy had impacted the ROK's civil–military relations (Lee, 2012; Palmer, 2013). In Park's first encounter with formal education in the 1920s, it was widely known that the previous indigenous Korean socio-political elite, the heavily Confucian-guided *yangban* literati, had already been eclipsed since the 1890s as the Japanese emphasized modern topics that embedded imported Western-originated sciences along with political role models from the West while relegating the study of Chinese classics (Lee, 2012, pp 32–3). According to available records, in spite of his financially challenged family background, Park excelled in elementary school in arithmetic, science, geography, physical education and moral education to the point that his teachers rewarded him with the position of the class monitor where he practised skills of command and enforcement. In fifth grade, the life and stories about Napoleon Bonaparte and Korea's own legendary 'Horatio Nelson equivalent' Admiral Yi Sun-shin deeply impressed the ambitious and disciplined young man. Yi secured his place in history as the steely commander who resisted the erstwhile Korean dynasty's mode of retreat, while single-handedly inflicting defeat on numerically superior Japanese invaders in the 1590s. Park admired these two figures for their defiance of the odds and ability to rise above selfishness and vainglory (Lee, 2012, pp 40–7).

Graduating to the next level of the 'Normal School', which is approximately today's equivalent of high school, Park developed a penchant for the military drills mandatory in its classes. He also enjoyed the Japanese sword fighting martial art called *kendo* and picked up the trumpet along with soccer. It helped that Park encountered gentlemanly and principled Japanese teachers who were associated with the liberal era of the so-called 'Taisho democracy'. These Japanese mentors at school showed affection and welfare towards their Korean charges, which in Park's case meant a great deal since he came from a poor family who mostly encountered discrimination even among Korean peers (Lee, 2012, pp 72–9). All these added up to the mental preparation of a future military commander who by 1938 implored the Japanese authorities to overlook his age, short build and other physical weaknesses to allow him to join the newly established Manchukuo Military Academy. Advised by a fellow Korean who had served as a soldier in the Japanese conquest of Manchuria (Manchukuo in Japanese) and who hailed from the Taegu area where Park had schooled, Park authored what appeared to be a sincere 'Oath in Blood' to the Japanese military trainers at Manchukuo who by 1939 were desperate to raise an army to further their campaign to advance further into China. This extraordinarily emotional pledge of loyalty to the Japanese cause was publicized as an instance of spontaneous patriotism by the Japanese-controlled Manchukuo newspaper (Lee, 2012, pp 103–05). It caught the attention of Japanese colonel Arikawa who recognized Park's background in Taegu. It would be Arikawa, invoking his seniority and influence with the commandant of the Manchukuo Military Academy, who got Park admitted on a special basis, paving the way for Park to become quintessentially the 'Japanized' Korean soldier (Lee, 2012, pp 103–11).

Nevertheless, it is also important to note that scholars such as Lee Chong-sik argue strongly that one should not label Park as an 'evil' collaborator who sold out to colonial power (Lee, 2012, pp 112–14). In fact, several thousand Koreans enlisted with the Japanese armies by the end of the Pacific War under the conviction of a sincerely embraced sense of a tutored nationalism that could lead towards social and economic betterment (Palmer, 2013, pp 67–91). The Japanese Empire of the 1930s heralded a different wave of Asian politico-cultural revival, that the preceding indigenous dynasties founded upon classical learning and social passivity among the commoners could not inspire. Japan's invasion of China symbolized the decline of rigid, socially decrepit dynastic Confucianism in the face of a modern militarized, scientific nationalism. Park did not perceive the modern Japan of the 1930s as the clumsy, immoral invader that his hero Admiral Yi Sun-shin had fought in the 1590s. It was a model that Park sincerely venerated (Lee, 2012, p 112). Like so many Asian nationalists in Southeast and South Asia, the political and social disruption wrought by the Japanese Occupation in World War Two served as a window of opportunity to learn modern ways of thought, discipline and empowerment (Cheah, 1983; Lee, 2000; Bose, 2011; Sengupta, 2011). Interestingly and by contrast, North Korea's founding leader Kim Il-sung boasted of his credentials as an anti-Japanese guerrilla fighter, taking advantage of the Japanese Occupation in a vastly different way (Baik Bong, 1973, pp 13–18).

Ultimately, as a direct product of Japanese rule, Park himself would go on to govern the ROK, filling the void his Japanese overlords would leave behind. Taking charge through a coup in 1961, after the tumultuous stewardship of Rhee Syng-man (1948–60), Park's grip on power would never be shaken to the extent that it was for his predecessors. Nor would he relinquish his post as primary overseer until his assassination in 1979, imprinting South Korea with his militant ethos for nearly two decades. Intriguingly, for historical onlookers such as Minji Jeong and Youseop Shin, accepting military insurrection as a legitimate means to 'save' and 'return' society to its intended state through the celebration of Japanese military elements who toppled the Shogunate to usher in the Meiji period most likely served as a template for Park's own uprising in 1961 when the opportunity presented itself (Jeong and Shin, 2018).

Shaped by such a heritage Charles Eckert has produced an articulate description of Park's 'guideposts' to governance, passed down from Japanese tutelage. More importantly, this provides a non-liberal reference point when scrutinizing South Korean civil–military relations:

1. A *political* conviction that in a national crisis of sufficient magnitude, the military had not only the right but duty to intervene in the political process.
2. An *economic* persuasion that saw unfettered capitalism as hazardous and that needed to be 'guided' for the sake of social stability and unity.
3. A *tactical orientation* devoted to daring and even dangerous acts for the sake of national goals.
4. A *disciplinary character* whereby the individual would ultimately give way to the needs of the collective (Eckert, 2016, pp 2–3).

These bearings would provide a reliable compass whereby all parties in state-building indirectly but perfectly understood where the 'true power' lay: the men in uniform.

Social militarism under the Cold War umbrella

Given their genesis under Japanese occupation, militaristic principles would soon find themselves crystallized in another occupation of sorts, save for this time under the tutelage of the United States and the Cold War (Beal, 2005). Modern, technologically equipped and managerially superior to all other social units in the country, South Korea's military would quickly establish itself as the readily available alternative to the political malaise of the moment. Sustained and propped up for years by the United States, by the time of Park's seizure of power in 1961, the structural imbalance between those with a uniform and those without would make the socio-political dominance of Park's men in green all but inevitable. All that was needed was the opening – a regime in peril in the case of Rhee Syng-man – and adequate time for military officers to become fully politicized (Anon, 2016).

As a consequence, the beginnings of South Korean politics during the Cold War can be described as a turning point for civil–military relations in which civilian factions were temporarily neutralized to effectively allow quasi-civilian, but in essence military personnel, to embark on their own version of nation building. As cold hard accounts have it, this was a local version of bootstrap capitalism whereby the militarily conscripted ex-servicemen filled out the factory floor lines of state-approved industrialists to mass produce goods the First World needed (Cumings, 2005, pp 302–5; Pirie, 2008, pp 59–75). South Korea's civil–military relations would allow for massive capitalist industrialization – subsidized and supervised by the state – but would allow little room for outside social or political forces to freely participate in state affairs. Park's governing philosophy was deliberately antagonistic to the Western ideal in which civilian control remains supreme, supported by a process in which those in uniform know their place and where civil society directs the national narrative. Conversely, Park and his fellow officers would waste no time eroding democratic civil–military relations practices once in higher office. Establishing the likes of the Supreme Council for National Reconstruction by the late 1960s, where the transition from uniform to business suits became more fluid, Park would quickly go on to create his own political party to fortify the official apparatus that he and his fellow agents already directed. Adding to the challenge to remain legitimate after such a brazen move by the early 1970s, a rapid shift in the global order would also intensify Park's sense of political encirclement. The US's efforts in Vietnam had gone awry signalling an aversion to Asian affairs and subsequently a withdrawal of a US division stationed in Korea would commence by 1971. Moreover, forging both amicable Sino-American and Sino-Japanese relations, something unfathomable in the Cold War narrative up till the 1970s, were being trialled by the Nixon administration. Combined with a belligerent North Korea that had just sent forces to attempt the assassination of Park in 1968, a serial psychosis of crises soon emerged in which the military elite had decided that the democratic optics would no longer suffice for the national interest and that a firmer hand would be needed (The Institute for East Asian Studies, 1975).

By October 1972, Park would inaugurate what he termed the Yushin (Reformation) Constitution legitimizing his authoritarian hold on power with more civilian appearances and constructed legality. Increasingly bolstered by an anti-communism that became more widespread due to the country's contention with its northern neighbour, and reinforced by the public's vague conception of wanting a Korean version of the 'American Dream' due to the US's ever domineering cultural and economic presence, South Korea's military would cunningly exploit such contexts to codify its own sense of political entitlement. The latter would be achieved through the ballot box and façade of rule of law, instead of the bullet. This burnished the optics of the militarization of society, fudging any possibility of delineating civil–military relations in terms of generals standing apart from actual politics and administration (Ahn, 2003, pp 7–10).

A change of command but not the command structure: bureaucratic authoritarianism

With Park's unanticipated assassination by his chief of intelligence Kim Jae Kyu, the Yushin system formally ended with Park's death, but its bureaucratic practices persisted. The preceding regimes under Syngman Rhee (1948–60) and the short-lived premiership of Chang Myon (1960–61) had acted to diffuse bureaucratic decision-making across different government ministries without allowing any to become dominant. Under Park, and continuing thereafter into the military presidencies of Chun Doo-hwan and Roh Tae-woo, some ministries that were regarded as strategic enjoyed the privilege of being *primus inter pares* over the rest with very few alterations between one president and the next. These were the Ministries of Finance, Agriculture, Commerce and Industry, Communication, Construction, Transportation, Public Information, Foreign Affairs and predictably National Defence. There was an abiding belief by the military elite that political functions could be replaced easily by administrative proficiency, thereby relegating most other priorities of government to the overriding goal of building economic growth (Ahn, 2003, pp 111–13). The main idea was to depoliticize the business of government so that national security in its twinned economic and military dimensions could be secured (Ahn, 2003, pp 114–17).

This particular governing style, with a cadre of military elite managing the administrative functions of the state, would quickly pass on to the next generation of coup enablers with Park's passing, commonly referred to as Hanahoe, or loosely translated as 'Group of One' or 'One Mind Society'. Led by General Chun Doo-hwan, the head of the Defense Security Command (DSC), the military's key intelligence branch charged with internal security, Chun and his fellow affiliates would not acquiesce to civilian oversight after Park's demise but would simply go on to mimic the subversive tactics that had catapulted Park to the Blue House. Using investigative powers granted to the unit to bring the perpetrators of Park's murder to justice, Chun would combine such authority with the strategic positioning of Hanahoe members in key military posts to quickly neutralize any obstacles to authoritarian continuity within the security apparatus. Swiftly taking control of Kim Jae Kyu's KCIA (Korean Central Intelligence Agency) and thereby appointing Chun himself as the sole proprietor of state intelligence, Hanahoe members would go on to methodically quell dissident voices within the civilian populace as well, as was the case in the Gwangju Uprising, thus enabling the foundation for Chun's own occupancy as President (Breen, 2010). Since then, the Hanahoe elite has been rebranded to include right wing lawyers and prosecutors under the umbrella label 'Yukbeop-dang'.

All the same, with Chun's personal promise to serve only one term, most likely impacted by the political scars of Gwangju, along with his inability to muster the same sort of 'justification' President Park had for his own seizure of power, compounded by a nascent political opposition taking clearer form, civil–military relations would take on a pattern of engaging in a makeover without a substantial reorientation. Any glimmers of liberal hope for civil–military relations would never materialize until the election of Kim Young-sam in 1993 some 13 years later. At this point, we can posit two factors to explain this transition of presidencies that occurred without altering civil–military relations at all.

First, despite the visible leadership succession within the executive, the removal of Park and his Yushin system did not come about by popular uprising or through an overwhelming nationally felt political consciousness. The events that incited the replacement of Park were mostly an internal affair in which the system itself was jolted but quickly adjusted to new realities and personnel. The often-used phrase 'palace coup' would be appropriate here.

Second, and perhaps more perversely impacting the Western psyche, South Korea's political culture, with its natural deference to hierarchy, inculcated by its extreme culture of Confucianism, combined with the nation's exposure to continuous 'strongman politics' for 30 years, may have subconsciously privileged the emergence of yet another 'strongman'. This may then be portrayed by the incoming presidency as a reassuring development for public consumption. The public appetite for strongman politics may be further reinforced by the fact that the daily contours of politics had not drastically changed. The inherent threat from North Korean communism justifies authoritarian vigilance. And an economy progressively elevating many South Koreans towards middle class status would also justify keeping politics *status quo*. It would appear to many Koreans that political alternatives with their bountiful divisions, as was the case between Kim Dae-jung's and Kim Young-sam's political clans, would hinder any structural capacity for installing a new version of civil–military relations (Rowl and Novak, 1987).

In the end, the *system* that gave rise to Park Chung-hee's ascendance would only last, at least in its most militant form, until Chun's successor Roh Tae-woo. By Roh's tenure, the nascent opposition, always simmering at society's margins, had advanced their presence by winning concessions from the regime for a constitutional amendment allowing the people to once again vote for their president. It is worth observing here that minor adjustments have always been undertaken in South Korea's civil–military relations with the passing of each General turned Executive. Such variations made for political and administrative conveniences at best, instead of serving as universal democratic governing principles between the military and civilian sectors. Only with the accession of Kim Young-sam to the presidency in 1993 did civil–military relations take a hesitant turn towards admitting civilian control. Although he was officially South Korea's first 'civilian' president, Kim had shrewdly joined forces with his predecessor Roh, and merged his Democratic Reunification Party with Roh's military-supported Democratic Justice Party to win the 1992 presidential elections under the banner of the new Democratic Liberal Party. However, once in office, Kim embarked on a campaign to strip Hanahoe associates of their positions and replace them with non-Hanahoe officers and civilian administrators (Kuehn, 2016). Ironically, both Chun and Roh would be tried for sedition during Kim Young-sam's tenure only to be pardoned at the behest of Kim Young-sam's successor, Kim Dae-jung, a man whom Chun had tried to sentence to death during his administration. Kim Dae-jung, a veteran of oppositional politics, would seek clemency for his predecessors as president-elect for the sake of national reconciliation in the aftermath of the 1997–98 Asian Financial Crisis. Judging the situation too dire by the time of his own inauguration, Kim Dae-jung mobilized state resources towards securing South Korea's economy first and foremost, with the hopes of moving towards conciliation with North Korea. Kim Dae-jung's presidency therefore represented the most earnest attempt to undo the inter-Korean antagonism which had lent consistent credibility to the military bureaucrats who had ruled behind the scenes for so long (Pollack, 1997). In the long run, Kim Dae-jung's efforts proved to be little more than taking infant steps in the Sisyphean task of reducing the threat from Pyongyang as the legitimating reason for militarizing South Korean politics.

Developmental authoritarianism as a national security state: virtue in Cold War paranoia

Developmental authoritarianism could not exist without its creators, its victims, and its beneficiaries, the South Korean population, ritualizing the national trauma that the world remembers as the Korean War of 1950–53 (Choi, 2015). The armistice or truce of 27 July 1953 lent considerable justification to General Park Chung-hee and his successors to justify the strategic need to militarize both society and the economy for national security purposes. Indigenous Korean scholarship and propagandistic history implied that the UN Command lost the opportunity after the Inchon landing in 1950 to unify the Peninsula (The Institute for East Asian Studies, 1975; Choue, 1985, pp 52–3). By extension, it was widely assumed by the South Korean elites that the North ought to have been thoroughly defeated and its leaders put on trial as warmongers and illegitimate representatives of the Korean people. It was believed that while Rhee Syng-man was elected under relatively free UN-administered elections in 1948, the communist supported Korean Workers' Party in Pyongyang gave Koreans in the north no such choice (Choue, 1985, pp 46–8). Between 1973 and 1975, Park's presidency has been described as pursuing a 'watertight' national security posture in the southern part of the Peninsula, calling on the North to swerve away from any ambitions to re-enact the war of 1950–53 as a route towards reunification, and instead engage in a peaceful competition for developing both Koreas economically (The Institute for East Asian Studies, 1975, pp 22–36).

The militarization of society and the economy was imparted with considerable momentum by Park Chung-hee's active mirroring of the South's sense of siege vis-à-vis the North's perceived advances in industrialization, urban renewal and military build-up. Park reasoned that if the South committed to heavy industrialization and a more disciplined society, the chances of the South's survival against either long-term military or non-military competition with the North would increase significantly (Clifford, 1998, pp 98–107). This translated into the creation of a 'national security state' that made no distinctions between civilian and military spheres of activity so long as policies were closely oriented towards national salvation vis-à-vis the perceived communist threat from the North. Park, for example, encouraged South Korean firms to borrow massively from overseas lenders to spur growth and export-oriented production ever since he became president in 1961. Within ten years, many Korean firms were faced with crushing debt servicing burdens that had become disproportionate loads on their still modest capital bases. In 1971, 200 firms went bankrupt and South Korea faced its first foreign debt crisis (Clifford, 1998, pp 102–3). This invited IMF intervention recommending devaluation of the Korean Won, raising debt servicing costs, cutting state subsidies to industry and penalizing the raising of new loans. Instead of taking the IMF's stiff prescriptions, President Park heeded the cries of Korean businesses and froze all private lending and extended debt moratoriums in the less-regulated curb market that acted in parallel to the formal market for banking loans. At the same time, subsidies for heavy and chemical industries continued. This marked the ever-deepening cosiness between Park Chung-hee's national security state and the many business elites (Clifford, 1998, pp 103–4).

The relationship between business elites and Park Chung-hee's militarized state was not always collegial. Park expected the former to respond raptly and obligingly whenever he summoned them for national programmes. But both found common cause in outdoing North Korea's obsession with the largest, the fastest or the grandest projects (Clifford, 1998, p 108). The most spectacular example of militarization of the economy came in the form of the creation of the Pohang Iron and Steel Company (POSCO). Park wanted this example of heavy industrialization in spite of the absence of either a credible domestic market for iron and steel products nor a demonstrable overseas one (Seok-man, 2011, pp 43–4). The Japanese occupation had seeded some aspects of an iron and steel industry through its munitions plants but these had all been laid waste during the Korean War. POSCO's rise was therefore spectacular, akin to the orders of a General raising an army out of raw recruits and establishing its battle experience overnight. In this story, the role of Park's friend, one time chief of staff, and ex-military confidant, the erstwhile Major-General Pak Tae-jun, looms large. Pak Tae-jun had been known to share Park Chung-hee's vision of 'make steel, serve the nation' and had retained a seat on the coup-installed Supreme Council for National Reconstruction following Park's seizure of political power in May 1961 (Seok-man, 2011, pp 54–5). Subsequently, Pak was appointed president of Korea Tungsten by fiat and went on to negotiate normalization with Japan. In the latter, he was instrumental in persuading his colleagues in redirecting 23.9 per cent of reparations towards constructing steelworks (Seok-man, 2011, p 48).

As expected, Pak Tae-jun imitated his superior's national security logic in compelling his POSCO employees to work as if the future of the nation depended upon it. He warned that if POSCO failed, its employees should 'drown themselves to redeem their historical sin for such a failure' (Seok-man, 2011, p 56). This maniacal pursuit of visible success led, for example, to the crash effort commencing in 1970 whereby both white collar executives and blue-collar employees worked marathon style to deliver its first phase hot-rolling plant with an annual production capacity of 1.03 million tons within 39 months. This contrasted favourably with 42 months and 49 months respectively for Japanese and Italian firms completing comparable large-scale steel mills in the early 1970s (Seok-man, 2011, p 57). Not unlike a meticulous field marshal commanding an army in war, Pak was personally involved in almost every aspect of POSCO's management and even encouraged ground level production and maintenance personnel to offer suggestions for improving workplace efficiency and product standards. Pak was reported to have shown zero tolerance of defects even in projects at 80 per cent completion status, preferring to destroy the faulty installation and rebuilding it, rather than having POSCO's reputation dented in the aftermath (Seok-man, 2011, p 59). Pak's clean, honest and disciplined reputation aligned with Park Chung-hee's mission and shielded POSCO considerably from political interference from all political parties and other ministries (Seok-man, 2011, pp 59–60).

It was also no secret that Park Chung-hee set a public precedent in declaring that the political and economic fortunes of a free South Korea were intimately tied to support for the US's anti-communist war in Vietnam between 1964 and 1975, and Washington's containment of Soviet influence everywhere else in general. In the words of Lee Jin-kyung, Park deliberately chose a strategy of 'justifying and displacing militarized politics in the domestic arena to militarism on foreign soil' (Lee, 2010, p 41). In exchange for solidly aligning with Washington against communism and specifically committing a number of combat brigades to the US effort in Vietnam, Seoul's soldiers were guaranteed salaries, combat experience and prestige while its workers and factories fulfilled lucrative contracts to build installations and logistics for US forces in their war effort. For nine years, the South Korean economy earned $200 million annually from the Vietnam War, and the earnings from combat military labour 'alone comprised 40% of the total earned from South Korean exports' during the same period (Lee, 2010, p 41). To consolidate these gains, Park Chung-hee ordered government ministries to stage multiple public ceremonies and foster popular culture productions to celebrate the patriotism of going off to war against the global communist enemy and reasserting the vitality of Korean ethnonational masculinity to the world. The development of this calculated domestic campaign of legitimizing anti-communist soldiering gave the rural young population of mostly males the prospect of gaining regular material comforts such as beds, uniforms and other garments as well as full daily meals even if they were combat rations (Lee, 2010, pp 43–5).

In fact, this war-driven economy had some distant precedents in the aftermath of the Korean War, when displaced peasants were gifted with battle scarred but arable land near the 38th parallel. Amid unmarked graves, spent shell casings and unexploded ordnance, these displaced farmers were told the land were theirs to keep if they farmed on it for ten years (Choe, 2021a). In the meantime, the ROK military continued to man checkpoints and impose curfews in the area. Today, the ownership of the land remains disputed under civilian ownership laws that technically allow the original owners from both North and South to contest land rights arising from military distribution. President Moon Jae-in (2017–22) responded to the plight of the settlers by re zoning the border farmlands as state land and enabling his government to negotiate either concessionary rights or compensation to both settlers and original owners (Choe, 2021a). Nonetheless, land disputes are a feature of a militarized political economy. Unsurprisingly, Lee Jin-kyung coined this the generation of a 'military proletariat' dedicated to serve nationalistic and military security objectives of the Park regime and its successors thereafter.

This was also a shrewd way for a militarized South Korean regime to act as a politically convenient surrogate for a US Cold War empire to the point of sharing the ignominy of having perpetrated atrocities against Vietnamese non-combatants during the US war in Vietnam (Choe, 2021b).

To all intents and purposes, this cult of militarization remains alive in the 2000s and 2020s given the steady raft of K-Wave movies (for example, *Operation Chromite, Brotherhood, My Way, Front Line, Joint Security Area, The Battle of Jangsari*) glamourizing Korean heroes in uniform on both sides of the Korean War between 1986 and 2019. Perhaps there is no surprise that Korean army, navy and air force soldiers have also appeared confident enough to undertake missions to complement HADR efforts by their US ally in Southeast Asia, and to a limited extent, in Iraq between 2004 and 2008. There is also intense public interest in scrutinizing whether popular Korean male actors actually serve out their compulsory period of military conscription today. Controversy continues to fester over whether young Korean male 'star' athletes and pop music icons – such as the boyband BTS – can be legally exempted from conscription under pre-existing legislation that treats acts that 'elevate national prestige' as the equivalent of complying with military conscription (Kwak, 2022). Understandably, this issue of 'national service' by other means falls squarely into the ongoing debate over armed patriotism. During the COVID-19 emergency lockdowns, ROK soldiers were visibly deployed to patrol martial law like zones while US military soldiers were permitted to assist in disinfection operations even in residential areas.

The politico-military-bureaucratic elite put in place under Park Chung-hee has mostly endured on the strength of the North's continued demonstrations of belligerence. The multiple narrowly failed assassinations carried out by North Korean agents against Park – one of which accidentally killed his wife in 1974 – provided vivid justifications for a national security state defined by the unyielding need to discipline economy and society for the eventuality of long-term strategic military and ideological competition with the North. There were also serial revelations that the North was actively building up armoured divisions, training saboteurs for large scale attacks behind South Korean lines at a moment's notice (these were compounded by the naked attempt to assassinate Park's successor, General Chun Doo-hwan in 1983 in Burma), the fatal aerial bombing of a Korean Air passenger jet in 1987, the attack on the South Korean frigate Cheonan in 2010, the artillery shelling of South Korea's Yeongpyeong island off the coast of the demilitarized zone at the 38th Parallel within the same year, and along with the North's recurring missile and nuclear tests, added up to an image of a fascist, militarized Pyongyang bent on armed reunification of the Korean Peninsula. This was a huge propaganda boon for Park and his successors who may have switched slogans for development under 'civilian rule' after 1988 but never wavered from entrenching authoritarian features in the South

Korean political system. The Korean version of an iron triangle between politicians, technocratic bureaucrats and soldiers was finessed under Chun Doo-hwan and subsequent presidents, including elected civilians with no significant military backgrounds. The current President Yoon Suk-yeol does not appear to possess tangible links to the aforementioned Yukbeop-dang right-wing elite of soldiers and lawyers. But his background as a career state prosecutor and pedigree of having graduated with a law degree from the nation's prestigious Seoul National University will undoubtedly make him an ardent supporter of pre-existing authoritarian institutions. This is notwithstanding his links to, and being beholden to, his predecessor, Moon Jae-in, for having promoted him to prosecutor-general (Draudt, 2022).

The military has therefore stoked considerable public ambivalence towards themselves. On the one hand, the threat from Pyongyang reifies the Park Chung-hee framework of civil–military fusion as a permanently defensive measure to defend against the standing North Korean contingency. On the other hand, the invocation of the memories of 1950–53 and the visibility of the threat from Pyongyang appear to cruelly justify, and abusively so, in the eyes of civilian public opinion the military's mandate to police against any deviation from a totalizing South Korean united front against Pyongyang (Moon, 2012, pp 27–69). The recurring tensions between 'mainlander Koreans' and the ROK military on one side against the native Koreans on strategically important Cheju Island off the southern coast have consistently stoked militant protests and armed incidents relating to the mistreatment of locals at the expense of preparing Cheju as a naval base for US and South Korean naval assets in anticipation of a looming war with either North Korea or China (Kirk, 2013). Cheju natives have chafed under the imposition of a 'Cold War society' since 1948 when mainland troops and police forcefully put down an uprising that had the appearance of defying a pro-US regime (Kirk, 2013, pp 1–32). The naval base protests that lasted from 2003 to 2016 drew anti-militarization and environmental protestors from Europe and North America to the cause of Cheju Koreans resisting the discipline of a national security logic (Moon, 2012, pp 141–74; Kirk, 2013, pp 97–126).

To date, the partisan political logic of a united national security state that tolerates no resistance against a totalizing socio-economic threat from the North has been manifested in a stunning *post facto* revelation in July 2018 by the DSC under then President Moon Jae-in's order. DSC documents showed that had his predecessor, the right-winger and daughter of Park Chung-hee, Park Geun-hye, been forced out of presidential office by candlelight holding protestors' appeals to the Constitutional Court, the military and intelligence agency would unilaterally implement martial law and deploy tanks at the culturally important Gwanghwamun park in the centre of Seoul (Kim Rahn, 2018). Even today, in the midst of Seoul's efforts to handle the COVID-19 pandemic, one of the 1970s-era protestors against Park Chung-hee at earlier

Gwanghwamun vigils recalls the ever-present threat of militarization against the civilian non-elites:

> But it is not over. The National Security Act is very much alive and well, and if we were to see the return of authorities who try to apply it to the letter, we could find ourselves once again headed to the prosecutors' offices and detention centers. I hope to see people endlessly standing before Gwanghwamun as the cold winds start to blow, posing their innocent queries to naked emperors. I can remember the wave of signs held by young students holding candles in Gwanghwamun Square. This is how South Korean democracy must be realized: by innocent minds revived across generations. (Jung, 2020)

Developmental authoritarianism persists through the mental construct of a national security state, and continues to provoke resistance to its once unassailable logic even if such resistance has yet to appear to be widespread.

Conclusion: The ROK national security state and consumerist democracy today

Failure to fully civilianize

With its origins in empire and its clever modifications during the Cold War, South Korea's security apparatus has certainly shown its facility to adapt and retrench itself with the political times. To many outsiders, the peaceful preservation of civilian rule since the mid-1990s to the ouster of Park Geun-hye through equally peaceful means in 2017 stand as sure symbols that the ROK has reached a Fukuyamian end when dealing with its political disputes. Yet to view South Korea's transition as something linear or binary in which the transformation from autocrats to democrats was a straight line, or that liberal forces can now flourish at the expense of illiberal elements, would be naïve to say the least. As the 'End of History' brought its own set of complications, many of which were inconclusive, so does South Korea's apparent 'End of Military History'. Distinct from other democracies, particularly of the Western design, a peculiarity of South Korea involves its inverse political character. The purpose of political parties and movements is not to organize and rule through grassroots glued together with an ideology *per se* but rather to be the expression and representation of the political leader itself. South Korea's 'entourage politics' feature strongmen/strongwomen at the centre, with political clusters that coalesce around them, in tandem with the personal ties that blur the professional limits of what is appropriate and what is not. This has been an enduring aspect of the country's governance dating back to Rhee Syng-man (Steinberg and Shin, 2005). The fact remains that a figure like Park Geun-hye was elected primarily because of the iconic name she carried – namely her father's – instead of her legislative achievements, is certainly a testament to the ingrained neo-Confucian Korean political culture of following a leader that mesmerizes and dominates through overwhelming promises.

Considering that the Ministry of Defence, the conduit through which civilians channel their directives to the military, has persistently filled its ranks with mostly military personnel despite the efforts to try and 'civilianize' the establishment, one could certainly imagine a situation in which *patronage* takes precedence over *procedure* in military affairs. As noted by Kuehn, since the founding of the republic in 1948 till 2007, only six of the 40 defence ministers did not come from a military background. Moreover, as of 2010, the crucial process of promoting leadership within its ranks lies exclusively within the ministry with active-duty generals and field-grade officers (Kuehn, 2016). Adding to such lingering habits in which civilians are given a minor voice when discussing military promotions, security outfits such as the DSC, Chun Doo-hwan's former and coup enabling unit, have only recently been disbanded under accusations of illegal surveillance and online operations at the behest of Park Geun-hye (KoreaTimes, 2018).

Authoritarian continuity in civilian form

Going forward, one must always be mindful of the disguised features of authoritarian continuity that hamstring any reform of civil–military relations. While not advertising themselves with military attire, the Korean Prosecution Service or KPS, with its vast powers for both investigations and indictment – at least prior to 2022 – like Park Chung-hee's formative experiences, locates its origins in colonial Japan with its own set of upgrades under each military-led administration (Arirang News, 2021). Under the auspices of the first coup, the enforcement body was given its most significant constitutional recognition, enshrined textually under Article 12 Section 3 (Korea Law Translation Center, 2018). As the sole entity capable of requesting warrants through the courts, thereby sidelining other investigative bodies and dictating its whims on police conduct, Park's regime would quickly determine that a strong prosecutorial arm would be necessary in providing legal legitimacy for their otherwise undemocratic programmes (Constitutionnet, 2018). As generals Chun and Roh had reified the 'military turned executive' tradition in addition to acclimatizing to democratic demands by putting on civilian suits, so too has the ROK's civil–military relations. While Park Chung-hee openly relied on the military and intelligence services as the backbone of his authority, Park's immediate successors would further enmesh their civilian counterparts into the authoritarian structure in order to legalize their activities across the entire spectrum of governance. The formation of the *Yukbeop-dang*, a conglomerate of key government personnel, all graduates of either the Military Academy or Seoul National University's School of Law, by itself a peculiar body of soldiers and prosecutors, would play a formidable role in guiding the country's direction well into the 1990s and up till the present (Park, 2014). Similarly, as the military turned executives of the 1960s and 1970s foresaw the merits of utilizing their Japanese and authoritarian inheritance, so too have the purely civilian executives democratically elected thereafter. The penchant for employing prosecutorial penalties under the ostensibly civilian presidents Kim Young-sam and Kim Dae-jung for either reform or political retribution, have repeatedly occurred in every transition dating back to Chun Doo-hwan's administration (Lee, 2016; YTN News, 2017; Choe, 2018). Perhaps the most potent example of just how far the KPS and its former members have come would be the election of Yoon Suk-yeol as president in 2022, a former prosecutor who investigated former president Park Geun-hye, Samsung Electronics Vice Chairman Lee Jae-yong and Hyundai Motor Group Honorary Chairman Chung Mong-koo (Kim, 2021).

It may serve this intellectual discourse then to conceive of South Korea's unique civil–military relations, with its Japanese legacies tailored for modern times, as having entrenched itself to the point of defying any conventional understanding of the term. To the Western mind at least, more influence under civilian control naturally carries with it an assumption of liberal and democratic norms taking hold within the levers of state power. Contrariwise, we suggest that traditional civil–military relations as a conceptual phrase may not suffice to capture the authoritarian mutation we see in present-day South Korea and that in place of *civil–military relations* perhaps we should consider *civil–ministry relations* in properly describing these residual legacies originating from military rule. If it was customary to envisage the battle for *civil–military relations* as the scuffle between civilian demonstrators against uniformed commanders, each vying for executive privilege, this imagery has now been supplanted in *civil–ministry relations* with that of the public and even elected representatives contending with business-suited bureaucrats. Having expanded its investigative monopoly under the Park regime, to being co-opted as equal players during the tenures of generals Chun and Roh, to now being viewed as the *go-to* political whip of convenience severely in need of being tamed, it has taken almost the entirety of President Moon's time in office to try and dilute the KPS' powers with the creation of the Corruption Investigation Office for High-ranking Officials (CIO). The latter is a separate investigative branch charged with cases deemed too politically sensitive or perhaps ripe for abuse by the KPS itself (Kyo-seok, 2021). Unsurprisingly, institutions that have long been privileged with autonomous enforcement powers are unlikely to bend their knees spontaneously to fresh civilianizing pressures, as is the case with the KPS' continual backlash against the publicly supported reforms (Jae-yeon, 2021). Whether the CIO will rein in the KPS, or should the mutual tension between these two agencies bring about an equilibrium more broadly palatable to the populace at large, remains to be seen. The assertion here is the lingering character of precisely those coercive measures, coordinated to neutralize the South Korean public's susceptibility towards left wing ideologies, surviving and even thriving, adapting themselves to the times with new hosts in civilian institutions. But perhaps the more disturbing aspect of South Korean politics lies in the ability of particular individuals to use or abuse their station, military or civilian, to simply transcend organizational limits. Initially centralized under Syngman Rhee, the ROK polity became fully militarized under the auspices of Park, Chun and Roh. With its mixture of presidential and parliamentary features, the South Korean Constitution can be claimed as the edifice that preserves authoritarian exploitation and its likely continuation. There are strong grounds for pessimism since every president from Kim Dae-jung onwards has either started too late into their term to enact democratic reform or has run into political gridlock (Kim, 2017). In this regard, South Korea ought not to be treated as a black and white contrast to the civil–military relations culture of the North or even of much of Southeast Asia. More importantly, South Korea's case reflects crucial characteristics of the hybridized Asian civil–military relations model that resonates across all the chapters of this book.

References

Adesnik, David A. and Kim, S. (2013) 'South Korea: the Puzzle of two transitions', in K. Stoner and M. McFaul (eds) *Transitions to Democracy: A Comparative Perspective*, Baltimore: The Johns Hopkins University Press, pp 266–90.

Ahmad, Z.H. (1985) 'Configurative and comparative aspects of military–civilian relations', in Z.H. Ahmad and H. Crouch (eds) *Military–Civilian Relations in South-East Asia*, Kuala Lumpur: Oxford University Press, pp 3–10.

Ahn, B-M. (2003) *Elites and Political Power in South Korea*, Cheltenham: Edward Elgar.

Akita, G. and Palmer, B. (2015) *The Japanese Colonial Legacy in Korea, 1910–1945: A New Perspective*, Portland: MerwinAsia distributed by University of Hawaii Press.

Anon. (2016) *Democracy in South Korea* [online], Available from: http://archive.much.go.kr/search.do [Accessed 17 January 2022].

Arirang News (2021) *Fighting Corruption in the Public Service* [Online] Available from: www.arirang.com/Tv2/TVCommon_NoStaff_Archive.asp?Prog_Code=TVCR0802&MENU_CODE=102346&view_seq=41516 [Accessed 18 January 2022].

Baik Bong. (1973) *Kim Il Sung – Biography (II): From Building Democratic Korea to Chullima Flight*, Beirut: Dar Al-Talia.

Beal, T. (2005) *North Korea: The Struggle Against American Power*, London: Pluto Press.

Bose, S. (2011) *His Majesty's Opponent: Subhas Chandra Bose and India's Struggle against Empire*, Cambridge: The Belknap Press of Harvard University Press.

Breen, M. (2010) 'General Chun Doo-hwan took power in a coup', *The Korea Times* 23 May, Available from: www.koreatimes.co.kr/www/news/nation/2016/11/117_66347.html [Accessed 23 December 2021].

Chae, O-B. (2013) 'Japanese colonial structure in Korea in comparative perspective', in G. Steinmetz (ed) *Sociology and Empire: The Imperial Entanglements of a Discipline*, Durham: Duke University Press, pp 396–414.

Cheah, B.K. (1983) *Red Star Over Malaya: Resistance and Social Conflict During and After the Japanese Occupation of Malaya, 1941–1946*, Singapore: Singapore University Press.

Choe, D-H. (2018) 'Prosecutors' role and their relationship with the police in South Korea: in a comparative perspective', *International Journal of Law, Crime and Justice*, 55: 88–96.

Choe, S-H. (2021a) 'Unsnarling land rights in South Korea', *New York Times International Edition*, 14 January, p 3.

Choe, S-H. (2021b) '"He kept begging for life"', *New York Times International Edition*, 23 August, p 3.

Choi, S. (2015) *Re-imagining North Korea in International Politics: Problems and Alternatives*, Abingdon: Routledge.

Choue, C-W. (1985) *The Integration of Korea: Theory and Research*, Seoul: Koreaone Press.

Clifford, M.L. (1998) *Troubled Tiger: Businessmen, Bureaucrats, and Generals in South Korea*, Armonk: M.E. Sharpe – an East Gate Book.

Constitutionnet (2018) *Republic of Korea (Recent Constitution Reform Efforts)*. [Online] Available at: https://constitutionnet.org/country/republic-korea [Accessed 12 February 2022].

Cotton, J. (1991) 'The military factor in South Korean politics', in R.J. May and V. Selochan (eds) *The Military, the State, and Development in Asia and the Pacific*, Boulder: Westview Press, pp 203–20.

Croissant, A., Kuehn, D. and Lorenz, P. (2012) *Breaking with the Past? Civil–Military Relations in the Emerging Democracies of East Asia. Policy Studies No 63*, Honolulu: East-West Center.

Cumings, B. (2005) *Korea's Place in the Sun: A Modern History*, 2nd edn, New York: W.W. Norton.

Draudt, D. (2022) 'What President Yoon Suk-yeol's election means for South Korean Democracy', *The Diplomat*, [online] 23 March, Available from: https://thediplomat.com/2022/03/what-president-yoon-suk-yeols-election-means-for-south-korean-democracy/ [Accessed 15 July 2022].

Eckert, C. (2016) *Park Chung Hee and Modern Korea: The Roots of Militarism (1866–1945)*, Cambridge: The Belknap Press of Harvard University Press.

Ha, Y.C. (2013) 'Colonial rule and social change in Korea: the paradox of colonial control', in H.Y. Lee, Y.C. Ha and C.W. Sorensen (eds) *Colonial Rule and Social Change in Korea, 1910–1945*, Seattle: Centre for Korea Studies UW and University of Washington Press, pp 39–75.

Jae-yeon, W. (2021) 'CIO's authority over indictments faces backlash from prosecutors', *Yonhap News Agency*, [online] 4 May, Available from: https://en.yna.co.kr/view/AEN20210504003100315 [Accessed 7 May 2021].

Jeong, M. and Shin, Y. (2018) 'Post-war Korean conservatism, Japanese statism, and the legacy of President Park Chung-hee in South Korea', *The Korean Journal of International Studies*, 16(1): 57–76.

Jung, B-H (2020) 'Tanks and BTS fans in front of Gwanghwamun', *Hankyoreh*, 12 November [column], Available from: www.hani.co.kr/arti/PRINT/969713.html [Accessed 28 August 2021].

Kim Rahn (2018) '"Tanks planned in Gwanghwamun under martial law"', *The Korea Times*, [online] 20 July, Available from: www.koreatimes.co.kr/www/nation/2019/11/113_252582.html [Accessed 28 August 2021].

Kim, J. (2021) 'Yoon Seok-youl wins South Korea opposition's presidential primary', *Nikkei Asia*, [online] 5 November, Available from: https://asia.nikkei.com/Politics/Yoon-Seok-youl-wins-South-Korea-opposition-s-presidential-primary [Accessed 10 March 2022].

Kim, S. (2017) 'Reforming South Korea's "Imperial presidency"', *Institute for Security and Development Studies*, Issue and Policy Briefs – October 2017, No 205, Available from: https://isdp.eu/publication/reforming-south-koreas-imperial-presidency/ [Accessed 16 April 2022].

Kim, Y.M. (1998) 'Patterns of military rule and prospects for democracy in South Korea', in R.J. May and V. Selochan (eds) *The Military and Democracy in Asia and the Pacific*, London: C. Hurst and Company Publishers, pp 119–31.

Kirk, D. (2013) *Okinawa and Jeju: Bases of Discontent*, New York: Palgrave Macmillan.

Korea Law Translation Center (2018) *Constitution of the Republic of Korea*. [Online] Available from: https://elaw.klri.re.kr/eng_service/lawView.do?hseq=1&lang=ENG [Accessed 9 January 2022].

KoreaTimes (2018) 'South Korea's military launches new security command', *The Korea Times*, [online] 1 September, Available from: www.koreatimes.co.kr/www/nation/2018/09/205_254865.html [Accessed 9 March 2021].

Kuehn, D. (2016) 'Institutionalising civilian control of the military in new democracies: theory and evidence from South Korea', *GIGA Working Paper* [Working Paper] Available from: www.giga-hamburg.de/en/publications/11572254-institutionalising-civilian-control-military-democracies-theory-evidence-from-south-korea/ [Accessed 10 February 2022].

Kwak, Y-S. (2022) 'Why are Koreans obsessed with "elevating national prestige"?', *The Korea Times*, [online] 21 April, Available from: www.koreatimes.co.kr/www/art/2022/04/398_327740.html [Accessed 14 July 2022].

Kyo-seok, S. (2021) 'Corruption-slaying CIO officially starts up', *Korea Joong Ang Daily*, [online] 21 January, Available at: https://koreajoongangdaily.joins.com/2021/01/21/national/politics/CIO-anticorruption-Kim-Jinwook/20210121180600598.html [Accessed 10 January 2022].

Lee, C-S. (2012) *Park Chung-Hee: From Poverty to Power*, Palos Verdes: Kyung Hee University Press.

Lee, H.Y. (2013) 'Introduction: A critique of "colonial modernity"', in H.Y. Lee, Y.C. Ha and C.W. Sorensen (eds) *Colonial Rule and Social Change in Korea, 1910–1945*, Seattle: Centre for Korea Studies, UW and University of Washington Press, pp 3–39.

Lee, J-K. (2010) *Service Economies: Militarism, Sex Work, and Migrant Labor in South Korea*, Minneapolis: University of Minnesota Press.

Lee, K.Y. (2000) *From Third World to First. The Singapore Story: 1965–2000*, Singapore: Times Editions.

Lee, S-W. (2016) 'The politics of prosecution service reform in new presidential democracies: the South Korea and Russia cases in comparative perspective', *Journal of Eurasian Studies*, 7(2): 141–50.

Luckham, R. (1991) 'Introduction: the military, the developmental state and social forces in Asia and the Pacific – issues for comparative analysis', in V. Selochan (ed) *The Military, the State, and Development in Asia and the Pacific*, Boulder: Westview Press, pp 1–50.

Moon, K.H. (2012) *Protesting America: Democracy and the US–Korea Alliance*, Berkeley: University of California Press.

Palmer, B. (2013) *Fighting for the Enemy: Koreans in Japan's War, 1937–1945*, Seattle: University of Washington Press.

Park, S.W. (2014) 'The President and the Yukbeop-dang', *Dong-A IlBo*, 8 May.

Pirie, I. (2008) *The Korean Developmental State: From Dirigisme to Neo-liberalism*, Abingdon: Routledge.

Pollack, A. (1997) 'New Korean leader agrees to pardon of 2 ex-dictators', *The New York Times*, 21 December.

Rowl, E. and Novak, R. (1987) 'South Korea's turn to democracy', *The Washington Post*, [online] 9 November, Available from: www.washingtonpost.com/archive/opinions/1987/11/09/south-koreas-turn-to-democracy/0bee41bb-7d27-4bc4-9e5c-30e5a23a5255/?noredirect=on&utm_term=.61bad951b0db [Accessed 12 January 2022].

Saxer, C.J. (2004) 'Generals and presidents: establishing civilian and democratic control in South Korea', *Armed Forces and Society,* 30(3): 383–408.

Sengupta, N. (2011) 'Introduction. A city and a soldier: Netaji in Singapore', in N. Sengupta (ed) *Netaji Subhas Chandra Bose: The Singapore Saga. Selected Writings, Rare Photographs, Oral History and Archival Documents on Subhas Chandra Bose and Singapore's Role in the Struggle for India's Freedom*, Singapore: The Nalanda-Sriwijaya Centre, pp 7–9.

Seok-man, Y. (2011) 'POSCO: building an institution', in H. Kim and C.W. Sorensen (eds) *Reassessing the Park Chung Hee Era, 1961–1979*, Seattle: Center for Korea Studies and University of Washington Press, pp 43–65.

Steinberg, D.I. and Shin, M. (2005) 'From entourage to ideology? Tensions in South Korean parties in transition', *East-West Center Working Papers: Politics, Governance and Security Series No 9,* Available from: www.eastwestcenter.org/system/tdf/private/PSwp009.pdf?file=1&type=node&id=32081 [Accessed 15 May 2022].

The Institute for East Asian Studies (1975) *Foreign Policy for Peace and Unification*, Seoul: The Institute for East Asian Studies.

Uchida, J. (2011) *Brokers of Empire: Japanese Settler Colonialism in Korea, 1876–1945*, Cambridge: Harvard University Press Asia Center.

YTN News (2017) *Former Presidents who have been through prosecution. From witness to confinement,* Available from: www.ytn.co.kr/_ln/0103_201703122120315830 [Accessed 9 March 2021].

13

Image Makeover: The Military Evolution of Japan's Self-Defense Forces

Yee-Kuang Heng

Debates on 'Japan's pivot in Asia' have highlighted how 'the Japanese government has been generating and deploying a fuller spectrum of strategic tools to position it to achieve its longer-term foreign policy objectives' (Samuels and Wallace, 2018, p 710). Many of these initiatives have involved the JSDF. While scholarly debate has questioned just how radical or transformative Japan's defence policy has been (Hughes, 2017), security practices have been more 'evolutionary' than revolutionary (Oros, 2008), even under a supposedly transformative leader like former Prime Minister Abe Shinzo (Liff, 2015). Military evolutions in Japan can be seen as an adaptive process whereby civil–military relations change and evolve slowly according to particular local concerns, interests, and tastes. The mechanisms can work in several ways over time incrementally. They can be developmentally driven, with initiatives launched by municipal authorities and/or private industry that relate to JSDF activities or bases. They can also be communication-driven, with initiatives coming from the JSDF to better explain and engage with the public.

This chapter investigates several key questions that underpin this volume as a whole. In stark contrast to other regional countries which suffered colonization, the JSDF has to deal with a colonial legacy whereby Japan was an imperial colonizer in Southeast Asia. Wartime history and past militarism have also doubtlessly shaped civil–military relations in Japan. As Japanese governments have worked to gain legitimacy and public acceptance for the JSDF both domestically and internationally, the effectiveness of civil–military relations here may be further viewed in terms of domestic/

regional acceptance of JSDF existence and roles, on top of the conventional emphasis in the civil–military relations literature on achieving developmental and modernization goals. A key evolutionary process for the JSDF has been to reach out to the civilian population through demonstrating its role in humanitarian and disaster relief missions (HADR) as well as cultivating an approachable image through the use of popular culture including *anime* or public events linked to military cuisine such as "kaigun kare" (navy curry). Adapting to local municipal concerns and interests, these have even brought some developmental benefits to large naval base communities such as Sasebo in the form of tourist attractions that are either anime-themed or military-related. Similar mechanisms are evident in how the JSDF explains its regional missions to its domestic audiences in Japan. Indeed, JSDF naval vessels cruising regional waters have even become somewhat routine and part of the new normal of Japan's regional defence diplomacy. Given this ramped up regional military profile, how does the JSDF present itself to regional audiences and its domestic public constituents, while communicating its mission of defending Japan, which potentially includes using lethal military force and taking/losing lives in the process?

Civil–military relations in Japan

This section situates civil–military relations in Japan within the existing academic literature as well as Japan's historical and constitutional context. In *The Soldier and the State*, Huntington (1957, p 2) argued that 'the military institutions of any society are shaped by two forces: a functional imperative stemming from the threats to the society's security and a societal imperative arising from the social forces, ideologies, and institutions dominant within that society'. For Huntington, the constitutional structure and ideology of a state are crucial: the United States' ideology of antimilitary liberalism was seen as a threat to military security. Huntington warned that the 'transmutation' of the military according to liberal values would diminish 'peculiarly military characteristics' (Owens, 2017). Huntington (1957, pp 14–15) also argued that the officer corps are entrusted with evaluating the security of the state and providing expert advice to its leaders, and society in turn must afford a measure of deference to their professional expertise and institutions. Referring to Japan, 'Japanese civil–military relations remained in a single relatively stable pattern from 1868 to 1945', and the 'military played a persistently active role in the politics of their country' (Huntington, 1957, p 98). Given its dark 20th-century history of militarism where its armed forces conducted assassinations, coup attempts and deposed civilian leaders, discussions of civil–military relations in post-war Japan have unsurprisingly centred on the issue of civilian control as well as the evolving power balances in policy, parliamentary and bureaucratic structures between civilian bureaucrats, the executive, legislatures and military officers (Koide, 2008; Hikotani, 2009; Hikotani, 2018). The principal focus of civil–military relations has for the most part been the relation of the officer corps to the state (Huntington, 1957). In Japan, the focus has also included rehabilitating the post-war image of the military in the eyes of the civilian population. Demonstrating that the JSDF serves a greater public good, such as disaster relief and humanitarian assistance and even defending the nation's territory, is a crucial element of the message to overcome wartime memories of militarists sacrificing civilians and the general population.

How far should a professional all-volunteer force reflect the society it protects and on whose behalf it stands ready to administer violence? Former US Defence Secretary Jim Mattis and Kori Schake (2016, p 3) warned of a military force that considers itself as 'a society apart, different from, and more virtuous than, the people they commit themselves to protecting, like praetorian guards at the bacchanalia, as one soldier described it'. On the other hand, another worry is that 'with little experience of warfare in the general population the public may have scant appreciation for what is needed to win our wars or become contemptuous of the military virtues necessary for winning on the battlefield when those virtues are out of sync with the values of our civil society' (Mattis and Schake, 2016, p 3). For Huntington (1957, p 2), a military that purely reflects only societal values may not perform its military functions effectively on the battlefield. However, at the same time, it may be impossible to recruit, train, and equip a military that solely fulfils its functional battlefield imperative, without reflecting some values of the society it protects: 'The interaction between these two forces is the nub of the problem of civil–military relations'(Huntington 1957, p2). Others such as Hikotani (2016, p 8) point out that in the case of Japan, the 'SDF is not necessarily meant to be reflective of society': a majority of public respondents reported having few friends in the Self-Defense Forces (SDF).

In his speech to the first graduating batch of cadets from the National Defence Academy in 1957, former Prime Minister Yoshida Shigeru referred in a rather stark and matter-of-fact manner to how

> it is possible that many of you might finish your career in the Self-Defense Forces without ever being thanked or welcomed by the people … because it is only when our country is facing crisis and confusion, when we are attacked by foreign forces or when necessity arises for you to embark on disaster relief missions that the people will praise and appreciate the Self-Defense Forces. I want you all to bear with the *life in the shadows*. (Yoshida Shigeru Memorial Foundation, 1991, p 458, emphasis added)

Under the second Abe Shinzo administration (2013–20), amending the constitution to make explicit reference to the actual existence of the JSDF was a key point of contention. A January 2018 poll by the Mainichi Shimbun newspaper found that 43 per cent of respondents were in favour of making such a change. Another poll by Kyodo News Agency in 2019 found similar results (The Japan Times, 2019). These results imply that even though few civilians may actually personally know a JSDF member, a reasonable wellspring of public understanding for JSDF does exist.

The challenges connecting the JSDF to the wider society are not unique, despite the peculiar constitutional and cultural context of Japan. Professional all-volunteer forces such as the US military too have confronted issues such as how to relate better to specific age groups who possess a 'knowledge deficit' when it comes to understanding basic principles and organization of the military. In a survey conducted by Stanford University, only 15 per cent of millennials claimed to be 'very familiar' with the military. Millennials also often responded with 'not sure' to factual questions about the military (Colford and Sugarman, 2016). Paradoxically, the United States had experienced its longest continued period of war in its history since 9/11. In Britain, the military has long struggled to recruit ethnic minorities who are under-represented as a proportion of the general population. The British Army's 2020 recruitment drive, in partnership with the contractor Capita, created captions such as 'social media addicts', 'gym junkies' and 'binge drinkers' on its campaign posters, while the 2019 campaign targeted 'snowflakes' and 'selfie addicts' (BBC, 2020).

Life in the shadows no more?

For a military force whose constitutional status remains subject to intense political debate and was once told to bear with living 'in the shadows' by former Prime Minister Yoshida, the JSDF has not been shying away from engaging with both its domestic constituents and foreign audiences. An official JSDF magazine called *MAMOR* (short for 'Mamoru' or 'to protect' in Japanese) caused a stir by featuring female 'idols' dressed in military uniform on its cover. Domestically, the JSDF has held frequent public open days at its bases to facilitate public interaction with its personnel and equipment. The Iruma Air Show is held every November in Saitama prefecture. The annual Higashi Fuji firepower demonstrations in summer attract massive crowds. The Blue Impulse aerobatics team performs across the country and tickets are highly sought after. There are also an array of private specialized military magazines such as *Panzer*, which is focused on tanks and armoured vehicles and has been published since 1975. Casual visitors to bookstores in Japan will also encounter magazines displayed prominently on shelves such as *J-Wings*, and *Koku Fan* (Aviation Fan) since 1952, which focuses on military aviation. The monthly *Arms Magazine* invariably features female models on its cover dressed in camouflage fatigues wielding an assortment of assault rifles and handguns. According to publisher Hobby Japan (nd), *Arms Magazine* 'aims to convey the charm of guns as an entertainment'. These magazines cater to a category of the public known as *gunji otaku* (military enthusiasts or, less politely, military-obsessed geeks). Even former defence minister and senior Liberal Democratic Party politician Ishiba Shigeru has been described in such terms.

The Japanese public is well-accustomed to seeing JSDF personnel on domestic HADR missions after natural calamities that often afflict the country. For instance, the JSDF were extensively deployed for the 2011 earthquake and the 2018 severe rains in the Western part of Japan. In 2018, major naval vessels including the large flat-top helicopter carrier *Kaga* were deployed to provide supplies and crucial public bathing facilities to the public near Kure city. The *Diamond Princess* cruise ship berthed off Yokohama in 2020 due to the coronavirus outbreak also saw JSDF personnel providing quarantine support and disinfection. JSDF personnel were furthermore sent to Narita and Haneda airports to support processing of passengers returning from virus-hit countries. The Tokyo Metropolitan Government and Hokkaido Prefecture have requested JSDF medical teams to help support infected persons. The JSDF also operated large-scale vaccination sites in Tokyo and Osaka.

The prominent role of the JSDF in domestic HADR operations explains why disaster relief topped the list of reasons why the public thought the JSDF should exist, in a public opinion poll conducted by the Ministry of Defense in 2012 (Public Relations Office, 2012). Of all respondents, 97 per cent appreciated positively the JSDF's roles in HADR after the 2011 Great East Japan Earthquake. The same poll also suggested that maintaining national security and preventing foreign invasion came in a close second. More recent poll data compiled by Hikotani (2018) from 2014 suggests that this positive view has been continuing, even in spite of public unease over a new security legislation under the Abe administration. Polling data from 2015 from the Cabinet Office revealed that a record high 30 per cent of respondents favoured strengthening the JSDF's capabilities (The Japan Times, 2015). Continuing this upward positive trend, data from Cabinet Office polling in 2018 found that 89.8 per cent of respondents had a 'good impression' of the JSDF (Yahoo News Japan, 2018).

While public opinion appears to be understanding of the JSDF role in defending against invasion and domestic HADR operations, public support is less clear when the JSDF is deployed overseas. NHK polling data in 2015 demonstrated an almost equal split in public opinion on whether the JSDF should be sent overseas or not (Tatsumi, 2015). Since the first 1992 peacekeeping deployment to Cambodia, there is precedent for JSDF personnel operating overseas, especially on regional HADR missions. The largest ever contingent of JSDF personnel deployed after World War Two headed to the Philippines after Typhoon Haiyan wreaked havoc in 2013. This included the flat-deck helicopter carrier *Ise*. However, as for Abe's pet project of constitutional amendment to Article 9, 2017 data from state broadcaster NHK suggested that 57 per cent of respondents still thought it was 'unnecessary'. NHK (2017) suggests that this caution arose from the Abe cabinet's move to exercise Japan's right to collective self-defence through a Cabinet decision and subsequent security legislation passed through the Diet.

JSDF and defence diplomacy

Increasingly frequent overseas deployments of the JSDF, especially in Asia, can be understood through the framework of defence diplomacy. The UK 1998 Strategic Defence Review highlighted the importance of defence diplomacy as one of the key tasks 'to dispel hostility, build and maintain trust and assist in the development of democratically accountable armed forces, thereby making a significant contribution to conflict prevention and resolution' (UK Ministry of Defence, 1998, p 6). The Strategic Defence Review points out how ship visits, exchanges with other countries' military forces and the training of foreign personnel are a long-established part of daily military business. The expansion of tasks associated with defence diplomacy has grown to include disaster relief as well as 'soft' power missions such as aerobatic performances. 'Defence engagement' is more recently the preferred term describing 'the non-combat use of military power' (UK MOD and Foreign and Commonwealth Office, 2017, p 6).

In terms of Japan's own defence engagement with Asia during the second Abe administration, Tokyo launched the Japan–ASEAN Ship Rider Cooperation programme in 2017 as part of the Vientiane Vision unveiled in 2016, which sets out for the first time guiding principles for Japan's defence cooperation with ASEAN. Press releases from the Ministry of Defense explained this Ship Rider initiative as part of an annual programme to build shared understandings of international law and maritime security with a representative from each ASEAN member state. The contents included seminars on HADR, international maritime and aviation law as well as opportunities to observe helicopter and communications operations (Japan Ministry of Defense, 2017). The first iteration of this programme was held on the JS *Izumo* for around a week in waters off Singapore.

A flotilla of Japanese naval vessels including destroyers and its largest helicopter carriers – JS *Izumo* and JS *Kaga* – has also deployed for extended periods of close to three months annually since the Indo-Southeast Asia Deployment 2018 (ISEAD18) and the Indo-Pacific Deployment 2019 (IPD19). These voyages have comprised port calls and exercises with

ASEAN countries and even further afield such as Sri Lanka and India. Multilateral exercises with navies of the US, UK, Australia and France have also been conducted as part of the deployments. As the Abe administration promoted its Free and Open Indo-Pacific vision, these naval deployments have been presented as concrete efforts demonstrating Japan's desire and commitment to support the rules-based maritime order. They are crucially designed to demonstrate Japan's 'presence' in the region (Interview, 2020). A Professional Airmanship Programme was launched in 2019 by Japan, to build understanding of international aviation law with ASEAN partners. This can again be read in terms of Tokyo's constant focus on supporting access not just to the maritime commons but also freedom of civil navigation. During former Philippine President Duterte's visit to JS *Izumo* in 2017 when it docked in Subic Bay, he highly commended the HADR capabilities of the state-of-the art Izumo: 'It's impressive and it's used for humanitarian and war reasons' (Mangosing, 2017). Duterte was accorded the honour of being the first head of state to visit *Izumo* as well as sister ship *Kaga* when the latter visited Subic in 2018. Likewise, during *Izumo*'s port visit to Sri Lanka, State Minister of Defence Wijayawardene praised the advanced HADR capabilities and stated his hope for the further enhancement of defence cooperation with Japan. At its launch, *Izumo* was explained as 'an escort vessel capable of serving international peace cooperation and disaster relief activities' (Japan MOD, 2013).

The HADR narrative has been quite prominent in how Japan Maritime Self-Defense Force (JMSDF) 'presence' overseas is being communicated both to overseas publics as well as domestic audience. Stressing the cooperative nature of such missions can make deployments more acceptable to overseas and domestic audiences. Speeches about HADR and upholding FOIP and rule of law are carefully drafted in advance for ship captains to deliver during media tours of the ships during port visits. These speeches are also sent to the National Security Secretariat for feedback, suggesting a coordinated approach (Interview, 2020). The reactions of overseas media to such visits are collected by Japanese Defence Attaches posted abroad. Japanese media such as the Asashi Shimbun that have correspondents posted in Singapore for instance have been briefed by the Japanese embassy in Singapore during JMSDF visits.

Naval deployments to the Indo-Pacific have been labelled in Japanese by the JMSDF (nd) as 訓練部隊 ('training units' or 'training task force'). In the naval port of Kure, there is a store that specializes in making and selling goods related to the JMSDF. There are even commemorative T-shirts and memorabilia on sale to mark for instance major deployments such as the Indo Pacific Deployment 2022 as well as mugs and towels of major surface vessels such as Izumo (Seifukunofuji 2022). (The same shop also offers keychains and handkerchief of the war-time Zero fighter.) Military magazine *Panzer* has featured articles and photos of the Professional Airmanship Programme while journalists from military magazines have been invited onto *Izumo* for parts of its deployments around Southeast Asia. The first Ship Rider Cooperation programme was reported during the valuable 'golden hour' of evening TV in Japan. The Ministry of Defense's Public Affairs Unit observes public social media responses to the JMSDF deployments on its SNS official page, and the response appears to be largely positive. However, there is no specially tailored official public opinion poll that currently exists to gauge how the Japanese public perceives such missions. One important reason is that such missions appear mainly targeted at the overseas audience, not domestic Japanese public opinion (Interview, 2020). Quite strikingly, these missions have attracted relatively little negative media reporting in a region once brutally occupied by Imperial Japan. Indeed, while official and media response has been more cautious in China and South Korea, Japan's growing presence in Southeast Asia is becoming part of the 'new normal'. In a 2020 opinion poll conducted by the Singapore-based Institute of South East Asian Studies for its 'The State of South East Asia: 2020 Survey Report', Japan emerged as the 'most trusted power among Southeast Asians', with 61.2 per cent of respondents expressing confidence in Japan to 'do the right thing' to contribute to global peace, security, prosperity and governance (Tang et al, 2020, p 4).

Despite the government's public emphasis on HADR exercises and maritime law, domestic newspapers like the Asahi Shimbun (2018) and online news portals such as Livedoor (2019) have pointed out that such deployments are meant to check Chinese power. The Mainichi reports that the *Izumo* deployment is an example of China and Japan sizing up each other's influence in the South China Sea (Mainichi Shimbun, 2019). The conservative-leaning evening daily Yukan Fuji (2018), in a report on the Ship Rider Cooperation Programme, praised the initiative and others as an example of Prime Minister Abe's leadership in regional peace. News magazine *Gendai Business* published by Kodansha, adopted a more cautious tone arguing that the JMSDF deployments and exercises in the South China Sea may exceed Japan's exclusively defence-oriented policies and heighten tensions, thus harming Japan's national security. It called for greater openness from the Abe administration on explaining the true purpose of these exercises for citizens to evaluate (Handa, 2018). Domestically, there have also been concerns about over-stretching the JMSDF. Retired Admiral Koda Yoji pointedly said: 'I am strongly against it (deploying JSDF on port visits and capacity-building throughout the region). Our navy was tasked to kill submarines in the Western Pacific and guarantee the safety of U.S. naval forces. That is enough, we can't do any more things' (Today, 2018). Other domestic critical voices such as the anti-war NGO Peace Forum warned of the Abe administration incrementally developing its 'gunboat diplomacy in peacetime' violating the past exclusively defence-oriented policies and pacifist constitution of Japan (Yuasa, 2020).

The Abe administration's 2019 order for a JMSDF destroyer to be deployed to the Gulf of Oman, without Diet parliamentary debate and approval, for 'research and study' purposes under Article 4 of the law establishing the Ministry of Defense, also generated unease in left-leaning *Asahi Shimbun* (2019). Smaller regional newspapers such as *Kochi Shimbun* expressed concern that such deployments that might involve using force could be incrementally expanded (2019). However, opinion polls by the *Yomiuri Shimbun* in January 2020 suggested that 50 per cent of respondents positively evaluated the dispatch. This deployment has been labelled differently in Japanese domestic media, as 'Despatch to the Middle East', rather than 'training exercises' in the case of the Indo-Pacific Deployment. The level of risk is certainly higher with tensions in the Gulf. This Middle East mission has drawn far more media and public attention than 'training exercises' in the Indo-Pacific deployment or the Ship Rider programme.

Reflecting the societal imperative through 'cuteness'?

Bearing harsh lessons of the militaristic past in mind, post-war Prime Minister Yoshida Shigeru (1948–54) strongly advocated that 'the people' should be the guiding tenet for the syllabus of the new National Defence Academy. Military personnel were reminded that they 'themselves were part of the Japanese people and remain in close touch with the people's needs' (Sasaki, 2015, p 56). Stones were once thrown by the public at JSDF personnel wearing uniform in city streets. 'Zeikin dorobo' (tax thieves) was another unwelcome label for the JSDF draining the coffers of Japan's economy (Bosack, 2019). Such sentiments have since softened as part of a military evolution. In the major naval base town of Sasebo that this author visited, movie discount tickets are now offered to JMSDF personnel. A top Sasebo tourist attraction is the JMSDF Naval Historical Museum 'Sail Tower'. Exhibiting the past and present of Japan's naval forces, the second floor focuses on JMSDF contributions to the civilian population and rapport with the local community. JMSDF Sasebo District pamphlets explain not only Japan's need to secure sea lines of communication for energy and food supplies, they also highlight 'Sasebo JSDF Gourmet' as a key public relations activity where the JMSDF has provided its famous curry recipes to restaurants in Sasebo. Military-themed gourmet such as 'military shokudo' (literally: military canteen) are hawked conspicuously to visitors at the tourist attraction 'Road Side Station Sasebox 99', serving '*kaigun kare*' (navy curry). An assortment of unique recipes of curry served on individual destroyers is also sold in souvenir packs. One can compare JS *Kongo*'s original beef curry with JS *Sawagiri*'s squid ink and beef tendon curry. JMSDF personnel even participate in local curry competitions such as Sasebo Goeikan (Escort Ship) Curry Grand Prix (GC1), which is a collaboration between the

JMSDF Sasebo District Headquarters and the Sasebo Yonka-cho Shopping Arcade. JSDF-themed cakes and sweets such as langues de chats are on sale as souvenirs in Sasebo's tourist spots, including boxes emblazoned with pictures of the Amphibious Rapid Deployment Brigade based nearby or cute keychains of the popular 'Kewpie' mayonnaise character dressed in military fatigues. The US military presence gave rise to another local speciality, Sasebo Burger, which is ubiquitously promoted to tourists. To protect the brand name, the local Sasebo Burger Association was launched to provide guides to the best certified burger joints and burger-themed merchandise like T-shirts and stickers. The four naval ports (Kure, Yokosuka, Sasebo and Maizuru) are collectively promoted to Japanese and overseas tourists as historical sites of Japan's modernization by the 'Former Naval Base City Development Council' (旧軍港市振興協議会), a joint initiative by the four city administrations. The goal is to promote tourism and revitalize local communities (Fujitsu Network Solutions, 2016). Driven by municipalities hosting bases, a military evolution in civil–military relations is reflected in this developmental-oriented approach.

The JSDF has made attempts through private television channels to connect with the people it serves. In February 2020, private television network TBS screened a special feature on the JSDF. A female announcer was taken aboard an F-15DJ Eagle interceptor, experiencing tight rolls and air-to-air refuelling. The programme (which is of the entertainment variety genre) also followed JMSDF units on anti-piracy missions in the Gulf of Aden, the first time television crews were granted access. A panel of serving officers from all branches of the JSDF appeared on the programme to answer questions. Another private TV station, Nippon Television, was allowed to join JSDF units preparing for the Fuji Firepower Demonstration in 2019. According to the station, the tickets for public attendance at this JSDF event were 27 times over-subscribed. TV personality Kazu Laser, a self-confessed '*gunji otaku*' was one of the guests on the show demonstrating his knowledge of howitzers and the Type 10 Main Battle Tank. This trend of entertainment variety programmes can be read as an attempt to broaden outreach to the public and enable better understanding of JSDF missions. This light-hearted format of typical Japanese TV 'variety' programmes featuring TV personalities and comedians trying out JSDF equipment, contained little serious discussion of the security and defence policy dimensions.

Pacifism is generally seen to shape public perceptions of the JSDF. However, as Midford (2011) has shown, pacifism may be over-stated and in fact, Japanese public sentiment may be more accurately described as "defensive Realism" with a belief in the necessity of defensive military capabilities to protect Japan's security. If this is the case, the JSDF should have no problems communicating its purpose to the public. Indeed, the Ground Self-Defense Force has focused on building domestic legitimacy and public acceptance. For instance, disaster relief operations have certainly helped in that regard (Eldridge & Milford 2017). A 2019 poll by the Jiji Press-affiliated Central Research Services Incorporated revealed that the JSDF was the most trusted institution by the public, followed by medical institutions (Japan Times 2019b).

While the JSDF is enjoying growing public trust as part of a military evolution, several challenges loom in its relationship with the public. Japan's population decline is reducing its pool of recruits, while JSDF leadership of the new generation have no recollection of the testy relations with the public in the early post-war years (Bosack, 2019). Risa Brooks (2016) argued that a paradox existed for civil–military relations in the United States whereby the public supports the military more than ever but knows less about it than ever. In Japan, the JSDF is dedicating more effort to communicate with a public that increasingly supports the JSDF, but the image communicated through 'cute' and fantasy cartoon characters in public recruitment campaigns may be further and further away from the reality of military life.

While the US military collaborates with Hollywood to showcase their latest hardware and cultivate a martial image, the JSDF utilizes popular fantasy games or anime-style characters in a society that is already over-saturated through anime and cartoon characters. Anime and manga hit *Girls und Panzer* for example takes a light-hearted tone, with high school girls competing in tank manoeuvres as a school sport. Staff from Bandai Visual, an animation unit of computer game maker Namco Bandai, were allowed to enter the Ground Self-Defense Force's tank school in an attempt to draw details of tanks accurately (Kelly and Kubo, 2014). In 2013, a Type 74 main battle tank was even exhibited at an event in the town Ōarai-machi, the fictional setting of the manga. However, Bandai is quite clear that their purpose was profit-driven, not to promote the JSDF. Die-hard manga and anime fans greatly value intricate details and accuracy of vehicles and equipment. Interestingly and perhaps bizarrely, one concern might be that the narrative presented to the public, at least through these anime cartoons, is that military equipment and the military vocation is not something dangerous, noble or threatening but rather cute and even 'fantastically' fun. For Huntington, the task and ethos of military officers was to 'manage violence' in a prudent and realistic way that was wary of going to war recklessly. However, in *Girls und Panzer*, nobody ever gets hurt in tank battles. 'We have presented it like a sports tournament. A real battle would mean people dying,' said producer Kiyoshi Sugiyama (Kelly and Kubo, 2014).

The Ministry of Defense website features a segment called 'Manga-Style Defense of Japan', which is a casual manga comic book introducing the defence policy of Japan to deepen people's understanding especially among the younger generation. For instance, the Defence White Paper 2017 is explained through this comic book pamphlet (Japan MOD, nd). In 2015, the MOD released a YouTube video of a cartoon talking bird called Bo-emon to introduce what it called the 'ABC of Self Defence Forces'. Bo-emon is a twist on the Japanese words (bo-ei) which means defence, while 'mon' refers to 'monster' in a cute sense like the well-known Pokemon. The Okayama Provincial Recruitment Centre reported a 20 per cent increase in volunteers in 2013 after three cute anime mascots appeared on their recruitment posters (Dong, 2014). Fumikane Shimada (an Okayama native and anime illustrator working on the military-themed anime series *Girls und Panzer*), was responsible for drawing the JSDF anime mascots for the Okayama office. Kanagawa Prefectural office, too, jumped onto the anime bandwagon, releasing posters that featured collaboration with the TV anime series *High School Fleet* (which featured locations in Kanagawa including naval base Yokosuka). In a modern twist on the ancient 88 Temple Pilgrimage in Shikoku Island, there is now the 88-spot Japanese anime pilgrimage. The naval base of Sasebo is one of the 88 sacred anime spots selected because of its association with *Kancolle* (short for Kantai Collection or Fleet Collection). Visitors to the Sasebo Machinaka Information Center's *Kukken Hiroba* can obtain a stamp to mark their visit (as they would with the temples on Shikoku). *Kukken Hiroba* also provides information on job vacancies at military bases as well as JSDF merchandise.

In March 2018, a recruitment office in Shiga Prefecture released a poster depicting female anime characters from *Strike Witches*, an aerial combat anime series clad in extremely short skirts, exposing what appeared to be underwear. The image has been used on the office's website, Facebook and Twitter accounts, as well as at some SDF regional offices across the prefecture. A spokesperson rejected claims that the image constituted sexual harassment, saying: 'We only used the existing anime work of Kadokawa Corp' (Koizumi, 2019). Asked why the office decided to use characters from *Strike Witches*, the spokesperson said: 'We thought that the content appeals to young people. We didn't really insist on using female character (sic).' One person who posted online suggested that 'images of SDF personnel working hard in disaster reconstruction are cooler', another wrote 'they should have used an image featuring a uniform that's befitting of SDF members' (Koizumi, 2019). Another collaboration in December 2019 involved the Air Self-Defense Force (ASDF) and Big West, the company behind popular space anime *Super Macross*. The resulting recruitment poster featured mainstay ASDF fighters such as the F-15 and F-2 flying alongside iconic VF-1 Valkyrie fighters from the anime series, with the slogan 'Towards the Future'.

Within wider society, there is a pre-existing stream of military-themed anime and manga that JSDF tapped into as part of its outreach adapting to public interests. As a result, the JSDF has become more 'warm and fuzzy' to appeal to people (Kelly and Kubo, 2014). This is not necessarily militarism *per se* but rather what Yamamura (2019) has argued is a fantasization of the military driven by private industry actors who seek profit and ever more realistic depictions of military hardware. While Huntington's concerns about societal pressure were related to how they might undermine the strict chain of command and discipline in the military, in the case of Japan, the ways through which the JSDF has sought to reflect societal interests in fantasy anime and manga for recruitment purposes raise several unanswered questions for future research. How far do fantasy-themed posters work and what 'reality' do recruits have in mind when joining the JSDF?

Conclusion

Japan as a democratic state with firm civilian control of its JSDF after 1945 does not face the challenges of SSR or severe threats to democracy that other Asian nations have experienced. The JSDF and the domestic communities it serves has undergone a military evolution where both partners have developed and adapted to each other's concerns, interests and needs. A developmental and economic regeneration agenda on the part of large base hosting communities has fed into a focus on promoting JSDF bases and the surrounding areas as tourism spots. On the other hand, the JSDF has promoted its HADR mission and tapped into popular culture such as anime and interest in military cuisine (for example, navy curry) as part of outreach with its host communities. Nevertheless, several challenges in civil–military relations remain. Domestic media such as the Mainichi and Asahi have reported extensively on the 2018 National Defence Programme Guidelines which unveiled plans to convert *Izumo*-class helicopter destroyers into an aircraft carrier capable of flying F-35 stealth fighters. It will be the first time since World War Two that Japan operates a flat-deck aircraft carrier. Officially, the ship will be called a multi-purpose vessel not carrying warplanes in peacetime. This is due to the longstanding official position not to own any 'offensive aircraft carriers'. Questions have been raised from senior retired JMSDF officers as to whether these two upgraded vessels are sufficient for combat operations. Two vessels would only allow for training operations, '[s]o this plan doesn't make sense for MSDF officers, frankly speaking', according to Ito Toshiyuki, a retired MSDF vice admiral. Another retired vice admiral, Koda Yoji, argued that a defence build-up programme must be based on the assumption 'that those [weapons] can actually be used in an emergency situation … Just showing off is not a legitimate way of thinking' (Yoshida, 2019).

Then-Defence Minister Iwaya Takashi claimed that 'this way of thinking was not formed because of specific needs or requests from the MSDF or Air Self-Defense Force. We reached this conclusion after conducting studies from defense policy perspectives' (Yoshida, 2019). There is no 'threat to democracy' in civil–military relations in that these decisions were made and implemented by democratically elected politicians accountable for their actions. Neither is there any concern of the military taking a more active role in politics, much less coups. The crux of concerns raised by retired senior JMSDF officers pertain to how far political leaders understand the operational implications of military decisions they are making.

In May 2017, orders were issued for the first time under new security legislation allowing the *Izumo* to escort US supply ships off the Boso peninsula amid fears of a North Korean missile threat. China looms large in the domestic debate, combined with deteriorating ties with Russia. Even a supposedly friendly nation, the Republic of Korea, has been involved in military incidents such as locking fire-control radar on a JMSDF patrol plane. With such a severe security environment, the Free and Open Indo-Pacific vision under the Abe administration was being promoted to regional partners in ASEAN through the Indo-Pacific Deployments and Ship Rider Cooperation Programme. Relatively little negative public backlash from the region has been observed, although eyebrows were raised initially. Domestically, the public reception has ranged from wariness over gunboat diplomacy and concerns over the implications for the pacifist constitution, to outright enthusiastic support by right-leaning media. As these deployments are labelled 'training exercises' in low-risk contexts, they seem to have attracted comparatively less public concern compared to the 'Middle East deployments', which constitute higher risks.

As for how the JMSDF communicates its missions domestically, JSDF outreach activities are of course not based entirely on fantasy characters and mascots. There are other, more realistic public outreach activities. The Ministry of Defense organizes one-day experiential events targeted at university students and females for a taste of military life. Private media such as Fuji TV have also produced programmes about part-time JSDF reservists. Taken together, these outreach projects convey a more realistic sense of what JSDF trains for in the ultimate employment of force.

However, the use of cartoon anime-themed characters in recruitment posters has not gone without a hitch. In 2016, Chiba prefecture's Ministry of Defense office released a rather disconcerting poster featuring a smiling disembodied head of the prefectural ministry mascot, Ei-Kun, being passed around by men in shadows. One Twitter user, Hiromi, posted: 'I wonder what they're trying to say with this passing-of-a-freshly-severed-head design … All I can say is, it's disturbing' (Murphy, 2016). At least to Hiromi as a member of the public, this official messaging did not work well. This also has implications for educating the public. In Japan, heiwa-boke (平和ボケ) or 'peace-boke', refers to complacency or misunderstanding induced by an excess of peacefulness or lack of exposure and understanding of the realities of combat. Communicating the military profession to the public through fantastical anime characters might help form some bond between the public and JSDF. This does not necessarily help the public or potential recruits make informed decisions about geopolitical threats that may require actual use of the JSDF in combat. This is partly why it has been suggested that the 'Japanese people have not experienced war directly since the end of the war in 1945 … in modern Japan, the war is just fantasy' (Alt, 2016, p 17).

Another question arises here regarding the specific process, motives and intentions of the JSDF recruitment posters. Ito Toshiyuki, the former head of the public relations division for the Maritime Staff Office, claimed that such publicity products are first and foremost to catch the eye of young people but clarified that: 'There are no members that have joined JSDF because something like this caught their attention' (Asahi Shimbun, 2016, p 17). Was the choice of anime or manga characters a result of intentional JSDF decisions to be 'closer to the public' or perhaps it was pitched to JSDF by advertising companies? Yamamura (2019) argues that in fact, it is anime companies that approach the JSDF for collaborations. The key driving force is the desire for anime companies to generate a larger market share and loyal fans through ever-more realistic depictions of military equipment (Yamamura, 2019). Accuracy and attention to detail are of huge importance for die-hard fans. This raises interesting aspects of how the JSDF has adapted and responded to local needs, in this case those of anime companies and fans. As Sugawa-Shimada (2019) shows, naval-themed anime such as Kantai Collection (with its collaboration with the JMSDF on events), has led to war-related contents tourism that is often light-hearted entertainment. Darker meanings and values associated with war have become displaced. One result is that anime fans of such military-themed series are relating themselves to JSDF through the sense of familiarity they achieve through watching their favourite anime (Sugawa-Shimada, 2019).

The JSDF is experiencing a military evolution in two senses. On the regional front, with lengthy deployments to communicate the message of a Free and Open Indo-Pacific and HADR capacity-building to ASEAN nations, domestic opinion in Japan remains somewhat mixed on the implications for Tokyo's hitherto defence-oriented policy and the pacifist constitution. On the other hand, JSDF attempts at domestic outreach through anime-themed posters run the danger of a disconnect with the increasingly harsh regional security environment that the JSDF is in fact grappling with. A developmental-oriented agenda focused on benefits from tourism and anime driven by local base-hosting communities and private industry has also emerged which the JSDF has adapted to. Despite these quirks that are particular to Japan, they reflect quite significant military evolutions in the civil–military relationship. As Sado (2017) has noted, in the early post-1945 years, the JSDF existed within a traditional form of negative civilian control designed mainly to actually avoid using the JSDF. This negativism is now displaced by a more positive form of civilian control geared towards how best to deploy the JSDF within existing constraints, both in terms of public opinion and constitutionally (Sado, 2017).

References

Alt, M. (2016) 'Senso-ga fantasy no kuni [The country where wars is fantasy]', *Asahi Shimbun*, [online] 27 February, Available from: www.asahi.com/ajw/ [Accessed 1 May 2022].

Asahi Shimbun (2016) 'Jieitai ga mijika yawaragu teiko [SDF is close, resistance softened]' *Asahi Shimbun*, [online] 27 February, Available from: www.asahi.com/ajw/ [Accessed 1 May 2022].

Asahi Shimbun (2018) 'インド太平洋で海自共同訓練へ 各国と協力、中国牽制', *Asahi Shimbun Digital*, [online] 22 August, Available from: www.asahi.com/articles/DA3S13645552.html [Accessed 1 May 2022].

Asahi Shimbun (2019) 'SDF deployment to Mideast raises a host of legal, strategic issues', *The Asahi Shimbun*, [online] 28 December, Available from: www.asahi.com/ajw/articles/AJ201912280010.html [Accessed 1 May 2022].

BBC (2020) 'Army urges young people lacking confidence to join', *BBC News*, [online] 2 January, Available from: www.bbc.com/news/uk-50966542 [Accessed 1 May 2022].

Bosack, M.M. (2019) 'New era, new self-defence forces', *Japan Times*, [online] 27 June, Available from: www.japantimes.co.jp/opinion/2019/06/27/commentary/japan-commentary/new-era-new-self-defense-forces/#.XlS5GSj7Q2w [Accessed 1 May 2022].

Brooks, R. (2016) 'Civil–military paradoxes', in J. Mattis and K. Schake (eds) *Warriors and Citizens,* Stanford, CA: Hoover Institution Press, pp 21–68.

Colford, M. and Sugarman, A.J. (2016) 'Millennials and the military', *Hoover Institution*, [online] 2 August, Available from: www.hoover.org/research/millennials-and-military [Accessed 1 May 2022].

Dong, B. (2014) 'Applications for Japan Self Defense Force Increase by 20% Thanks to Moe', *Anime News Network,* [online] 13 January, Available from: www.animenewsnetwork.com/interest/2014-01-13/applications-for-japan-self-defense-force-increase-by-20-percent-thanks-to-moe [Accessed 1 May 2022].

Eldridge, R.D. and Milford, P. (eds) (2017) *The Japanese Ground Self-Defense Force: Search for Legitimacy*, London: Palgrave Macmillan.

Fujitsu Network Solutions (2016) '旧軍港市振興協議会 様', *Fujitsu*, [online] 18 March, Available from: www.fujitsu.com/jp/group/fnets/about/resources/case-studies/2016/kyugunkoshi.html [Accessed 1 May 2022].

Handa, S. (2018) '海上自衛隊が南シナ海で異例の「対潜水艦戦訓練」を決行した事情.', *Gendai Business*, [online] 22 September, available from: https://gendai.ismedia.jp/articles/-/57618?page=3 [Accessed 1 May 2022].

Hikotani, T. (2009) 'Japan's changing civil–military relations: from containment to re-engagement?', *Global Asia*, 4(1): 22–6.

Hikotani, T. (2016) 'From containment to engagement: Japan's civil–military relations in a time of change', *Suntory Foundation Research Project*, [online] 10 August, Available from: www.suntory.com/sfnd/jgc/forum/010/pdf/010.pdf [Accessed 1 May 2022].

Hikotani, T. (2018) 'The Japanese diet and defence policy making', *International Affairs*, 94(4): 791–814.

Hobby Japan (nd) 'Monthly Hobby Japan', *Hobby Japan*, [online] nd, Available from: https://hobbyjapan.co.jp/en/publications.html [Accessed 19 March 2020].

Hughes, C.W. (2017) 'Japan's strategic trajectory and collective self-defense: essential continuity or radical shift?', *Journal of Japanese Studies*, 43(1): 93–126.

Huntington, S. (1957) *The Soldier and the State: The Theory and Politics of Civil–Military Relations*, New York: Belknap Press.

Japan Maritime Self-Defense Force (nd) '平成３１年度インド太平洋方面派遣訓練部隊(IPD19)', *Ministry of Defense*, [online] nd, Available from: www.mod.go.jp/msdf/operation/cooperate/IPD19/ [Accessed 9 August 2018].

Japan Ministry of Defense (MOD) (2013) 'Naming and launch ceremony of new escort vessel 'IZUMO'', *Japan Defense Focus*, [online] September, Available from: www.mod.go.jp/e/jdf/sp/no44/sp_activities.html [Accessed 1 May 2022].

Japan MOD (2017) 'Japan-ASEAN Ship Rider Cooperation Program: a Vientiane Vision Initiative', *Ministry of Defense*, [online] 19 June, Available from: www.mod.go.jp/e/press/release/2017/06/19b.html [Accessed 1 May 2022].

Japan Public Relations Office (2012) 'Outline of 'Public Opinion Survey on the Self-Defense Forces (SDF) and Defense Issues'', *Ministry of Defense*, [online] March, Available from: https://nation.time.com/wp-content/uploads/sites/8/2012/04/public_opinion.pdf [Accessed 1 May 2022].

Kelly, T. and Kubo, N. (2014) 'Tank girls lead the charge', *Japan Times*, [online] 19 March, Available from: www.japantimes.co.jp/news/2014/03/19/national/tank-girls-lead-the-charge/ [Accessed 1 May 2022].

Kochi Shimbun (2019) '【海自の中東派遣】「なし崩し」は許されない', *The Kochi Shimbun*, [online] 28 December, Available from: www.kochinews.co.jp/article/334970 [Accessed 1 May 2022].

Koide, T. (2008) 'Civil–military relations in Japan', *Kokusai Seiji*, 154: 79–94.

Koizumi, M. (2019) 'SDF draws fire for recruitment poster featuring female anime characters in skimpy costumes', *Japan Times*, [online] 1 March, Available from: www.japantimes.co.jp/news/2019/03/01/national/sdf-draws-fire-recruitment-poster-featuring-anime-style-female-characters-skimpy-costumes/ [Accessed 1 May 2022].

Liff, A. (2015) 'Japan's defence policy: Abe the evolutionary', *The Washington Quarterly*, 38(2): 79–99.

Livedoor News (2019) 'バーティゴも体験　日本とASEAN、初の空軍パイロット交流会実施 その本当の目的は…？', *Livedoor News*, [online] 8 August, Available from: https://news.livedoor.com/article/detail/16897051/ [Accessed 1 May 2022].

Mainichi Shimbun (2018) '43% want existence of SDF mentioned in revised Constitution: Mainichi poll', *Mainichi Shimbun*, [online] 22 January, Available from: https://mainichi.jp/english/articles/20180122/p2a/00m/0na/020000c [Accessed 1 May 2022].

Mainichi Shimbun (2019) '南シナ海舞台に日中、影響力探り合い 護衛艦「いずも」多国間訓練', *Mainichi Shimbun*, [online] 1 July, Available from: https://mainichi.jp/articles/20190701/k00/00m/010/300000c [Accessed 1 May 2022].

Mangosing, F. (2017) 'Duterte tours Japan's biggest warship', *Philippine Daily Inquirer*, [online] 4 June, Available from: https://globalnation.inquirer.net/157605/duterte-tours-japans-biggest-warship#ixzz6H6xxAjV4 [Accessed 1 May 2022].

Mattis, J. and Schake, K. (2016) 'A great divergence?', in J. Mattis and K. Schake (eds) *Warriors and Citizens*, Stanford, CA: Hoover Institution Press.

Midford, P. (2011) *Rethinking Japanese Public Opinion and Security: From Pacifism to Realism?*, Stanford, CA: Stanford University Press.

Murphy, M. (2016) 'Japan Self-Defence Force poster seems to be repelling more people than it's recruiting', *Sora News 24*, [online] 6 March, Available from: https://soranews24.com/2016/03/06/japan-self-defence-force-poster-seems-to-be-repelling-more-people-than-its-recruiting/ [Accessed 1 May 2022].

NHK (2017) 'Changes in the public attitudes towards the constitution', *NHK Broadcasting Culture Institute*, [online] 1 October, Available from: www.nhk.or.jp/bunken/english/research/yoron/20171001_9.html [Accessed 1 May 2022].

Oros, A. (2008) *Normalizing Japan: Politics, Identity, and the Evolution of Security Practice*, Stanford, CA: Stanford University Press.

Owens, M.T. (2017) 'Civil–military relations', *Oxford Research Encyclopaedia of International Studies*, [online] 30 November, Available from: http://internationalstudies.oxfordre.com/view/10.1093/acrefore/9780190846626.001.0001/acrefore-9780190846626-e-123 [Accessed 1 May 2022].

Sado, A. (2017) *The Self-Defense Forces and Postwar Politics in Japan*, trans. Makito Noda, Tokyo: Japan Publishing Industry Foundation for Culture (JPIC).

Samuels, R.J. and Wallace, C. (2018) 'Introduction: Japan's pivot in Asia', *International Affairs*, 94(4): 703–10.

Sasaki, T. (2015) *Japan's Postwar Military and Civil Society: Contesting a Better Life*, London: Bloomsbury Publishing.

Seifukunofuji, "Seifukunofuji Web Shop", https://seifukunofuji.co.jp/ [Accessed 5 October 2022].

Sugawa-Shimada, A. (2019) 'Playing with militarism in/with *Arpeggio* and *Kantai Collection*: effects of *shōjo* images in war-related contents tourism in Japan', *Journal of War and Culture Studies*, 12(1): 53–66.

Tang, Siew Mun, Hoang Thi Ha, Glenn Ong, Anuthida Saelaow Qian and Pham Thi Phuong Thao (2020) *The State of Southeast Asia: 2020 Survey Report*, ISEAS-Yusof Ishak Institute, [online] 16 January 2020, Available from: https://think-asia.org/bitstream/handle/11540/11709/TheStateofSEASurveyReport_2020.pdf?sequence=1 [Accessed 1 May 2022].

Tatsumi, Y. (2015) 'The Japanese defense reform no one is talking about', *The Diplomat*, [online] 16 May, Available from: https://thediplomat.com/2015/05/the-japanese-defense-reform-no-one-is-talking-about/ [Accessed 1 May 2022].

The Japan Times (2015) 'Record 30% of Japanese want SDF beefed up: Cabinet survey', *Japan Times*, [online] 8 March, Available from: www.japantimes.co.jp/news/2015/03/08/national/politics-diplomacy/record-number-of-japanese-want-beefed-up-sdf-capabilities-cabinet-survey/#.Xk4l1Sj7Q2w [Accessed 1 May 2022].

The Japan Times (2019) 'Poll shows 54% oppose revision of Japan's pacifist Constitution under Abe's watch', *Japan Times*, [online] 11 April, Available from: www.japantimes.co.jp/news/2019/04/11/national/politics-diplomacy/poll-shows-54-oppose-revision-japans-pacifist-constitution/#.XlS5Lij7Q2w [Accessed 1 May 2022].

Today (2018) 'As Chinese influence grows, Japanese warship visits Sri Lanka', *Today Online*, [online] 1 October, Available from: www.todayonline.com/world/chinese-influence-grows-japanese-warship-visits-sri-lanka?cid=h3_referral_inarticlelinks_03092019_todayonline [Accessed 1 May 2022].

UK Ministry of Defence (1998) 'Supporting essay four: defence diplomacy' *Strategic Defence Review*, [online] 15 October, Available from: https://researchbriefings.files.parliament.uk/documents/RP98-91/RP98-91.pdf [Accessed 1 May 2022].

UK Ministry of Defence and Foreign and Commonwealth Office (2017) 'UK's international defence engagement strategy', UK Ministry of Defence and Foreign and Commonwealth Office, [online] 17 February, Available from: https://assets.publishing.service.gov.uk/government/uploads/system/uploads/attachment_data/file/596968/06032017_Def_Engag_Strat_2017DaSCREEN.pdf [Accessed 1 May 2022].

Yahoo News Japan (2018) '自衛隊への好印象度は89.8％.' *Yahoo! Japan*, [online] 19 March, Available from: https://news.yahoo.co.jp/byline/fuwaraizo/20180319-00082828/ [Accessed 1 May 2022].

Yamamura, T. (2019) 'Cooperation between anime producers and the Japan Self-Defense Force: creating fantasy and/or propaganda?', *Journal of War and Culture Studies*, 12(1): 8–23.

Yomiuri Shimbun (2020) '海自中東派遣「評価する」５０％… 読売世論調査.', *Yomiuri Shimbun*, [online] 19 January, Available from: www.yomiuri.co.jp/election/yoron-chosa/20200119-OYT1T50120/ [Accessed 1 May 2022].

Yoshida Shigeru Memorial Foundation (eds) (1991) *Ningen Yoshida Shigeru*, Tokyo; Chuoukouronnshinsha.

Yoshida, R. (2019) 'Japan's plan to remodel Izumo-class carriers: needed upgrade or mere show of force?', *Japan Times*, [online] 23 May, Available from: www.japantimes.co.jp/news/2019/05/23/national/izumo-needed-upgrade-mere-show-force/ [Accessed 1 May 2022].

Yuasa, I. (2020) '自衛隊の砲艦外交を定着させてはならない，―定期化するインド太平洋派遣訓練.', *Peace Forum*, [online] 31 January, Available from: www.peace-forum.com/p-da/200131.html [Accessed 1 May 2022].

Yukan Fuji (2018) '【アジアを先導する日本】トランプ氏を突き動かした「自由で開かれたインド太平洋戦略」 北京の拡張主義に対抗.', *Zakzak by Yukan Fuji*, [online] 9 January, Available from: www.zakzak.co.jp/soc/news/180109/soc1801090006-n2.html [Accessed 1 May 2022].

PART III
South Asia

14

The Deficient Evolution of Civil–Military Relations in India

Harsh V. Pant and Tuneer Mukherjee

> Military strength should be proportional to the threats confronting the polity. It serves no purpose to establish a protection force and then to vitiate it to the point where it can no longer protect. Indeed, an inadequate military institution may be worse than none at all. (Feaver 1999, p 215)

In August 2019, Indian Prime Minister Narendra Modi announced the nation's most significant defence reform since its establishment as a constitutional republic – the institution of the post of Chief of Defence Staff (CDS) (Unnithan, 2019). By appointing a four-star general and establishing the Department of Military Affairs inside the Ministry of Defence, the government sought to address the array of issues that afflict India's military effectiveness. The post of the CDS has been a core recommendation of almost all defence review committees set up in India to scrutinize the armed forces' workings. With its realization, the government has demonstrated intent in implementing more systematic reforms that will have a broader impact on India's defence organization.[1] According to Prime Minister Modi, 'the CDS would be the government's single-point military advisor and sharpen coordination between the forces making them even more effective' (Unnithan, 2019). While the CDS' investiture is no silver bullet, it assuages the paucity in synergy between the different elements that constitute India's higher defence management [the political leadership, the bureaucracy and the military] – which have traditionally operated in silos. A similar fragmented relationship also exists among the armed forces' respective services, severely impacting India's jointness in operations and defence planning. The CDS is mandated to bind together all these disjointed sections and restructure India's armed forces. Under his command, India is now undergoing a fundamental recalibration from segregated service-based commands to integrated functional commands. The plans to establish an Air Defence Command and a Maritime Theatre Command (MTC) are already in progress and could herald the most extensive organizational restructuring in the history of the Indian armed forces (Dhoundial, 2021).

This government's intent to restructure the dogmatic organization of India's civil–military relations reflects the evolution of the country's national security objectives and political priorities. India's present dictum as a 'net security provider in the Indian Ocean' has broadened the framework of its civilian and military principals, and their synchronization needs to be commensurate with this new strategic posture. Comparably, the political leadership's determination to make the armed forces more effective stems from India's external security challenges involving its geopolitical adversaries – Pakistan and China. Prime Minister Narendra Modi's centre-right government has displayed an increased propensity to use military action as a tool to counter the two hostile neighbouring states. The longstanding policy of 'strategic restraint' has given way to a policy of 'punitive retaliation' in Pakistan's case (Tarapore, 2020). While on the eastern border with China, the political leadership has exhibited strategic resolve in reinforcing border infrastructure and deterring Chinese 'land-grabs' through counter-coercion (Tarapore, 2020). In addition, the conceptualization of 'Indo-Pacific' as a paradigm of Asian geopolitics has further manifested India's position as a consequential military power in the region's evolving security dynamics. As such new paradigms change the calculus of Asian security, this chapter seeks to study *how India can achieve military effectiveness while fulfilling its self-mandated role as a regional security provider.*

The current scholarship on civil–military relations of democratic societies has moved beyond the aspect of 'civilian control' and focuses on second order challenges of military effectiveness and efficiency (Bruneau and Matei, 2013; see also Chapter 1 in this volume). Scholars are deliberating finer theoretical frameworks that can better decipher how nation-states achieve greater usefulness of their military power while adhering to civilian oversight (Bruneau and Matei, 2013). As the chapter proceeds to argue, India's approach to civil–military relations has successfully instituted civilian control but achieved limited military effectiveness. The evolution of civil–military relations in India is reflective of the adaptive processes by which the Indian state has graduated from a post-colonial state with multiple security challenges that searched for a favourable configuration in the relationship between the 'political principal' and its 'security agent', to a nation that has acknowledged its role as a leading military power in Asia and is organizing its civil–military relations apposite to its geopolitical disposition (Feaver, 2003).

The fundamental evolution of Indian civil–military relations has come in the form of constant competition for influence between the country's political executive, bureaucracy and military leadership. The successes and shortcomings resulting from the various formal and non-formal arrangements of control between these three entities has resulted in India evolving through different patterns of civil–military relations over the last 70 years. Circumstances in the immediate neighbourhood, major geopolitical shifts and the rise of modern military technology have similarly played a key role in shaping the current contour of Indian civil–military relations. Indian defence institutions and their procedures reflect these adaptive processes and are indicators as to which direction the pendulum of India's civil–military relations swayed in the various phases of its evolution.

In contrast to other South Asian states, which have been subject to periods of military intervention in the country's administration, India has stayed true to its democratic ideals, and its trajectory is most closely comparable in the Asian context to the Japanese experience of civil–military relations. The application of the traditional Huntington-Feaver model to analyse India's civil–military relations is common since the nation shares constitutional ideals with Western liberal democracies, but the evolving nature of civil–military relations in India, driven by its unique experience as a post-colonial developmental state mired with multiple conflicts with neighbouring countries necessitates observers to consider its distinct position. India's experience is only similar to other Asian nations in areas such as defence diplomacy and MOOTW, as they have progressively evolved as an important confidence-building tool to showcase the nation's defence preparedness. Contrastingly, India has seamlessly instituted the military as an essential organ in its civilian-directed geopolitical strategy and is therefore progressively ahead in the evolutionary curve distinctive to Asian civil–military relations. As a flagbearer of Asian democracy that needs to constantly condition its armed forces with military preparedness, wide-ranging defence diplomacy roles and large-scale humanitarian operations, while simultaneously ensuring overall military effectiveness, the multifaceted operating landscape of India's defence forces is an illustration of India's importance in the examination of Asian civil–military relations.

Conventionally, civil–military relations in India have conformed to a predictable pattern of rigorous civilian oversight of an operationally autonomous military. Existing scholarship on India's civil–military relations maintains that this arrangement based on Huntington's mode of 'objective civilian control' has created a gap in transmission of defence policy from those in government to those in uniform (Huntington, 1957; Raghavan, 2009; Mukherjee, 2020; Tarapore, 2020). Mukherjee's seminal work on India's civil–military relations titled 'The Absent Dialogue' addresses this problem and claims that 'the pattern of civil–military relations in India compromises the effectiveness of the military' (Mukherjee, 2020, p 5). India's political leadership has relegated essential functions of defence management to the bureaucracy, which has instituted strong procedural control over the armed forces, leading to a dissonance between civilian and military institutions (Cohen, 2001; Wilkinson, 2018; Mukherjee, 2020). Illuminating the constraints that arise from this arrangement and building upon Mukherjee's 'absent dialogue' argument, this chapter proceeds to understand how civil–military relations have evolved in India and why the present arrangement of 'objective control' has compromised the nation's military effectiveness.

The authors of this chapter rely on the vast body of existing work that has analysed and debated the relationship between the political leadership and armed forces of the country. The historical evolution of India's civil–military relations in various stages from the initial phase as a post-colonial state to a rising military power has been enunciated in detail by relying on the work done by several experts (Chari, 1977; Cohen, 2001; Wilkinson, 2015; Wilkinson, 2018; Mukherjee, 2020). The edited volume by Ganguly, Blarel and Pardesi provides a broad appraisal of India's defence organization and its various structures and their functions (Ganguly et al, 2018). Additional commentary and academic research, dealing directly with topics such as weapons procurement, defence planning, force structuring and defence diplomacy (Jaishankar, 2016; Narang and Staniland, 2018; Behera, 2018; Bitzinger, 2018; Joshi and Rej, 2018; Tarapore, 2020; Shukla, 2021), have aided the authors in providing a comprehensive insight into the internal functioning of the Indian civil–military organization. One of the authors' own works, specifically focussing on interactions between the military and the political class in the Indian nuclear weapons programme, has been vital to understanding how the modern Indian state has instituted civilian control over one of the most complex elements of military power (Pant, 2007).

Building upon such exhaustive work and taking into consideration recent developments, this chapter marks an important investigation into India's civil–military relations evolution and allows the reader to compare it with other Asian nations analysed in this volume. By answering specific questions raised by the editors of this volume, the authors tease out the specific nature of processes that shape civil–military relations in India. The chapter contributes to the ongoing dialogue on what plagues the effectiveness and efficiency of India's higher defence establishment, and what course correction is required to catalyse India's fulfilment of its goal of being a 'net security provider' in the Indian Ocean region. In a deferential inference to the existing literature on civil–military relations in India, this chapter presents a comprehensive examination of all topics that form India's present-day civil–military relations. The chapter tracks the evolutionary processes and units that make up Indian civil–military relations, while simultaneously detailing the internal structures of the military and how they are positioned in a broader sense to help realize India's security objectives. Finally, the authors researched the subject at a time when a fundamental recalibration is underway in civil–military relations in

India. This provides the unique opportunity to deliver a novel perspective as to what can be expected out of these reforms, and how India's civil–military principals are preparing themselves for the security and organizational challenges that lie ahead of them.

The chapter is arranged into six distinct sections. The first section provides a historical overview of civil–military relations in India and deduces its changing nature from nodal events that have moulded the relationship. The second section outlines India's current approach to national security, examining defence planning procedures and force structuring doctrines. In the subsequent sections, the chapter engages with three questions raised by the editors in this volume. The third section traces the colonial origins of civil–military relations in India and tries to understand how the colonial regime influenced the Indian military's self-definition of its role in independent India. The fourth section tracks India's approach to defence diplomacy and its political direction, detailing India's external political-military engagements as an instrument in articulating its strategic posture in the Indo-Pacific. The penultimate section examines India's military effectiveness through the frame of force modernization and how it is tailored to achieve long-term strategic objectives. The chapter concludes with an overview of the salient issues forming civil–military relations in India and considers future debates as its civilian and military leaders experiment with new mechanisms to synergize their interactions.

The evolution of India's civil–military relationship

The trajectory of civil–military relations in India has been shaped by the post-colonial state's distinct political phases, in conjunction with its military conflicts at various junctures. This section attempts to trace that journey by deducing the various inflection points of India's military operations while reflecting on the nature of civil–military interactions of that time.

The Nehruvian era: foundations of civilian control

Jawaharlal Nehru, independent India's first prime minister, emphasized strong procedural control over military matters and shaped norms and institutions in a manner that would protect the nascent state from a military coup. He made four significant changes to the existing colonial structure of defence management to subjugate the military and reduce its political influence. First, Nehru abolished the office of the 'commander-in-chief', who had until then been the highest-ranking military official in the land. Second, he established the Ministry of Defence to take procedural control over military matters and replaced the commander-in-chief of the Indian Army with a civilian defence minister in his cabinet (Cohen, 2001; Wilkinson, 2018;

Mukherjee, 2020). Third, he split up the unified armed forces into three separate branches – the army, the navy and the air force, assigning a separate chief of staff to each of them. Fourth, he reduced the tenure of the service chiefs from four years to three years.

Wilkinson (2018, p 170) argues that the reduction in tenure 'created some problems for military effectiveness, since the top Indian officers ascended to high rank after Independence at young ages, given the mass exodus of British senior officers from India in 1947–49, could have potentially provided valuable military experience for many more years than they did.' Around the same time, Nehru also gradually demoted military officers in the Warrant of Precedence, positioning them lower than their civilian counterparts. Examining Nehru's reforms, Cohen (2001, p 173) contends that 'all these organizational changes had the effect of reducing the military's role in the decision-making process. The military was thoroughly indoctrinated with the principle of civilian control'. While these changes increased the power of the civilian leadership vis-à-vis the military, they had a detrimental effect on India's military effectiveness. Especially Nehru's decision to separate the armed forces would institute a disjointed approach to defence decision-making.

The Sino-Indian War: establishment of objective control

While Nehru's policies successfully instituted civilian control, India's loss to China in the border conflict of 1962 under his leadership left an enduring legacy of military failure in India's institutional memory. Nehru's appointment of Krishna Menon as defence minister in 1957 is viewed as a major reason behind the defeat. In the years preceding the war, Menon introduced rigorous procedural control over the military and imposed himself on the service chiefs in matters of military strategy, officer promotion policies, military risk assessment and operational planning (Wilkinson, 2018, p 174). The military leadership despised Menon for his interference as they considered these areas to be their own domain (Mukherjee, 2020, p 53). As a result, when India lost the war to China owing to an ineffectual defence strategy, Nehru and Menon received the blame.

Existing scholarship acknowledges that one of the primary reasons behind India's defeat to China in 1962 was the political interference of the civilian leadership in operational issues (Chari, 1977; Cohen, 2001; Wilkinson, 2015; Mukherjee, 2020). However, Srinath Raghavan has offered an alternative explanation, exonerating the civilian leadership from complete culpability. He argues that the civilian leadership had to intervene in operational issues because the armed forces were unable to conceive a strategy to counter the impending threat of Chinese territorial aggression (Raghavan, 2009). While the defeat's actual causes are still up for debate, it was evident that India's defence leadership had failed to discharge its duty during the war, resulting in the cessation of territory to China. Consequently, the loss to China entrenched the perception of civilian incompetency in military strategy and established the format of 'objective civilian control' in the nation. Thereafter, political leaders would refrain from interfering in operational matters. Speaking to his military chiefs shortly after the war, Nehru himself would accept a clear delineation, remarking that, 'broader strategy must be governed by political factors, but detailed strategy – and tactics especially – have to be judged by military considerations' (Raghavan, 2009, p 166).

India's wars with Pakistan: institutionalization of objective control

Following its defeat by China in 1962, India would get embroiled in two different wars with Pakistan – one in 1965 during Prime Minister Lal Bahadur Shastri's tenure and another one in 1971, under Indira Gandhi's leadership. In compliance with the template established after the war in 1962, this phase was characterized by a civilian leadership that set broader political objectives and provided the military complete autonomy over strategy and operations. While the war in 1965 ended in a *status quo ante bellum*, India claimed military success on account of its forces ending Pakistan's attempted insurgency in Kashmir. The lessons learned from the 1962 War, coupled with India's assumed military success in 1965, created the belief that India's military effectiveness is greater when civilians delegate operational matters to the military (Raghavan, 2009). This notion would be further cemented when India achieved a decisive victory in the 1971 War.

Essentially, both conflicts reinforced the claim that there should be a strict separation between civilian and military domains but had distinct variations on how the political leadership communicated operational objectives to the military establishment. Prime Minister Shastri provided substantial autonomy to the military and was minimally involved in coordinating the war effort, creating a disconnect between the strategic decisions made by field commanders from political considerations, thus impacting India's military effectiveness in the war (Raghavan, 2009). In contrast, Indira Gandhi's approach involved closer coordination with the military establishment and engendered better military effectiveness. Mukherjee alludes to this when discussing the 1971 war, stating that 'civilians played a much more active role … ensuring greater coordination between the services and marked a departure from the previous model of civil–military relations' (Mukherjee, 2020, p 74). While other factors also contributed to India's varying military effectiveness in these two wars, the broader outcome was the validation of the blueprint of 'objective control' as the appropriate framework for India to achieve military success.

Civil–military relations post-1971: bureaucratization of objective control

Starting with Indira Gandhi's second term in office in 1971, civil–military relations in India became increasingly dominated by bureaucratic authority. She emboldened the civilian bureaucracy to take complete control of defence decision-making in India, and in that process side-lined the military leadership (Mukherjee, 2020). Assessing this period, Mukherjee states that 'the underlying compact of civil–military relations was set during Indira Gandhi's extended premiership. This compact consisted of two main features – bureaucratic control and military autonomy. Under Indira Gandhi, civilian bureaucrats played an increasingly important role in framing defence policies, and at times, excluded the military from this process' (Mukherjee, 2020, p 79). On the other end, the Indian Army was occupied with internal security challenges. Starting from the Naxalite insurgency of 1967, the Army was involved in counter insurgency operations in different parts of the country, which redefined its political role. Chatterjee (2013) argues that insurgencies validated the armed forces' autonomous nature, as when they were deployed against civilian populations, their role widened to include administrative and governance procedures, increasing their political influence. In effect, an authoritative bureaucracy along with an autonomous military resulted in the fragmentation of India's civil–military relationship, with defence institutions arranging themselves into different factions and each unit preserving its own interests.

Rajiv Gandhi, who succeeded Indira Gandhi as prime minister, attempted to bridge this schism between the political leadership and the military by minimizing the bureaucracy's role. His government significantly increased the defence budget and promoted jointness in defence planning (Mukherjee, 2020, p 81). However, this proximity between the political leadership and the military was short-lived due to two separate crises precipitated by an ambitious chief of army staff, General K. Sundarji. The first was Operation Brasstacks, wherein the three services of the armed forces under the instructions of General Sundarji conducted India's largest peacetime military exercise near the India–Pakistan border, thereby fomenting political tension with Pakistan. The second was the involvement of Indian armed forces in a peacekeeping operation in Sri Lanka, which ended in a strategic failure. Both instances caused serious political crises for Rajiv Gandhi's government and the blame would be squarely laid on the enhanced authority given to General Sundarji, who had failed to deliver the operational successes that he had guaranteed the civilian leadership. Following Rajiv Gandhi's term, civil–military relations resumed functioning on previously established arrangements. The bureaucracy reassumed its role as the intermediary between the political leadership and the military principals, reinforcing the idea that India is best suited to a model in which the bureaucracy, the political leadership and the military each operate in their separate domain.

Atal Bihari Vajpayee's election as the leader of India's first centre-right government ushered in a new era in India's civil–military relations. His government made its strategic priorities clear from the outset by conducting nuclear weapons tests a few months after coming into office. And, after Pakistan conducted similar tests of its own, it was assumed that nuclear weapons would moderate conventional hostilities between the two nations. However, the opposite happened, and India would become entangled in a limited war with Pakistan in 1999 when Pakistani troops would cross the international boundary separating the two nations and occupy strategic positions in the mountains of Kargil. The Kargil conflict is of particular significance because, during the conflict, Prime Minister Vajpayee instructed his military principals not to cross the international border under any circumstances when pursuing the more critical operational directive of reclaiming the strategic heights. Vajpayee issued these operational instructions to avoid escalating the conflict to the nuclear threshold. Mukherjee remarks that Vajpayee's actions 'reflected maturity and confidence in civil–military relations that contrasted from earlier years' (Mukherjee, 2020, p 88). The eventual success of the Indian armed forces, despite the operational restraint, has corrected previous conjectures about civilian involvement in strategizing operations.

Post-Kargil, Vajpayee's government instituted the Kargil Review Committee to restructure India's higher defence management and promote jointness among the different branches of the Indian military (Mukherjee, 2020). At the same time, the National Security Council, established by Vajpayee in 1998, formulated a civilian-dominated nuclear command structure and outlined the nation's nuclear weapons doctrine of 'no-first-use' (Pant, 2007). However, apart from the formation of the 'Integrated Defence Staff' (IDS), other vital reforms recommended by the Kargil Review Committee and other subsequent defence reform committees formed after it were never implemented.[2] This fundamental inability to execute reforms illuminates the deficient processes that mark civil–military relations in India, which as a result, undermine military effectiveness. The current government under Narendra Modi has demonstrated intent in shaping a new trajectory for defence management by undertaking long-pending reforms, the institutionalization of the CDS being one. However, it is too early to determine whether these reforms will be able to alter the fundamental principles upon which civil–military relations function in India.

India's national security strategy

Defence planning in India

India's national security strategy has undergone multiple renovations through the years but remains acutely fixated on cross-border transgressions from

Pakistan and China. However, despite unambiguous security threats, the political leadership's precise organizational mandate regarding defence policy remains unclear due to the absence of a coherent strategic document. While the presence of a document outlining India's national security strategy has been alluded to by officials in the Modi government, it has not been released for public scrutiny. The absence of a clear security formulation has two major consequences. First, it widens the gap between military strategy and fiscal outlays, and second, it engenders the disjointed approach towards defence planning among the three services. Multiple governments have attempted to improve defence planning by forming new institutions, but mostly all of them have failed to assimilate the various stakeholders of India's higher defence management into the planning process (Mukherjee, 2020, pp 227–42).

Under Prime Minister Modi's leadership, there has been another attempt to mend this process by creating the Defence Planning Committee (DPC). The DPC is headed by the national security advisor and includes senior officials from the civilian bureaucracy and the armed forces. According to one defence analyst:

> the DPC is tasked to prepare at least five different sets of drafts including: 'national security strategy, strategic defence review and doctrines; international defence engagement strategy; roadmap to build defence manufacturing eco-system; strategy to boost defence exports; and prioritized capability development plans for the armed forces over different timeframes in consonance with the overall priorities, strategies and likely resource flows.' (Behera, 2018)

For the DPC to succeed in these tasks, it should avoid the mistakes made by the previous renditions of defence planning institutions and give equal standing to all the stakeholders of India's higher defence management in the planning process. Ideally, such a planning process would then incubate a continuous dialogue that generates transparency in strategic goals, fiscal planning, threat assessment mechanisms and force structuring.

India's force structuring

The Indian armed forces' current force structure is primarily geared towards negating a conventional continental threat from Pakistan. The army's most clearly formulated strategic plan called 'Cold Start' envisages a limited conventional war where integrated battle groups of the Indian Army would conduct a shallow thrust offensive into Pakistan to capture territory, which would then be used as leverage in political negotiations (Tarapore, 2020, p 13). The key to the 'Cold Start' manoeuvre is the designated 'holding corps', which would transform into 'pivot corps' once armoured brigades are attached to them (Joshi and Rej, 2018, p 13). However, this strategy has two main drawbacks. First, the 'Cold Start' manoeuvre assumes that it would not invite a nuclear retaliation from Pakistan. Analysts like Tarapore have argued against this assumption stating that, 'Pakistan has made tactical nuclear weapons an integral part of its military strategy and consistently warns that it will not hesitate to escalate a crisis past the nuclear threshold' (Tarapore, 2020, p 18). Second, given the recent accentuation of the security threat from China, a 'Cold Start' doctrine imperils India's forced preparedness in the eastern sector. Recent developments suggest that the government has acknowledged this reality and redesignated two divisions of the Mathura based 1 Corps, previously designated as one of the holding corps under the 'Cold Start' doctrine, into becoming 'mountain strike corps' that could be deployed to strike into Chinese territory from Ladakh (Shukla, 2021).

Consequently, the recalibration of forces from the western sector (directed towards Pakistan) to the eastern sector (for countering Chinese coercion) could be a precursor for future force-structuring computations, whereby the eastern sector becomes the primary focus of combat operations for the Indian Army. Before this redeployment 'of the army's 38 divisions, just 12 divisions faced China, while 25 divisions were deployed on the India-Pakistan border' (Shukla, 2021). This alteration in force structure comes in the wake of recent incursions by Chinese forces across the Line of Actual Control (LAC), which functions as an international boundary between the two countries. Starting from May 2020, Chinese forces occupied tactical positions in multiple sectors and engaged in grey zone aggression to establish their dominance over strategic mountain heights. The Indian Army's current strategy to counter such actions is centred around the 17 Corps, which were raised as India's first mountain strike corps to undertake counter-offensive operations against China. The addition of the 1 Corps as another mountain strike corps reinforces this strategy. However, for the most part, the army's approach vis-à-vis China has remained reactionary, and despite multiple Chinese incursions over the past few years along the LAC, it has failed to pre-empt Beijing's manoeuvres. Arguably, India's counter-coercion strategy brought it limited success during the Dokhlam standoff in 2017, and the same could be construed after disengagement began in parts of eastern Ladakh following the latest series of clashes. Yet, at present, this counter-coercion strategy is devoid of a design that will deter future Chinese encroachment.

India released its joint doctrine for the armed forces in 2017 (Ministry of Defence, Government of India, 2017). While the doctrine is supposed to provide a template for jointness in operations between the three services, it has a serious flaw in that it is an army-centric doctrine that fails to incorporate the other two services – the air force and the navy – into India's defence posture. The Indian Air Force (IAF) is relegated to a supporting role in the army-centric doctrine, which is adapted from the United States Army's

Air–Land battle doctrine of the 1980s (Joshi and Rej, 2018). This limits the ability of the IAF to project force beyond India's borders. As such, the IAF is currently functioning below capacity with 30 operational squadrons against a sanctioned strength of 42, with many obsolete aircraft in line to be retired out in the near future (Peri, 2020a). Similarly, the Indian Navy's ability to project sea power beyond its near seas is mismatched by the scarce resources available for extensive long-range missions (Mukherjee, 2019). While the Air Force and the Navy have outlined plans to project Indian air power and sea power, respectively, the joint-force doctrine limits the ambit of both services to a constabulary role (Joshi and Rej, 2018). The government's strategy to reshape the armed forces needs to acknowledge these facets and empower the projection of India's aviation and naval capabilities.

The chief of defence staff and integrated theatre commands

The appointment of the CDS by the Modi government has instigated a broader transformation in the structure of the Indian armed forces. Presently, the armed forces are being reorganized from disjointed service-based commands towards more integrated theatre-based commands. Plans are already in progress to establish a National Air Defence Command (NADC) and an MTC by the end of 2021 (Dhoundial, 2021). The logic behind the formulation of integrated theatre commands is to foster jointness in operations between the different branches of the military while simultaneously easing logistical nodes for the various assets available to India's military planners. Reports indicate that the proposed MTC would 'subsume all operational aspects of the four existing naval commands, and also include IAF fighter jets, helicopters and transport aircraft on the Indian peninsula, two Indian Army brigades for amphibious operations and all Coast Guard patrol vessels, helicopters and aircraft' (Unnithan, 2020). Similarly, the NADC 'would integrate the air defence and assets of the Army, Air Force and Navy and jointly provide air defence cover to the country' (Negi, 2020). Both commands are likely to be placed under the operational control of a three-star officer, who would further operate under the direction of the Department of Military Affairs, headed by the CDS. Once operational, these commands will allow better force projection of India's aviation and naval capabilities. Similar plans also exist to reorganize the Indian Army into at least three theatre commands – Western, Northern and Eastern. Moreover, the military is considering setting up a new joint training command to complement the new unified command structure (Dutta, 2020). The government expects this remodelled force structure to improve jointness in operations, enabling the Indian armed forces to tackle multiple security threats across different theatres.

The colonial legacy of India's civil–military relations
Legacy of civilian control

The mentalities that shape India's civil–military relations are deeply rooted in the British colonial rule that lasted on the Indian sub-continent for close to two hundred years. The organizational structure of higher defence management formed during the British colonial rule established strict provisions of civilian control over the armed forces (Chari, 1977; Cohen, 2001; Wilkinson, 2018). Chari (1977, p 7) argues that '[c]ivil–military relations developed over the long period of British rule in India, crystallized into a well-defining pattern – a tradition of civil supremacy over the military apparatus'. After independence, Nehru retained this policy of civilian control and shaped norms and institutions to favour the civilian leadership. He clearly stated to the new commander-in-chief in August 1947 that:

> While I am desirous of paying attention to the views and susceptibilities of our senior officers, British and Indian … In any policy that is to be pursued, in the Army or the otherwise, the views of the Government of India and the policy they lay down must prevail. If any person is unable to carry out this policy, he has no place in the Indian Army. (Wilkinson, 2018, p 169)

Likewise, the institutional dissonance that is characteristic of India's present-day higher defence management is a legacy of the colonial era. The colonial British administration's primary objective was to exercise control over the Indian sub-continent and maintain civil order (Wilkinson, 2018, p 167). To this end, the defence administration was highly decentralized and closed to public scrutiny. The political administrators of the British Indian Empire, namely the governor-general and the secretary of the state, strived to keep the domains of the civilian bureaucracy and the armed forces separate. According to Cohen, the defence decision-making process of post-colonial India followed similar principles and in the post-colonial state, 'the process had become more decentralized and more compartmentalized than the British Indian system' (Cohen, 2001, p 174). Ergo, this overly decentralized system has created a massive gap in accountability mechanisms for defence decision-making in India and given rise to a system where the civilian bureaucracy, the political leadership and the military heads function in oscillating isolation from one another. Over the years, this arrangement has been entrenched further, causing massive inefficiency in long-term defence planning. Cohen (2001, p 175) aptly states that 'the attitudes inherited from the British have turned out to be a crippling legacy, providing neither theoretical nor practical guidance'.

Colonial influence on military philosophy

Similarly, the colonial legacy of military professionalism also shaped the thoughts of officers who formed the initial leadership of independent India's armed forces. Cohen (2001, p 176) states that '[t]he British tradition of separate spheres of military and civilian activity carried over … Indian officers like to boast that politics and military don't mix; that the two are immutably different and separate, and that the military, is and should forever be, outside politics'. Thus, the military's self-definition of its role in the new state remained politically neutral, upholding previously established norms. The armed forces viewed themselves as one of the most professional and well-rounded institutions in the newly created nation and as a force that existed only to protect the country's sovereignty from external and internal threats (Cohen, 2001). In contrast to other post-colonial states in the region that have seen military involvement in state administration, the Indian officer brass has stayed true to their professional ideology and remained impartial to political developments.

Furthermore, in the initial years after independence, British thinking on military planning and professional military education profoundly influenced Indian military philosophy. The new Indian government retained the entire structure of professional military education instituted by the colonial state with minimal changes. Consequently, the Indian military's relation with the British armed forces in the initial years after independence was collegial and included 'close association between Indian and British officers, the deputation of Indian officers to British schools of instruction, and the retention of British officers after independence' (Mukherjee, 2020, p 180). These contacts systemized a military education system derived entirely from British concepts of warfare. Likewise, India's initial civilian leadership sought frequent counsel from prominent British defence planners such as P.M.S Blackett and former Governor-General Lord Mountbatten. Nehru appointed Blackett for advice on military and defence affairs, which resulted in Blackett producing a report on India's strategic position and its military spending in 1948 (Cohen and Dasgupta, 2010, p 6). Comparably, Mountbatten contributed significantly to India's initial defence policy making, influencing Nehru's government on issues such as weapons procurement, higher defence organization and civil–military relations (Mukherjee, 2020, p 46–52). Such close coordination between the new Indian government and the British state on various issues of higher defence management attests to the reality that the colonial legacy had endured well past the date of independence.

Defence diplomacy in India

India's status as one of Asia's leading military powers has always had a bearing on its foreign policy discourse. Consequently, beginning from the early days of the Cold War, when India championed itself as a leader of the post-colonial world, to its present-day rendition as a 'net security provider in the Indian Ocean', defence diplomacy has been a critical instrument in communicating India's strategic posture to the world. In pursuit of defence diplomacy, the government participates in multiple politico-military interactions, which include military exercises, strategic dialogues, goodwill visits by chiefs of staff, foreign officer training and education, extra-territorial humanitarian assistance and disaster relief operations and weapons procurement (Dutta, 2009; Jaishankar, 2016). Appreciating the significance of defence diplomacy, India created the 'Directorate of International Defence Co-operation' within the IDS in 2007, to channel its global politico-military engagements. The directorate's website states that 'India uses the Armed Forces to further India's national interests by contributing proactively to achieve international peace and security as well as creating conducive conditions for accelerating India's ongoing transformation' (Ministry of Defence, Government of India, 2021).

Ideologically, India defines its military–diplomatic policy through the lens of 'strategic autonomy', which allows the country to maintain its longstanding policy of non-alignment while seeking beneficial foreign partnerships across geopolitical fissures. Prime Minister Modi's government comprehends India's unique strategic position and has made a concerted effort to link India's foreign policy postures with its national security policy. Compared to other areas of civil–military interactions, defence diplomacy has been a bright spot of success. According to Jaishankar (2016, p 21), this is because 'unlike many other aspects of military preparedness, which are based to a certain degree on strategic foresight, military diplomacy tends to be more demand-driven and commensurate with Indian interests and extant capabilities.' Presently, in the domain of defence diplomacy, the government is prioritizing its engagement with countries in the Indo-Pacific to better manoeuvre the region's changing security dynamics.

India's strategic outreach in the Indo-Pacific

India's enunciation of its role as a net security provider in the Indian Ocean comes at a time when the strategic concept of Indo-Pacific is being proclaimed as the new framework for maritime security dynamics in Asia. To this effect, India's politico-military diplomacy in the Indo-Pacific finds its essence in engaging different partners on maritime security. The maritime arena grants numerous opportunities for cooperation, ranging from port visits to joint naval exercises, to foster familiarity between India and its strategic partners. Over the years, India has sharply accelerated its naval contacts in the region, specifically focusing on Indian Ocean island nations. Concomitantly, it has expanded cooperation with major

Indo-Pacific naval powers such as Australia, Japan, the United States, France and Indonesia, by conducting routine naval exercises and instituting dialogue mechanisms on maritime security (Mukherjee, 2019). The maritime domain is important to both littoral and non-resident nations, as they all want to ensure unimpeded navigation on the high seas. An important institution to this end is the Indian Ocean Naval Symposium, which was established in 2008 to foster cooperation and exchange between littoral states of the Indian Ocean. The symposium provides India with a platform to enhance maritime cooperation with naval professionals in the Indian Ocean region and seek politico-military solutions to regionally relevant maritime issues (Indian Ocean Naval Symposium, 2021). Likewise, an important component of India's maritime outreach is its maritime information sharing hub – the IFC-IOR (Information Fusion Centre-Indian Ocean Region) which supports regional maritime domain awareness operations with real-time information on shipping. To this end, the Indian Navy has secured White Shipping agreements with several nations and also hosts international liaison officers from multiple foreign nations, including maritime security partners such as Japan, France and the U.S. The IFC-IOR substantiates India's position as a regional security provider by helping mitigate local security challenges while supporting the larger objective of maintaining sea-control over the IOR (Peri 2020b; Indian Navy, 2021).

Another example of India's defence diplomacy thrust in the Indo-Pacific is the Malabar naval exercise. Initially, a bilateral venture between India and the United States, the training exercise has recently expanded to include the naval forces of Japan and Australia. Effectively, the Malabar exercise mirrors the security consultations between the four nations under the Quadrilateral Security Dialogue mechanism, which seeks to establish a 'Free and Open Indo-Pacific', through policy coordination and naval interoperability. This compact is especially significant given China's belligerent attitude towards its maritime neighbours in the South China Sea, where it has coerced nations by militarizing artificial islands and restricting access to common maritime territory. Accordingly, India's approach to defence diplomacy in Southeast Asia aims to bring it closer to countries that share its apprehensions about China's growing naval might. Apart from providing these countries a line of credit for the purchase of defence equipment, India has also initiated defence cooperation with multiple Southeast Asian nations for joint training of officers. Given that India's military diplomacy approach has strong underpinnings in officer-to-officer contact, it would benefit India to improve the quality of its officer training programmes, since consequently countries would logically be attracted to increase their strategic engagement with New Delhi (Jaishankar, 2016).

Net importer of defence equipment

Defence diplomacy in India has also articulated itself through weapons procurement from foreign nations. India's strategic proximity to a partner nation has at times been exhibited through valuable purchases of high-end military assets from them. This trend can be traced back to the Cold War era, when India's strategic closeness to the Soviet Union coupled with its underdeveloped indigenous defence industry, led to Soviet weapons being licensed for production in India. This parochial attitude of building relations with major defence partners by complementing them with weapons purchases continue. The procurement of Rafale fighter jets from France, P8-I maritime surveillance aircraft from the United States and the S-400 Triumf missile defence system from Russia conform to this narrative. These weapons purchases serve as a critical element of India's strategic cooperation with these countries. For example, India's growing strategic relationship with the United States has been accompanied by an increase in the supply of defence equipment from Washington to New Delhi. Both countries have lately increased their strategic engagement by signing 'foundational agreements' on military cooperation and instituted the 2+2 dialogue mechanism to conjoin their defence and diplomatic approaches (Ministry of External Affairs, Government of India, 2020; Philip 2020b). Expectedly, these developments in the strategic relationship were accompanied by a visible uptick in India's weapons procurement from the United States (The Times of India, 2020).

Military effectiveness in India

Traditionally, the parameter to measure India's military effectiveness has been determined by its armed forces' success on the battlefield, especially against Pakistan and its terrorist proxies. As Narang and Staniland contend, 'Pakistan is both a high-salience issue in Indian politics and the public also overwhelmingly views Pakistan as a serious threat' (Narang and Staniland, 2018, p 20). Comparatively, they argue, '[d]efence acquisition and procurement is generally an area … even when it comes to provisioning against Pakistan and China, where both political salience and public clarity surrounding the issue is low' (Narang and Staniland, 2018, p 30). Because of this indifferent mindset, institutions in India have not prioritized any reform in procurement mechanisms despite having multiple committees set up to improve procurement effectiveness. According to Mukherjee, 'it is the pattern of interaction between civilians and the military combined with the processes within their organizations that contribute to long delays, misplaced priorities, wasteful expenditure, and sub-optimal weapons' in India's procurement process (Mukherjee, 2020, p 97).

Weapons procurement

India's weapons procurement has a long history of fostering military inefficiency (Cohen and Dasgupta, 2010; Bitzinger, 2018; Mukherjee, 2020). Traditionally, indigenous defence procurement in India is routed through state-owned enterprises which include eight large government-owned defence public sector undertakings and 41 ordinance factories (Bitzinger, 2018, p 133). The research and development are done by another government agency – the Defence Research and Development Organization [DRDO], which runs 52 laboratories. Despite having such a sizeable indigenous defence industrial base, India has failed to develop critical weapons systems on its own. Cohen and Dasgupta have even argued that the 'DRDO has not delivered a single major weapon system to the armed forces in five decades of existence' (Cohen and Dasgupta, 2010, p 32). The deficiency in indigenization indicates an absence of clarity and foresight on the part of India's defence industrial base. Comparably, among the armed forces, there exists an inclination to repeatedly amend the technical specifications of its weapons requirements, further lengthening the procurement process (Mukherjee, 2020). Legacy procurement projects such as the Tejas Light Combat Aircraft, Netra Airborne Early Warning and Control System, Astra Air to Air Missile system, Arjun Main Battle Tank, Close Quarter Battle Carbines and so on, have all failed to follow pre-determined timelines, with many of these prototype weapons systems encountering protracted technical glitches. This ultimately results in the nation's continued dependence on imported military assets and technology to meet the requirements of its armed forces.

To this end, Prime Minister Modi launched the 'Make in India' programme to stimulate the defence industrial base. The programme aims to instigate greater involvement of private companies in defence production. According to Mukherjee, under Modi, 'the government brought clarity in granting industrial licenses, tried to level the field between public and private sectors, increased the automatic foreign direct investment limit to 49%, simplified rules for offsets and public-private partnerships, and made it easier to export defence material' (Mukherjee, 2020, p 121). While such developments suggest a positive change, India's present weapons procurement strategy is still unable to meet its military's needs.

During the 2020–21 border skirmish with China, the government accorded emergency procurement mechanisms to the military, mirroring a similar exercise in the aftermath of the Uri attacks in 2016 (Philip, 2020a). Such instances of ad-hoc weapons procurement during security crises reveal the absence of an integrated defence planning process. Similarly, India has revised its military acquisition handbook 8 times in the last 18 years, indicating a persistent lack of clarity in incubating a successful defence acquisition ecosystem (Singh, 2021). Defence analyst Sushant Singh painted a grim picture when he alluded to the fact that 'India is completely unprepared in the event of a two-front conflict with Pakistan and China … ammunition stocks are below the minimum acceptable risk level [that is] meant to last 20 days of warfighting, and certain types of ammunition were not sufficient for even 10 days of intense warfighting' (Singh, 2020). In the future if India wants to possess a combat effective military, the civilian leadership needs to address such capability gaps and remedy the cumbersome procurement process.

The civilian bureaucracy

Existing literature suggests that the over-arching powers accorded to the civilian bureaucracy in India's civil–military relationship is the main detriment to military effectiveness (Cohen and Dasgupta, 2010; Narang and Staniland, 2018; Mukherjee, 2020). The civilian bureaucracy, which lacks the technical expertise of the military and the political legitimacy of the elected government, is delegated with considerable authority by the political leadership in areas of defence planning, weapons procurement and budgetary outlays. However, in its directive to ensure civilian control over the armed forces, the bureaucracy has over time established maladroit institutional procedures restricting the military's involvement in key policy decisions, resulting in a weak system of defence management (Ray, 2015, p 57). This institutional structure erodes inter-agency coordination and essentially handicaps India's ability to translate its resources into military effectiveness. At a time when the nation's defence leadership is charting a new course to accomplish its strategic objectives, it is imperative that this institutional arrangement that impedes military effectiveness be reformulated. The appointment of the CDS is a step in that direction. The presence of the CDS as the head of the Department of Military Affairs in the Ministry of Defence has the potential to bridge the gap between the bureaucracy and the military and ameliorate inter-agency coordination. However, in the long-term, procedural controls that have become commonplace under the sway of oversight mechanisms need to be replaced with a system that catalyses the smooth conduct of defence policy, without compromising accountability measures.

Conclusion

This chapter has examined the current state of civil–military relations in India and illustrated the different factors that have hindered military effectiveness and efficiency. The most significant among them is the institutional structure of civil–military interactions. As explicated in the chapter, India remains rooted in 'Huntingtonian' paradigms that advocate separate domains for the political leadership and the military (Huntington, 1957). This separation of roles has over time been institutionalized and legitimized to a degree where procedures have taken precedence over the tangible enhancement of military capability. Although there have been successful instances of collaboration between the civilian leadership and the military brass, their overall relationship has been strained by a bureaucracy that continuously seeks to protect its own role in India's civil–military arrangement.

The evolutionary transformation in India's civil–military relations is characterized by the ever-changing relationship between these three forces that constitute its higher defence management. At different points in time, the organizational structure of its defence decision-making has been reflective of the shifting nature of this complicated arrangement, rendering the Huntington–Feaver model insufficient to fully discern the evolution of India's civil–military relations. Making progress, scholars attempting to understand India's civil–military relations need to widen their scope to include paradigms that are better able to answer questions that deal with the multiple roles assigned to the Indian military apparatus by the civilian leadership and incorporate local factors. The central focus of any body of work examining India's civil–military relations should be able to clearly answer if any processes, procedures or structures exist at the expense of the military's fundamental role as the protector of the polity.

Revisiting the central question posited at the beginning of this chapter, the authors attempted to understand how India can achieve military effectiveness in fulfilling its self-mandated role as a regional security provider. The answer is two-fold. First, India's political leadership needs to demonstrate resolve and change deep-seated assumptions that have shaped the nature of civil–military relations in the country. Second, as a democratic nation that aims to provide regional security, India needs to be transparent with its defence policies and objectives. The fundamental assumption that civilian control and military effectiveness are exclusive, needs to be repudiated. India needs to invoke more acuity in its defence policy making and condition institutions towards achieving time-bound objectives. To this end, the government needs to introduce better accountability mechanisms for weapons procurement, improve budgetary spending through sophisticated monitoring and evaluation practices, and most important of all, recruit civilians with specialized competency to the defence bureaucracy. In the future, India's aim for the defence planning process should be to incubate a continuous dialogue between the various stakeholders of India's defence management. Such a dialogue will help cultivate jointness in defence decision-making and create congruity between financial planning and force structuring. Likewise, the government needs to release its national security strategy for public scrutiny to create transparency on defence policy. In the same vein, the government also needs to clearly communicate India's agenda for regional security. The world needs to unambiguously understand what India's manifesto of being a security provider in the Indian Ocean region entails.

Civil–military relations in India are currently going through a period of transformation, wherein the different components of India's defence leadership are coming together to synergize their internal functions to generate greater effectiveness of the armed forces. By undertaking long-pending reforms, Modi's government has demonstrated explicit intent to the military and the civilian bureaucracy. His government has repeatedly promoted indigenization as a solution to India's defence problems, whether it be indigenization of the weapons industry, defence technology or developing an indigenous approach to military doctrines (Kartha, 2021). Such an approach is crucial at a time when technological progress is fundamentally altering the definition of military effectiveness. Armed forces are increasingly leaning towards doctrines suited for network-centric warfare, adapting new concepts of tactics and strategy to their force structures. While India has already embarked on this process by establishing agencies tailored to this new generation of warfare, it needs to develop critical civilian expertise for skilful tactical and strategic management of network-centric operations. India will also need to develop technological capabilities that seamlessly integrate information sharing among its different services and agencies. For India's security strategy to succeed in this technology-driven ecosystem, the political leadership, the civilian bureaucracy and the armed forces need to work together to improve the transmission of political objectives into military capability. This necessitates the dissolution of the functional boundaries that currently separate the various factions of India's higher defence management.

Notes

[1] India's first CDS, General Bipin Rawat, died in a helicopter accident on 8th December 2021. His successor, General Anil Chauhan, was appointed on 30th September 2022. This gap of more than 9 months in the appointment of the CDS created a vacuum in civil–military relations as there was no pre-established order of succession for India's top military office. After General Rawat's death, the Chief of Army Staff General Manoj Mukund Naravane assumed the position of Chairman of the Chiefs of Staff Committee, which was supposed to be held by the CDS. Subsequently, on General Naravane's superannuation on 30th April 2022, even that post fell vacant. Essentially, until General Chauhan's appointment, the Indian government was without a principal military advisor for five months. These developments cast serious aspersions on the government's willingness to reform India's civil–military relations. Most importantly, General Rawat's plans to implement theatre-based commands hangs in the balance, and it is up to General Chauhan to take this agenda forward. This uncertainty is unbecoming of a nation of India's stature that faces multiple security challenges and is attempting a fundamental transformation in its civil–military relations. For future stability, the government needs to institute a better standard operating procedure for the CDS' line of succession (Bedi, 2022; Singh, 2022; Peri, 2022).

2   Defence Review Committees instituted in India after the Kargil War: Kargil Review Committee (1999), Report of the Group of Ministers on National Security (2001), Naresh Chandra Committee (2012), Shekatkar Committee (2015).

References

Bedi, R. (2022) 'Is the Centre Quietly Trying Do Away With the Post of Chief of Defence Staff?', *The Wire*, [online] 15 September, Available from: https://thewire.in/government/chief-of-defence-staff-end-of-the-road-government-bipin-rawat [Accessed 12 October 2022].

Behera, L. (2018) 'Creation of defence planning committee: a step towards credible defence preparedness', *Institute for Defence Studies and Analyses*, [online] 19 April, Available from: https://idsa.in/idsacomments/creation-of-defence-planning-committee-lkbehera-190418 [Accessed 7 April 2021].

Bitzinger, R. (2018) 'India's defence industrial base: decay and reform', in S. Ganguly, N. Blarel and M.S. Pardesi (eds) *The Oxford Handbook of India's National Security*, New Delhi: Oxford University Press, pp 132–48.

Bruneau, T. and Florina, M. (eds) (2013) *The Routledge Handbook of Civil–Military Relations*, Abingdon: Routledge.

Chari, P. (1977) 'Civil military relations in India', *Armed Forces and Society*, 4(1): 3–28.

Chatterjee, A. (2013) 'Shifting lines of governance and in insurgencies: India', in T.C. Bruneau and F.C. Matei (eds) *The Routledge Handbook of Civil–Military Relations*, Abingdon: Routledge, pp 167–80.

Cohen, S. (2001) *The Indian Army: Its Contribution to the Development of a Nation*, New Delhi: Oxford University Press.

Cohen, S. and Dasgupta, S. (2010) *Arming without Aiming: India's Military Modernization*, Washington DC: Brookings Institution Press.

Dhoundial, S. (2021) 'India likely to get air defence command, maritime command by August 15', *News 18*, [online] 30 March, Available from: www.news18.com/news/india/india-likely-to-get-air-defence-command-maritime-command-by-august-15-3589595.html [Accessed April 7 2021].

Dutta, A. (2009) 'Role of India's defence cooperation initiatives in meeting the foreign policy goals', *Journal of Defence Studies*, 3(3): 31–47, [online], Available from: https://idsa.in/system/files/jds_3_3_adutta.pdf [Accessed April 7 2021].

Dutta, A. (2020) 'Joint training command for Army, Navy & IAF in the works, Nagpur the likely base', *The Print*, [online] 18 March, Available from: https://theprint.in/defence/joint-training-command-for-army-navy-iaf-in-the-works-nagpur-the-likely-base/382427/ [Accessed April 7 2021].

Feaver, P. (1999) 'Civil military relations', *Annual Review of Political Science*, 2(1): 211–41.

Feaver, P. (2003) *Armed Servants: Agency, Oversight and Civil Military Relations*, Cambridge, MA: Harvard University Press.

Ganguly, S., Blarel, S. and Pardesi, M.S. (eds) (2018) *The Oxford Handbook of India's National Security*, New Delhi: Oxford University Press.

Huntington, S. (1957) *The Soldier and the State: The Theory and Politics of Civil–Military Relations*, Cambridge, MA: Harvard University Press.

Indian Navy (2021) 'Information Fusion Center-Indian Ocean Region', *Indian Navy Government of India*, [online] nd, Available from: https://www.indiannavy.nic.in/ifc-ior/about-us.html [Accessed 7 April 2021].

Indian Ocean Naval Symposium (2021) 'Indian Ocean Naval Symposium', *Indian Ocean Naval Symposium*, [online] nd, Available from: http://www.ions.global/ [Accessed 7 April 2021].

Jaishankar, D. (2016) 'India's military diplomacy', in S. Singh and P. Das (eds) *Defence Primer: India at 75*, Observer Research Foundation, pp 18–24, [online], Available from: https://www.orfonline.org/wp-content/uploads/2016/03/Military_Layout-.pdf [Accessed April 7 2021].

Joshi, S., and Rej, A. (2018) 'India's joint doctrine: a lost opportunity', *Observer Research Foundation*, Occasional Paper No 139, [online], Available from: https://www.orfonline.org/research/india-joint-doctrine-lost-opportunity/ [Accessed 7 April 2021].

Kartha, T. (2021) 'Modi is right about indigenous defence doctrine: Army staff colleges cannot keep studying US', *The Print*, [online] 5 April, Available from: https://theprint.in/opinion/modi-is-right-about-indigenous-defence-doctrine-army-staff-colleges-cant-keep-studying-us/633538/ [Accessed 7 April 2021].

Ministry of Defence, Government of India (2017) 'Joint doctrine Indian Armed Forces', Integrated Defence Staff, Ministry of Defence, Government of India, [online] April, Available from: www.ids.nic.in/IDSAdmin/upload_images/doctrine/JointDoctrineIndianArmedForces2017.pdf [Accessed 7 April, 2021].

Ministry of Defence, Government of India (2021) 'International defence co-operation', *Integrated Defence Staff, Ministry of Defence, Government of India*, [online] nd, Available from: https://ids.nic.in/international-defence-co-operation.php [Accessed 7 April 2021].

Ministry of External Affairs, Government of India (2020) 'Joint Statement on the Third India-US 2+2 Ministerial Dialogue', *Ministry of External Affairs, Government of India*, [online] 27 October, Available from: www.mea.gov.in/bilateral-documents.htm?dtl/33145/Joint_Statement_on_the_third_IndiaUS_2432_Ministerial_Dialogue [1 May 2022].

Mukherjee, A. (2020) *The Absent Dialogue: Politicians, Bureaucrats, and the Military in India*, New Delhi: Oxford University Press.

Mukherjee, T. (2019) 'Maritime security and India: India as a regional security provider', in H.V. Pant (ed) *India's Evolving National Security Agenda: Modi and Beyond*, New Delhi: Konark, pp 45–71.

Narang, V, and Staniland, P. (2018) 'Democratic Accountability and Foreign Security Policy: Theory and Evidence from India', *Security Studies*, 27(3): 410–47.

Negi, M. (2020) 'India's integrated air defence command to come up by October 8: Defence Ministry', *India Today*, [online] 27 August, Available from: https://www.indiatoday.in/india/story/india-s-integrated-air-defence-command-to-come-up-by-october-8-defence-ministry-1715716-2020-08-27 [Accessed 7 April 2021].

Pant, H. (2007) 'India's nuclear doctrine and command structure: implications for civil–military relations in India', *Armed Forces & Society*, 33(2): 238–64.

Peri, D. (2020a) 'How is India building up the squadron strength of its air force?', *The Hindu*, [online] 12 July, Available from: https://www.thehindu.com/news/national/the-hindu-explains-how-is-india-building-up-the-squadron-strength-of-its-air-force/article32053910.ece [Accessed 7 April 2021].

Peri, D. (2020b) 'India looks at integrating more countries into coastal radar network', *The Hindu*, [online] 20 December, Available from: www.thehindu.com/news/national/india-looks-at-integrating-more-countries-into-coastal-radar-network/article33379243.ece [Accessed 12 October 2022].

Peri, D. (2022) 'Lt. General Anil Chauhan (retd.) appointed next Chief of Defence Staff', *The Hindu*, [online] 28 September, Available from: www.thehindu.com/news/national/lt-general-anil-chauhan-appointed-as-new-cds/article65946805.ece [Accessed 12 October 2022].

Philip, S. (2020a) 'Armed forces working on 100 emergency procurement contracts amid tensions with China', *The Print*, [online] 21 July, Available from: https://theprint.in/defence/armed-forces-working-on-100-emergency-procurement-contracts-amid-tensions-with-china/465408/ [Accessed 7 April 2021].

Philip, S. (2020b) 'The 3 foundational agreements with US and what they mean for India's military growth', *The Print*, [online] 27 October 27, Available from: https://theprint.in/defence/the-3-foundational-agreements-with-us-and-what-they-mean-for-indias-military-growth/531795/ [Accessed 7 April 2021].

Raghavan, S. (2009) 'Civil–military relations in India: the China crisis and after', *Journal of Strategic Studies*, 32(1): 149–75.

Ray, A. (2015) 'Indian civil–military relations', in H.V. Pant (ed) *The Handbook of Indian Defence Policy, Themes, Structures and Doctrines*, Abingdon: Routledge, pp 48–63.

Shukla, A. (2021) 'Army's pivot to the north', *Business Standard*, [online] 7 January, Available from: www.business-standard.com/article/opinion/army-s-pivot-to-the-north-121010701572_1.html [Accessed 7 April 2021].

Singh, A. (2021) 'Indian defence procurement: righting the ship', *Observer Research Foundation*, Issue Brief No 443 [online] 10 February, Available from: www.orfonline.org/research/indian-defence-procurement-righting-the-ship/#_ednref1 [Accessed 7 April 2021].

Singh, D. (2022) 'General Naravane hangs boots, but mystery over next CDS remains', *The Hindu Business Line*, [online] 30 April, Available from: www.thehindubusinessline.com/news/general-naravane-hangs-boots-but-mystery-over-next-cds-remains/article65369968.ece [Accessed 12 October 2022].

Singh, S. (2020) 'Can India transcend its two-front challenge?', *War on the Rocks*, [online] 14 September, Available from: https://warontherocks.com/2020/09/can-india-transcend-its-two-front-challenge/ [Accessed 7 April 2021].

Tarapore, A. (2020) 'The army in Indian military strategy: rethink doctrine or risk irrelevance', *Carnegie Endowment for International Peace*, [online] 10 August, Available from: https://carnegieindia.org/2020/08/10/army-in-indian-military-strategy-rethink-doctrine-or-risk-irrelevance-pub-82426 [Accessed 7 April 2021].

Times of India (2020) 'India's weapons procurement from the US jumps to $3.4 billion in 2020', [online] 9 December, Available from: https://timesofindia.indiatimes.com/india/indias-weapons-procurement-from-the-us-jumps-to-3-4-billion-in-2020/articleshow/79637133.cms [Accessed 7 April 2021].

Unnithan, S. (2019) 'Chief of defence staff: can the new superchief call the shots', *India Today*, [online] 23 August, Available from: https://www.indiatoday.in/magazine/cover-story/story/20190902-enter-the-superchief-1590316-2019-08-23 [Accessed 7 April 2021].

Unnithan, S. (2020) 'The high seas command', *India Today*, [online] 7 December, Available from: www.indiatoday.in/magazine/special-report/story/20201207-the-high-se-as-command-1744377-2020-11-27 [Accessed 7 April 2021].

Wilkinson, S. (2015) *Army and Nation: The Military and Indian Democracy since Independence*, Ranikhet: Permanent Black.

Wilkinson, S. (2018) 'Civil–military relations', in Sumit Ganguly, Nicolas Blarel and Manjeet S. Pardesi (eds) *The Oxford Handbook of India's National Security*, New Delhi: Oxford University Press, pp 165–83.

15

Defence Diplomacy and Civil–Military Relations: The Case of Bangladesh

Rashed Uz Zaman

In late May 2020, George Floyd, a middle-aged African American was killed by police in Minneapolis, Minnesota, during an arrest for an alleged misdemeanour. The resulting outcry against the killing convulsed the United States. Its impact was felt across a world already numbed by the death and mayhem caused by the COVID-19 pandemic. While protestors made their rage felt on the streets, President Donald J. Trump threatened to use the military to bring order back to the cities. The situation took a new turn when on 1 June, the President accompanied by the US's top military officer, Chairman of Joint Chiefs of Staff Mark Milley in combat uniform, walked over for a photo opportunity in front of Washington DC's St John's Episcopal Church through an area that had just been violently cleared of demonstrators. The resulting furore led General Milley to issue a remarkable apology, admitting his presence had raised an uncomfortable perception of the US armed forces getting involved in domestic politics. While the apology put an end to the immediate uproar, the event raised questions about the state of civil–military relations in an established democracy like the US. Writing in *Foreign Policy*, one commentator forewarned that problems in civil–military relations in the country have been simmering for decades and, if the present trend of relying on the military to take sides to protect democracy continues unchecked, the future of US democracy will be imperilled (Golby, 2020).

The US example is interesting for it questions the state of civil–military relations in a country where democracy has been a stable feature for centuries and, in spite of challenges, is considered as a 'shackled Leviathan' (Acemoglu and Robinson, 2019, pp 24–7). In this connection, one may wonder about the state of civil–military relations in countries where democracy is more of a recent phenomenon and has faced many bumps on the road.

Bangladesh, the eighth most populous country in the world, and also the youngest nation-state in South Asia, is one such country. It emerged in 1971 as an independent state after a nine-month long war that devastated the country, displaced millions, and led to killings and rape on a horrific scale. Since then, the country has traversed a long and winding path which often witnessed a volatile political environment, multi-faceted challenges to governance and political violence. While critics have raised questions about the state of the country's political system, it is true that over the last one decade and a half political stability has been more the norm than experienced in the past (Fair, 2019). At the same time, the country has also been identified as a development success story with steady economic growth, a nominal current account deficit and stable macroeconomic indicators (Saez, 2018, pp 130–1). In Bangladesh's quest for political development and economic growth, its nearly 200,000 strong military remains an important factor (The International Institute for Strategic Studies, 2021). While the world is now more familiar with the image of Bangladesh's military members in United Nations peacekeeping operations (Zaman and Biswas, 2017) and its evolving domestic politics, factors like the growth and existence of the military as a potent force and its organizational and economic interests require serious and constant attention from politicians and governing elites (Hasanuzzaman, 2016, p 117). It is fitting that the Bangladesh military should be subjected to an academic study. In keeping with the guidelines set by the editors, this chapter seeks to provide answers to the following questions: How do colonial legacies influence the evolution of civil–military relations and the Bangladesh military's self-definition of vital roles? Is the Bangladesh military socially, politically, and economically embedded to the point that civil–military relations cannot be viewed as a gap between civilian and military elements? Is Bangladesh's civil–military relations equilibrium a strength in handling various facets of defence diplomacy, and in what way?

Bangladesh's military, while locating its origins in the colonial and post-colonial militaries of British India and Pakistan, has a different trajectory from both. First, the chapter explains the birth of the Bangladesh military from the British Indian and, after 1947, Pakistan militaries and the impact this evolution had on the nature of the institution and civil–military relations in post-1971 Bangladesh. The next section will highlight several cases of defence diplomacy and show how civil–military relations and certain elements of defence diplomacy have often become embedded to the point that it is difficult to identify civil–military relations in terms of a gap between the civilian and military domains in Bangladesh. In the last section, the chapter traces the pathways of Bangladesh's defence diplomacy after the COVID-19 pandemic.

Bangladesh's military: genesis and development

The beginning of the Bangladesh military goes back more than 300 years to the mercantile period of British expansion. Representatives of British commercial capital arrived on the Indian subcontinent to trade and plunder. The first army comprised Indian troops led by Europeans and these forces were organized by government-sponsored business companies such as the British East India Company (Mason, 1988). Not surprisingly, the legacy of three hundred years of British military presence in India is most apparent in the two successor establishments, the Indian Army and the Pakistan Army. The Bangladesh military, tracing its origins from both these institutions, shares both similarities and differences with them and it will be helpful to discern such features for properly understanding civil–military relations in Bangladesh.

At the beginning, the British Indian Army recruited from areas which first came under the domination of the British: Bombay, Madras and especially Bengal. However, after the Sepoy Mutiny of 1857, most of the Bengal Army units were disbanded and a freeze on recruitment from this area was imposed until 1910 (Lindquist, 1977, p 10; Omissi, 1994, pp 6–10). At the same time, the British developed the myth of the martial races which was to have a profound impact upon the development of the military and civil–military relations on the Indian subcontinent.

Lord Roberts of Kandahar, who served as commander-in-chief of the Indian Army from 1885 to 1893, can be credited with (or blamed for) introducing the policy fostering this myth. Roberts' theory of the military superiority of certain Indian classes never waned and continued long after the British left India (Cohen, 2001, pp 45–7; Wilkinson, 2015). Acting on this principle, most recruitment for the British Indian army from the latter part of the 19th century onwards was carried out in India's northwest regions from among the Punjabis, Pathans, Dogras, Jats and the Gurkhas of Nepal (Lindquist, 1977, p 10; Nawaz, 2008, pp 11–13; Caplan, 2010) that were considered as vigorous, courageous and warlike. At the same time, other 'races' were identified as not possessing the required martial spirit and the Bengalis were placed in this category.

The newly formed Pakistan Army which emerged from the 1947 partition of the Indian subcontinent continued to adhere to the myth of the martial races. As Cohen points out, the Pakistan Army in the years 1947–71 was ethnically more imbalanced than the British Indian or Indian Army of the same period, as people from East Bengal, which became a part of Pakistan and was subsequently called East Pakistan, were grossly under-represented in the Pakistan Army. In fact, many Pakistani officers regarded the Bengalis as particularly unsuited for military life (Cohen, 2001, p 193; Cloughley, 2016, pp 146–7). The Pakistan Army, therefore, continued the British tradition of recruiting mainly from the 'martial races' of West Punjab and North-West Frontier Province. The result of such a recruitment policy was obvious. In spite of the fact that the Bengalis made up more than 50 per cent of Pakistan's population, they were a paltry 5 per cent in the military elite (Jahan, 1994, pp 24–6). Bare numbers tell the story. Out of 897 officers holding the rank of major or above in the Pakistan Army in 1956 only 15 were Bengalis, the majority of them majors (Rizvi, 2000, pp 128–9; Maniruzzaman, 2003, p 7).

Such discrimination, along with lopsided economic development, rankled Bengali political elites. The sense of alienation experienced by the Bengalis had deep roots in the way the Pakistan state was constituted and dominated from the West Pakistani side. The inability of the Bengalis who formed the majority population of Pakistan to secure a meaningful and balanced representation in the two main non-elected institutions of the state – the military and the civilian bureaucracy – was made worse by the fact that democratic political processes were derailed in the 1950s and never got back on track. The politics of exclusion and the economies of inequality forced Bengalis to push, at first, for provincial autonomy. The struggle between Bengali politics and the imperatives of the civil–military bureaucratic state which existed in undivided Pakistan proved irreconcilable and contributed ultimately to the armed struggle for independence in 1971 (Alavi, 1972, pp 76–81; Bose and Jalal, 2004, pp 177–81).

Bangladesh was born in a war and so was its army. When the Pakistan Army began to move against the Bengali population on the night of 25 March 1971, its first objective was to disarm the Bengali units of the Pakistan Army. These units comprised six battalions of the East Bengal Regiment (EBR), numbering about 6,000 men. In addition, there were 13–14,000 lightly armed troops of the border security force, the East Pakistan Rifles (Lindquist, 1977, p 11). Disarming these units proved more difficult than expected and resulted in a good number of Bengali officers and men taking up arms against the Pakistan state. It was around this nucleus of trained fighters that the Bangladesh independence movement gathered and gelled into a fighting force (Maniruzzaman, 2003, pp 103–25; Raghavan, 2013).

The 1971 war obliterated the distinction between soldiers and civilians and erased the traditional barriers between officers and ordinary troops. A sense of brotherhood forged during the War of Liberation replaced the conventional armed forces' traditional hierarchy. Such bonds, tempered by the heat of a vicious conflict, turned the majority of soldiers into an exclusive fraternity that posed a serious challenge to the peacetime civilian and military chains of command when these were restored after the war. As Ahmed notes, 'participation in the war was a political act and had fully politicized them' (Ahmed, 1995, p 8). What would be the role, if any, of such soldiers in the development of the newly independent country was a question to which there were no quick or easy answers.

To such a politically conscious military was added another unique characteristic: the issue of 'repatriated' officers and soldiers, Bengali servicemen who were confined in West Pakistan and could not take part in the war (Codron, 2007). A total of 28,000 (including 1,100 officers) were 'repatriates' and their arrival from Pakistan virtually doubled the Bangladesh Army's ranks overnight and added to the military's skillset (Ali, 2010, p 105). Their return, however, was not easily accepted and led to resentment and divisions within the newly formed armed forces of Bangladesh (Baxter and Rahman, 1991, p 44; Riaz, 2016, p 60). Moreover, the officers and men carried with them a strong anti-Indian attitude and this was to have important consequences for the future of Bangladesh-India relations (Mohsin, 1992, p 65).

The problems faced by the Bangladesh military did not stay confined within the controversy over the nature of the officer class. Difficulties also arose over the characteristics of the military itself. One group of officers and troops favoured the retention of the conventional army patterned after the British Indian and Pakistan armies (Milam, 2010, p 36). This group, comprising mostly 'repatriates', were deemed to be holding conservative viewpoints, and a strong distrust of India shaped by training in the Pakistan Military Academy (PMA) and service in the Pakistan armed forces (Kabir, 1999, p 43). This group's views on the future of the Bangladesh military were opposed by many of the soldiers and officers who had taken part in the 1971 war. For them, a return to the norms and behaviour of a conventional army establishment was unacceptable. Participation in the war had fully politicized them and influenced their opinion and respect for the command and allegiance found in traditional armies. Added to this volatility was the emergence of a group within the military that advocated removal of the trappings of the old order and aimed to form a classless military that was to engage in construction and productive tasks so as not to be a burden on the peasantry (Lindquist, 1977, p 13; Ahmed, 2014). The majority of this group joined the underground wing of *Jatiya Samajtantrik Dal* (JSD), a leftist party, and formed cells of *Biplobi Shainik Sangstha* (Revolutionary Soldiers' Association) on the pattern of the 'Soviet of Soldiers' which had emerged in the Tsarist Russian Army prior to the 1917 Revolution. The growth of such a leftist group within the armed forces was an unprecedented development in the military annals of South Asia (Maniruzzaman, 2003, p 173). These cleavages and rancour within the Bangladesh military along with the challenges to governance in the newly formed state led to a profound sense of disillusionment. It was under such circumstances that Bangladesh experienced a series of coups, counter-coups, uprisings and disturbances which led to bloodshed and political uncertainty (Islam, 1984; Khondker, 1986; Riaz, 2016, pp 59–75).

From the mid-1980s, Bangladesh experienced relative stability and this also influenced the military. As the years progressed, both the military and, after the restoration of democracy in 1990, democratic rulers took measures to alleviate the concerns of the military. A good salary, lucrative fringe benefits and the prospect of rapid promotion within an expanding military all helped to keep the armed forces reasonably satisfied (Hakim, 1998, p 286). Since 1982, the country has not experienced any military coup which has led to regime change and in spite of a raucous political atmosphere, the military has refrained from directly assuming control over the levers of the state. In 1996 and in 2013–14, when political turbulence badly affected the country and speculation was rife about an imminent coup, the military refused to carry it out and insisted on political solutions to the crisis. In 2007, the military did intervene but acted in an indirect manner and left a façade of civilian rule in place during the two-year-long hiatus (Lorch, 2017, pp 192–6).

While the academic debate on the trajectory of the Bangladesh military continues, politics in the country has moved at a fast pace that has put civil–military relations in a new light. Turning a page on Bangladesh's tumultuous past, the Fifteenth Amendment Bill was passed by parliament on 30 June 2011. Among other laws, the Bill added one provision to the constitution: Article 7A. Given the country's past experience with violent political transfers, Article 7A declares any attempt to abrogate or suspend the constitution an act of sedition, punishable by death (Riaz, 2016, pp 91–2). Supporters of the amendment believe that this clause will shut the door to extra-constitutional moves and democracy's journey may continue unimpeded. Of course, this does not mean the importance of the military is in any way underestimated. Fair notes how the present prime minister, who is serving her third consecutive term in office and is the daughter of the country's founding father Bangabandhu Sheikh Mujibur Rahman (who was assassinated by members of the military on 15 August 1975), has reiterated her close ties with the military and commitment to ensure the development of the country's armed forces (Wolf, 2013, p 34; Fair, 2019, p 126). Also, the political system cannot disregard the fact that the military is a powerful bloc and one of the all-important factors in any power calculation. This has strong implications for civil–military relations. Looking at the country's chequered political history, one observer noted that attempts were never made to design civil–military relations in such a manner to ensure objective control of the military and this has resulted in a political culture where control over the military by political authority has always been 'subjective' with no clear boundary of military activism (Kabir, 1999, p 170).

The Bangladesh military has gradually undergone significant changes in the 50 years of its existence. One is the identification of the military as an institution that represents the people. Since its creation, the military has expanded its recruitment base and became a geographically, economically, ethnically, and religiously representative force. As the Bangladesh military – a key provider of social advancement and other benefits – became more accessible it came to represent greater national cohesion. It is interesting to note that in united Pakistan, the image of the Punjabi-dominated military was such that Bengalis more often than not perceived it as an alien entity and showed little interest in joining it. The number of applications received from Bengalis was strikingly much less than those from West Pakistan (Fair and Nawaz, 2011, p 75). In an independent country, the situation has changed and officers and troops of the Bangladesh military, though moulded differently due to the very nature of the military profession, are an integral part of the Bangladeshi society and 'watches the same television programmes and listens to the same music as society at large' (Tarafdar, 2020). Moreover, with the broadening of the recruitment base has also come the issue of how, in many parts of the world, today's serving men and women perceive the military more as an occupation than as an institution (Moskos, 1977). The Bangladesh military is no exception to this trend (Tarafdar, 2020) with the current recruitment of the Bangladesh Army being more heterogeneous than earlier. At the same time, the tendency to respect the chain of command as set by the constitution has gained deep roots within the institution. Also, as the PMA commissioned officer corps have retired from service and graduates of the Bangladesh Military Academy (BMA), which was set up in 1974, rose up the ranks and took command of the military, the issue of 'freedom fighters vs. repatriate officers' and the factionalism which it caused within the military has disappeared. While professional competition will continue as a feature common to all institutions, the disappearance of a strong contentious issue has positive implications for civil–military relations. The participation of the Bangladesh military in UN peacekeeping is also seen as yet another positive step for the consolidation and preservation of democracy and improved civil–military relations (Kabir, 1999, p 254). It is in this context that the next section discusses defence diplomacy under which such peacekeeping operations are carried out and analyses how and to what extent civil–military relations in Bangladesh has influenced defence diplomacy.

Bangladesh: the tides of defence diplomacy

Defence diplomacy has increasingly come to play an important role in the world of diplomacy. While defence diplomacy's origins lie in the classic military diplomacy practised since ancient times, it is only in the 1990s in a changing world of complex interdependence, plurality of actors and the advent of public diplomacy, that a new and expanded conception of defence diplomacy emerged (Cheyre, 2013, p 374). The concept is not easy to define and one author warns that while military diplomacy and defence diplomacy are often used interchangeably, they have different meanings (Du Plessis, 2008, p 93). Moreover, at present, defence diplomacy's civilian facets are increasingly pursued by their military counterparts and have further complicated the definitional issue between the two types of diplomacy (Tan, 2016, p 594). The chapter takes into cognizance the definitional ambiguity but for the sake of clarity sets the parameter that defence diplomacy is one of the tools used in the conduct of a country's foreign policy. Defence diplomatic activities are conducted in tandem with the general foreign policy guidelines set by the state and guided, first and foremost, by its national strategic interests (El Morabety, 2017, p 241). The traditional aspects of defence diplomacy, that is, the placement of defence attachés, exchange of visits between military teams, as well as conferences on military and security issues, are practised by Bangladesh. However, while such practices are important, they say little about Bangladesh's defence diplomacy and its ties with civil–military relations. Therefore, the chapter discusses several case studies where the military was a factor to further Bangladesh's vital interests. The case studies span the five decades since the country's inception and took place under both democratic and military regimes. Defence diplomacy has been a part of Bangladesh's diplomatic repertoire since the very beginning and the selected cases had far-reaching implications for the country. The following discussion will shed light on the link between civil–military relations and defence diplomacy.

Defence diplomacy: the early years (1971–75)

In order to understand the position of the Bangladesh military in society, this chapter draws attention to an important event in the history of the military. Curiously, this event has largely been overlooked in the existing literature on civil–military relations in Bangladesh.

The passing-out ceremony of the Gentlemen Cadets (GC) of the 1st BMA Short Course took place on 11 January 1975 at Cumilla Cantonment, where the Academy was temporarily situated. The Father of the Nation, Bangabandhu Sheikh Mujibur Rahman, who was the prime minister and head of the government, was the chief guest and took the salute of the graduating cohort. A brief speech was given by Bangabandhu on the occasion and in it he firmly set the tone for the pattern of civil–military relations in the country. Addressing the cadets, Bangabandhu made it clear that they should never forget that they were a part of the Bangladeshi society and a 'public force' (Rahman, 1975). He reminded them that unlike other armies, they were not to be a professional army but a people's army. It is the common people who paid taxes that sustained the armed forces and the newly minted officers were urged to note the common people comprised their own parents and siblings. The military was not to be the master of the people but to serve the people (Rahman, 1975).

The speech is important as it charts a course for the military. It should be emphasized that the call not to be a professional army did not imply an army that lacked proper training, a strict chain of command or equipment. Rather, coming at the end of the Bengali people's unhappy experience with the military–bureaucratic state called Pakistan, it was a vision for a military that would epitomize the aspirations and will of the people of Bangladesh. A vital aspect of the speech was the emphasis on the symbiotic relationship between the Bangladeshi society and the military and, of course, this only serves to reinforce the idea that it is not possible to separate the military and politics in a democratic setting. It is interesting to note that US President John F. Kennedy often spoke of the need for the US military's future leaders to study economics, politics, diplomacy and history along with military studies as they were expected to play a constructive role in national politics (Slater, 1977, p 104). Bangabandhu's 1975 speech found a theoretical shape when, years later, a political theorist observed that it is not possible to separate politics from the army (Barany, 2012, p 16). It is a political institution and there is no such thing as an apolitical military. The focus should be on 'democratic army', an organization that is not partisan but supports the principles of democratic governance (Barany, 2012, p 16). For this chapter, it is important to note that Bangladesh under Bangabandhu Sheikh Mujib's government had already used the military as a tool to further the country's foreign policy goals. How this was done is described in the following paragraphs.

Bangladesh's emergence from united Pakistan, an Islamic state, had not gone down well with many Muslim countries and diplomatic recognition of the new state had been withheld for some time. For Bangladesh it was imperative to change this state of affairs and the 1973 Arab-Israeli war offered an opportunity to do so. As soon as the war broke out, Bangladesh not only sent a message of support to Egypt but also decided to send tea and an army medical unit to Syria, both of which were needed at the front. The supplies went to Syria via Libya and the army medical unit landed in Lebanon and quickly joined the action. The 28-member team comprising seven officers and 21 men of other ranks were deployed four kilometres west of Damascus and set up a field hospital there. During its month-long stay at the hospital the team provided medical treatment to both military and civilian casualties (Sarwar, 2016, pp 763–5). The result of Bangladesh's adroit use of military diplomacy was not long in coming. Egypt and Syria gave diplomatic recognition to Bangladesh promptly, followed within days by Kuwait and Jordan. The frosty climate brought on by false propaganda spread in the Middle East about Bangladesh's status dissipated rapidly and relations flourished (Hossain, 2013, p 189; Majumder, 2021). The normalization of ties with the Muslim world was sought both by the government and the people of the country, the majority of whom profess the Muslim faith. The unstinting support provided by Bangabandhu Sheikh Mujibur Rahman to the Muslim countries and the Palestinian cause reflected the feeling of the majority and is an interesting but seldom discussed early example of synchronization of civil–military relations and defence diplomacy in Bangladesh.

From August 1975, Bangladesh went through a turbulent phase and entered a period of nearly 15 years of military rule under Lieutenant General Ziaur Rahman (1975–81) and Lieutenant General H.M. Ershad (1982–90) until the restoration of democracy in December 1990. The next section scrutinizes this period under the lens of defence diplomacy.

Defence diplomacy under military rulers (1975–90)

While India's role in the 1971 war had been pivotal, events during the war and in its aftermath cast an ominous shadow over Bangladesh's relations with India. The mainstream media portrayal of the 1971 war as an Indo-Pakistan war, the absence of Bangladesh's top military official at the surrender ceremony of the Pakistan Army's Eastern Command and the fate of arms and ammunition surrendered by members of the Pakistan armed forces all seemed to point to high-handedness on the part of India. This added fuel to a lingering anti-Indian attitude both in the civil and military sectors of the society, a legacy of two and a half decades of Pakistani rule (Rahman, 2016, p 379). Issues of smuggling, construction of a dam on one of the important transboundary rivers and a cooperation and friendship treaty signed hurriedly did not help in dissipating the mounting distrust of a powerful and overbearing neighbour. The administration of Bangabandhu was able to keep these feelings under wraps. With his assassination in August 1975 and the subsequent military takeover, domestic and foreign policies of the two countries no longer converged. Rather, the new military ruler Ziaur Rahman, whose power base in the mid-1970s lay in a military which harboured strong anti-Indian feelings, had ample opportunities to ride on this popular fear of a hegemonic and hostile India, and he had no qualms in doing so. Jacques argues that regardless of Zia's true intentions towards India, the deeply ingrained distrust prevailing within Bangladesh swamped the precariously balanced ties between the two countries and Zia could not take any course in foreign policy which would appear as pro-Indian (Jacques, 2000, p 102). As a natural corollary, the Zia regime sought to build strong ties with China to lessen the influence of the 'India factor' in Bangladesh (Yasmin, 2016, p 393). China did not disappoint Ziaur Rahman nor the military and civilian governments that followed him. Over the past few decades, the civil and military elites of Bangladesh came to view China as a balancer against India and an alternate source of military and economic aid and a trading partner. China has emerged as the largest supplier of military hardware to Bangladesh (Jain, 2017, p 191; Diplomatic Risk Intelligence, 2021), and though Sheikh Hasina's government is perceived to be friendlier to India than any other regime since 1975, defence diplomacy engagement with China has remained one of the most important pillars of Bangladesh's foreign policy.

President Zia was assassinated in 1981 and, after a brief democratic hiatus, the armed forces under Lieutenant General Hussain Muhammad Ershad took over in a bloodless military coup in March 1982. Hussain M. Ershad's tenure as the Chief Martial Law Administrator (CMLA) and later as president has been the subject of many studies (van Schendel, 2009, pp 194–97; Lewis, 2011, pp 85–90). In both the military regimes, the military-backed executive power dominated the judicial and legislative branches though the executive had to adjust and compromise with increasing pressure to civilianize the administration. However, in one particular instance, the military ruler, nudged by his civilian foreign minister, took a decision that went a long way in strengthening the country's defence diplomacy.

On 2 August 1990, Iraq under President Saddam Hussein invaded and occupied the small oil-rich state of Kuwait. The action shook the world and the tremors were strongly felt in South Asia. Bangladesh was no exception and with soaring oil prices, a precipitous drop in remittance sent by thousands of its nationals in Iraq, Kuwait and Saudi Arabia, the three states most affected by the crisis, and a major humanitarian crisis that entailed planning for the safe return of its citizens from the war zone, the country faced a major foreign policy challenge.

As the world scrambled to deal with the crisis, Bangladesh's General-turned-President Ershad decided to stand by Kuwait and support the US and Saudi-led military coalition against Iraq. This was a surprise as Ershad was known to be particularly close to Saddam Hussein (Khan, 2012, pp 181–2, 187). Moreover, in spite of the fact that Iraq had invaded and occupied a Muslim state, a sizeable and vocal majority of Bangladeshis supported Saddam Hussein who was seen as an Islamic hero standing firm against pro-Western Muslim regimes and the US. While Ershad was aware of the groundswell of support in Bangladesh for Iraq's action and his own personal rapport with the Iraqi leader, he took a quick and firm decision to condemn the Iraqi aggression and send Bangladeshi troops to the Saudi-led coalition, which was getting ready to eject the invading army and free Kuwait. The decision to join the coalition against Iraq was a manifestation of an all-powerful executive decision taken by a president who had only recently exchanged his khakis for a safari suit. Eventually, Bangladesh sent 2,300 troops to the coalition led by Saudi Arabia and the US. While these troops were mostly in support units and deployed in staging areas rather than at the front, the gesture gained much appreciation and gratitude from Saudi Arabia (Hossain, 1997, p 42).

Bangladesh's foreign policy decision in the 1990–91 Gulf War did not end with only a declaration of gratitude from Saudi Arabia. On a more concrete level, the country's steadfast and unequivocal position on Iraq's wrongdoing led the Kuwaiti government to offer Bangladesh's military an opportunity to send an army engineering contingent to clear Kuwait City of mines, bombs and other military debris strewn all over the city and to repair various utilities. Also, Kuwait was divided into six sectors for mine-clearing operations and Bangladesh was offered one sector. Eventually, Bangladesh and Kuwait signed agreements through which Bangladesh's military contingents were to work on the agreed tasks on generous terms. In addition, Kuwait also offered to ship a large amount of abandoned military equipment to the Bangladesh military in return for little or no payment (Shehabuddin, 2006, pp 269–73). The arrangement between Bangladesh and Kuwait on cooperation in the defence field has been further strengthened since then. Starting from the de-mining tasks, today the cooperation has extended to different sectors like health care services provided by members of the Bangladesh military medical corps, support for Kuwait's information technology and other sectors by members of the Bangladesh military. Such cooperation has allowed Bangladesh to emerge as a friendly and reliable partner for powerful Arab countries and reap economic and political benefits.

Defence diplomacy in the post-Cold War era (1990–2020)

In 1988, just 17 years after Bangladesh's independence and the creation of an army virtually from scratch, Dhaka sent 31 military observers to the UN Iran–Iraq Military Observation Group (UNIIMOG) mission. Over the years, Bangladesh contributed more peacekeepers to other missions as well. Within a short period of time, Bangladesh became a leading provider of UN peacekeepers and as of February 2022, Bangladesh stands as the top military and police contributing country (United Nations Peacekeeping, 2022). Apart from increasing its participation, Bangladesh also sought to diversify its contribution. Thus, the country was a strong supporter of the women, peace and security (WPS) agenda during its membership of the UN Security Council in 2000, when Resolution 1325 emphasized for the first time the central role of gender equality in the maintenance of international peace and security. Since then, Bangladesh has made concrete efforts to recruit, train and eventually deploy female soldiers as peacekeepers and in February 2019, female soldiers were deployed as an engagement team alongside an infantry unit. So far, a total of 701 female peacekeepers have participated in UN peace operations (Armed Forces Division, 2022), which allowed the country to successfully project itself as firmly committed to the WPS agenda. In 2016, the Bangladesh Army deployed its first female military contingent commander in the UN mission in Côte d'Ivoire (The Daily Star, 2016). Two female pilots of the Bangladesh Air Force (BAF) were deployed in the Democratic Republic of Congo in 2018 where they successfully completed a year-long deployment as aviators flying BAF

Mi-6 helicopters. These examples underscore Bangladesh's commitment to achieving the UN's Sustainable Development Goals 15 and 16 on gender equality and women's empowerment, and the promotion of peaceful and inclusive societies (UN Women, 2021).

While Bangladesh's turbulent history and political, economic and social challenges can help us understand why the country has achieved such an enviable record, it should be remembered that many troop-contributing countries are also pushed into peacekeeping for similar reasons (Flammia, 2005; Liegeois and Deltenre, 2017; Adhikari, 2020). A cursory response to why Bangladesh provides so many UN peacekeepers includes the following points. First, participation in UN peacekeeping operations fulfils the country's constitutional and international aspirations. Second, involvement with such missions allows troops and officers of the Bangladesh military to interact with members of foreign armed forces and improve their professional skills. Such multi-national exposure helps them gain operational expertise and first-hand knowledge of the latest military doctrines and equipment. Third, financial incentives are a powerful reason why Bangladesh takes part in UN missions. They allow the armed forces to reward personnel and to purchase and maintain military equipment that would otherwise be difficult to obtain. In other words, peace operations help subsidize Bangladesh's armed forces (Islam, 2001, pp 50–8; Cunliffe, 2013, pp 207–9).

Analysts have offered additional reasons as to why there are so many Bangladeshi peacekeepers. Banerjee identified the fulfilling of international commitments, the need to project a positive image of the country, diverting the army's attention away from any praetorian desire, subsidizing the army with reimbursement obtained from peacekeeping missions and the financial benefit accrued to members of the armed forces as reasons behind Bangladesh's policy (Banerjee, 2008, pp 195–6). It has also been argued that economic, normative and political-institutional rationales explain Bangladesh's emergence as a top peacekeeping personnel contributor (Zaman and Biswas, 2013, pp 194–8). This is a status that political elites, the military and the citizenry have attained a significant degree of consensus upon (Zaman and Biswas, 2014, pp 324–44). The traditional theories of separation of civil–military relations have proven inadequate for the Bangladesh armed forces as they were never separated from politics. The unique political nature of the Bangladeshi military, arising phoenix-like out of the fire and ashes of the 1971 war, made it difficult for traditional models of civil–military relations to be applied to Bangladesh. The post-independence historical trajectory, as depicted in the preceding pages, demonstrates that the process of separation has never been successful. Instead, for the last 50 years Bangladesh has been involved in an on-going quest for an appropriate framework to govern civil–military relations and delineate the armed forces' role vis-à-vis Bangladeshi society. It is contended here that it is this fluid nature of civil–military relations, a sort of a 'work in progress', that features peacekeeping as an element of defence diplomacy that has been vigorously pursued. Participation in UN peace operations has created a sort of concordance whereby politicians and the officer corps agree not to allow any situation where the military reverts to praetorian tendencies in internal politics and participation in peace missions performs a critical role in diverting the military's attention from any plans to rock the boat.

Civil–military relations in the COVID-19 pandemic and afterwards

As it became clear that the COVID-19 pandemic was going to affect the country, the government swiftly mobilized the armed forces. While soldiers patrolled designated areas to ensure people obeyed health guidelines, the Combined Military Hospitals (CMH) were thrust forth to deal with the flow of patients requiring critical care (Rahman, 2020). At the same time, a Bangladesh Navy ship sailed to the Indian Ocean Island state of Maldives with 100 metric tons of food, medicine and medical assistance (Bhuyan, 2020). The Air Force was also involved in providing humanitarian assistance as it flew missions to Maldives carrying doctors and daily essential items (Rashid, 2020).

While Bangladesh has pursued defence diplomacy to the best of its ability in the midst of the global pandemic, the country itself has been dealt a blow on the diplomatic front: in early December 2021, the US government imposed human rights-related sanctions on the Rapid Action Battalion (RAB), an elite security force under the Ministry of Home Affairs, together with seven current and former top officials of the force, including Benazir Ahmed, the incumbent Inspector General of Police (The Daily Star, 2021). The actions by the US State and Treasury Departments were hotly contested by the Bangladesh government and strenuous efforts were made to overturn the sanctions (Palma, 2022). While the RAB episode caused a stir in bilateral relations, defence diplomacy has emerged as an important arena through which Bangladesh has been able to project a positive image of the country and its security institutions to the US audience. In the third week of April 2022, the chief of army staff of the Bangladesh Army, General Shafiuddin Ahmed, made a high-profile visit to the US where he met with the chief of staff of the US Army, General James C. McConville and other top US Army, Marine and Defence Department officials (The Business Standard, 2022). He also addressed a selected audience at the Near East South Asia (NESA) Center for Strategic Studies, National Defence University in Washington DC where he was inducted into the NESA Hall of Fame as the ninth distinguished alumnus (NESA, 2022). In his speech at NESA, General Shafiuddin presented Bangladesh's position on matters of global and regional security, reiterated Bangladesh's commitment to international norms and highlighted the country's contribution to upholding international peace (Ahmed, 2022). The Bangladesh Army chief's visit is part of a regular process whereby top officials from both Bangladesh and US armed forces visit each other's country. However, coming at a time when bilateral relations between Bangladesh and the US are under some pressure, General Ahmed's visit helped in presenting a positive image of the country and strengthened Bangladesh's efforts toward mitigating the damage brought on by imposition of sanctions by the US government.

Conclusion

For Bangladesh, civil–military relations have been an important dimension of its politics and as this chapter has shown, the unique nature of this relationship pattern has shaped Bangladesh's defence diplomacy in many ways. This deserves close scrutiny and by answering the questions asked at the very outset, this chapter has shown how colonial and post-colonial legacies helped shape the Bangladesh military. The 1971 war, the expansion of the military and the adoption of a non-discriminatory recruitment policy helped make the military an inescapable part of the country's social and political (and one may add economic) landscapes. Given the nature of the country's political system and its historical, social, and even geographical baggage, it will be a challenge to theorize about its civil–military relations. Like many Latin American states, democratic leadership in Bangladesh will not willingly refrain from using the military and its capabilities to address domestic challenges (Pion-Berlin and Trinkunas, 2005, p 23). What this study has to add is that Bangladesh's civil–military relations have operationalized the warp and woof of its diplomacy and this trend is likely to continue in the foreseeable future.

References

Acemoglu, D. and Robinson, J.A. (2019) *The Narrow Corridor, States, Societies, and the Fate of Liberty*, New York: Penguin Press.

Adhikari, M. (2020) 'Breaking the balance: the impact of peacekeeping missions on civil–military relations', *International Peacekeeping*, 27(3): 369–94.

Ahmed, M. (1995) *Democracy and the Challenge of Development: A Study of Politics and Military Interventions in Bangladesh*, Dhaka: The University Press Limited.

Ahmed, M. (2014) *Jashoder Uthan Poton: Osthir Somoyer Rajniti*, Dhaka: Prothoma Prokashan.

Alavi, H. (1972) 'The state in post-colonial societies: Pakistan and Bangladesh', *New Left Review*, Jul/Aug 72: 59–81.

Ali, S.M. (2010) *Understanding Bangladesh*, New York: Columbia University Press.

Armed Forces Division (2022) 'Female participation of Bangladesh in UN peace operation', *Prime Minister's Office Armed Forces Division*, [online] nd, Available from: https://afd.gov.bd/un-peacekeeping/female-participation [Accessed 30 April 2022].

Banerjee, D. (2008) 'South Asia: contributors of global significance' in D.C.F. Daniel, P. Taft and S. Wiharta (eds) *Peace Operations*, Washington DC: Georgetown University Press, pp 187–202.

Barany, Z. (2012) *The Soldier and the Changing State: Building Democratic Armies in Africa, Asia, Europe, and the Americas*, Princeton and Oxford: Princeton University Press.

Baxter, C. and Rahman, S. (1991) 'Bangladesh military: political institutionalisation and economic development', *Journal of Asian and African Studies*, 26(1–2): 43–60.

Bhuyan, O. (2020) 'Bangladesh Navy ship sets sail with food, medicines for Maldives', *New Age*, [online] 16 April, Available from: www.newagebd.net/article/104475/bangladesh-navy-ship-sets-sail-with-food-medicines-for-maldives?fbclid=IwAR0jqaHDLm8yKgfslZEplOG8Wjq_JAkVA_b2PSndgjOVkvX5G2K829NzV-Q [Accessed 30 April].

Bose, S., and Jalal, A. (2004) *Modern South Asia: History, Culture, Political Economy* , New York: Routledge.

Caplan, L. (2010) 'Martial Gurkhas: the persistence of a British military discourse on "race"', in K. Roy (ed) *War and Society in Colonial India*, 2nd edn, New Delhi: Oxford University Press, pp 225–45.

Cheyre, J.E. (2013) 'Defence diplomacy', in A.F. Cooper, J. Heine and R. Thakur (eds) *The Oxford Handbook of Modern Diplomacy*, Oxford: Oxford University Press, pp 369–82.

Cloughley, B. (2016) *A History of the Pakistan Army, Wars and Insurrections*, New York: Carrel Books.

Codron, J. (2007) 'Putting factions "back in" the civil–military relations equation, genesis, maturation and distortion of the Bangladeshi Army', *South Asian Multidisciplinary Academic Journal*, [online] nd, Available from: https://journals.openedition.org/samaj/230 [Accessed 30 April 2022].

Cohen, S.P. (2001) *The Indian Army: Its Contribution to the Development of a Nation*, New Delhi: Oxford University Press.

Cunliffe, P. (2013) *Legions of Peace: UN Peacekeepers from the Global South*, London: C. Hurst & Co Ltd.

Diplomatic Risk Intelligence (2021) 'Bangladesh–China Relations', *Diplomatic Risk Intelligence*, [online] 8 October, Available from: https://dri.thediplomat.com [Accessed 30 April 2022].

Du Plessis, A. (2008) 'Defence diplomacy: conceptual and practical dimensions with specific references to South Africa', *Strategic Review for Southern Africa*, 30(2): 87–119.

El Morabety, A. (2017) 'Evolution of Moroccan defence diplomacy', *Contemporary Arab Affairs*, 10(2): 241–55.

Fair, C.C. (2019) 'Bangladesh in 2018, careening toward one-woman rule', *Asian Survey*, 59(1): 124–32.

Fair, C.C. and Nawaz, S. (2011) 'The changing Pakistan Army Officer Corps', *Journal of Strategic Studies*, 34(1): 63–94.

Flammia, R.R. (2005) *Copper Soldiers Forging New Roles for the Chilean Military*, MA thesis. Monterey: Naval Postgraduate School, [online] September, Available from: https://apps.dtic.mil/sti/pdfs/ADA439294.pdf [Accessed 30 April 2022].

Golby, J. (2020) 'America's politicized military is a recipe for disaster', *United States Studies Centre*, [online] June 18, Available from: https://foreignpolicy.com/2020/06/18/us-military-politics-trump-election-campaign/ [Accessed 30 April 2022].

Hakim, M.A. (1998) 'Bangladesh: the beginning of the end of militarized politics?', *Contemporary South Asia*, 7(3): 283–300.

Hasanuzzaman, A.M. (2016) 'Civil–military relations' in A. Riaz and M.S. Rahman (eds) *Routledge Handbook of Contemporary Bangladesh*, London and New York: Routledge, pp 109–18.

Hossain, I. (1997) 'Bangladesh and the Gulf War: response of a small state', *Pakistan Horizon*, 50(2): 39–55.

Hossain, K. (2013) *Bangladesh: Quest for Freedom and Justice*, Dhaka: The University Press Limited.

Islam, M.A. (2001) 'Peacekeeping operations and its legal implications', *Bangladesh Army Journal*, January: 50–8.

Islam, S.S. (1984) 'The state in Bangladesh under Zia (1975–81)', *Asian Survey* 24(5): 556–73.

Jacques, K. (2000) *Bangladesh, India and Pakistan, International Relations and Regional Tensions in South Asia*, Basingstoke, Hampshire and London: Macmillan Press Ltd.

Jahan, R. (1994) *Pakistan: Failure in National Integration*, 1st Bangladesh edn, Dhaka: The University Press Limited.

Jain, B.M. (2017) *China's Soft Power Diplomacy in South Asia, Myth or Reality?*, Lanham, Lexington, Boulder and London: Lexington Books.

Kabir, B.Md.M. (1999) *Politics of Military Rule and the Dilemmas of Democratization in Bangladesh*, New Delhi: South Asian Publishers.

Khan, M.R. (2012) *Amar Sainik Jiban: Pakistan Theke Bangladesh*, Dhaka: Prothoma Prokashan.

Khondker, H.H. (1986) 'Bangladesh: anatomy of an unsuccessful military coup', *Armed Forces & Society*, 13(1): 125–43.

Lewis, D. (2011) *Bangladesh: Politics, Economy and Civil Society*, Cambridge: Cambridge University Press.

Liegeois, M. and Deltenre, D. (2017) 'Astuteness is commitment: Rwanda and UN peacekeeping 1994–2014', *The Round Table*, 106(4): 421–35.

Lindquist, A. (1977) 'Military and development in Bangladesh', *The IDS Bulletin*, 9(1): 10–18.

Lorch, J. (2017) 'Civil society support for military coups: Bangladesh and the Philippines', *Journal of Civil Society*, 13(2): 184–201.

Majumder, M.H. (2021) 'Bangabandhu and the inception of defence diplomacy: Bangladesh perspective', *NDC Journal*, Special Issue: December: 153–65.

Maniruzzaman, T. (2003) *The Bangladesh Revolution and Its Aftermath*, Dhaka: The University Press Limited.

Mason, P. (1988) *A Matter of Honour: An Account of the Indian Army, Its Officers and Men*, Dehradun: EBD Educational Private Limited (Indian edition).

Milam, W.B. (2010) *Bangladesh and Pakistan: Flirting with Failure in South Asia*, Dhaka: The University Press Limited.

Mohsin, A. (1992) 'Bangladesh-India relations: limitations and options in an evolving relationship', in E. Ahamed and A. Kalam (eds) *Bangladesh, South Asia and the World*, Dhaka: Academic Publishers, pp 59–73.

Moskos, C.C. (1977) 'From institution to occupation: trends in military organization', *Armed Forces & Society*, 4(1): 41–50.

Nawaz, S. (2008) *Crossed Swords: Pakistan, Its Army, and the Wars Within*, Karachi: Oxford University Press.

Near East South Asia Center for Strategic Studies (2022) 'Distinguished alumni award for Bangladesh CSA Gen S.M. Shafiuddin Ahmed', *Nesa-Center*, [online] nd, Available from: https://nesa-center.org/distinguished-alumni-award-for-bangladesh-csa-gen-s-m-shafiuddin-ahmed/?utm_source=rss&utm_medium=rss&utm_campaign=distinguished-alumni-award-for-bangladesh-csa-gen-s-m-shafiuddin-ahmed [Accessed 30 April 2022].

Omissi, D. (1994) *The Sepoy and the Raj: The Indian Army, 1860–1940*, Basingstoke, Hampshire and London: Macmillan Press Ltd.

Palma, P. (2022) 'Dhaka–Washington ties: 'feast' ends, now it's time for action', *The Daily Star*, [online] 23 April, Available from: www.thedailystar.net/news/bangladesh/news/dhaka-washington-ties-feast-ends-now-its-time-action-3010371 [Accessed 30 April 2022].

Pion-Berlin, D. and Trinkunas, H. (2005) 'Democratization, social crisis and the impact of military domestic roles in Latin America', *Journal of Political and Military Sociology*, 33(1): 5–24.

Rahman, Bangabandhu Sheikh Mujibur (1975) 'Father of the Nation of Bangladesh Bangabandhu Sheikh Mujibur Rahman at BMA's 1st Graduation Parade', *Bangladesh24-7*, [online] nd, Available from: https://youtu.be/1QMKKYg2xc0 [Accessed 30 April 2022].

Rahman, Md.M. (2020) 'Impacts of Covid-19 in Bangladesh, mitigation strategy and role of Bangladesh Army', *The Security World*, 2(June): 4–23.

Rahman, M.S. (2016) 'Bangladesh and its neighbors', in A. Riaz and M.S. Rahman (eds) *Routledge Handbook of Contemporary Bangladesh*, London and New York: Routledge, pp 378–88.

Raghavan, S. (2013) *1971: A Global History of the Creation of Bangladesh*, Ranikhet: Permanent Black.

Rashid, M. (2020) 'BAF aircraft flies to Maldives with physicians' *New Age*, [online] 17 May, Available from: www.newagebd.net/print/article/106621 [Accessed 30 April 2022].

Riaz, A. (2016) *Bangladesh: A Political History since Independence*, London and New York: I.B. Tauris.

Rizvi, H-A. (2000) *Military, State and Society in Pakistan*, Basingstoke, Hampshire and London: Macmillan Press.

Saez, L. (2018) 'Bangladesh in 2017, bloggers, floods, and refugees', *Asian Survey*, 58(1): 127–33.

Sarwar, Md.B. (2016) *Cambodia: Shantisenar Journal*, Dhaka: Prokriti Publishers.

Shehabuddin, K.M. (2006) *There and Back Again: A Diplomat's Tale*, Dhaka: The University Press Limited.

Slater, J. (1977) 'Apolitical warrior of soldier-statesman, the military and the foreign policy process in the post-Vietnam era', *Armed Forces & Society*, 4(1): 101–18.

Tan, S.S (2016) 'Military diplomacy' in C.M. Constantinou, P. Kerr and P. Sharp (eds) *The Sage Handbook of Diplomacy*, Los Angeles, London and New Delhi: Sage, pp 591–600.

Tarafdar, A. [Brigadier General, Director General (DG), Inter Services Selection Board (ISSB).] (2020) Interview by Rashed Uz Zaman [telephone], 9 May.

Tarafdar, A. [Brigadier General, Director General (DG), Inter Services Selection Board (ISSB).] (2020) Interview by Rashed Uz Zaman [email], 27 May.

The Business Standard (2022) 'Army chief returns from US', *The Business Standard*, [online] 29 April, Available from: www.tbsnews.net/bangladesh/army-chief-returns-us-411630 [Accessed 30 April 2022].

The Daily Star (2016) 'First female officer leads contingent', *The Daily Star*, [online] 29 February, Available from: www.thedailystar.net/frontpage/first-female-officer-leads-contingent-783856 [Accessed 30 April 2022].

The Daily Star (2021) 'Human rights abuse: US sanctions Rab, seven top officials', *The Daily Star*, [online] 11 December, Available from: https://www.thedailystar.net/news/bangladesh/news/us-sanctions-rab-six-high-ups-2914466 [Accessed 30 April 2022].

The International Institute for Strategic Studies (2021) *The Military Balance*, London: Routledge.

United Nations Peacekeeping (2022) *Troops and Police Contributors*, [online] August, Available from: https://peacekeeping.un.org/en/troop-and-police-contributors [Accessed 30 April 2022].

United Nations Women (2021) 'From where I stand: "you can very well be a mother and a front-line combatant"', *United Nations Women*, [online] 22 February, Available from: https://asiapacific.unwomen.org/en/news-and-events/stories/2021/02/fwis-nayma-haque [Accessed 30 April 2022].

Van Schendel, W. (2009) *A History of Bangladesh*, Cambridge: Cambridge University Press.

Wilkinson, S.I. (2015) *Army and Nation: The Military and Indian Democracy since Independence*, Ranikhet: Permanent Black.

Wolf, S.O. (2013) 'Civil–military relations and democracy in Bangladesh', *Spotlight South Asia*, Special Issue, October.

Yasmin, L. (2016) 'Bangladesh and the great powers', in A. Riaz and M.S. Rahman (eds) *Routledge Handbook of Contemporary Bangladesh*, London and New York: Routledge, pp 389–401.

Zaman, R.U. and Biswas, N.R. (2013) 'Bangladesh', in A.J. Bellamy and P.D. Williams (eds), *Providing Peacekeepers: The Politics, Challenges, and Future of United Nations Peacekeeping Contributions*, Oxford: Oxford University Press, pp 183–203.

Zaman, R.U. and Biswas, N.R. (2014) 'Bangladesh's participation in UN peacekeeping missions and challenges for civil–military relations: a case for concordance theory', *International Peacekeeping*, 21(3): 324–44.

Zaman, R.U. and Biswas, N.R. (2017) 'The contribution of Commonwealth armed forces in UN peacekeeping: the case of Bangladesh', *The Round Table*, 106(4): 437–52.

16

Conclusion: Asian Military Evolutions as a Contribution to Civil–Military Relations Thought

Alan Chong and Nicole Jenne

In closing this attempt to plumb an Asian contribution to civil–military relations, we will revisit the six research questions set out in Chapter 1. Before doing so, it is appropriate to preface the conclusion with a reflection upon a representative perspective from a grounded Asian approach to civil–military relations. The following excerpts come from Malaysia's first ever Defence White Paper, published in 2020 (Ministry of Defence of Malaysia, 2020). We chose Malaysia because it has been a country very much neglected, or at best under-studied in the field of civil–military relations, as David Han pointed out in Chapter 6.

Concentric Deterrence, the principal pillar, involves primarily the role of the MAF (Malaysian Armed Forces) in protecting national interests, particularly defending the sovereignty and territorial integrity by dissuading all forms of external intrusion and conflicts. National defence is pursued along the concentric areas that cover land, maritime, air and cyber electromagnetic domains.

Comprehensive Defence involves the synergistic application of both whole-of-government and the whole-of-society approaches to defend the nation in line with the concept of HANRUH [an abbreviation of *Pertahanan Menyeluruh* in Malay, signifying 'Total/Comprehensive Defence']. The process encompasses a continuous effort to build internal cohesion, enhancing defence preparedness, improving inter-agency coordination, strengthening nation-building, as well as boosting economic capacity and other aspects of national resilience in a thorough and sustainable manner. The nation's defence is also enhanced through KESBAN [an abbreviation of *Keselamatan dan Pembangunan* in Malay, meaning 'Security and Development'] that emphasises on pursuing security and development simultaneously.

Credible Partnerships refers to bilateral or multilateral defence cooperation with external partners. These partnerships are credible from two angles. First, Malaysia's credibility as a dependable partner is the foundation of our defence engagements with countries in the region and the wider world. Second, these engagements benefit Malaysia and our partners in terms of defence readiness, security needs and regional stability.

The Government is committed to implement all three pillars to achieve the National Defence Vision. *The three pillars mirror the cohesion and combination of efforts by the government and the society in keeping Malaysia as a secure, sovereign and prosperous nation.* (Ministry of Defence – Malaysia, 2020, p 41, emphasis added)

The concept of concentric deterrence cannot be found in the vast majority of Western textbooks on civil–military relations, let alone in practical works of strategy produced by military veterans of the likes of Liddell-Hart, Fuller, Mahan, Corbett, Douhet or Seversky. Parts of it might be found in double readings of Clausewitz, Sun Tzu and Kautilya. However, the emphasis on comprehensive defence involving the general population planting their stakes alongside soldiers in expediting a common nationhood and economic prosperity is clearly developmental in nature. Some might claim that the ideas of HANRUH and KESBAN have been borrowed from the writings of the theorists of modernization *qua* development popular in the 1960s (Apter, 1965; Black, 1967). This is not completely wrong, since Malaysia was indeed granted its independence by Britain after considerable political agitation by nationalist forces (1946–63) on the ground during the Cold War on the basis that the future of an independent Malaysia will be charted according to some version of capitalist modernity that would uplift economically all citizens.

Still, the idea of melding civilian progress and material well-being in a defence statement is surely an Asian formulation that echoes across the 13 country studies in this volume. Indonesian development under Soekarno and Soeharto exhibited ideological formulations that included military personnel as integral streams of development. Singapore's PAP government treated synergies between the civilian population and military service as a cornerstone of 'total defence' anchored to a corporatist notion of economic progress for its entire population. Vietnam likewise witnessed the doctrinal incorporation of the Vietnam People's Army into a totalizing vision of a postcolonial socialist republic. China's party–military dynamics featured a constant struggle to define the place of the PLA within schemes of an economically centred modernization vision articulated by various communist 'paramount' leaders since 1949. Both Koreas too witnessed strongmen leaders jockeying to retain military-like discipline to simultaneously tamp down opposition to their regimes while also conscripting a deliberately repressed civilian population to work for state-directed economic growth. Similarly, the Philippine case reveals that the Armed Forces of the Philippines' senior officers are always being co-opted into public offices by civilian strongmen bent on improving population docility towards an authoritarian vision of progress. The case of Myanmar and the rule of the *Tatmadaw*, along with Thailand's military elites, equally echo the need for military ruling elites to legitimize praetorian rule through some vision of nation-making and so-called 'rightly ordered' national rejuvenation. In Japan's case, the role of the JSDF since 1952 had to be dressed up in discreet or politically correct discourses to avoid conflicting with Japan's thoroughly civilianized high technology first world economy. Although modernization ideology scarcely dominated front and centre in the cases of India and Bangladesh, such considerations have been salient in the political manoeuvres to either enlarge the room for military involvement in politics or to keep it acquiescent to civilian politicians.

The following sections turn to the three big themes raised by the initial six research questions: the enduring impact of colonialism by foreign powers and other legacies of the past, civil–military fusion and its links to development and political guardianship of the nascent modern Asian state and lastly, civil–military relations and its connection with defence diplomacy and MOOTW. In each section we seek to highlight and contextualize commonalities across cases without delving too closely into national contexts as these have been carefully described in the contributions to this volume.

The enduring legacies of colonialism and the precolonial past

Colonialism is more than the experience of physical occupation and domination of geography and economic activities by European and Japanese powers across Asia between the 1500s and 1950s. The psychological impacts of nearly five centuries of colonial governance translated into patterns of civil–military fusion and modes of domestic security governance.

First, as the cases of Malaysia, Indonesia, Myanmar, Vietnam, India and Bangladesh illustrate, organizing indigenous civilians for defence meant maintaining law and order domestically, which added to an already strong and lasting preoccupation with internal security. Second, in a number of contexts within the same above-mentioned cases, militarization for nationalism meant politicizing soldiers for ousting European and Japanese colonial powers. On the other hand, North and South Korea, India, and to some extent, Bangladesh, very visibly picked up many ideas for organizing their future armed guardians from their erstwhile colonial overlords. In the two Koreas, Japanese domination either induced dedicated arms training, habits of sacrifice for a greater good, or illuminated possibilities for disciplining and improving civilian populations' mindsets and skills for seeding *dirigiste* economics.

In cases like Indonesia, Myanmar, Vietnam, North Korea, China and Bangladesh, the respective national militaries could claim revolutionary status and portray themselves as 'above normal politics' because of their historical roles in the fight against foreign rule and in most of these cases, the creation of new states. In situations where the postcolonial Asian states were led by indigenized Marxist-Leninist regimes such as Vietnam, North Korea and China, the primary issue that vexed the new governments was how to incorporate the armed vanguards of the anti-imperialist struggle into the new ideological regime. Despite divergences between the political climates of Hanoi, Pyongyang and Beijing, all three countries found ways to fuse the patriotic roles of the military into civilian economy, construction and even in business and MOOTW. Revolutionary goals from the era of armed struggle were transformed into nation-building and all manner of political vigilance against polluting ideas from hostile neighbours or the Western powers. In Indonesia and Myanmar, the armed forces have viewed themselves as eternal protectors against domestic civil disturbances and other centrifugal forces that would imaginably destroy the hard-earned independence from foreign imperialism half a century ago. These internal threats are often classified through assorted labels as anti-national groups to tar ethnic insurgencies and democratic movements, even civil society. Chapter 7 by Alex Vuving on Vietnam suggests a useful phrase in this regard that stands in stark contrast to the Huntingtonian paradigm of the professional aka apolitical soldier: 'the primacy of politics'. Policing against domestic threats however does not mean that 'neocolonial' territorial actions emanating from hostile neighbours and revanchist great powers do not constitute a serious threat on a more conventional scale. North Korea's practice of *Songun* politics, or 'Military First' politics, could not have been possible if the South did not present itself as a permanent threat to Pyongyang in alliance with an 'imperialist USA'. South Korea's persistent authoritarian civil–military relations practices, in turn, have been nurtured by the siege mentality of the national security state constructed to survive competition with the North, as Lee and Chong's original contribution in Chapter 12 demonstrates. Likewise, the VPA, the PLA and the TNI continue to earn domestic plaudits and civilian politicians' favour by appearing to maintain patrols against malevolent intrusions by foreign craft into sovereign water, land and air spaces.

Thailand and Japan necessarily stand out from these broader patterns of colonial impact. The Japanese Self Defense Forces (JSDF) are a post-Pacific

War creation that have been in need of a politically correct, non-imperialist posture intended for both domestic and foreign consumption. At the same time, the JSDF in its maritime component can only stage foreign deployments in tandem within coalitional parameters, usually together with the US. The Army and Air Force equivalents of the JSDF are thus far forbidden from foreign belligerent operations and as Yee-Kuang Heng points out in Chapter 13, has had to even mask their roles with intensive popular culture-infused public relations campaigns. Thailand's civil–military relations represent an even more distinct lineage from a confluence of ancient and early modern pasts. It dates back to the era when monarchs like Chulalongkorn learnt that protecting both the sovereignty of Siam and the legitimacy of the throne meant keeping temptations for imperial acquisitions of Siamese territory at bay through modernizing the military. The military was transformed through imitation of principally Western European powers, for two reasons. One was to undercut the nobles who controlled private armies made loyal through clientelist ties. Another reason was to convince the would-be Western aggressors of the 1800s and early 1900s that a Westernized Siamese military adept at Western ways of drills, tactics and firearms could realistically demonstrate territorial defence of, and maintain internal stability within Siam's royal boundaries and remove any excuse for colonial style interventions. As Greg Raymond's Chapter 8 details it, the modern RTA has inherited a simultaneously domestic and foreign security function. In short, Thailand's civil–military dynamics, described by Raymond as 'trialectical' involving also the actions of democratic politicians and civil society upon the monarchy and the interests of the military, is descended from a 19th-century reaction against colonial encroachments that were both physical and ideological.

Civil–military fusion and its links to development and political guardianship

The aforementioned Thai case sketched in considerable detail by Greg Raymond is nonetheless representative of an Asian preference for civil–military fusion to power national development. As we have stated in Chapter 1, development is widely understood in Asia (and by its militaries) as the pursuit of the consolidation of statehood and nationhood, actions ensuring political stability that do not exclude violent put downs of civilian 'misrule', and the involvement by militaries in direct contributions to the economy, social rehabilitation and disaster relief. Several mainstream studies continue to insist that democracy and its legal framework, is the yardstick or at least one of the central standards by which Asia's civil–military relations are to be assessed (Alagappa, 2001a; Alagappa, 2001b; Croissant et al, 2013; Bruneau and Croissant, 2019; Matei et al, 2022). In this line of thinking, Asian militaries ought to follow their Western counterparts in returning to the barracks and confining themselves to externally oriented defence and foreign policy missions. This volume disagrees that this is possible or even necessarily desirable without unravelling larger national configurations both in terms of their legal-institutional set up and their everyday practices. Military roles in Asia have *evolved* within the paradigm of national development and are therefore inextricably intertwined with the prevailing socio-political, economic and cultural contexts. Military roles may be domestic in orientation like in Indonesia and Myanmar or be treated as a nation-building mission with both domestic and external facets such as in Bangladesh, China, Singapore, Vietnam and, to some extent, Malaysia, but they are never completely separate from developmental efforts leveraged for a declared national cause. Failure to take this into consideration explains why unaccustomed observers of the Indonesian, Myanmar, Vietnam and Philippine cases find it difficult to fathom why Huntington, Feaver and Janowitz-influenced modelling hardly helps with policy-relevant prognoses. Terence Lee's work positing that the TNI often faces the dilemma of defecting from or defending civilian politicians is helpful in pointing the way to this developmentalist logic where the stakes are invested directly in the survival of the nation (Lee, 2015). However, we contend that it is much more than that. Much of Asia has not arrived at first world standards of consumerist, middle class modernity. Modernity, however defined via civil–military relations, must be considerate towards the identities and welfare of the populations caught up in the drama of socio-economic progress (Rosen, 1996; Grabowsky and Rettig, 2019; Ratuva et al, 2019).

We propose that even if Asia modernizes, it will *not* mirror the West authentically in formal terms nor in practice. Instead, civil–military relations in tandem with most Asian political systems will evolve in a hybridized distinctiveness evidencing attempts to fit successful foreign models into local circumstances. The Singaporean and Malaysian cases – arguably the most modern political and economic systems in Southeast Asia – reveal a superficially apolitical military. But closer scrutiny in Chapters 5 and 6 by Jun Yan Chang and Shu Huang Ho and David Han, respectively, have revealed that a fusion of military functions and socioeconomic progress arbitered by civilian leaders has occurred. Chang and Ho have facetiously titled their chapter 'mind the gap' to draw the readers' attention to the 'everyday quality' of Singaporeans transiting between military and civilian roles in order to sustain a corporatist strategy to engineer unrelenting economic growth. One can choose to label this some shade of authoritarianism or militarism, but first and foremost it is a variation of an Asian way to modernization. The cases of the two Koreas are even more obvious – developmental guardianship meant blending the military's mores into the civilian spheres. In many cases, the particular mould of civil–military fusion has served to keep ruling elites in power and yet, such strategies of political struggle would not have emerged had it not been for developmental ideologies mobilized in pursuit of state and nation-building.

Of course, not all countries have succeeded in expediting economic growth and enlarging the middle class as the Philippine and Myanmar cases show. Civil–military fusion for development can lead to cronyism and corruption. Nonetheless, all the Asian countries included in this volume have tried some form of fusion responding to the particular circumstances at any given time. Notably, in the Vietnamese, Chinese, Indian and Bangladeshi cases, the military has been gradually tutored or learnt through trial-and-error experiences to mind their place in keeping development in positive motion. In the Japanese case, the military tries hard to endear itself as part of the civilian mainstream, and this is performed almost to a fault with the adoption of metaphors of popular culture.

Civil–military relations and its impacts on defence diplomacy and MOOTW

In tandem with experiments in civil–military fusion, MOOTW has rapidly been emerging as a major everyday mission for Asian militaries. As Nicole Jenne's chapter argues via studies of Southeast Asian peacekeeping manoeuvres, MOOTW offers a politically neutral or inoffensive functionalist paradigm for military-to-military ties. Additionally, when it comes to operationalizing civil–military fusion in the eyes of domestic and foreign public opinion, MOOTW earns legitimacy for each national military, adding another dimension to but also simultaneously reinforcing its role in national development, as Chapter 15 on Bangladesh argues. HADR missions are media-friendly, including social media accessibility, and allow militaries to attain high profile non-combat achievements that directly contribute to some notion of peace and economic positivity. Peacekeeping, like the rest of MOOTW is also socially and politically progressive in the mode of military evolutions when it comes to gradually empowering women in the armed forces as Chapters 9 and 15 by Jenne and Zaman respectively point out. Additionally, some MOOTW missions like peacekeeping, HADR, simple SAR, or even elementary passing exercises between navies, army map exercises and exhibitions of military hardware and training operations all allow what Chong and Chang and Jenne have dubbed 'security competition by proxy'. Thus, MOOTW allow indirect, non-aggressive intelligence gathering about erstwhile rivals' military readiness, morale and other indices of military competence short of actual combat.

MOOTW is also inured to the broad idea of civil–military fusion, an idea that is discussed at length in Chapter 6 on Malaysia. According to Han, a stable civil–military relations pattern allowed extensive and successful engagement in defence diplomacy activities by the MAF while, at the same time, civilian politicians used such deployments to reinforce civilian superiority. HADR and joint exercises involve civilian diplomatic legwork and logistical collaborations that feature non-combat skills. One thinks of any number of earthquake, tsunami and storm relief efforts whereby Asian militaries have to work closely with governments, relief agencies and local civic associations both in the sending and recipient countries. The same applies to peacekeeping where experiences need to be shared across the civil–military spectrum, as Jenne points out. Military effectiveness in this regard is hence commensurate with the strength of civilian state structures and therefore fits neatly with the general understanding of the military as a guardian of national progress. Unsurprisingly, none of the Asian militaries surveyed in this book appears to have opposed MOOTW as one might expect it to be the case in Western militaries that see warfighting as their exclusive prime focus.

Looking ahead, this book with its country studies by younger or up and coming scholars that train fresh scholarship on a hitherto jaded subject hopes to be productively incendiary in setting off multiple fronts for research into Asian militaries. Asian military evolutions are revealing of cumulative and synthetic slow-motion phenomena unfolding across the region's politico-security landscape, but it will prove rewarding to study them if one does not always associate the Asian military in stark formations like authoritarianism versus democracy.

References

Alagappa, M. (ed) (2001a) *Military Professionalism in Asia: Conceptual and Empirical Perspectives*, Honolulu, HI: East West Center.

Alagappa, M. (ed) (2001b) *Coercion and Governance: The Declining Political Role of the Military in Asia*, Stanford, CA: Stanford University Press.

Apter, D.E. (1965) *The Politics of Modernization*, Chicago, IL: University of Chicago Press.

Black, C. (1967) *The Dynamics of Modernization: A Study in Comparative History*, New York: Harper and Row / Harper Torchbooks.

Bruneau, T. and Croissant, A. (2019) *Civil-Military Relations: Control and Effectiveness Across Regimes*, Boulder, CA: Lynne Rienner Publishers.

Croissant, A., Kuehne, D., Lorenz, P. and Chambers, P.W. (2013) *Democratization and Civilian Control in Asia*, Houndmills, Basingstoke: Palgrave Macmillan.

Grabowsky, V. and Rettig, F. (eds) (2019) *Armies and Societies in Southeast Asia*, Chiang Mai: Silkworm Books.

Lee, T. (2015) *Defect or Defend: Military Responses to Popular Protests in Authoritarian Asia*, Baltimore: Johns Hopkins University Press.

Matei, F., Halladay, C. and Bruneau, T. (eds) (2022) *The Routledge Handbook of Civil-Military Relations*, Abingdon, Oxon, New York: Routledge.

Ministry of Defence – Malaysia (2020) *Defence White Paper*, Kuala Lumpur: Ministry of Defence.

Ratuva, S., Compel, R. and Aguilar, S. (2019) 'Guns and roses: the nexus between the military and citizenry in the new security environment', in S. Ratuva, R. Compel and S. Aguilar (eds) *Guns and Roses: Comparative Civil–Military Relations in the Changing Security Environment*, Singapore: Springer Nature, pp 1–14.

Rosen, S.P. (1996) *Societies and Military Power: India and its Armies*, Ithaca, NY: Cornell University Press.

Index

A

Abe, Shinzo 272, 275
Alagappa, Muthiah 3, 11
Andika Perkasa 60
Arab Israeli War 1973
  Bangladesh support for Egypt and Syria 328
Asian values debate 99
Association of Southeast Asian Nations (ASEAN) 17, 38, 53, 122, 124, 140, 189, 277–278, 385–386
  defence diplomacy
    ASEAN Defence Ministers Meeting (ADMM) 171, 186
      Plus (ADMM+) 117, 143
        Expert Working Group on Peacekeeping 121, 183
    ASEAN Regional Forum (ARF) 117
      Inter sessional Meeting on Peacekeeping Operations 182
  integrated Southeast Asian force
    Indonesia proposal 184–185
    Malaysia proposal 185
  member states' bilateral military drills
    Cambodia 170–171, 173, 178, 180–181, 185
      Angkor Sentinel 184
    Indonesia 170–171, 173, 176, 178, 180–181, 183–185, 187
      Garuda–Shield 184
    Thailand–US 177
      Cobra–Gold 162, 184
  member states' participation in peace operations other than UN
    European Union Mission to Aceh 2005 187
    Organisation of Islamic Cooperation Mission in Mindanao 1995–96
    International Monitoring Team (IMT) 187
  Military Ready Group (AMRG) 117
  non–interference 21, 116
  peacekeeping in ASEAN 184–185, 174
    ASEAN Peacekeeping Centre Association 183
    Peacekeeping Experts' Meeting 182
  Political–Security Community (APSC) 171–176, 182, 186, 188, 189
    track II diplomacy 18, 111, 124
  ASEAN Defence and Security Initiative (NADI) 117, 118
  peacekeeping 112, 117, 118, 121, 175, 182
Aquino, Benigno Simeon 72, 80
Aquino, Corazon 68–72
Aung San Suu Kyi 29, 34, 36, 38

B

Bangabandhu Sheikh Mujibur Rahman 325, 327–328
Bangladesh 2, 5, 11, 24, 38, 116, 320–331, 334, 342–343, 345–346
  participation in UN peace operations 332–333
Basuki Tjahaja Purnama 56
battle of Dien Bien Phu 1954 130
battle of the Capitol 1
Bhumipol Adulyadej 158–160
Biden, Joseph 53
Black, Cyril 8
Blackett, P.M.S. 308
Boxing Day Tsunami 2004 116
Bruneau, Thomas 5–7
bumiputera (Sons of the Soil) 115, 121
Burma *see also Myanmar* 10–11, 13, 31–33, 262
  Anglo–Burmese War 1824–26 153

C

Chambers, Paul 12–14
Chaovalit Yongchaiyudh 163
China *see People's Republic of China*
Chuan Leekpai 163, 178
Chulalongkorn 153–156, 160, 344
Civil Disobedience Movement (CDM) 38–39
civil-military relations
  Global South perspectives 3, 8, 10
  non–Western 5–6
  orthodox theorizing 3

practices 255, 343
structural theories 103
traditional paradigm *see civil-military relations orthodox theorizing*
Communist Party 137
 Burma 32
 China 197–214, 217–219
 Indonesia 48, 52, 57
 North Korea 232, 236
 Vietnam 14, 20, 129–133, 144–145
comprehensive defence 340–341
concentric deterrence 340–341
counterterrorism 19, 46–48, 50, 54, 56, 60, 92, 122
Croissant, Aurel 7, 12
crony capitalism 51
Crouch, Harold 10–12
cyber 96, 122, 340
 warfare 34, 55
cyclone Nargis 116

D

defence diplomacy 3, 16–18, 21–24, 59, 110–119, 121–124, 143, 171–175, 182, 184–186, 188–189, 173, 277, 297–299, 308–311, 320–321, 326–327, 329–331, 333–334, 432, 346–347
 multilateral 2, 15, 171, 174–175, 182–184
democracy 2, 4, 8, 11–12, 19, 29, 47, 50–51, 57, 69, 72, 77, 85–87, 113, 120, 134, 140, 150, 156, 158–163, 248, 250, 253, 264, 284, 297, 320–321, 325–326, 329, 344, 347
 liberal 5, 13, 22, 48, 60, 82, 131, 249
democratic 1, 6–8, 12, 14, 18–19, 21, 41, 50, 52, 69–72, 74, 76–77, 79–80, 82, 84–87, 110–114, 120–121, 124, 132, 144, 157–159, 161–162, 178, 236, 249–250, 255, 258, 265–267, 276–277, 284, 296–297, 314, 323, 325, 327–328, 330–331, 334, 343–344
 armies 5
 control 3–5, 48
 transition 5, 15, 58, 68, 119
democratization *see also democratic transition* 6, 13, 18–19, 22, 30, 61, 69–70, 79, 130, 138, 151–152, 171, 178
 third wave 5, 68
Deng Xiaoping 198, 199, 201
Desch, Michael 93, 103
development 3–11, 13–14, 16, 20, 23, 29, 32, 34–35, 41, 49, 71, 76, 79–80, 83, 85, 90–91, 94, 96, 100, 111–112, 114, 117, 123, 133, 136, 138, 151–153, 156, 158–159, 162–163, 172–173, 188, 197–198, 202, 249, 257, 261–262, 277, 281, 304, 312, 321–325, 332, 341–342, 344–346
 technological 33, 315
developmental 8–10, 13, 15, 18, 23, 91, 114, 152, 158, 172, 248, 272–273, 281, 284, 286, 297, 341, 346

authoritarianism 22, 249–250, 258, 264
 guardianship 29–32, 36, 39–41, 345
disaster relief 3, 17, 24, 117, 121, 143, 164, 175, 185, 186, 273, 274, 276, 277, 278, 309, 344
Duterte, Rodrigo 19, 70–71, 82–87, 278
 War on Drugs 69, 80

E

East Timor 49, 55, 115, 172, 178, 181
Edmunds, Timothy 7
effectiveness (as a measure of civil-military relations) 3, 5–7, 11, 18, 23, 73–74, 80, 91, 142, 172, 188, 272, 295–297, 298, 301, 303, 311, 313, 314
efficiency (as a measure of civil-military relations) 3, 5–7, 11, 69, 82, 91, 100, 296, 298, 313, 315, 347
Ershad, H.M. 329, 330
Estrada, Joseph 68
export–oriented liberalization 114

F

Farage, Nigel 56
Feaver, Peter 4–5, 7, 11, 90, 92, 103, 111, 297, 314, 345
Forster, Anthony 15
Free Aceh Movement (GAM) 51
Free Papua Movement (OPM) 52

G

Gandhi, Indira 301–302
Gandhi, Rajiv 302
Gatot Nurmantyo 50–53, 55, 57
Giap Vo Nguyen 137–139
Goh Keng Swee 95
Group of 20 (G20) 60

H

Ho Chi Minh 130, 132
Hu Jintao 198, 201–203, 205, 217, 218
human rights 47, 49, 51, 54, 55, 57, 59, 60, 69, 73, 80, 182, 189, 333
human trafficking 35
humanitarian assistance and disaster relief (HADR) 17–18, 20, 58, 111–118, 121–124, 262, 273, 276–279, 284, 286, 346–347
Huntington, Samuel 4, 8, 11, 23, 48, 60, 92, 98, 102–103, 111, 113, 162, 198, 201, 218, 230, 244, 274, 282, 284, 314, 343, 345
 constitutional structure and ideology of state
 US ideology of antimilitary liberalism 273
Huntington-Feaver approach, school 5
military professionalism 3, 6, 93
objective civilian control 91, 94, 112, 297, 301
Huxley, Tim 94, 98

INDEX

I

India 5, 11, 17, 23, 31, 53, 76, 183, 278, 295–298, 305–306, 309, 313, 315, 321–322, 324, 330, 333, 342, 346
  border skirmishes with China 312
  National Security Strategy 303–304, 314
  Nehru, Jawaharlal 299–300, 307–308
  relations with the US 310–311
  war with Pakistan 302, 304
    1965 301
    1971 301, 329
    Kargil War 1999 303
indigenized Marxist–Leninist regimes
  China 343
  North Korea 343
  Vietnam 343
Indonesia 2, 5, 10, 13–14, 17–18, 76, 116, 170–171, 173, 176, 178, 180–181, 183–185, 187, 310, 341–342
  anti-communist violence 1965–66 46, 49, 56–57
  dwifungsi 46–49, 51–52, 58, 60
  Guided Democracy 1957–65 11, 48
  New Order 9, 46–47, 49–51, 55–57, 60
  new-style communism (Komunisme Gaya Baru) 57
  reformation (*reformasi*) 47
  TNI (Tentara Negara Indonesia) 19, 46–61, 343, 345
Indo-China War, Third 139
Indo-Pacific 18, 23, 111, 285–286, 296, 299, 309
  Deployment 277, 280
  Free and Open (FOIP) 278, 310
  Malabar Naval Exercise 310
  Quadrilateral Security Dialogue (QUAD) 310
Indo-Pakistani War 1971 329
Islamic State in Iraq and Syria (ISIS) 54, 178, 328
Israel 100

J

Jaishankar, S. 309
Janowitz, Morris 6, 92, 103, 111, 113, 201, 345
Japan 10–11, 16–17, 23, 31, 130, 158, 183–184, 187, 230–231, 234–235, 237–238, 251–255, 260, 265, 266, 272, 274–281, 297, 310, 342–343, 346
  anime and manga 282–286, 273
  colonialism 22, 248, 250
  militarism 5
Jiang Zemin 198, 201–202, 205, 212, 217
Johnston, John J. 9

K

Kim Dae-jung 257–258, 266–267
Kim Il-sung 22, 229–240, 242–254
Kim Jong-un 229–231, 233, 235, 241–244

Korean War 236, 249–250, 258, 260–262
Kuehn, David 12, 265
Kopassus 50–51
Kuomintang (KMT) 32, 199

L

Le Duc Anh 136–137, 139–141
Lee Hsien Loong 95, 102
Lee Kuan Yew 95
Lee, Terence 12, 345
LeoGrande 131, 133–134, 199
LGBTQ+ 46, 55–56
Liew Chin Tong 121
Lin Biao 200
Linz, Juan 5, 234
Long March 200
Lord Mountbatten 308
Lord Roberts of Kandahar 322
Lorenz, Philip 12
Luckham, Robin 11

M

Mahathir Mohamad 114–115, 119
Malaysia 10–11, 14, 17, 76, 99, 110, 112–113, 116–117, 120, 122, 124, 170, 173, 176–181, 185–187, 340, 342, 345–346
  Airlines flight MH370 118–119
  communalism 20, 111, 115, 121
  Keselamatan dan Pembangun (KESBAN) 114–115, 118, 341
  racial riots 123
Mao Zedong 32, 130, 198–201, 205–206, 212–213, 234
Marcos, Ferdinand 15, 68, 71, 87
Matei, Florina 5–7
Mattis, James 60
Menon, Krishna 300
military
  constabulary role 113–114, 306
  counterinsurgency operations 32–33, 71, 112
  culture 98–100, 103
  evolutions 91, 113, 171, 272, 280, 281–282, 284, 286
  government 8–9, 34, 39, 236
  operations other than war (MOOTW) 2–3, 7–8, 17, 24, 35, 47–48, 53, 59, 111–112, 115, 118, 121, 171, 182, 188, 203, 297, 34–343, 346–347
  professionalism 3, 6, 87, 93, 103, 113, 308
Modi, Narendra 295, 296, 303
Moon Jae-in 261, 263
Min Aung Hlaing 29, 30, 34–35, 37
Mindanao conflict 69
Modelski, George 152
Moskos, Charles 98
Muhyiddin Yassin 122
Mukherjee, Anit 297–298, 301–304, 308, 311–312

Myanmar 2, 9–11, 13–14, 18, 30–31, 34–35, 41, 59, 116, 171, 177, 181, 342–343, 345–346
  constitution 2008 36–40
  military coup 2021 29, 38
  secessionist movements 40
    Kachin Independence Army (KIA) 38
    Karen National Defence Organization 32
    Karen National Union 38
    Ta'ang National Liberation Army 38
Myint Swe 36

N

Najib Razak 116, 119
Nasution, Abdul Harris 48, 49
nationalism 4, 10, 55, 59, 158, 234, 250, 251, 253, 342
Natuna Islands 53–54
narcotics 35
Naxalite insurgency 1967 302
Ne Win 31, 177
nepotism 49
New Order *see Indonesia*
North Korea 23, 249, 254–255, 257–258, 260, 262–263, 285, 343
  anti-imperialism 237
  Juche ideology 231–232, 237–238, 240, 244
  Kim family 22, 230, 238, 240, 243–244
    hereditary successions 229, 234, 241
    personality cult 231, 234, 237
    politico-ideological authority, legitimacy 233
    patrimonial leadership 235
  Songun (military-first) 229–232, 234, 238–244
  nuclear weapons 229, 244, 249, 262, 298, 305
  tests
    North Korea 303
    Pakistan 303

O

Opium War 1839–42 153

P

Pandjaitan, Luhut Binsar 50–51, 53
Pakistan 8, 11, 296, 301–302, 304, 311, 313, 321
  armed forces 322–324, 326, 329
  democratic processes 5
  nuclear weapons test *see nuclear weapons*
Park Chung Hee 248, 249, 252, 258–263, 265
Park Geun-hye 263, 265–266
Papuan independence 52
paramilitary institutions 6, 156, 249
Patriotic Burma Forces (PBF) 31
peacekeeping *see track II diplomacy*

People's Republic of China 11, 13–14, 17, 22, 60, 113, 137–140, 142, 153, 161–162, 182–184, 202, 205, 214, 219, 234–237, 244, 251, 253, 263, 285, 296, 301, 304–305, 311–313, 329–330, 343, 345
  China-US rivalry 122, 204
  Chinese Civil-War 1949 199–200
  Cultural Revolution 212, 218
  Party Congress, 18th 22, 197, 203, 206
  People's Liberation Army (PLA)
    big army mentality 217
    Joint Command Centre 217
    Military Regions system 206, 213
    modernization 197, 341
  territorial disputes
    Sino–India border 300
    South China Sea 16, 53–54, 80, 122, 204, 279, 310
Perlmutter, Amos 131, 133, 134, 199
Phibun Songkhram 157–158
Philippines 10, 13–15, 68, 74–75, 77, 85–87, 116–117, 171, 173, 176–178, 180–187, 277, 342
  colonialism 69
  constitution of 1987 72–73, 84
  foreign relations
    China
      territorial disputes in the South China Sea 80
    United States 69
      US bases in the Philippines 71
  Moro secessionism 71
  militarization 19, 70, 80, 82–83
  patronage politics 76
Prabowo Subianto 51, 53, 54, 60
Prayuth Chan-ocha 149–150, 178, 180
Prem Tinsulanonda 160
Przeworski, Adam 5–6
Puangthong Pawakapan 153, 159
Putin, Vladimir 60
Pye, Lucian 9

R

Reform and Opening-up 201–202, 218
Rostow, Walt 8
Russia 2, 60, 76, 93, 156, 161–162, 183, 285, 311, 324
Responsibility to Protect (R2P)
  principle 34, 185
Rhee Syng-man 9, 254–256, 259, 264, 267
Ryamizard Ryacudu 50–55, 57

S

Saddam Hussein 330
Sarit Thanarat 157–159
Schiff, Rebecca 93, 103
Schmitter, Philippe 5
Shigeru, Ishiba 276

INDEX

Search and Rescue Operations 2, 118, 119, 121, 143
security 4–5, 7–9, 12–15, 18–23, 32–34, 36–40, 46, 48–49, 51–52, 54–55, 58–59, 68–76, 78, 80, 82–83, 85–86, 91–92, 94–98, 100, 111–117, 119–120, 123–124, 137–138, 140–142, 154, 156–158, 160–161, 163, 170–171, 174, 176–178, 180, 182–189, 204–214, 218, 230, 239, 243–244, 248, 250, 256–265, 272–273, 276, 278–279, 281, 285–286, 296, 298–299, 302–306, 312, 314–315, 323, 327, 331, 333–334, 341–344, 346
  democratic 6
  human 2, 3, 16, 17
  maritime 53, 60, 122, 173, 181, 277, 309–310
  non-traditional 2, 35, 118, 122, 143
  soft 172, 175
Selochan, Viberto 11, 12
Shafiuddin Ahmed 333
Siam *see also Thailand* 164, 344
  absolute monarchy 21, 150–151
    Mongkut *see Rama IV*
    founding of the professional Thai military 153
    Rama II 153
    Rama III 153
    Rama IV 153
    Rama V 153
    Rama VI
      Ror Sor 130 rebellion 156
    Rama VII 157
  conscription law of 1902 155
  Pak Nam Crisis 1893 155
  sakdina system 154
Singapore 10–11, 14, 17, 20, 170, 177–178, 181, 185–187, 277–279, 345
  Armed Forces (SAF) 19, 90 91, 94–104
  civil servants in the SAF 95, 99
  Code of Conduct 100
  conscription 100, 103
  core values 101
  soldier–scholar 95–96
  Civil Defence Force (SCDF) 97
  National Service (NS) 96
  People's Action Party (PAP) 95, 103, 341
  racial riots 1964 94
  total defence 96, 103, 341
Sino-Indian War 1962 300–301
Sino-Vietnamese War 1979 136
Soeharto 19, 46–47, 49–51, 57, 59, 341
soft power 2, 16, 277
South Korea 5, 8–9, 23, 177, 236, 252, 254–256, 266–267, 279, 342
  Cheju Island 263
  HADR efforts
    in Southeast Asia 262
    in Iraq 262
  K-Wave movies 262
  national security state 22, 248, 250, 258–259, 262–264, 343
  Manchukuo Military Academy 253
  political culture 251, 265
    confucianism 253, 257
    deference to hierarchy 257
    authoritarian vigilance 257
  support for the Vietnam War 261
  tensions with North Korea
    bombing of Korean Air passenger jet 1987 262
    Cheonan sinking in 2010 262
    nuclear tests *see nuclear weapons*
    shelling of Yeongpyeon island 262
Shils, Edward 8–9
Smelser, Neil 8
Stepan, Alfred 5, 234
Suharto *see Soeharto*
Sukarno
  Guided Democracy *see Indonesia*

T

Tan Shwe 29
Tat (volunteer army corps in colonial Burma) 31
terrorism 7, 35, 52, 54, 55, 56, 80, 173
Thailand 2, 5, 11, 17, 20, 153, 155, 162, 176–178, 181, 183–185, 187, 342–344
  Cold War 156, 158, 160, 163–164, 170
  monarchy-military complex 152
    Vajiralongkorn Rama X 160–161
    Royal Security Command 160
    control over the King's Guard Units 161
  revolution
    1932 10, 14, 21, 150–151, 156–157, 164
    constitution 1932 158
    1973 159
  coup 149, 154, 157, 159, 163
    2006 14, 150, 160
    2014 14, 161, 180
  Red Shirt riots in Bangkok 161
Thaksin Shinawatra 160
Thanom Kittikachorn 157
Thayer, Carlyle 14, 141, 181
Thein Sein 29
Thirty Comrades 31
Tiananmen protests 1989 219
Tilly, Charles 152
transnational crime 35
Trump, Donald 1, 53, 56, 320
Tunku Abdul Rahman 114
Typhoon Haiyan 2013 116, 277

U

United Nations 21, 24, 51, 118, 121, 143, 172, 176, 186–189, 259, 321, 326, 332–333
  Charter 173
  Chapter VIII 173

General Assembly 60
peacekeeping
　Cambodia 115, 170–171, 173, 178,
　　180–181, 184–185
　hybrid missions
　　regional organisations
　　　African Union 173
　　　European Union 173
　Security Council (UNSC) 116, 170, 174,
　　177, 180, 183, 185, 331
United States of America (US) 1, 4, 49–52,
　56, 60, 100, 117, 137, 140, 142, 151,
　158–159, 161–163, 177, 204, 237, 244,
　255, 273, 275, 282, 305, 310–311, 320

V

Vietnam 9–11, 20, 129, 144, 163, 170,
　173–174, 180–181, 183, 185, 342, 344, 346
　doi moi 136
　foreign relations
　　China 140, 341
　　United States 140, 255, 261–262
　Independence League (Vietminh) 130
　Party Congresses 139
　　4th Party Congress 134
　　6th Party Congress 136
　　7th Party Congress 136, 138
　People's Army (VPA) 14–15, 130–133,
　　136–137, 139, 141, 145, 343
　　forward defence 142
　party in uniform 134
　peacekeeping 135, 143, 175, 184
　Vietnam War 14, 134, 136, 261

W

Waitoolkiat, Napisa 13
Waltz, Kenneth 152
War on Terror 50, 204
Western liberal values 99, 273
Win Myint 36
Women, Peace and Security (WPS)
　agenda 180, 331
World War Two 23
　impact 10–11
　lessons learned 5
　occupation 14, 31, 130, 254
Wuhan, lockdown 219

X

Xi Jinping 22, 197, 198, 199, 201, 203, 204,
　205, 206, 212, 214, 217, 219

Y

Yangon 32, 36
Yoon Suk-yeol 263, 266
Yoshida Shigeru 274, 275, 280

Z

Zakaria Haji Ahmad 10–12
Ziaur Rahman 329

www.ingramcontent.com/pod-product-compliance
Lightning Source LLC
Chambersburg PA
CBHW070802040426
42333CB00061B/1769